Distributed
and
Multi-Database
Systems

The Artech House Computer Science Library

For further information on these and other Artech House titles, contact:

Artech House
685 Canton Street
Norwood, MA 02062
617-769-9750
Fax: 617-769-6334
Telex: 951-659
email: artech@world.std.com

Artech House
Portland House, Stag Place
London SW1E 5XA England
+44 (0) 171-973-8077
Fax: +44 (0) 171-630-0166
Telex: 951-659
email: bookco@artech.demon.co.uk

Distributed and Multi-Database Systems

Angelo R. Bobak

Artech House
Boston • London

Library of Congress Cataloging-in-Publication Data
Bobak. Angelo R.
    Distributed and multi-database systems/Angelo R. Bobak
      p. cm.
    Reprint. Originally published: New York: Bantam, 1993
    Includes bibliographical references and index.
    ISBN 0-89006-614-0 (alk. paper)
    1. Distribution databases. 2. Database design. I. Title.
  QA76.9.D3B618   1995
  005.75'8–dc20

                         95-42035
                         CIP

British LibraryCataloguing in Publication Data
Bobak, Angelo R.
    Distributed and Multi-Database Systems
    I. Title
    005.758

ISBN 0-89006-614-0

© 1996 ARTECH HOUSE, INC.
685 Canton Street
Norwood, MA 02062

International Standard Book Number: 0-89006-614-0
Library of Congress Catalog Card Number: 95-42035

10 9 8 7 6 5 4 3 2 1

This book is dedicated to my wife, Cathy,
and, of course, Toby

Preface

There are many good books available now that discuss distributed and multi-databases using highly theoretical approaches. My intent in this book, however, is to provide a practical source of information for the programmer or technical manager whose responsibilities include the design and implementation of distributed or multi-database systems. At the same time I feel it is important to supply some theoretical discussions that are easy to read and useful for the novice to the field. Including such discussions makes this book an ideal introduction for the student as well as a comprehensive source of practical information for experienced technical users. Complex topics such as serialization and table fragmentation are discussed in an easy, informal manner so that both groups of readers can grasp the basic concepts and formulas used.

I have also included basic chapters on relational theory, relational calculus, and algebra for readers unfamiliar with these disciplines. Some time spent with these chapters will help with the remainder of the text.

Upon completing this book, the reader may go on to the earlier, more traditional books and papers of the pioneers in the field, which are referenced in the end notes.

For any trivia buffs out there, parts of this book were written in London, England. (Special thanks go to the staff of the Gore Hotel, who supplied me with an endless stream of cappuccino, and an incredible Victorian environment!) Parts were written in Cirencester, while I taught some technical courses at QA Training. And, finally, some chapters were researched while I visited Torino, Italy, where I grew up as a child. A view of the Alps is certainly inspiring when writing a book.

This second edition of the book has been enhanced with a chapter on object-oriented databases. This technology allows us to realize not only multi-databases, but federated databases as well. We will see how object brokers can be used to locate and communicate with databases that participate in what is known as a federation of cooperating databases. These databases agree on what data to share and view by setting up specialized data dictionaries called import/export schemas. These topics are all covered in the last chapters of the book.

Angelo R. Bobak
September 1995

Contents

2   Relational Algebra, Calculus, and Fundamental Database Concepts   9

3   Database Models   33

PART II   Distributed Database Architectures   139

PART III Multi-Database Architectures 307

Acknowledgments

Special thanks go to Tom Johnson, who produced the line art in this book. How he was able to understand my attempts at drawing I'll never know! Next, Lauralee Reinke deserves credit for her fine desktop publishing skills and infinite patience. Much of what is positive about this book is due to the efforts of these fine people.

Finally, I would like to thank George Zaruba, John Monnet, Todd Whitman, and Jan Moyaux of ISSC in Southbury, Connecticut, for having reviewed selected chapters. Their suggestions and comments are greatly appreciated and contributed extensively to the book.

P A R T I

Theory and Supporting Topics

1

How to Use This Book: A Road Map

1.1 INTRODUCTION

Everything requires a starting point. This is the starting point of a book on a very complex but interesting topic: distributed and multi-database systems. I have tried to keep the book interesting (and, hopefully, at times entertaining) for as wide a scope of readers as possible. This was accomplished by keeping the theory down to a minimum and focusing on the practical design aspects of the architecture. With this goal in mind, I divided the book into the following three parts:

   I.   Theory and Supporting Topics

   II. Distributed Database Architectures

  III. Multi-Database Architectures

Part I, Theory and Supporting Topics, is where the bulk of the theory and math can be found. Advanced readers can skip Part I and come back to it later, although I recommend Chapter 3 (Database Models) and Chapter 4 (SQL Basics) be read before other chapters in the book are read. If the reader requires a review on basic relational theory concepts, Chapter 2 is a must!

Part II, Distributed Database Architectures, is what this book is all about. Here the reader is introduced to homogeneous distributed database architectures. Distributed transactions and query processing are also discussed.

Part III deals with multi-database architectures. Multi-database or heterogeneous databases are what one can expect to find in business enterprises today. Multi-database sytems are simply diverse databases connected by a layer of communication and control software. By diverse I mean databases that run on different hardware platforms and are based on different data models and/or vendor DBMS (database management systems).

Let's start by examining each of the three parts of the book, then continue by discussing the scope of each chapter.

1.2 PART OVERVIEW

As mentioned earlier, this book is divided into three parts. Part I is included for readers who have no relational or database background. It also provides a good refresher for those who are a bit rusty on the subject.

The following two chapters form the foundation for subsequent theory and discussions in the rest of the book:

- All of Chapter 4, SQL Basics
- All of Chapter 5, Concurrency and Recovery

The contents of these two chapters must be fully understood to benefit from the topics discussed in the remainder of the book.

Distributed database architectures can be broadly categorized as either homogeneous or heterogeneous database architectures. Parts II and III reflect this division. Part II is dedicated to homogeneous distributed databases.

Throughout each chapter, numerous references are made to research papers that the reader can obtain to gain a deeper knowledge of the topic.

Part III deals with the second type of distributed architecture, namely, multi-database architectures. I focus on multi-database systems and include two example architectures: multi-database and federated architectures. The latter is a further subtype of heterogeneous distributed databases. The main distinction is that the federated databases are completely autonomous.

1.3 WHAT EACH CHAPTER COVERS

This section outlines the scope of every chapter in the book. The reader is encouraged to read this section so that he or she may decide which chapters to examine first.

Chapter 1 Overview (How to Use This Book: A Road Map)

This chapter serves not only as a guide to the book but also as an introduction to each chapter. The reader can select topics he or she may wish to concentrate on.

Chapter 2 Overview (Relational Algebra, Calculus, and Fundamental Database Concepts)

This is an important chapter. Understanding distributed architectures requires a solid foundation in relational algebra and relational calculus. These two disciplines are a prerequisite for properly understanding the relational model and further discussions on distributed database design.

Chapter 3 Overview (Database Models)

This chapter is required reading for anyone not familiar with the three principal data models used to implement databases.

Chapter 3 concludes with a section describing the transition from the entity-relationship model to each of the three database models. An example database, which will be used throughout the rest of the book, is created in this chapter.

Chapter 4 Overview (SQL Basics)

This chapter serves as a compact (although complete) tutorial on the Structured Query Language. SQL is composed of three subdivisions called the data declaration language, the data control language, and the data manipulation language.

Chapter 5 Overview (Concurrency and Recovery)

This chapter forms the foundation for later chapters that discuss concurrency and recovery in distributed and multi-database architectures.

Chapter 6 Overview (Introduction to Distributed and Multi-Database Systems)

This is the last chapter in Part I and serves as an introduction to Parts II and III. I begin the chapter by classifying each type of distributed database architecture and follow up with sections focusing on the most important categories.

Chapter 7 Overview (Introduction to Distributed Database Systems)

This chapter deals with homogeneous distributed databases. The chapter serves as an introduction by discussing the data and software components of a typical architecture.

Chapter 8 Overview (Homogeneous Distributed Database Design)

Chapter 8 deals with the design of a distributed database architecture from the data model point of view. Table fragmentation and table replication issues are discussed together with algorithms that can be used to properly distribute relation attributes to various sites.

Chapter 9 Overview (Distributed Query Processing)

This chapter is dedicated to describing the steps required to process a distributed query.

Chapter 10 Overview (Transaction Processing, Concurrency, and Deadlocks in Distributed Architectures)

Chapter 10 expands on the discussion of transaction processing in the centralized database environment that was included in Part I.

The chapter concludes with a discussion on deadlocks in a distributed environment together with possible resolution techniques.

Chapter 11 Overview (Distributed and Local Recovery Strategies)

This chapter is divided into two parts. The first part deals with various techniques discussed in the literature for implementing recovery systems in centralized architectures. The second part of the chapter discusses the coordination of the centralized systems in order to enable transaction recovery in a distributed environment.

Chapter 12 Overview (Introduction to Multi-Database Architectures)

This chapter marks the beginning of Part III, which deals with the topic of multi- or heterogeneous database architectures.

Chapter 13 Overview (Multi-Database Design Issues)

Chapter 13 begins with discussions on the design of the global schema and views, followed by a section on the global data model.

Chapter 14 Overview (Case Study 1: MDBMS Using OS/2 and OS/2 Database Manager)

Now that all the pertinent areas of this architecture have been explored, I include an example of a multi-database architecture using real-world technology. Chapter 14 begins with a section describing the environment followed by a section on the hardware and software components required to implement the example system.

Chapter 15 Overview (Case Study 2: A Federated Architecture Using IBM's OS/2)

Federated multi-databases are a special case of multi-databases. This chapter discusses the implementation of a simple federated database using IBM's operating system OS/2 and OS/2 Database Manager.

Chapter 16 Overview (Object-Oriented Databases)

This is the last chapter of the book. We wrap things up by discussing object-oriented databases and how they relate to traditional relational databases, client/server environment, and distributed and federated architectures.

1.4 SUMMARY

The primary goal of this book is to provide the reader with a pratical guide for the design and implementation of distributed database architectures. I have tried to keep the theory down to a minimum.

By now you should have a basic understanding of what this book is all about. After you have finished this book, you will know how to design distributed databases (homogeneous and heterogeneous), be aware of the pitfalls and trouble areas, and be prepared to recommend design strategies for implementing distributed databases.

2

Relational Algebra, Calculus, and Fundamental Database Concepts

2.1 INTRODUCTION

This is the first theoretical chapter of the book. Our discussions on distributed and multi-databases will rely heavily on relational databases and theory. For this reason, the topics covered in this chapter are included for the novice reader or for those who may require a quick refresher.

Chapter 2 begins with a review of relational algebra (Section 2.2) and relational calculus (Section 2.3). Relational databases were introduced by E. F. Codd of IBM in 1970 and have a solid foundation in set theory and relational calculus. Subsequent query language development was based on the work of Codd and others.

Because relational algebra is used heavily in query optimization and distributed query processing, the basics for these disciplines will also be reviewed in this chapter. (Relational calculus-based languages can be translated into relational algebra.) The reader will find these topics of value when reading Parts II and III of the book.

Section 2.4 is dedicated to the architecture of a relational database. The main components of a database are discussed: tables, views, indexes, plans, and procedures. Section 2.5 examines the database catalog, the component that is used to describe and maintain database objects. Database catalogs play an integral role in the generation of access plans for query execution. Important information and statistics are kept in these catalogs and are used by the database manager to maintain the database.

Without further ado, let us delve into the mysteries of relational algebra.

2.2 RELATIONAL ALGEBRA

Relational algebra defines a set of operators and formulas for manipulating sets of data. In our case, the sets are database relations. The data in question are the attributes and tuples that make up these relations. An example best clarifies the terms relation and attributes:

```
EMP_TABLE = {LAST_NAME,FIRST_NAME,EMP_ID}
```

Here we have a relation named EMP_TABLE. It contains attributes LAST_NAME, FIRST_NAME, and EMP_ID. The range of values for each attribute is defined as its domain. Figure 2.1 shows this relation initialized with data. As can be seen, the term relation is just another name for a flat two-dimensional file or, in the case of relational databases, a table.

Our relation contains four tuples (rows). With this information, we can plainly state that a relation is a two-dimensional entity that contains rows and columns. The columns are its attributes and the rows are its tuples.

```
EMP_TABLE = {LAST_NAME,FIRST_NAME,EMP_ID}
```

LAST_NAME	FIRST_NAME	EMP_ID
MURREY	SAM	E1
SMYTHE	REGINALD	E2
MCDONALD	MIKE	E3
PICCADILLY	MARY	E4

Figure 2.1 The EMP_TABLE relation

Before studying the operations that can be performed on relations, let us examine some commonly used symbols used in formulas that operate on relations.

Relational Algebra Symbols

Π	PROJECT a column from a relation
σ	SELECT a vertical row or tuple from a relation
⋈	natural JOIN between two relations
⋉	a semi JOIN between two relations
θ	theta JOIN between two relations
F	a formula used in one of the above operations
∪	UNION between two relations
∩	INTERSECTION between two relations
−	the DIFFERENCE between two relations
÷	DIVISION between two relations
X	the CARTESIAN PRODUCT between two relations

Before discussing what each symbol means and how it is used, I would like to introduce two simple relations that will assist us in this section, namely, the relation R and the relation S:

```
R: A  B  C     S: A  C  E
   1  1  2        1  2  2
   2  2  1        4  3  3
   3  3  2
```

The two relations are derived from the set of domains A, B, C, and E. These domains are defined over the natural numbers 0, 1, 2, 3, and so on. Relation R is composed of the domains A, B, and C. We will refer to these domains of R as the attributes of relation R. Therefore, R = {A,B,C}.

Relation S is composed of the domains A, C, and E. Therefore, S = {A,C,E}. Relation R contains three tuples (rows) and relation S contains two tuples. Now we will proceed to use each of the symbols that were introduced.

The Π symbol is used to extract a vertical attribute from a relation. The common term for this extraction is "PROJECT." Therefore, if we wish to PROJECT attributes A and C from relation R, a typical relational algebra formula would look like this:

$$R'_{A,C} = \Pi(R)$$

The result after executing this formula would be a new relation called R':

```
R'A,C = Π(R)  = A   C
                1   2
                2   1
                3   2
```

The σ symbol is used to SELECT horizontal tuples from a relation. Usually, a formula is used together with this symbol to further define the criteria for the selection. For example, to SELECT all tuples from relation R where B >= 2, the following formula would be used:

```
R'B>=2 = (R)  = A   B   C
                2   2   1
                3   3   2
```

If we wish to see only attributes A and C, the following formula would be used:

```
R'A,C = ΠB>=2((R))  = A   C
                      2   1
                      3   2
```

Notice that the selection formula is nested within parentheses inside the PROJECT formula.

The next symbol is slightly more involved. The natural JOIN is used in operations that involve two relations. The JOIN operation is used to concatenate two relations over a common attribute. An example best illustrates this concept:

```
R'R.A=S.A = R ⋈ S =  A   B   C   E
                     1   1   2   2
```

The formula R.A = S.A is used to specify that we want to concatenate the tuples of the two relations over attributes that have identical values. In this case, the result is only one tuple. Notice that the redundant attribute is removed from the results; that is, only one A attribute is shown. This characteristic is specific to the natural JOIN.

A variation of the natural JOIN is the equi JOIN. In the equi JOIN, the redundant attribute is not removed from the final result set:

```
R'A=A = R ⋈ S    A   B   C   C   E
                 1   1   2   2   2
```

Notice the appearance of redundant attribute names in the result. Unquestionably, a means of uniquely identifying each attribute to avoid any confusion should be used. This problem is solved by prefixing the relation name to each attribute in the final result set:

```
R'A=A = R ⋈ S     R.A   R.B   R.C   S.C   S.E
                    1     1     2     2     2
```

If we had wanted to PROJECT only attribute A from relation R and attribute E from relation S, our relational algebra query formula would look like this:

```
R'A,E = Π((RA=A ⋈ S)) =  R.A   S.E
                          1     2
```

(Once again, notice the inclusion of the nested SELECTION formula!)

The next symbol that we examine is used to perform the semi JOIN operation. The semi JOIN is used in operations similar to the natural JOIN except that only attributes from the left-hand relation are returned in the final result set:

```
R'A=A = R ⋉ S = R.A   R.B   R.C
                 1     1     2
```

This particular formula is very helpful in distributed environments where communications costs are to be kept to a minimum. Only the tuples and attributes from the first relation are returned in the result set. (This particular concept will be discussed in Chapter 9.)

The theta JOIN is discussed next and is similar to the natural JOIN except that the following operators are used in the JOIN formula: <=, >=, >, <, <>. (The symbol = is implied in the natural JOIN!) Another example further illustrates the use of this symbol:

```
R' = RA>2 θ S = R.A   S.A   R.B   R.C   S.C   S.E
                 3     4     3     2     3     3
```

The symbol F represents the subformulas that we have been using all along with the major formula symbols; therefore, we will not elaborate on it any further.

We conclude this section by discussing the five remaining relational algebra operators: UNION, INTERSECTION, DIFFERENCE, DIVISION, and the CARTESIAN PRODUCT. The convention used will first show an example of each operator in a formula together with the result. Following this, an explanation and an analysis of the formula and output are given.

Union

Given the following two relations:

```
R:  A   B   C      S:  A   B   C
    1   3   2          1   1   2
    1   4   5          2   1   2

R' = R UNION S =   A   B   C
                   1   3   1
                   1   4   5
                   1   1   2
                   2   1   2
```

Unions are used between relations with common attributes. The result is the concatenation of the attributes as shown in the final result set R'. This particular operation requires that each relation involved have the same number of attributes. Additionally, the domains in each of the attributes must match the domains of the attributes in the other relation involved in the operation.

Intersection

Given the following two relations:

```
R:  A   B   C      S:   A   B   C
    1   2   3           3   1   2
    5   5   5           1   1   2
    4   5   6           5   5   5
```

The intersection of R and S:

```
R' = R ∩ S =   A   B   C
               5   5   5
```

The result yields all tuples that are common to both of the relations. In this case, only one tuple is in the result set: A = 5, B = 5, and C = 5. As in the previous operation, each relation must have the same number of attributes and the domains of the attributes in the first relation must match the domains of the attributes in the second relation.

Difference

Given the following two relations:

```
R:  A   B   C      S:  A   B   C
    1   2   3          3   1   2
    5   5   5          1   1   2
    4   5   6          5   5   5
```

The difference of R and S:

```
R'  =  R  -  S   =  A   B   C
                    1   2   3
                    4   5   6
```

That is, all tuples that appear in relation R but not in relation S are generated in the result table.

The difference of S and R:

```
R'  =  S  -  R  =  A   B   C
                   3   1   2
                   1   1   2
```

In this case, all tuples contained in relation S but not in relation R appear in the result set.

Division

Given the following two relations:

```
R:  A   B      S:  A
    5   3          3
    5   2          2
    5   1          1
    6   4          2
    1   1          1
    2   2
    1   1
```

The result of R divided by S:

```
R'  =  r  ÷  S  =  A
                   5
                   5
                   5
```

There are two conditions to satisfy for this operation:

1. The sequence of the matching domains must be identical; in this case, 3, 2, 1.
2. The values of the resulting attributes must all be the same; in our case, the values are 5, 5, 5.

Cartesian Product

Given the following two relations:

```
R: A  B  C    S: A  B  C
   1  1  2       1  1  1
   2  2  2       2  2  3
   3  3  3
```

The Cartesian product between these two relations is generated by the following formula:

```
R' = R X S = R.A  R.B  R.C  S.A  S.B  S.C
              1    1    2    1    1    1
              1    1    2    2    2    3
              2    2    2    1    1    1
              2    2    2    2    2    3
              3    3    3    1    1    1
              3    3    3    2    2    3
```

Notice that the number of tuples in the result set of a Cartesian product operation is the product of the number of tuples in the first relation multiplied by the number of tuples in the second relation. In this case, 3×2 or six tuples are generated in the result set.

Note: A Cartesian operation is a special case of the equi JOIN that we previously discussed. It is an equi JOIN without the JOIN occurring over two common attributes.

2.3 RELATIONAL CALCULUS

E. F. Codd introduced the relational databases and theory to the database community in 1970 when his famous paper was published: "A Relational Model of Data for Large Shared Data Banks."[1]

From this work, others, such as D. D. Chamberlin and R. F. Boyce, developed query languages to manipulate and extract data from relational databases. Chamberlin and Boyce developed a query language called SEQUEL in 1974. The language was first introduced in their paper titled "SEQUEL = A Structured English Query Language."[2]

SEQUEL eventually evolved to SEQUEL 2 and was used in IBM's implementation of relational database systems called System R. Finally, in 1980 it was renamed SQL (Structured Query Language). It has been enhanced over the years to further increase its features and power and is currently used in many vendor database management systems such as ORACLE, Informix, Gupta Technologies SQLBase, and IBM's OS/2 Database Manager.

Two variations of the relational calculus exist: tuple and domain calculus. As promised, I will keep the theory to a minimum and present just the bare features and concepts of each language category.

Tuple Calculus

The basic underlying mechanism in a tuple calculus formula is the concept of a tuple variable. These variables represent tuples in a relation and are used to extract data from the relation. Other components of the tuple calculus formula qualify the data by restricting the values of the specified attributes. The best way to understand this concept is to look at a typical SQL query:

```
SELECT  EMP_TABLE.LAST_NAME,  EMP_TABLE.SALARY,
        EMP_TABLE.DEPT
FROM    EMP_TABLE
WHERE
EMP_TABLE.DEPT = 'd1'
AND
EMP_TABLE.SALARY >= 50000
```

This query is basically saying two things:

1. We wish to extract tuples from the relation EMP_TABLE whose DEPT attribute contains the value "D1" and whose attribute SALARY is equal to or greater than the value 50,000.

2. From these tuples, we wish to display the attributes LAST_NAME and SALARY.

Roughly speaking, the attributes EMP_TABLE.DEPT and EMP_TABLE.SALARY are the tuple variables. A generic tuple calculus formula takes the following form:

```
TV1 operator TV2 or constant
```

where

TVi= tuple variable, where i = 1 to m tuple variables
operator= >, <, >=, <=, <>, =
constant= any numerical or string value

The constraint is that the tuple variables and the constants must belong to the same domain. These formulas can be connected with the familiar Boolean operators AND, OR, and NOT:

```
TV1 operator TV2 or constant
AND
TV3 operator TV4 or constant
AND
*
*
*
OR
TVm operator TVn or constant
```

That's really all there is to it. Simple, isn't it?

As stated earlier, the SQL is based on the tuple calculus.

Domain Calculus

The second variation of the relational calculus is domain calculus. As the name implies, the variables in this language are based on the domains (attributes) of a relation, instead of tuples. An IBM product called QBE (query by example) is based on the domain calculus.

A typical domain calculus formula takes the following form:

```
DOMAIN VARIABLE LIST, CONDITION
```

CONDITION is either a formula imposing constraints on one of the domain variables or a formula imposing a constraint on one of the attributes involved in the formula itself. This latter formula takes the following form:

```
RELATION NAME(ATTRIBUTE BELONGING TO RELATION
DOMAIN VARIABLE OR CONSTANT)
```

An example will clarify this concept. Given the following relation:

```
EMP_TABLE = EMP_NAME    SALARY    LOCATION
            SMYTHE      50000     LONDON
            COLLINS     75000     LONDON
            FERGISON    80000     EDINBURGH
            BOLLOCK     45000     LONDON
```

A typical domain calculus formula to extract the attributes EMP_NAME, SALARY, and LOCATION for all employees in London making more than £45,000 would be:

```
EMP_DV,SALARY_DV,LOCATION_DV
CONDITION(EMP_TABLE(LOCATION = 'LONDON')
AND
      (SALARY_DV >= 45000))
```

The QBE (query by example) product mentioned earlier allows users to specify the domain variable formulas by filling in values on an interactive data entry template. The formula just described is shown in Figure 2.2 as it would appear on a simple facsimile of a QBE entry screen. The items displayed on the BEFORE screen represent what the user types in. The results are displayed in the AFTER screen.

Let's continue by examining the components that make up an actual relational database.

BEFORE

EMP_NAME	SALARY	LOCATION
	>=45000	=LONDON

AFTER

EMP_NAME	SALARY	LOCATION
SMYTHE	50000	LONDON
COLLINS	75000	LONDON

Figure 2.2 EMP_TABLE

2.4 DATABASE OBJECTS

In this section we study the components that constitute a typical relational database:

- tables
- views
- indexes
- plans

Tables are another term for relations. Whereas relations contain vertical objects called attributes and horizontal objects called tuples, tables contain columns and rows. That is, an attribute is equivalent to a column, and a row is equivalent to a tuple.

Views are virtual tables constructed from existing tables. Indexes are data structures used to increase performance when accessing tables. Plans are algorithms that can be stored in special tables so that they can be repeatedly retrieved and executed without the need to be recompiled. Last, but not least, database catalogs are special tables that contain information and parameters that are used to manipulate the database residing on the system.

Let's continue by first examining a conceptual view of a typical database after which we will examine each object in greater depth.

Database Overview

Databases reside on high-end servers and host mainframe computers, usually configured with one or more high-capacity hard disk drives and internal memory storage in the range of 16 or more megabytes. (The CPUs on the server have very fast clock speeds.)

The server is usually connected to a local area network (LAN) or a communications network such as IBM's SNA. Since multiple users simultaneously access the databases residing on these servers, sophisticated database management system software is required to coordinate the multiple user transactions. Central host systems and midrange machines such as IBM's S/370 (host) and AS/400 (midrange) are used for this purpose.

Popular LAN database servers such as IBM's models 90 and 95 serve as hosts to such relational DBMS as IBM's OS/2 Database Manager, Informix RDBMS, and Gupta's SQLBase. Distributed database environments involve the connection of any combination of these products over a communications network.

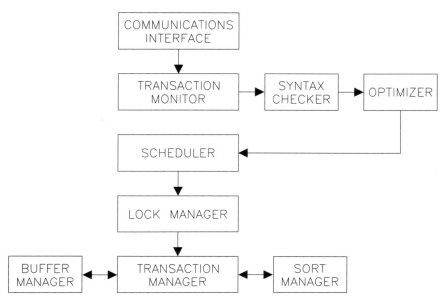

Figure 2.3 Internal components of a typical RDBMS

Associated with the database is software used to manage and access data residing in each of the databases. Figure 2.3 shows the basic components of an RDBMS (relational database management system).

This piece of software is called the database management system (DBMS). The top layer usually contains the necessary software modules and entry points for interfacing to a communications network.

The transaction monitor checks these entry points for user transactions. Once a transaction is received, it is passed to the syntax checker and then to the optimizer.

Once the transaction satisfies the syntax requirements and any optimization on the transaction is performed, it is passed to the scheduler module. The scheduler builds an access plan, ensures that the plan does not conflict with the plans of any other concurrent transactions, and then passes it to the lock manager. Once the required objects are locked (tables and/or rows), the transaction schedule is passed on to the transaction manager, which works together with the sort manager (to order temporary result sets) and a buffer manager (to allocate internal memory) to process the transaction. A log is kept of all this activity storing important information that might be required to restore the database if a system crash occurs.

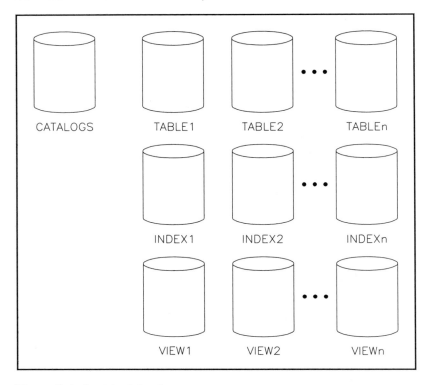

Figure 2.4 A typical database

In later chapters on distributed and multi-database systems we will see that other software components interface with the DBMS to allow distributed transactions to occur.

Figure 2.4 shows a conceptual view of a typical database. The basic components are the database catalogs, tables, indexes, and views. We now proceed to examine each of these components in detail.

Tables

As stated earlier, a table is a relation; the attributes are called columns and the tuples are called rows. Figure 2.5 shows a simple example of a small table called REST_EMP. The table is made up of three columns (or attributes) called EMP_ID, TITLE, and SALARY. The table is meant to represent staff members of a small restaurant.

The schema below the table describes each column in terms of its data type and size. The EMP_ID column is defined over the domain

TABLE REST_EMP

EMP_ID	TITLE	SALARY
1	CHEF	50,000
2	WAITER	25,000
3	MAITRE'D	40,000
4	SOMALIER	45,000

SCHEMA

COLUMN NAME	DATA TYPE	LENGTH
EMP_ID	INTEGER	2
TITLE	CHARACTER	20
SALARY	DECIMAL	10.2

Figure 2.5 Restaurant database

ranging over the integer values 0, 1, 2, 3, and so on. The TITLE column domain ranges over the alphabet characters and is represented by a 15-character string. Finally, the SALARY column domain ranges over decimal values. Each column also has an associated length. A typical relational algebra formula to retrieve the EMP_ID and TITLE columns for employees earning more than £25,000 is shown below:

$$\Pi_{\text{EMP ID,TITLE}} \, (\sigma_{\text{SALARY}>25,000} \, (\text{REST EMP}))$$

An equivalent SQL query would be:

```
SELECT EMP_ID,TITLE
FROM REST_EMP
WHERE SALARY > 25,000
```

We now proceed by looking at a special type of table called a view.

Views

Views are considered to be virtual tables because physically they do not exist. All that does exist is the description of the view. This description is stored in special tables called catalogs. (Catalogs will be discussed in Section 2.6.) Views can be based on one, two, three, or more base tables.

Figure 2.6 shows a view based on two tables, A and B. The view contains four columns: V_A1, V_A2, V_A3, and V_A4. The table below illustrates how the view columns map to the columns in the original base tables:

View Column	Base Table	Base Table Column
V_A1	A	A1
V_A2	A	A2
V_A3	B	A3
V_A4	B	A4

In relational databases, views are created by executing the following SQL command:

```
CREATE VIEW V
( V_A1 CHAR NOT NULL,
  V_A2 CHAR NOT NULL,
  V_A3 DECIMAL,
  V_A4 INTEGER)
AS
SELECT A.A1,A.A2,B.A1,B.A3
FROM A,B
WHERE A.A2 = B.A2
```

The SQL create statement for both tables and views will be discussed in Chapter 4. For now, the concept of views as being virtual tables will suffice. In conclusion, each time a view is used, its description is loaded into memory by the database management system. Views are used either to restrict access to tables or to define new ways of looking at existing base tables.

Indexes

The next database object that we examine is the index. Indexes are used to improve performance when accessing large tables. Imagine a table with 100,000 rows. (The key values for this table range from 1

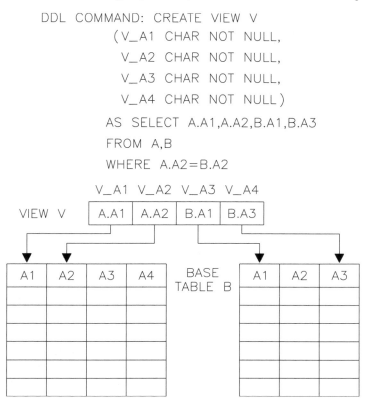

```
DDL COMMAND: CREATE VIEW V
                (V_A1 CHAR NOT NULL,
                 V_A2 CHAR NOT NULL,
                 V_A3 CHAR NOT NULL,
                 V_A4 CHAR NOT NULL)
             AS SELECT A.A1,A.A2,B.A1,B.A3
             FROM A,B
             WHERE A.A2=B.A2
```

Figure 2.6 View defined from two base tables

to 100,000.) If a query were to retrieve rows whose key values are between 45,000 and 50,000, a sequential search would have to be performed. Furthermore, assume that the rows in the table did not appear in sequential order. Indeed, the performance for retrieving the desired rows would be poor. In each row, every key value would have to be checked to see if it fell within the range specified in the query.

Indexes alleviate this problem by providing a structure that drastically reduces the search time involved in processing a query. Figure 2.7a shows a relation with seven rows and Figure 2.7b shows an index based on an inverted tree structure called a B+ tree.

Assume the following SQL command is executed:

```
SELECT A1, A2, A3
FROM TABLE
WHERE KEY = 'E'
```

REC	KEY	A1	A2	A3
1	C	—	—	—
2	B	—	—	—
3	F	—	—	—
4	E	W	X	Y
5	A	—	—	—
6	D	—	—	—
7	G	—	—	—

Figure 2.7a Base table

A program that executed this query would operate in the following manner: Starting at the root of the index, the algorithm would follow the pointer to the first node of the tree. The first node contains the key value "D." We are searching for the value "E," which is higher than "D," so the right pointer is followed to the next node. This next node contains the letter "F." Since "F" is higher then the letter "E," the left pointer is followed to the next node in the index. Lo and

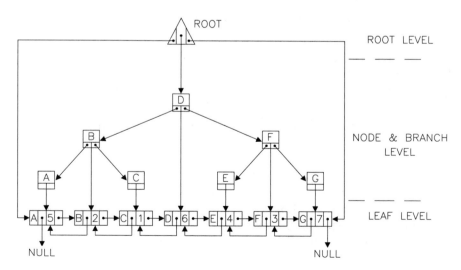

Figure 2.7b Index architecture

behold, this node contains the letter "E," which matches the value we are looking for. The pointer to the leaf node is followed where we find the node that contains the record number of the row in the table. The fourth row is accessed and the query is executed with the following result:

```
A1       A2       A3
W        X        Y
```

As stated earlier, this index is based on a B+ tree structure. B implies a binary tree and the "+" symbol implies that the lower leaves are linked in a fashion similar to a linked list. If a report is requested that requires the rows to appear in sorted ascending order, the left pointer of the root is followed to the first leaf. Each leaf contains a pointer to the next leaf, which contains the next ascending key value.

Backward pointers that allow traversal from the last leaf to the first to produce output in descending order are also present.

Notice that it took only three traversals of the tree to get to the desired key. Had we searched the table in sequential order, it would have taken us four sequential accesses to get to the desired row. Our three-level index represented seven records. A 16-level tree would represent $2 \wedge 16 + 1$ or 65,537 records. From these figures we can see that only a maximum of 16 accesses is required in order to reach 65,537 rows. This is a considerable improvement over 65,537 sequential accesses.

In an actual B+ tree implementation, each node would hold more than one key in order to significantly improve the number of records that could be referenced. A 16-level tree that contained four key values per node would support $4 \pm 65,536$ or 246,142—roughly a quarter of a million records.

Indexes play an integral role in the access plans for executing queries. These objects are examined in the next section.

Access Plans

Access plans can be considered stored algorithms that are used by the database management system to execute queries. Since the algorithms are stored, the DBMS does not have to recompile them prior to execution. The plan is derived from a query, compiled once, and then stored in the SYS_PLANS catalog table.

Typical components of an access plan are whether or not to use an index, what type of sorting must be performed prior to displaying the results, and what type of joins to execute for queries that involve more than one table. We will examine access plans in detail when we discuss query optimization in Chapters 5 and 9.

2.5 CATALOGS

The final topic of discussion in this chapter is database catalogs. Associated with each database is a specialized set of tables that can be manipulated only by the database management system. An exception to this rule is that read-only privileges are granted to the database administrator.

These tables contain information that describes each of the database objects on the system. Additionally, statistical information is stored and used to build access plans for the execution of transactions. Figure 2.8 shows a diagram of a simplified catalog. This catalog is composed of the following tables:

- SYS_TABLES
- SYS_INDEXES
- SYS_VIEWS
- SYS_COLUMNS
- SYS_PLANS

Let's examine the components of each table.

SYS_TABLES Catalog Table

Figure 2.9 shows the schema of the SYS_TABLES catalog. This catalog table is used to define each of the tables that resides on a data-

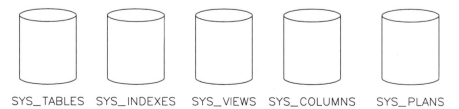

SYS_TABLES   SYS_INDEXES   SYS_VIEWS   SYS_COLUMNS   SYS_PLANS

Figure 2.8 Database catalog

TABLE NAME	TYPE	CARDINALITY	CREATOR	COMMENT
T1	T	1000	BOBAK	LARGE TABLE
T2	T	100000	BOBAK	LARGER TABLE
T3	T	500	BOBAK	MEDIUM TABLE
T4	T	100	BOBAK	SMALL TABLE
V1	V	1000	BOBAK	LARGE TABLE

Figure 2.9 The SYS_TABLES catalog table

base. In our case, the catalogs contain five rows—four rows for the table entries and one row for a view entry. The cardinality column contains the value for the number of rows in each table. This value is obtained by running a utility that maintains statistics for each database object. This utility is usually run after significant changes to the tables have been made (such as updates, deletes, and inserts) in order to keep the statistics up-to-date.

The last two columns in this table are self-explanatory. They contain the name of the table's creator and a place for comments that can be entered to supply the system administrator with additional information about the table.

The SYS_INDEXES Catalog Table

Next we examine the SYS_INDEXES catalog table, which can be seen in Figure 2.10. This table is used to store descriptive and statistical information pertaining to each index residing in a database. The following columns are found in this table:

index name	The name of the index.
table	The table that the index is based on.
key column	The column that was designated as the key for the index. The "+" symbol indicates that the sort order used by the index is in ascending order. If the "–" symbol appeared, the sort order would be in descending order.
creator	Person who created the index.

INDEX NAME	TABLE	KEY COLUMN	CREATOR	% UNIQUE VALUES	COMMENT
I1	T1	+C1	BOBAK	100	INDEX FOR TABLE 1
I2	T2	+C1,C2	BOBAK	100	INDEX FOR TABLE 2
I3	T3	−C1	BOBAK	80	INDEX FOR TABLE 3
I4	T4	+C1	BOBAK	100	INDEX FOR TABLE 4

Figure 2.10 The SYS_INDEXES catalog table

unique values percentage
: Percentage of unique values in the column. One method for calculating this value is to use this formula: ((#unique keys / #rows) × 100).

comment
: Helpful comment to aid the database administrator.

The SYS_VIEWS Catalog Table

Figure 2.11 shows an example of the SYS_VIEWS catalog table. It contains the following columns:

view name
: The name of the view.

creator
: The creator of the view.

query
: The SQL query used to create the view.

comment
: Helpful comment to aid the database administrator.

The SYS_COLUMNS Catalog Table

The SYS_COLUMNS catalog table contains descriptive and statistical information for each column belonging to each table in the data-

VIEW NAME	CREATOR	QUERY	COMMENT
V1	BOBAK	SELECT C1,C2,C3 FROM T1	VIEW BASED ON TABLE T1
V2	BOBAK	SELECT C1,C4 FROM T1,T2 WHERE T1.C1 = T2.C2	VIEW BASED ON TABLES T1 AND T2

Figure 2.11 The SYS_VIEWS catalog table

COLUMN NAME	TABLE	CREATOR	UNIQUE VALUES	COMMENT
C1	T1	BOBAK	1000	THIS COLUMN BELONGS TO TABLE T1
C2	T1	BOBAK	100000	THIS COLUMN ALSO BELONGS TO TABLE T1
			⋮	
C1	T4	BOBAK	100	THIS COLUMN BELONGS TO TABLE T4

Figure 2.12 The SYS_COLUMNS catalog table

base. Figure 2.12 shows an example of this catalog table, which contains the following columns:

column name	The name of the column.
table	The name of the table that contains the column.
creator	The name of the database administrator who created the table that contains the column.
unique values	The number of unique values in the column.
comment	Helpful comment for the database administrator.

The SYS_PLANS Catalog Table

The final table that we examine is the SYS_PLANS table, which is used to store the access plans for the precompiled transactions. A simple example can be seen in Figure 2.13. The following columns are found in this table:

plan name	The name of the plan.
creator	User ID of the person who created the plan.
access plan	Vendor-specific implementation of the access plan.
comment	Helpful comment describing the plan.

All of the tables I have just discussed and shown are greatly simplified versions of actual vendor implementations. They do convey that

PLAN NAME	CREATOR	ACCESS_PLAN	COMMENT
P1	BOBAK	CREATE TEMP. TABLE, PERFORM ASCENDING SORT, ...	PLAN BASED ON TABLE T1
P2	BOBAK	CREATE TEMP. TABLE, CREATE TEMP. TABLE 2, PERFORM NESTED LOOP JOIN...	PLAN BASED ON TABLE T2

Figure 2.13   The SYS_PLANS catalog table

very important descriptive and statistical information is kept in these tables. This information is used to maintain the database and to supply information for creating access plans or executing queries. The reader is referred to implementations of various vendor products such as IBM's DB2 for large host systems or OS/2 Database Manager for server systems.

2.6 SUMMARY

The purpose of this chapter was to provide an overview of key theoretical concepts that the reader requires to understand the implementation and workings of a relational database. These concepts will come in handy when distributed and multi-databases are introduced. But first, we'll examine the data models that are used in a database.

2.7 END NOTES

1. Codd, E. F. "A Relational Model of Data for Large Shared Data Banks," *Communications of the ACM* 13 (October 6, 1970): pp. 337–387.

2. Chamberlin, D. D., and R. F. Boyce. "SEQUEL = A Structured English Query Language," *Proceedings of the ACM-SIGMOD Workshop on Data Description, Access and Control,* Ann Arbor, MI (May 1974): pp. 249–264.

3

Database Models

3.1 INTRODUCTION

In this chapter, the data models that are traditionally used to create databases are introduced. Popular database structures come in four flavors:

- Entity-relationship
- Relational
- Hierarchical
- Network

The discussions on the relational, hierarchical, and network models will be loosely based on the features of three popular systems:

- Relational: IBM's DB2
- Hierarchical: IBM's IMS
- Network: Cullinet's IDMS

Multi-database systems can be composed of one, two, or three of these models. Distributed databases can be designed around one of the above models. Understanding these three database models will prepare us for the logic, theory, and protocols that will be used to distribute and translate database objects among the three architectures.

We will begin the chapter with the entity-relationship model, which is typically used as the starting point for any database design process. Examples of the three principal database models follow.

Of major importance in this section is the logic of translating one model to another—that is, how to perform the following schema mappings:

- Relational to network and vice versa
- Relational to hierarchical and vice versa
- Hierarchical to network and vice versa

In Section 3.8 the reader will be shown how to formally translate the entity-relationship model to each of the three principal models. These translations will be encountered in subsequent chapters and are key in the design of multi-database systems.

3.2 THE ANSI/SPARC DATABASE MODEL

In 1972, a study group was established by a committe of the American National Standards Institute (ANSI) to research and recommend a model for database management systems. This study group was called the Standards and Planning Architecture Requirements Committee (SPARC). This committee published two reports, an interim report in 1975[1] and a final report in 1978.[2] These two reports defined an architecture for database management systems called the ANSI/SPARC architecture. This architecture is used today as the de facto standard, so it will be used in this book.

The architecture defines a database model composed of three layers:

1. The external view layer
2. The conceptual view layer
3. The internal view layer

A representation of this model can be seen in Figure 3.1.

Layer 1, the user/application view, defines how the user and applications see the database—for example, as data entry panels. Layer 2, the conceptual view, is how the enterprise sees the database—that is, the layout of the database is defined at this layer from the database administrator's point of view. Layer 3, the final layer, is defined from the systems programmer's point of view. At this layer, the actual fields and record structures together with the physical storage requirements are specified.

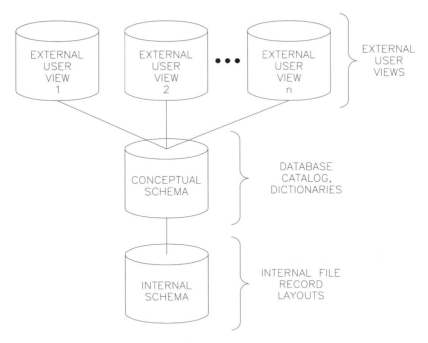

Figure 3.1 ANSI/SPARC model

3.3 THE ENTITY-RELATIONSHIP MODEL

The entity-relationship model[3] is usually used to first describe the data objects that are used to create the database. Entity-relationship diagrams are typically used in the first step of the design process.

Figure 3.2a shows a database made up of four entities. Each of these four entities will be converted to tables (in the relational model) and files (in the network and hierarchical models). The lines between each of the entities represent the relationships between the entities.

The relationship between entity 1 and entity 2 is a many-to-many relationship. Another example of a many-to-many relationship is a college course with many students enrolled. A student can be enrolled in many courses and each course contains many students.

The relationship between entity 1 and entity 3 is one-to-many. An example of the one-to-many relationship is that a course can require more than one book for the subject.

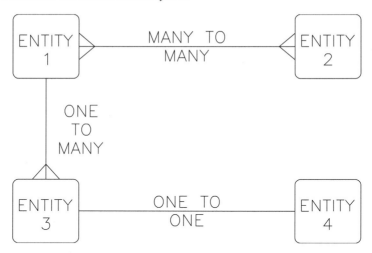

Figure 3.2a Many-to-many relationship

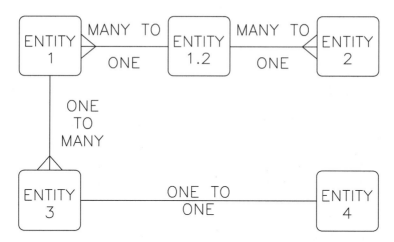

Figure 3.2b Many-to-many relationship removed

Finally, the relationship between entity 3 and entity 4 is one to one. For example, if entity 3 represents a book to be used for a course, entity 4 could contain the name of the publisher for the book. That is, a book can have only one publisher.

Figure 3.2a contains a many-to-many relationship. These types of relationships are undesirable as they are cumbersome to process. A solution to this dilemma is to bridge the entities with an intermediate entity so that the many-to-many relationships are split into a pair of many-to-one relationships. This concept is illustrated in Figure 3.2b. Entity 1.2 was introduced to connect entity 1 with entity 2.

From this final entity-relationship diagram a logical database can be designed. Let us continue by discussing our first database model, the relational model.

3.4 THE RELATIONAL MODEL

We are now ready to discuss what is probably the most popular of the three data models: the relational model. The relational model was introduced by E. F. Codd in his two famous papers.[4,5] Figure 3.3 shows a database made up of three tables. The tables are blown up to show their attribute components.

Table 1 contains 7 columns and 10 rows, the columns being labeled C1 through C7. Table 2 contains 4 columns and 5 rows. The last table, Table 3, contains 5 columns and 8 rows.

Another name for a table is a relation. A relation is composed of attributes (columns) and can have 0, 1, 2, or more tuples (rows). Therefore, we can plainly state that a database is composed of one or more relations. Each relation is defined by its attributes and each can contain 0 or more rows. (English translation: A database can be made up of one or more tables, each table composed of rows and columns that form a two-dimensional grid.)

Figure 3.4 shows the same three relations with one of the attributes of each relation shaded. These shaded attributes are used to uniquely identify each tuple in the relation. These attributes are called indexes. Queries spanning more than one relation are linked together via the common attributes. These links are referred to as joins and will be covered in Chapter 4 where Structured Query Language is discussed.

Notice the dotted lines connecting the links in Figure 3.1. These lines represent the links between tables. (These are virtual links—that is, they do not physically exist.) As we will see in the other two models, pointers are required to link tables in order to retrieve related information. Pointers are not required in the relational model.

The links between tables in a relational database are described in a special database called a catalog. Queries spanning more than one table consult the catalogs to establish the links during query execu-

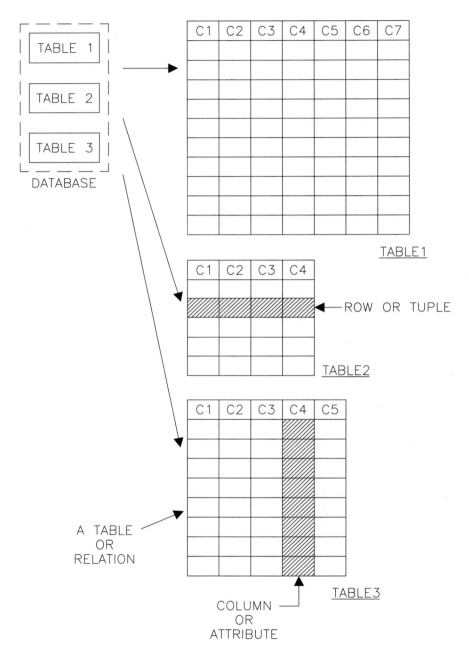

Figure 3.3 A relational database with three tables

38

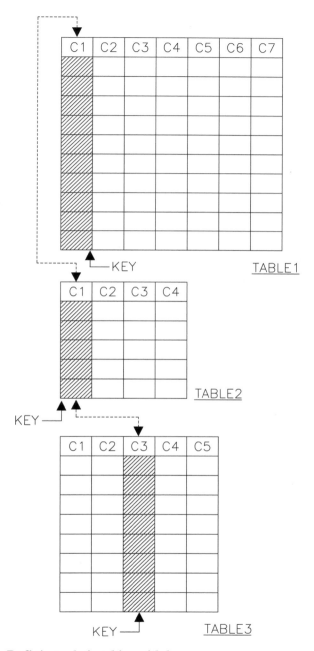

Figure 3.4 Defining relationships with keys

tion. This process is called building an access plan. Queries that are executed frequently can store the access plan so that the cost of building the plan is incurred only once. We will see in later chapters how the access plans are built.

3.5 THE NETWORK MODEL

The network database model is composed of files. Unlike the relational model, it requires physical pointers to establish the links between the tables. Figure 3.5 shows a simplified block diagram of a network database made up of four files.

The four files are connected by special records called DBTG sets. DBTG stands for the database task group and has no bearing on the function of this database object. The name was adopted by the CODASYL committee and has been used ever since.[6,7] DBTG sets are used to connect related records between files. Figure 3.6 illustrates this mechanism.

Navigation between records is accomplished by following the pointers contained in the DBTG sets. To go from record 1 in file 1 to record 1 in file 2 the application must access the DBTG set. The

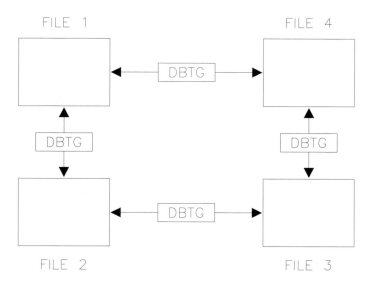

Figure 3.5 A database based on the network data model

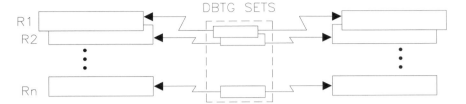

Figure 3.6 Physical link pointers in the network database model

DBTG set is read and the pointers are retrieved so as to allow access to the related records in file 2. Navigation from file 2 to file 1 is accomplished in a similar manner.

We can see how the "JOIN" method used in the relational database to link the tables is easier and less complex than this method. The hierarchical model (which is discussed next) also establishes relationships by using physical address pointers. For further discussions on the network model refer to S. Atre[8] and R. Hogan.[9]

3.6 THE HIERARCHICAL DATABASE MODEL

The discussions that follow are loosely based on the implementation features of IBM's IMS database management system. Figure 3.7 contains a diagram of a database based on the hierarchical data model. This database is made up of five files. Like the network model, this model also requires physical pointers to establish relationships among data files.

Notice the resemblance this model has to an inverted tree structure. The top file, file 1, is the root file (or parent file). This file is parent to two child files, file 2 and file 3. File 2, in turn, is parent to two more files, file 4 and file 5.

A child can have only one parent, a parent can have more than one child, and a child can be a parent to other tables. (In the network model a child file can have one, two, or more parent files.)

The one-parent rule in the hierarchical database model poses a problem in that certain relationships cannot be implemented. To solve this problem, a special record called a dummy or virtual record is introduced. Virtual records contain pointers (similar to DBTG sets) that connect files requiring more than one parent.

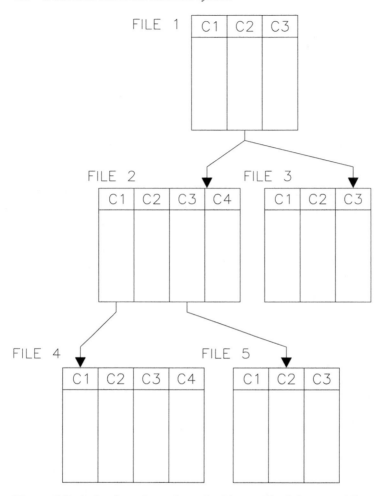

Figure 3.7 A database based on the hierarchical data model

Let us explore this concept further by designing a hierarchical database from an entity-relationship diagram that contains multi-parent relationships. The diagram can be seen in Figure 3.8.

This database is composed of three entities. Notice that entity 2 has two parent entities, entity 1 and entity 3. The relationship between entity 1 and entity 2 is one to many, and a similar relationship exists between entity 2 and its other parent, entity 3.

This design could be easily implemented as a network model by creating a DBTG set for each relationship. Since the hierarchical

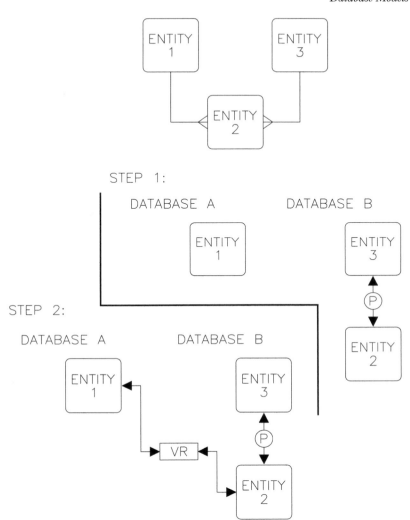

Figure 3.8 Design of a hierarchical database

database requires a strict adherence to the one-parent rule, we must take special steps to implement these relationships.

The first step is to create a forest of trees from the relationships. (Remember that a hierarchical database structure is based on an inverted tree structure.) This is accomplished by dividing the database schema into multiple schemas that adhere to the one-parent rule. An example of this can be seen in Figure 3.8, step 1.

Database A consists of entity 1. Database B consists of entity 2 and entity 3. The relationships between these two entities are implemented via a set of pointers that implement the links between each related record. This set of pointers is labeled "P" in the diagram.

To implement the relationships between entity 1 and entity 2, we introduce a virtual record that was discussed earlier in the chapter. This step can be seen in Figure 3.8, step 2.

Our design is now complete. We have satisfied the one-parent rule by splitting the entity-relationship diagram into two databases. Entity 2 is connected to its parent, entity 3, via a set of pointers embedded in each of the headers in the records. The relationship between entity 2 and entity 1 (which is now in database A) is satisfied by the introduction of the virtual record. Navigation between entity 2 and entity 3 can be accomplished by accessing the pointers in the virtual record. For further discussions on the hierarchical database model, refer to S. Atre[8] and R. Hogan.[9]

3.7 THE TRADITIONAL FISH 'N' CHIPS ENTERPRISE

Now that we have studied the architectural features of the three principal database models, we will continue by designing a database schema for a fictitious company called the Traditional Fish 'n' Chips enterprise. This enterprise maintains central office locations in three major cities in the United Kingdom: London, Edinburgh, and Bath. Each location has several branch restaurants that sell fish and chips and other assorted regional delicacies such as jellied eel! The database that we will design for each location will be used throughout the discussions and examples in the book. The first step will be to design a schema based on the entity-relationship model.

Following the design, three databases will be created, each based on one of the three principal database models that have just been discussed.

Figure 3.9a contains the entity-relationship diagram for the fictitious Traditional Fish 'n' Chips enterprise. As can be seen, it is composed of the following entities: DEPT, EMP, BMGR, and BRANCH.

The DEPT entity contains information that describes each of the departments that make up the Traditonal Fish 'n' Chips enterprise.

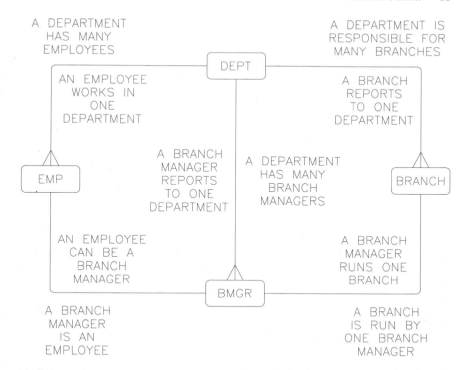

Figure 3.9a Entity-relationship diagram for the Traditional Fish 'n' Chips enterprise

The EMP entity contains information describing each of the employees in the company. The BRANCH entity contains information describing each of the branch locations that belong to the company. Finally, the BMGR entity contains information pertaining to each branch manager who is responsible for the operations of each branch location.

Let us examine the relationships between each entity as defined by our diagram:

- A department is responsible for MANY branches.
- A branch reports to ONE department.
- A department has MANY employees.
- An employee belongs to ONE department.
- A department has MANY branch managers.

- A branch belongs to ONE department.
- An employee can be A branch manager.
- A branch manager is AN employee.
- A branch manager runs A branch.
- A branch is run by A branch manager.

Based on the entity-relationship diagram, let us define a database schema for the Traditional Fish 'n' Chips company.

Figure 3.9b contains the definitions for each attribute belonging to each of the four entities we have just discussed. We will base the design of the relational, network, and hierarchical databases on this schema.

Of particular interest are the assignments of the primary and foreign keys in each entity. Primary keys are columns that are used to uniquely identify the rows in a table. Foreign keys are columns that are used to establish links with primary keys belonging to other tables. The primary key, foreign key combination allows tables to be joined, thereby establishing the relationships that were specified in the entity-relationship diagrams when the database was designed.

The DEPT_ID attribute of the DEPT entity has been assigned as the primary key. No foreign keys have been assigned. The primary key for the EMP entity is the EMP_ID attribute.

The EMP_DEPT attribute has been assigned as a foreign key to the DEPT entity.

The BRANCH entity has the BRANCH_ID attribute as its primary key. The DEPT_ID attribute is a foreign key to the DEPT entity.

Finally, the BMGR entity has the BRANCH_MGRID attribute as its primary key. The remaining three attributes are assigned as foreign keys to each of the other three entities in the database. The DEPT_ID attribute is the foreign key to the EMP entity. The last attribute, BRANCH_ID, is a foreign key to the BRANCH entity.

We can now proceed to design each of our databases. Let us begin with the relational version of our enterprise, which will be located in London. The Edinburgh location database will be based on the hierarchical model. The Bath location database will be based on the network model.

ENTITY NAME: DEPT

ATTRIBUTES	DATA TYPE	KEY
DEPT_ID	CHARACTER STRING	*
DEPT_MGR_ID	CHARACTER STRING	
DEPT_LOCATION	CHARACTER STRING	
DEPT_NAME	CHARACTER STRING	
NUM_EMP	NUMERIC	

ENTITY NAME: EMP

ATTRIBUTES	DATA TYPE	KEY
EMP_ID	CHARACTER STRING	*
EMP_NAME	CHARACTER STRING	
EMP_DEPT	CHARACTER STRING	**
EMP_TITLE	CHARACTER STRING	
EMP_SALARY	CURRENCY	
EMP_WORK_DATE	DATE	

ENTITY NAME: BRANCH

ATTRIBUTES	DATA TYPE	KEY
BRANCH_ID	CHARACTER STRING	*
DEPT_ID	CHARACTER STRING	**
BRANCH_NAME	CHARACTER STRING	
BRANCH_LOCATION	CHARACTER STRING	
PROFITS_TO_DATE	CURRENCY	
BRANCH_MANAGER	CHARACTER STRING	

ENTITY NAME: BMGR

ATTRIBUTES	DATA TYPE	KEY
BRANCH_MGRID	CHARACTER STRING	*
DEPT_ID	CHARACTER STRING	**
EMP_ID	CHARACTER STRING	**
BRANCH_ID	CHARACTER STRING	**

NOTE:

* = PRIMARY KEY
** = FOREIGN KEY

Figure 3.9b Entity-relationship diagram for the Traditional Fish 'n' Chips enterprise

3.8 MODEL TRANSLATION CONCEPTS

There are two goals to this section. The first is to design each of the three principal database models based on the specifications of the entity-relationship diagram and schema that were just developed. The second goal is to discuss the logic required to translate schemas from one model to the other.

The techniques learned here will be most valuable in Part III. There, we will design a multi-database system based on each of the three database models. Distributed query processing for queries accessing more than one database model will rely on these techniques to properly access each data object. Let us continue by first mapping our entity-relationship diagram to the relational, network, and hierarchical models.

Entity-Relationship to Relational Schema Translation

Figure 3.10 shows the relational database derived from the entity-relationship diagram developed earlier in this chapter. (The entity-relationship diagram is included for easy reference.) Each entity is implemented as a relational table. (Relational tables are discussed in detail in Chapter 4.)

Notice that each table contains a primary key and that each table has one or more foreign keys (the FNC_DEPT_TBL has no foreign keys). The combinations of primary key and foreign keys implement the relationships between each of the entities. Let us examine each one in detail, beginning with the DEPT entity.

The DEPT entity is implemented as a table called FNC_DEPT_TBL. This table has relationships between each of the other three tables in the database. Let us examine the primary–foreign key combinations that implement each relationship. The convention used is

```
<table 1 name>.<column name> = <table 2 name>.<column name>
```

- The "a department has MANY employees" relationship is defined by the FNC_BMGR_TBL.DEPT_ID = FNC_EMP_TBL. EMP_DEPT equation.
- The "department has MANY branch managers" relationship is defined by the FNC_DEPT_TBL.DEPT_ID = FNC_BMGR_TBL. DEPT_ID equation.

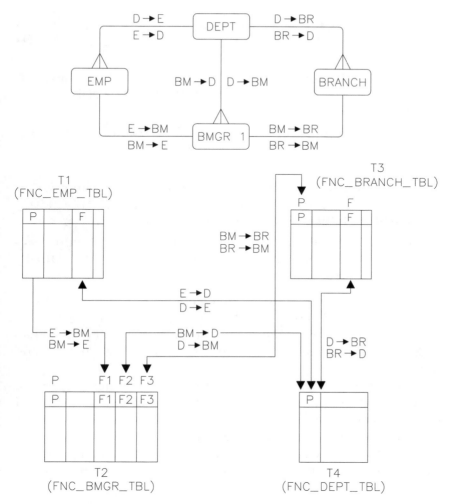

Figure 3.10 Entity-relationship to relational translation

- The "department is responsible for MANY branches" relationship is defined by the FNC_DEPT_TBL.DEPT_ID = FNC_BRANCH_TBL.DEPT_ID equation.

- The "employee belongs to ONE department" relationship is defined by the FNC_EMP_TBL.EMP_DEPT = FNC_DEPT_TBL.DEPT_ID equation.

- The "employee can be A branch manager" relationship is defined by the FNC_EMP_TBL.EMP_ID = FNC_BMGR_TBL.EMP_ID equation.

- The "a branch manager is AN employee" relationship is defined by the FNC_BMGR_TBL.EMP_ID = FNC_EMP_TBL.EMP_ID equation.

- The "branch manager belongs to A department" relationship is defined by the FNC_BMGR_TBL.DEPT_ID = FNC_DEPT_TBL. DEPT_ID equation.

- The "branch manager runs ONE branch" relationship is implemented by the FNC_BMGR_TBL.BRANCH_ID = FNC_ BRANCH_TBL.BRANCH_ID equation.

- The "a branch is run by ONE branch manager" relationship is defined by the FNC_BRANCH_TBL.BRANCH_ID = FNC_ BMGR_TBL.BRANCH_ID combination.

- The "branch reports to ONE department" relationship is defined by the FNC_BRANCH_TBL.DEPT_ID = FNC_DEPT_ TBL.DEPT_ID combination.

I have gone to considerable (and tedious) lengths to describe how each relationship is implemented. My purpose is to stress that in the relational model, navigation from one table to another is implemented via the primary and foreign key combinations between related tables.

Chapter 4 will discuss the Structured Query Language (SQL), which is used to retrieve information from a relational database. I sneak in an example of a SQL query at this time to show the reader how relationships between tables are defined.

Assume we want to see all the branch managers from a particular department in London. The SQL query would look something like this:

```
SELECT BRANCH_MGRID,DEPT_ID,BRANCH_LOCATION
FROM FNC_BMGR_TBL,FNC_BRANCH
WHERE FNC_BMGR_TBL.DEPT_ID = FNC_BRANCH_TBL.DEPT_ID
AND
FNC_BRANCH_TBL.BRANCH_LOCATION = 'London'
```

The above command is submitted to the relational database management system as is. Imagine the equivalent query in a network or hierarchical database! A complex application would have to be written to access the record pointers in the files so that the required relationships to process the query could be built.

Entity-Relational to Network Schema Translation

We continue by developing the network version of our database. (The central office in Bath will use a database based on this model.) Recall from Section 3.4 that relationships between files in a network database are implemented via sets of pointers called DBTG sets (Database Task Group sets). Figure 3.11 shows the entity-relationship diagram together with the derived network database design. Each of the entities is implemented as a file.

The employee entity is now called the FNC_EMP_FILE. The DEPT entity is implemented as a file called FNC_DEPT_FILE. The BMGR entity is implemented as the FNC_BMGR_FILE and the BRANCH entity is implemented as the FNC_BRANCH_FILE.

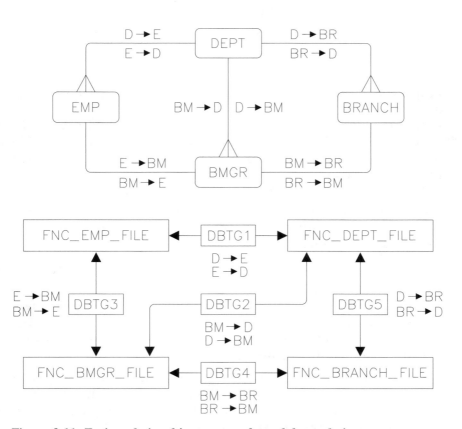

Figure 3.11 Entity-relationship to network model translation

The relationships between the entities are implemented as DBTG sets. We can immediately see that this design is much more complicated than the relational model that was developed earlier. Applications must access the DBTG sets in order to navigate between files. (Below each DBTG set is the relationship that was specified in the entity-relationship diagram.)

The point to stress in this subsection is that the relationships are implemented as DBTG sets in a network database. The relationship between the DEPT entity and the EMP entity is implemented as a DBTG1. The relationship between the DEPT entity and the BRANCH entity is implemented as DBTG5. DBTG2 implements the relationship between the DEPT entity and the BMGR entity. DBTG3 implements the relationship between the EMP entity and the BMGR entity. Finally, DBTG4 implements the relationship between the BMGR entity and the BRANCH entity.

Let's continue by deriving the hierarchical database from our entity-relationship diagram.

Entity-Relationship to Hierarchical Schema Translation

Next, we examine the procedure to design a hierarchical database from our previously defined entity-relationship diagram. Figure 3.12 depicts the entity-relationship diagram together with the derived hierarchical database.

There are two steps to this transition. Remember that unlike network databases, a child entity can have only one parent in a hierarchical database. In order not to violate this requirement, we must split our database into two databases, as follows:

- Database 1 contains the entities FNC_DEPT_FILE and FNC_EMP_FILE. FNC_DEPT_FILE is the parent of FNC_EMP_FILE. Navigation between the two files is via a two-way pointer between each of the related records of the files. The pointer is labeled P1 and implements the one-to-many relationship between the two entities.

- Database 2 contains the remaining two files. The FNC_BRANCH_FILE is the parent of the FNC_BMGR_FILE. Again, navigation between the files is with a two-way pointer between each record. The pointer is labeled P2.

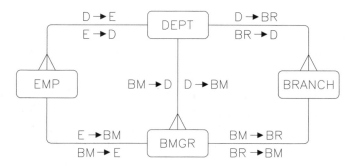

HIERARCHICAL MODEL:

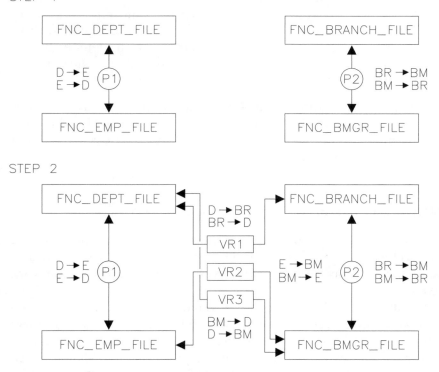

Figure 3.12 Entity-relationship to hierarchical model translation

Phase 2 of the transition phase requires the declaration of virtual records to connect the two databases together. Virtual record VR1 is used to connect FNC_BRANCH_FILE to FNC_DEPT_FILE, virtual record VR2 connects FNC_BMGR_FILE to FNC_EMP_FILE, and, finally, virtual record VR3 connects records in FNC_BMGR_FILE with records in FNC_DEPT_FILE. These virtual records implement the one-to-many relationships specified in the entity-relationship diagram. Two concepts are worth stressing:

1. The use of virtual or "dummy" records allows the original relationships that were specified in the entity-relationship diagram to be preserved. This technique prevents violation of the one-parent rule in the hierarchical database.

2. The second concept is that the navigation between a parent and a child file is via pointers embedded in the header sections of records. Informally, the design steps are as follows: Given any entity-relationship diagram, if an entity has more than one parent, split the database and use virtual records to preserve the relationship. Use pointers to implement the remaining parent-child relationships as specified in the entity-relationship diagram.

To summarize, a hierarchical database can be compared to a forest of inverted trees where each leaf is a record of a file for that tree. Interconnection between databases is via virtual records that contain pointers between related records in related files.

Network to Hierarchical Schema Translation

We now discuss how to translate a network database schema into a heirarchical database schema. The discussion that follows is also valid for the translation of a hierarchical database to a network database.

Recall from earlier sections that relationships in a network database were implemented as DBTG sets. Relationships in a hierarchical database were implemented as record pointers and virtual records. Therefore, we can safely state that the process of translating a network model schema to a hierarchical model schema is to substitute each DBTG set with the proper combination of record pointers and/or virtual records between files.

To facilitate this process, we can translate the network model back to the entity-relationship model. From the entity-relationship model we can derive the equivalent hierarchical model by applying the techniques that were discussed in earlier sections of this chapter. Figure 3.13 shows the transition steps.

NETWORK MODEL:

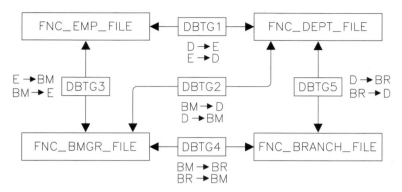

ENTITY—RELATIONSHIP MODEL:

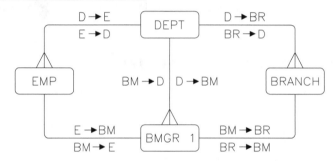

HIERARCHICAL MODEL:

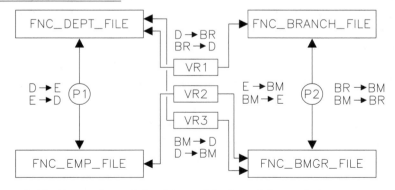

Figure 3.13 Network model to hierarchical model translation

The small labeled squares in the top portion of the figure represent the DBTG sets that are used as links between files. The relationship that each DBTG set implements appears immediately below each DBTG set and can be traced back to the entity-relationship diagram.

In the bottom portion of the figure, pointers and virtual records replace the DBTG sets. The following substitutions are required:

Network Schema (replace)	Hierarchical Schema (with)
DBTG1	P1
DBTG2	VR3
DBTG3	VR2
DBTG4	P2
DBTG5	VR1

Although this is not the most optimal design, it illustrates the logic behind the transition: Replace each DBTG set with a pointer or a virtual record as required.

Relational to Hierarchical Schema Translation

Figure 3.14 shows the transition diagram for mapping a relational database schema to a hierarchical schema. (Recall that the entity-relationship diagram is used as an intermediate step to facilitate this translation process.)

Earlier we examined how relationships between tables in relational databases are defined via the primary to foreign key combinations. Also recall that in the hierarchical model, the relationships are defined via the use of pointers and virtual records that are used to facilitate navigation between related files. Our goal is to translate each primary–foreign key pair with the equivalent combination of pointers and/or virtual records in the hierarchical model. The table below illustrates the required translations:

Relational Schema (replace)	Hierarchical Schema (with)
T1.F = T4.P	P1
T1.P = T2.F1	VR2
T2.F3 = T3.P	P2
T2.F2 = T4.P	VR3
T4.P = T3.F	VR1

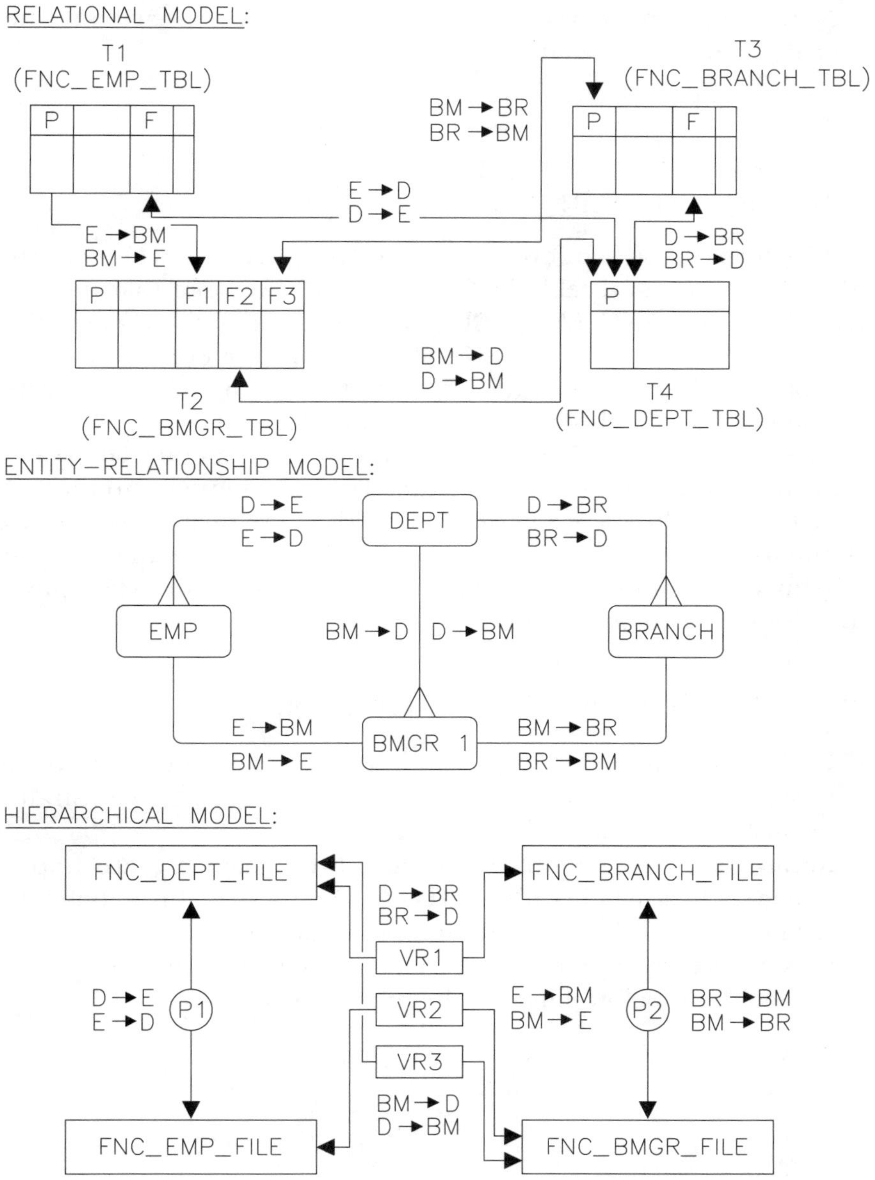

RELATIONAL MODEL:

ENTITY—RELATIONSHIP MODEL:

HIERARCHICAL MODEL:

Figure 3.14 Relational model to hierarchical model translation

Notice that the tables have been given aliases to facilitate the specifications of the relationships:

T1 = table FNC_EMP_TBL
T2 = table FNC_BMGR_TBL
T3 = table FNC_BRANCH_TBL
T4 = table FNC_DEPT_TBL

Therefore, to specify the relationship between table FNC_EMP_TBL and table FNC_BMGR_TBL we state that the primary key in the FNC_EMP_TBL (T1.P) must equal the value in the foreign key (T2.F1) in the FNC_BMGR_TBL for every row being compared. The formula T1.F = T4.P is actually the JOIN predicate that appears in a SQL statement that joins the two tables.

The equivalent JOIN in the hierarchical version of our database is implemented as VR2 in our diagram. That is, an application would have to access the record in order to retrieve the related records. In summary, to translate the relational schema to the hierarchical schema we substitute each primary key–foreign key pair to its equivalent pointer or virtual record.

Network to Relational Schema Translation

Finally, let's examine the steps required to translate a network database schema to a relational database schema. Figure 3.15 illustrates the translation diagrams for this process.

Recall that the relationships in a network database are implemented via physical links called DBTG sets. Our goal in this section is to translate the DBTG sets in the network database to the proper primary key–foreign key pairs in the relational database model.

The columns below illustrate the translations:

Network Model (replace)	Relational Model (with)
DBTG1	T1.F = T4.P
DBTG2	T2.F2 = T4.P
DBTG3	T1.P = T2.F1
DBTG4	T2.F3 = T3.P
DBTG5	T4.P = T3.F

NETWORK MODEL:

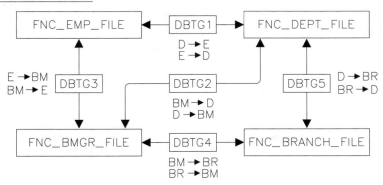

ENTITY–RELATIONSHIP MODEL:

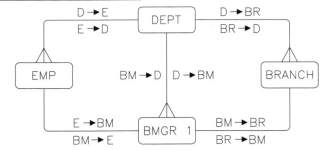

RELATIONAL MODEL:

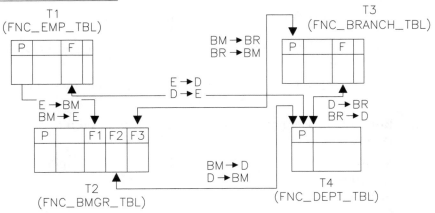

Figure 3.15 Network model to relational model translation

One can clearly see that the DBTG sets must be replaced with the proper JOINs between the primary keys and the foreign keys in the tables. Although I have not used it in my examples, JOINs can also be implemented between primary keys or between foreign keys. For example:

T1.P = T2.P
T1.F = T2.F

Recall that the following aliases were used for each table:

T1 = table FNC_EMP_TBL
T2 = table FNC_BMGR_TBL
T3 = table FNC_BRANCH_TBL
T4 = table FNC_DEPT_TBL

Conclusions

To recapitulate our discussion of the principal database models, we recall that translation from one model to the other was faciliated by using the entity-relationship diagram as an interim model that permitted the mapping of the relationship mechanism.

The key concepts that were pertinent in this chapter are:

1. Use entity-relationship diagrams as starting points in the database design process.

2. Relationships in relational databases are implemented by the primary–foreign key combinations.

3. Relationships in network databases are implemented by DBTG sets.

4. Relationships in hierarchical databases are implemented by record pointer links between parent-child files and virtual records between files in separate databases.

5. Translations between models consist of translating the relationship mechanism to its counterpart in the target model. The table below summarizes this concept:

Model From	Relationship To	Relationship Mechanism
Relational Network	P-F keys	DBTG sets
Relational Hierarchical	P-F keys	Pointers and virtual records
Hierarchical Network	Pointers	DBTG sets and virtual records

Note: P-F means primary to foreign key combinations. Primary to primary and foreign to foreign key combinations are also permissible.

3.9 SUMMARY

The reader has now seen how to design a database from an entity-relationship diagram. Additionally, three schemas based on the relational, hierarchical, and network database models were designed for the fictitious Traditional Fish 'n' Chips company. This company has locations in the following three cities:

Location	Database Model	Vendor Implementation
London	relational model	IBM's DB2
Edinburgh	hierarchical model	IBM's IMS
Bath	network model	Cullinet's IDMS

Each location uses a database to store enterprise data. Each database is based on one of the principal database models discussed earlier in the chapter. We now have a situation where the company must support three different vendor implementations for each database. We will see in Part III of this book how to build and process transactions that span more than one database. We will also confront several complex issues that arise when attempting to process transactions in a distributed and multi-database design.

Several references were cited for discussions on the ANSI/SPARC data model and the three principal database models. Additional information on database design and systems can be found in Atre,[8] Yao,[10] and Date.[11]

3.10 END NOTES

1. ANSI/X3/SPARC Study Group on Database Management Systems. Interim Report, *ACM FDT Bulletin* (1975).

2. Tsichritzis, D. C., and A. Klug. "The ANSI/X3/SPARC DBMS Framework Report of the Study Group on Database Management Systems," *Information Systems* (1978): pp. 173–191.

3. Ullman, J. D. *Principles of Database Systems*, 2d ed., Rockville, MD: Computer Science Press, 1982.

4. Codd, E. F. "A Relational Model of Data for Large Shared Data Banks," *Communications of the ACM*, vol. 13 (October 6, 1970): pp. 377, 387.

5. Codd, E. F. "Relational Completeness of Database Sublanguages," *Database Systems*, R. Rustin, ed. Englewood Cliffs, NJ: Prentice Hall, 1972, pp. 65–98.

6. CODASYL Programming Committee. *Database Task Group Report to the CODASYL Programming Language Committee*, New York: ACM, October 1969.

7. CODASYL Programming Committee. *CODASYL Database Task Group, April 1971 Report*, New York: ACM, 1971.

8. Atre, S. *Database—Structured Techniques for Design, Performance and Management*, 2d ed., New York: John Wiley & Sons, 1988.

9. Hogan, R. *A Practical Guide to Database Design*, Englewood Cliffs, NJ: Prentice Hall, 1990.

10. Yao, S. Bing, ed. *Principles of Database Design, Vol. 1—Logical Organizations*, Englewood Cliffs, NJ: Prentice Hall, 1985.

11. Date, C. J. *An Introduction to Database Systems*, 3d ed., Reading, MA: Addison-Wesley, 1981.

4

SQL Basics

4.1 INTRODUCTION

This chapter is dedicated to the Structured Query Lanaguage, affectionately known by the moniker SQL. SQL is divided into the following sublanguages:

- The data declaration language (DDL)
- The data control language (DCL)
- The data manipulation language (DML)

The data declaration language is used to create the various component objects of the database. The data control language is used to implement and control data security and consistency. The data manipulation language forms the core of SQL. It is used to retrieve data from each of the tables by forming relationships over columns called indexes. This part of the SQL language will be examined in great detail.

We will also create an example database from the entity-relationship diagram that was introduced in Chapter 3 (see Figure 3.9a). Recall that the diagram represented a database with the following four entities:

1. EMP
2. DEPT
3. BMGR
4. BRANCH

The following four tables will be created from these entities:

1. FNC_EMP_TBL
2. FNC_DEPT_TBL
3. FNC_BMGR_TBL
4. FNC_BRANCH_TBL

As we proceed through the chapter, these tables will be created with the proper DDL statments. Rows will then be inserted into the tables and indexes and views will be created. The core of the chapter will concentrate on retrieving data from the tables by using the DML sublanguage of SQL. Let us now proceed by introducing the data declaration language portion of SQL.

4.2 DATA DECLARATION LANGUAGE

DDL is made up of commands that allow database administrators the capability to create and declare objects in the database. The primary DDL keywords are listed below:

- CREATE
- DROP
- ALTER
- COMMENT ON

In this section I will show how to use each of these keywords in a DDL statement that will create objects, drop objects, alter existing objects, and enter descriptive text for each object into the database catalog. (For those requiring a quick review, database catalogs were discussed in Chapter 2.)

Before we continue, let me reintroduce the entity-relationship diagram and database schema for the Traditional Fish 'n' Chips enterprise. Figure 4.1 shows the entity-relationship diagram and Figure 4.2 depicts the database schema. The CREATE statements to build the tables defined in the schema are introduced next.

CREATE

Below is the template for the CREATE TABLE DDL statement:

```
CREATE TABLE <tablename>
(column 1 name column 1 type NULL/NOT NULL,
```

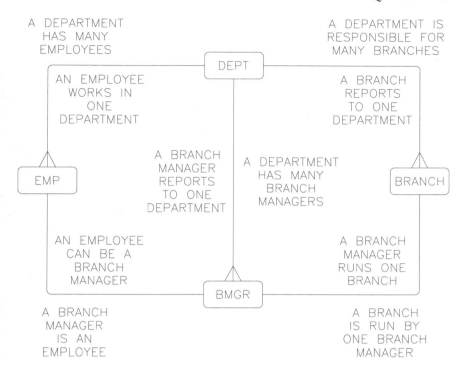

Figure 4.1 Entity-relationship diagram for the Traditional Fish 'n' Chips enterprise

```
column 2 name column 2 type NULL/NOT NULL,
*
*
column N name column N type NULL/NOT NULL)
```

This is a generic form of the statement, and it may vary slightly with other forms of SQL dialects implemented by various vendors. The statement is very simple. It begins with the "CREATE TABLE" keywords followed by the table name. Enclosed within parentheses is a list of column names, column data types, and notation to state whether NULL values are allowed in the column.

In Section 4.8 of this chapter I will discuss referential integrity, a mechanism whereby related data that span multiple tables can be manipulated by the database management system. This mechanism maintains data consistency by allowing the database administrator the capability to define rules and conditions for deleting, inserting, and updating related rows of information. Additionally, referential

ENTITY NAME: DEPT

ATTRIBUTES	DATA TYPE	KEY
DEPT_ID	CHARACTER STRING	*
DEPT_MGR_ID	CHARACTER STRING	
DEPT_LOCATION	CHARACTER STRING	
DEPT_NAME	CHARACTER STRING	
NUM_EMP	NUMERIC	

ENTITY NAME: EMP

ATTRIBUTES	DATA TYPE	KEY
EMP_ID	CHARACTER STRING	*
EMP_NAME	CHARACTER STRING	
EMP_DEPT	CHARACTER STRING	**
EMP_TITLE	CHARACTER STRING	
EMP_SALARY	CURRENCY	
EMP_HIRE_DATE	DATE	

ENTITY NAME: BRANCH

ATTRIBUTES	DATA TYPE	KEY
BRANCH_ID	CHARACTER STRING	*
DEPT_ID	CHARACTER STRING	**
BRANCH_NAME	CHARACTER STRING	
BRANCH_LOCATION	CHARACTER STRING	
PROFITS_TO_DATE	CURRENCY	
BRANCH_MANAGER	CHARACTER STRING	**

ENTITY NAME: BMGR

ATTRIBUTES	DATA TYPE	KEY
BRANCH_MGR_ID	CHARACTER STRING	*
DEPT_ID	CHARACTER STRING	**
EMP_ID	CHARACTER STRING	**
BRANCH_ID	CHARACTER STRING	**

NOTE:

    * = PRIMARY KEY
  ** = FOREIGN KEY

Figure 4.2 Relational schema for the Traditional Fish 'n' Chips enterprise

integrity requires the definition of primary keys and foreign keys. The CREATE statements that are declared in this section will be enhanced to include referential integrity constraints in Section 4.8.

Let us proceed by creating the four tables with the following SQL DDL statements:

```
CREATE TABLE FNC_DEPT_TBL (
DEPT_ID          CHAR(4)   NOT NULL,
DEPT_MGR_ID      CHAR(4)   NOT NULL,
DEPT_LOCATION    CHAR(20)  NOT NULL,
DEPT_NAME        CHAR(20)  NOT NULL,
NUM_EMP          INTEGER,
PRIMARY KEY (DEPT_ID))

CREATE TABLE  FNC_EMP_TABLE (

EMP_ID           CHAR(5)   NOT NULL,
EMP_NAME         CHAR(20)  NOT NULL,
EMP_DEPT         CHAR(4)   NOT NULL,
EMP_TITLE        CHAR(20)  NOT NULL,
EMP_SALARY       DECIMAL   NOT NULL,
EMP_HIRE_DATE    DATE      NOT NULL,
PRIMARY KEY (EMP_ID),
FOREIGN KEY (EMP_DEPT) REFERENCES  FNC_DEPT_TBL)

CREATE TABLE FNC_BRANCH_TBL (
BRANCH_ID        CHAR(4)   NOT NULL,
DEPT_ID          CHAR(4)   NOT NULL,
BRANCH_NAME      CHAR(20)  NOT NULL,
BRANCH_LOCATION  CHAR(20)  NOT NULL,
PROFITS_TO_DATE  DECIMAL   NOT NULL,
BRANCH_MANAGER   CHAR(5)   NOT NULL,
PRIMARY KEY (BRANCH_ID),
FOREIGN KEY (DEPT_ID) REFERENCES FNC_DEPT_TBL,
FOREIGN KEY (BRANCH_MANAGER) REFERENCES
FNC_BMGR_TBL)

CREATE TABLE FNC_BMGR_TBL (
BRANCH_MGR_ID    CHAR(5)   NOT NULL,
DEPT_ID          CHAR(4)   NOT NULL,
EMP_ID           CHAR(5)   NOT NULL,
BRANCH_ID        CHAR(4)   NOT NULL,
PRIMARY KEY (BRANCH_MGR_ID),
```

```
FOREIGN KEY (DEPT_ID)    REFERENCES FNC_DEPT_TBL,
FOREIGN KEY (EMP_ID)     REFERENCES FNC_EMP_TBL,
FOREIGN KEY (BRANCH_ID)  REFERENCES FNC_BRANCH_TBL)
```

Notice how these DDL statements directly reflect the relationships defined in the entity-relationship diagram that was created in Chapter 3. Each CREATE statement has a line that defines the table's primary key and foreign keys that are required to establish relationships with other tables. Let us continue by creating a view that accesses several columns based on the tables in our database. To create a view, the same DDL statement is used except that the keyword TABLE is replaced with the keyword VIEW. The command below creates a view called LONDON_BRANCH_INFO:

```
CREATE VIEW LONDON_BRANCH_INFO (
BRANCH_ID CHAR(4),
DEPT_ID   CHAR(4),
EMP_ID    CHAR(5) )
AS
SELECT BRANCH_ID,DEPT_ID,EMP_ID
FROM   FNC_BRANCH_TBL,FNC_BMGR_TBL
WHERE  BRANCH_LOCATION = 'LONDON'
AND    BRANCH_MANAGER = BRANCH_MGR_ID
```

Notice how the command uses a SELECT statement to join two tables and retrieves only the rows whose BRANCH_LOCATION column contains the string "London." The SELECT statement is part of the DML sublanguage, which will be discussed in Section 4.4. I include a sample here to show the reader how it can be used to create views.

The data declaration language also allows the database administrator the capability to create indexes for accessing the tables in ascending or descending order. This mechanism will be examined next.

Creating Indexes

Indexes are required so as to allow fast performance when retrieving rows from tables. Indexes are usually based on the B+ tree structure and are defined over one or more columns of the table. Below are four commands required to create indexes for each of the four tables:

```
CREATE INDEX INX_EMP_TBL1
ON TABLE FNC_EMP_TBL
USING (EMP_ID, ASC)

CREATE INDEX INX_DEPT_TBL1
ON TABLE FNC_DEPT_TBL
USING (DEPT_ID,ASC)

CREATE INDEX INX_BRANCH_TBL1
ON TABLE FNC_BRANCH_TBL
USING (BRANCH_ID)

CREATE INDEX INX_BMGR_TBL1
ON TABLE FNC_BMGR_TBL
USING(BRANCH_MGR_ID)
```

You can see that the syntax is similar to the syntax of the command that was used to create the four tables. The basic format of the command is

```
CREATE INDEX

USING (<columnname>,ASC/DESC>,...)
```

The keywords to remember are CREATE, INDEX, ON, USING, and ASC or DESC. After each column name the database administrator can define whether the sort order of the index is in ascending (ASC) or descending (DESC) order. The two keywords ASC and DESC are optional and if left out the sort order will be ascending by default.

DROP

Now that we have defined and created our objects, we will delete them. Yes, that's right, after all our hard work we will delete every object that was just created. Below are the commands required to drop each of the tables, indexes, and the view that was just created:

```
DROP TABLE FNC_EMP_TBL
DROP TABLE FNC_DEPT_TBL
DROP TABLE FNC_BRANCH_TBL
DROP TABLE FNC_BMGR_TBL
```

```
DROP INDEX INX_EMP_TBL1
DROP INDEX INX_DEPT_TBL1
DROP INDEX INX_BRANCH_TBL1
DROP INDEX INX_BMGR_TBL1
DROP VIEW FNC_LONDON_BRANCH_INFO
```

As can be seen, the syntax is very simple. A general template for this command is:

```
DROP <objecttype> <objectname>
```

The keyword DROP is followed by the keyword for the object type and then the object name itself. Remember to use this command with care, for once an object is dropped it cannot be restored unless a backup of the database is available.

The tables, indexes, and view can be recreated by running the commands that were introduced in the earlier sections of the chapter. Next we examine how to alter database objects by using the ALTER command.

ALTER

The ALTER command is basically used to change existing table schemas by adding columns to the table or adding or dropping referential constraints. The following is the general syntax for this command:

```
ALTER TABLE <tablename>
DROP or ADD <type objectname>
```

The following object types can be added:

- REFERENTIAL CONSTRAINT
- PRIMARY KEY
- COLUMN

The following object types can be deleted:

- PRIMARY KEY
- FOREIGN KEY

Let us now take a look at an example database.

```
INSERT INTO FNC_BMGR_TBL
(BRANCH_MGR_ID,DEPT_ID,EMP_ID,BRANCH)
VALUES(
'BM001',   'D001',   'E0005',   'B001',
'BM002',   'D002',   'E0006',   'B002',
'BM003',   'D003',   'E0007',   'B003',
'BM004',   'D004',   'E0008',   'B004',
'BM005',   'D005',   'E0009',   'B005',
'BM006',   'D006',   'E0011',   'B006',
'BM007',   'D007',   'E0012',   'B007',
'BM008',   'D008',   'E0013',   'B008'
)
```

Figure 4.3 INSERT row command for the FNC_BMGR_TBL table

4.3 THE EXAMPLE DATABASE

Now that the database has been created, data must be inserted into it. We will preview the SQL INSERT command, which will be covered in Section 4.5. Below are the four commands required to fill each table with the rows of data (see Figures 4.3–4.6).

Data can now be retrieved from the tables by issuing various DML commands.

4.4 THE DATA MANIPULATION LANAGUAGE

Now that all of the tables have been created and filled with rows of information, we must execute several DML commands to produce reports. The easiest way to accomplish this is by using the SELECT

```
INSERT INTO FNC_BRANCH_TBL
(BRANCH_ID,DEPT_ID,BRANCH_NAME,BRANCH_LOCATION,
PROFITS_TO_DATE,BRANCH)
VALUES(
'B001', 'D001','CASTLE HILL',      'PRINCE ST',                500000, 'BM001',
'B002', 'D002','BATCH CRESCENT', 'CRESCENT MEWS',        400000, 'BM002',
'B003', 'D003','MAYFAIR 1',        'HAY'S MEWS',               375000, 'BM003',
'B004', 'D004','MAYFAIR 2',        'AUDLEY SQUARE',          750000, 'BM004',
'B005', 'D005','KENSINGTON 1',   'ABINGDON ROAD',         650000, 'BM005',
'B006', 'D006','KENSINGTON 2',   'KENSINGTON HIGH ST',550000, 'BM006',
'B007', 'D007','PICCADILLY 1',    'OLD PARK LANE',          400000, 'BM007',
'B008', 'D008','PICCADILLY 2',    'BOLTON',                    310000, 'BM008'
)
```

Figure 4.4 INSERT row command for the FNC_BRANCH_TBL table

```
INSERT INTO FNC_DEPT_TBL
(DEPT_ID,DEPT_MGR_ID,DEPT_LOCATION,DEPT_NAME,NUM_EMP)
VALUES(
'D001',  'E0001',  'LONDON',      'EXECUTIVE',          1,
'D002',  'E0010',  'EDINBURGH',   'PRINCE ST',          3,
'D003',  'E0015',  'BATH',        'MINISTER SQUARE',    3,
'D004',  'E0002',  'LONDON',      'MAYFAIR',            5,
'D005',  'E0003',  'LONDON',      'KENSINGTON',         5,
'D006',  'E0004',  'LONDON',      'PICCADILLY',         5
)
```

Figure 4.5 INSERT row command for the FNC_DEPT_TBL table

statement of the SQL language. This statement is similar to an English sentence in that it is composed of clauses and predicates. We will dedicate a subsection to each clause so that we can examine this powerful feature of the Structured Query Language.

A typical SQL statement can be made up of two or more of the following clauses:

  * SELECT clause
  * FROM clause
  WHERE clause
  GROUP BY clause
  HAVING clause
  ORDER BY clause

The SELECT and FROM clauses are marked with asterisks because they are the only two clauses required in a SQL SELECT statement. That is, a SQL SELECT is minimally composed of a SELECT and a FROM clause. Let's continue by first examining the SELECT clause.

The SELECT Clause

The basic format of the SELECT clause is shown below:

```
SELECT column 1, column 2, ..., column N
```

or

```
SELECT *
```

Let's examine the last form first. The keyword SELECT followed by an asterisk will retrieve all of the columns in a table. If a table called T1 contains the following five columns—C1, C2, C3, C4, and

```
INSERT INTO FNC_EMP_TBL
EMP_ID,EMP_NAME,EMP_DEPT,EMP_TITLE,EMP_SALARY,EMP_HIRE_DATE)
VALUES(
'E0001', 'SMYTH',            'JOHN',     'D001', 'PRESIDENT',    100000, '01/01/89',
'E0002', 'FURLOUGH',         'STEVE',    'D004', 'DEPT MGR',      75000, '01/01/89',
'E0003', 'BURLIN',GTON',     'JAMES',    'D005', 'DEPT MGR',      75000, '01/01/89',
'E0004', 'MAC MOE',          'MARY',     'D006', 'DEPT MGR',      75000, '01/01/89',
'E0005', 'MC MULLINS',       'PETER',    'D002', 'BRANCH MGR',    40000, '02/01/89',
'E0006', 'BEDLOE',           'SUSAN',    'D003', 'BRANCH MGR',    40000, '02/01/89',
'E0007', 'BROOME',           'PEGGY',    'D004', 'BRANCH MGR',    40000, '02/01/89',
'E0008', 'BRONTON',          'SALLY',    'D004', 'BRANCH MGR',    40000, '03/01/89',
'E0009', 'CHELSEA',          'JOSEPH',   'D005', 'BRANCH MGR',    40000, '03/01/89',
'E0010', 'DOVE',             'MICHEAL',  'D002', 'DEPT MGR',      75000, '03/01/89',
'E0011', 'DOVIN',GTON',      'BARRY',    'D005', 'BRANCH MGR',    40000, '01/01/89',
'E0012', 'THAMES',           'DOUGLAS',  'D006', 'BRANCH MGR',    40000, '09/01/89',
'E0013', 'WHITMAN',          'KEN',      'D006', 'BRANCH MGR',    40000, '09/01/89',
'E0014', 'BOULDER',          'KEVIN',    'D003', 'STAFF',         20000, '09/01/89',
'E0015', 'SMEDLEY-'SMYTHE',  'LORETTA',  'D003', 'DEPT MGR',      75000, '10/01/89',
'E0016', 'FINSTER',          'PAMELA',   'D002', 'STAFF',         20000, '01/01/89',
'E0017', 'HOLYHOKE',         'PEGGY',    'D004', 'STAFF',         20000, '10/01/89',
'E0018', 'ORLOWE',           'CATHY',    'D004', 'STAFF',         20000, '10/01/89',
'E0019', 'BEASLEY',          'LAURA',    'D005', 'STAFF',         20000, '10/01/89',
'E0020', 'WITHERSPOON',      'STEVE',    'D005', 'STAFF',         20000, '10/01/89',
'E0021', 'WILLIAMS',         'BOB',      'D006', 'STAFF',         20000, '10/01/89',
'E0022', 'JONES',            'AL',       'D006', 'STAFF',         20000, '10/01/89'
)
```

Figure 4.6 INSERT row command for the FNC_EMP_TBL table

C5—then the command SELECT * and the command SELECT C1, C2, C3, C4, C5 would be equivalent. SELECT * is just a shorthand notation and comes in handy when a table has a large number of columns.

The first style format is the longhand form of the syntax. It contains the SELECT keyword followed by a list of column names separated by commas. These column names can be fully qualified; that is, they can be preceded by the table name in which they can be found. For instance, if table T1 described above is used in this style, our select clause would look like this:

```
SELECT T1.C1, T1.C2, T1.C3, T1.C4, T1.C5
```

This format is necessary because if columns from another table with the same name are included in the SELECT list, it is important to be able to distinguish between the two columns. For example: Table T1 contains columns C1, C2, C3 and table T2 contains columns C1, C2, C3, C4. We want to select C1, C2 from table T1 and C2 and C5 from table T2. The syntax to accomplish this task would be:

```
SELECT T1.C1, T1.C2, T2.C2, T2.C3
```

Qualifying the column name with the table name and a period to separate both the names ensures uniqueness, as each table in a database must have a unique name. Let us now continue by examining the second required clause in a SQL statement, the FROM clause.

The FROM Clause

To project columns from a table in a SELECT clause, a "FROM" clause must be included to specify the tables from which the data are to be retrieved. The syntax for a SQL statement projecting columns from a table is

```
SELECT <column list or *>
FROM   <table name list>
```

Column list is a list of qualified or simple column names separated by commas. (The asterisk stands for all columns.) To retrieve columns from more than one table, the following syntax is used:

```
SELECT <column list>
FROM   <table name list>
WHERE  <join conditions>
```

This form requires special attention. When more than one table is included in the FROM clause, the relationship between the tables must be specified in the WHERE clause. The JOIN conditions of the WHERE clause are defined by equating the columns between two tables. An example best clarifies this concept. Assume that we have the following two tables shown in Figure 4.7.

The following query retrieves column EMP_ID and column SALARY from table EMP and column DEPT_LOCATION from table DEPT by joining the two tables over the DEPT_ID column:

```
SELECT EMP_ID,SALARY,DEPT_LOCATION
FROM EMP,DEPT
WHERE EMP.DEPT_ID = DEPT.DEPT_ID
```

Notice that we had to fully qualify the column names in the WHERE clause with the table names, as the two column names are exactly the same.

An alternate form of the same query would be to give each table name an alias in the FROM clause as follows:

```
FROM EMP A,DEPT B
```

```
INSERT INTO FNC_BMGR_TBL
(BRANCH_MGR_ID,DEPT_ID,EMP_ID,BRANCH)
VALUES(
'BM001',  'D002',  'E0005',  'B001',
'BM002',  'D003',  'E0006',  'B002',
'BM003',  'D004',  'E0007',  'B003',
'BM004',  'D004',  'E0008',  'B004',
'BM005',  'D005',  'E0009',  'B005',
'BM006',  'D005',  'E0011',  'B006',
'BM007',  'D006',  'E0012',  'B007',
'BM008',  'D006',  'E0013',  'B008'
)
```

Figure 4.7 INSERT row command for the FNC_BMGR_TBL table

The new form of the query would be

```
SELECT A.EMP_ID,A.SALARY,B.DEPT_LOCATION
FROM EMP A,DEPT B
WHERE A.DEPT_ID = B.DEPT_ID
```

This feature of SQL comes in handy particularly when the table names are either long or cryptic; that is, the table name is something like DS000451.

Executing either of these queries produces the following report:

EMPID	SALARY	LOCATION
E1	20000	London
E2	30000	Edinburgh
E3	40000	Swindon
E4	50000	Cirencester

The above query is rather restricting, as it always returns every row in the tables involved. The optional WHERE clause contains predicates that can be used to restrict the range of rows we want to access. These predicates are covered next.

The WHERE Clause

The third clause that makes up a DML SELECT query is optional although it is often used. The WHERE clause contains predicates that restrict the range of the rows that a user or application wants to access. The syntax for the WHERE clause is shown below:

```
WHERE column name = value or column name
column name < value or column name
```

```
column name > value or column name
column name <> value or column name
column name >= value or column name
column name <= value or column name
column name IN (value list)
column name NOT IN (value list)
column name LIKE value
column name NOT LIKE value
column name BETWEEN value 1 and value 2
column name NOT BETWEEN value 1 and value 2
```

We will see how the order of these predicates affects performance when I discuss query optimization and scheduling in Chapter 7.

Next, we'll use each of these predicates in a SQL statement that can be executed against the Traditional Fish 'n' Chips database.

```
column name = value or column name
```

The above predicate is used to check the condition where a column is equal to a value or another column name; the latter is a join between two tables. The following two queries illustrate both forms of the predicate:

```
SELECT DEPT_ID,DEPT_NAME
FROM FNC_DEPT_TABLE
WHERE NUM_EMP = 1

OUTPUT
DEPT_ID  DEPT_NAME
D001     EXECUTIVE


SELECT DEPT_ID, DEPT_NAME,EMP_ID,EMP_SALARY
FROM FNC_DEPT_TBL,FNC_EMP_TBL
WHERE DEPT_ID = EMP_DEPT
AND   DEPT_ID = 'D001'

OUTPUT
DEPT_ID  DEPT_NAME   EMP_ID   EMP_SALARY
D001     EXECUTIVE   E0001    100000
```

column name < value or column name

This next predicate is used to test the "less than" condition between a column and a value or between two columns. The query below illustrates the condition for departments having fewer than five employees:

```
SELECT DEPT_ID,DEPT_LOCATION,NUM_EMP
FROM FNC_DEPT_TBL
WHERE NUM_EMP < 5

OUTPUT

DEPT_ID   DEPT_LOCATION   NUM_EMP
D002      Edinburgh       3
D003      Bath            3
```

column name > value or column name

This predicate tests the condition for a column having a value greater than the specified value or column:

```
SELECT DEPT_ID,DEPT_LOCATION,NUM_EMP
FROM FNC_DEPT_TBL
WHERE NUM_EMP > 3

OUTPUT

DEPT_ID   DEPT_LOCATION   NUM_EMP
D004      London          5
D005      London          5
D006      London          5
```

This query tells us that the departments in London have the greatest number of employees.

column name <> value or column name

The above predicate tests for inequality between a column and a value or between two columns. Let's use the FNC_DEPT_TBL table one more time to illustrate this predicate:

```
SELECT DEPT_ID,DEPT_LOCATION
FROM FNC_DEPT_TBL
WHERE FNC_DEPT_LOCATION <> 'London'
```

OUTPUT

```
DEPT_ID   DEPT LOCATION
D002      Edinburgh
D003      Bath
```

column name >= value or column name

This next predicate tests for the "greater than or equal" condition between a column and a value or between two columns. The query below accesses the FNC_EMP_TBL table to illustrate the usage of this predicate:

```
SELECT EMP_NAME,EMP_SALARY
FROM FNC_EMP_TABLE
WHERE EMP_SALARY >= 75000
```

OUTPUT

```
EMP_NAME           EMP_SALARY
Smythe             100000
Furlough           75000
Burlington         75000
Mac Moe            75000
Dove               75000
Smedley-Smythe     75000
```

column name <= value or column name

This predicate is used to test the "less than or equal" condition between a column and a value or between two columns:

```
SELECT EMP_ID,EMP_NAME,EMP_TITLE
FROM FNC_EMP_TBL
WHERE EMP_SALARY <= 20,000
```

OUTPUT

```
EMP_ID   EMP_NAME    EMP_TITLE
E0014    Boulder     STAFF
E0016    Finster     STAFF
E0017    HolyHoke    STAFF
E0018    Orlowe      STAFF
E0019    Beasley     STAFF
```

```
E0020    Witherspoon   STAFF
E0021    Williams      STAFF
E0022    Hones         STAFF
```

From this query we can see that STAFF members make £20,000 or less. We will see in Section 4.6 how we can use SQL to give them a raise.

column name IN (value list)

This predicate is used to test the condition that the column have a value that is included in the provided list. The keyword IN is followed by a list of comma-separated values enclosed in parentheses. The query below accesses the FNC_BRANCH_TBL to illustrate the use of this predicate:

```
SELECT BRANCH_ID, BRANCH_LOCATION, PROFITS_TO_DATE
FROM FNC_BRANCH_TBL
WHERE DEPT_ID IN ('D003','D005','D006')
```

OUTPUT

BRANCH_ID	BRANCH_LOCATION	PROFITS_TO_DATE
B002	Crescent Mews	400000
B005	Abingdon Road	650000
B007	Old Park Lane	400000

column name NOT IN (value list)

The above predicate is the negation of the prior predicate that was just examined. It tests for the condition that the contents of the column not be equal to any member of the supplied value list:

```
SELECT BRANCH_ID, BRANCH_LOCATION, PROFITS_TO_DATE
FROM FNC_BRANCH_TBL
WHERE DEPT_ID NOT IN ('D003','D005','D006')
```

OUTPUT

BRANCH_ID	BRANCH_LOCATION	PROFITS_TO_DATE
B001	Prince St	500000
B003	Hay's Mews	375000
B004	Audley Square	750000

column name LIKE value

This next predicate is used to test the condition that a column is like the supplied value. In this type of predicate, two wild card symbols, "_" or "%," can be used. The first symbol is used to replace any single character. For example,

```
SELECT BRANCH_ID,DEPT_ID
FROM FNC_BRANCH_TBL
WHERE DEPT_ID LIKE '_004'

OUTPUT

BRANCH_ID  DEPT_ID
B003       D004
B004       D004
```

The second wild card predicate replaces one or more characters:

```
SELECT BRANCH_ID,DEPT_ID
FROM FNC_BRANCH_TBL
WHERE DEPT_ID LIKE 'D%6'

OUTPUT

BRANCH_ID  DEPT_ID
B007       D006
B008       D006
```

column name NOT LIKE value

This next predicate tests the negative condition of the prior predicate; that is, we use this predicate to test for columns not like the supplied value:

```
SELECT BRANCH_NAME,BRANCH_ID,DEPT_ID
FROM FNC_BRANCH_TBL
WHERE   DEPT_ID NOT LIKE 'D%5'
AND     DEPT_ID NOT LIKE 'D%6'

OUTPUT

BRANCH_NAME    BRANCH_ID  DEPT_ID
Hill           B001       D002
```

```
Bath Crescent   B002        D003
Mayfair 1       B003        D004
Mayfair 2       B004        D004
```

Notice that multiple predicates can be connected with the "AND" keyword.

The final two predicates we examine are BETWEEN and NOT BETWEEN.

column name BETWEEN value 1 and value 2

This predicate is used to test for the condition that a column falls within the range of two supplied values:

```
SELECT BRANCH_ID,BRANCH_LOCATION,PROFITS_TO_DATE
FROM FNC_BRANCH_TBL
WHERE PROFITS_TO_DATE BETWEEN 550000 and 750000

OUTPUT

BRANCH_ID   BRANCH_LOCATION      PROFITS_TO_DATE
B004        Audley Square        750000
B005        Abingdon Road        650000
B006        Kensington High St   555000
```

column name NOT BETWEEN value 1 and value 2

This last predicate tests for the condition that a column NOT be within the range of the two supplied values:

```
SELECT BRANCH_ID,BRANCH_LOCATION,PROFITS_TO_DATE
FROM FNC_BRANCH_TBL
WHERE PROFITS_TO_DATE NOT BETWEEN 550000 AND 750000

OUTPUT

BRANCH_ID   BRANCH_LOCATION   PROFITS_TO_DATE
B001        Prince St         500000
B002        Crescent Mews     400000
B003        Hay's Mews        375000
B007        Old Park Lane     400000
B008        Bolton            310000
```

The GROUP BY Clause

The GROUP BY clause in the SQL SELECT statement is used to group common information when querying the tables of a database. An example best illustrates this command:

```
SELECT BRANCH_ID,DEPT_ID,BRANCH_LOCATION
FROM FNC_EMP_TABLE
WHERE PROFITS_TO_DATE > 400000
GROUP BY DEPT_ID

OUTPUT
```

BRANCH_ID	DEPT_ID	BRANCH_LOCATION
B001	D002	Prince St
B002	D003	Crescent Mews
B004	D004	Audley Square
B005	D005	Abingdon Road
B006	D005	Kensington Road
B007	D006	Old Park Lane
B008	D006	Bolton

Notice how the output was grouped by common departments. The column named in the GROUP BY clause must appear in the SELECT clause.

The HAVING Clause

The HAVING clause is considered as the "WHERE" clause for groupings of information. Again, an example best illustrates this command:

```
SELECT DEPT_ID,DEPT_LOCATION,NUM_EMP
FROM FNC_DEPT_TBL
GROUP BY DEPT_LOCATION
HAVING NUM_EMP >= 3

OUTPUT
```

DEPT_ID	DEPT_LOCATION	NUM_EMP
D003	Bath	3
D002	Edinburgh	3
D004	London	5
D005	London	5
D006	London	5

As can be seen, the output was grouped by the locations for the departments having three or more employees.

The ORDER BY Clause

The ORDER BY clause is used to specify the sort order that will be used to generate the query output. The sort order can be based on one or more columns in the SELECT clause:

```
SELECT *
FROM FNC_BRANCH_TBL
WHERE BRANCH_ID BETWEEN B005 and B008
ORDER BY BRANCH_ID DESC, PROFITS_TO_DATE ASC

OUTPUT

BRANCH_ID   DEPT_ID   BRANCH_NAME    BRANCH_LOCATION
B008        D006      Piccadilly 2   Bolton
B007        D006      Piccadilly 1   Old Park Lane
B006        D005      Kensington 2   Kensington High St
B005        D005      Kensington 1   Abingdon Road

PROFITS_TO_DATE   BRANCH_MANAGER
310000            BM008
400000            BM007
550000            BM006
650000            BM005
```

4.5 THE SQL INSERT COMMAND

Inserting data into tables is accomplished via the INSERT DML command. The format for this command is

```
INSERT INTO <table name >
(list of values for row 1,
 list of values for row 2,
 *
 *
 *
 list of values for row n)
```

```
INSERT INTO FNC_BRANCH_TBL
(BRANCH_ID,DEPT_ID,BRANCH_NAME,BRANCH_LOCATION,
PROFITS_TO_DATE,BRANCH)
VALUES(
'B001', 'D001', 'CASTLE HILL',       'PRINCE ST',                500000, 'BM001',
'B002', 'D002', 'BATCH CRESCENT',    'CRESCENT MEWS',            400000, 'BM002',
'B003', 'D003', 'MAYFAIR 1',         'HAY'S MEWS',               375000, 'BM003',
'B004', 'D004', 'MAYFAIR 2',         'AUDLEY SQUARE',            750000, 'BM004',
'B005', 'D005', 'KENSINGTON 1',      'ABINGDON ROAD',            650000, 'BM005',
'B006', 'D006', 'KENSINGTON 2',      'KENSINGTON HIGH ST', 550000, 'BM006',
'B007', 'D007', 'PICCADILLY 1',      'OLD PARK LANE',            400000, 'BM007',
'B008', 'D008', 'PICCADILLY 2',      'BOLTON',                   310000, 'BM008',
)
```

Figure 4.8 INSERT row command for the FNC_BRANCH_TBL table

The following four figures (Figures 4.8–4.11) show the INSERT command used to insert information into each of the tables in the Traditional Fish 'n' Chips database.

This is not the only way of inserting rows into the tables. The DML SELECT statement can be included in the INSERT statement to extract rows from the existing tables and insert them into a target table.

```
INSERT INTO FNC_DEPT_TBL
(DEPT_ID,DEPT_MGR_ID,DEPT_LOCATION,DEPT_NAME,NUM_EMP)
VALUES(
'D001', 'E0001', 'LONDON',      'EXECUTIVE',            1,
'D002', 'E0010', 'EDINBURGH',   'PRINCE ST',            3,
'D003', 'E0015', 'BATH',        'MINISTER SQUARE',      3,
'D004', 'E0002', 'LONDON',      'MAYFAIR',              5,
'D005', 'E0003', 'LONDON',      'KENSINGTON',           5,
'D006', 'E0004', 'LONDON',      'PICCADILLY',           5
)
```

Figure 4.9 INSERT row command for the FNC_DEPT_TBL table

```
INSERT INTO FNC_EMP_TBL
(EMP_ID,EMP_NAME,EMP_DEPT,EMP_TITLE,EMP_SALARY,EMP_HIRE_DATE)
VALUES(
'E0001', 'SMYTH',            'JOHN',     'D001', 'PRESIDENT',   100000, '01/01/89',
'E0002', 'FURLOUGH',         'STEVE',    'D004', 'DEPT MGR',     75000, '01/01/89',
'E0003', 'BURLINGTON',       'JAMES',    'D005', 'DEPT MGR',     75000, '01/01/89',
'E0004', 'MAC MOE',          'MARY',     'D006', 'DEPT MGR',     75000, '01/01/89',
'E0005', 'MC MULLINS         'PETER',    'D002', 'BRANCH MGR', 40000, '02/01/89',
'E0006', 'BEDLOE',           'SUSAN',    'D003', 'BRANCH MGR', 40000, '02/01/89',
'E0007', 'BROOME',           'PEGGY',    'D004', 'BRANCH MGR', 40000, '02/01/89',
'E0008', 'BRONTON',          'SALLY',    'D004', 'BRANCH MGR', 40000, '03/01/89',
'E0009', 'CHELSEA',          'JOSEPH',   'D005', 'BRANCH MGR', 40000, '03/01/89',
'E0010', 'DOVE',             'MICHEAL',  'D002', 'DEPT MGR',     75000, '03/01/89',
'E0011', 'DOVINGTON',        'BARRY',    'D005', 'BRANCH MGR', 40000, '01/01/89',
'E0012', 'THAMES',           'DOUGLAS',  'D006', 'BRANCH MGR', 40000, '09/01/89',
'E0013', 'WHITMAN',          'KEN',      'D006', 'BRANCH MGR', 40000, '09/01/89',
'E0014', 'BOULDER',          'KEVIN',    'D003', 'STAFF',        20000, '09/01/89',
'E0015', 'SMEDLEY-SMYTHE', 'LORETTA', 'D003', 'DEPT MGR',     75000, '10/01/89',
'E0016', 'FINSTER',          'PA',MELA', 'D002', 'STAFF',        20000, '01/01/89',
'E0017', 'HOLYHOKE',         'PEGGY',    'D004', 'STAFF',        20000, '10/01/89',
'E0018', 'ORLOWE',           'CATHY',    'D004', 'STAFF',        20000, '10/01/89',
'E0019', 'BEASLEY',          'LAURA',    'D005', 'STAFF',        20000, '10/01/89',
'E0020', 'WITHERSPOON',      'STEVE',    'D005', 'STAFF',        20000, '10/01/89',
'E0021', 'WILLIAMS',         'BOB'       'D006', 'STAFF',        20000, '10/01/89',
'E0022', 'JONES',            'AL',       'D006', 'STAFF',        20000, '10/01/89
)
```

Figure 4.10 INSERT row command for the FNC_EMP_TBL table

```
INSERT INTO FNC_BMGR_TBL
(BRANCH_MGR_ID,DEPT_ID,EMP_ID,BRANCH)
VALUES(
'BM001',  'D001',  'E0005',  'B001',
'BM002',  'D002',  'E0006',  'B002',
'BM003',  'D003',  'E0007',  'B003',
'BM004',  'D004',  'E0008',  'B004',
'BM005',  'D005',  'E0009',  'B005',
'BM006',  'D006',  'E0011',  'B006',
'BM007',  'D007',  'E0012',  'B007',
'BM008',  'D008',  'E0013',  'B008'
)
```

Figure 4.11 INSERT row command for the FNC_BMGR_TBL table

4.6 THE SQL UPDATE COMMAND

The DML sublanguage also provides a command for updating existing rows. In an earlier section a query was executed that showed us that STAFF members of the Traditonal Fish 'n' Chips enterprise earned a salary of only £20,000. The president of the company has decided to give each STAFF member a generous salary increase. The following SQL statements can be used to accomplish this task:

```
UPDATE FNC_EMP_TBL
SET EMP_SALARY = EMP_SALARY * 1.25
WHERE EMP_TITLE = 'STAFF'
```

Notice the syntax of this statement:

```
UPDATE <table name>
SET
<column name 1> = value,
<column name 2> = value,
*
*
<column name N> = value
WHERE
<condition predicates>
```

The keywords for this command are UPDATE, SET, and WHERE. The user supplies the table name, a list of column = values (separated by commas) and a WHERE clause containing the predicates that were discussed earlier. This is the WHERE clause as it would appear in an SQL SELECT statement.

Let us look at one more example. The hire dates for the STAFF members in department D005 were entered incorrectly. The actual hire dates for these STAFF members is 11/01/89. The following UPDATE query will correct the error:

```
UPDATE FNC_EMP_TBL
SET EMP_HIRE_DATE = '11/01/89'
WHERE EMP_DEPT = 'D005'
```

4.7 THE DATA CONTROL LANGUAGE

For the sake of completeness I include a brief discussion on the security aspects of Structured Query Language. To control user access to database objects, the data control language provides two commands, GRANT and REVOKE. The GRANT command is used by the database administrator to grant privileges to users. The RE-VOKE command is issued to revoke privileges from users. The syntax for each command is briefly discussed below.

The GRANT Command

The syntax for this command is

```
GRANT <privilege> to <userid>
```

The keywords for this command are GRANT and TO. A privilege is typically a SQL command such as UPDATE, DROP, or CREATE. The user ID is the identification code of the user to whom the database administrator wants to grant the specific privilege. For instance, if the DBA wants to grant user ARB the capability to UPDATE and CREATE tables, the following commands would be issued:

```
GRANT TABLE CREATE TO ARB
GRANT DROP TO ARB
```

The REVOKE Command

The opposite of the GRANT command is the REVOKE command. The syntax for this command is

```
REVOKE <privilege> FROM <userid>
```

If we wish to revoke the privileges that were previously granted to user ARB, the following commands would be issued:

```
REVOKE CREATE TABLE FROM ARB
REVOKE DROP FROM ARB
```

4.8 REFERENTIAL INTEGRITY

The best way to explain referential integrity to the reader is by referring to the Traditional Fish 'n' Chips database and posing the following question: What happens to employee records in the FNC_EMP_TBL table when a department is deleted from the FNC_DEPT_TABLE? As we know, the FNC_EMP_TBL table is linked to the FNC_DEPT_TBL over the department ID columns; that is, every employee belongs to a department.

Referential integrity maintains database consistency and integrity by allowing database administrators the capability to declare rules that will take care of circumstances such as the one we have just examined. That is, we can define what actions the database management system will take when rows that establish relationships between parent and dependent tables are deleted.

Referential integrity also has built-in rules that maintain integrity when rows that establish relationships between tables are inserted or updated. Let us examine the delete rules first, after which we will modify our SQL create statements to implement referential integrity.

Maintaining Integrity When Deleting Rows

SQL DML now provides three rules for maintaining integrity upon occurrences of row deletions between tables:

RESTRICT   If a row exists that has a foreign key linked to a row of another table that is being deleted, do not allow the row deletion.

CASCADE   If a row exists that has a foreign key linked to a row of another table that is being deleted, also delete the row with the foreign key.

SET NULL   If a row exists that has a foreign key linked to a row of another table that is being deleted, set the foreign key to NULL so as to reflect the absence of the row that was just deleted.

The integrity rules are specified in the DML create command when the table is being created. Let us now modify each of the CREATE statements that were introduced earlier to allow for referential integrity between tables.

```
CREATE TABLE FNC_DEPT_TBL (
DEPT_ID         CHAR(4)     NOT NULL,
DEPT_MGR_ID     CHAR(4)     NOT NULL,
DEPT_LOCATION   CHAR(20)    NOT NULL,
DEPT_NAME       CHAR(20)    NOT NULL,
NUM_EMP INTEGER,
PRIMARY KEY (DEPT_ID))
```

```
CREATE TABLE  FNC_EMP_TABLE (
EMP_ID      CHAR(5)   NOT NULL,
EMP_NAME    CHAR(20)  NOT NULL,
EMP_DEPT    CHAR(4)   NOT NULL,
EMP_TITLE   CHAR(20)  NOT NULL,
EMP_SALARY  DECIMAL   NOT NULL,
EMP_HIRE_DATE  DATE   NOT NULL,
PRIMARY KEY  (EMP_ID),
FOREIGN KEY  (EMP_DEPT) REFERENCES  FNC_DEPT_TBL
ON DELETE SET NULL
ON UPDATE RESTRICT)

CREATE TABLE FNC_BMGR_TBL (
BRANCH_ID         CHAR(4)    NOT NULL,
DEPT_ID           CHAR(4)    NOT NULL,
BRANCH_NAME       CHAR(20)   NOT NULL,
BRANCH_LOCATION   CHAR(20)   NOT NULL,
PROFITS_TO_DATE   DECIMAL    NOT NULL,
BRANCH_MANAGER    CHAR(5)    NOT NULL,
PRIMARY KEY  (BRANCH_ID),
FOREIGN KEY (DEPT_ID) REFERENCES FNC_DEPT_TBL,
FOREIGN KEY (BRANCH_MANAGER) REFERENCES FNC_BMGR_TBL
ON DELETE SET NULL
ON UPDATE RESTRICT)

CREATE TABLE FNC_BMGR_TBL (
BRANCH_MGR_ID  CHAR(5)   NOT NULL,
DEPT_ID        CHAR(4)   NOT NULL,
EMP_ID         CHAR(5)   NOT NULL,
BRANCH_ID      CHAR(4)   NOT NULL,
PRIMARY KEY (BRANCH_MGR_ID),
FOREIGN KEY (DEPT_ID) REFERENCES FNC_DEPT_TBL,
FOREIGN KEY (EMP_ID) REFERENCES FNC_EMP_TBL,
FOREIGN KEY (BRANCH_ID) REFERENCES FNC_BRANCH_TBL
ON DELETE SET NULL
ON UPDATE RESTRICT)
```

As the reader can see, I've decided to play it safe. On any deletes in the parent table, I've decided to set the affected values to NULL. The CASCADE rule is dangerous and should be used with care. A rule is included to restrict updates in each table. This capability is discussed next.

Maintaining Referential Integrity When Inserting or Updating Rows

Referential integrity can also be maintained when inserting or updating rows. If a row is to be inserted into a dependent table, the key for that row must exist in the parent table. When updating rows, two rules exist. If a key value inside a row of a dependent table is being updated, the new updated value must exist in a row of the parent table. If a key in the parent table is being updated, and the key does not exist in the dependent table, the transaction is denied. This is the "ON UPDATE RESTRICT" rule that was used in the revised DDL CREATE statements.

Let us conclude this chapter with a brief discussion on distributed SQL queries. The next section should raise some issues that will be resolved in Parts II and III of the book.

4.9 EXAMPLES OF DISTRIBUTED QUERIES

Now that we have a solid foundation of the SQL, we sneak a peek at what's coming up in Parts II and III by introducing an example of a distributed query.

Assume that the FNC_DEPT_TBL table of our database is located on a server in London and the FNC_BRANCH_TBL table is on a server in Edinburgh. Since the two tables are now in physically different locations, a way is required to identify the servers so the location can be determined. Assuming both servers are on the same wide area network (WAN), we give the server located in London the name SITEL and the server located in Edinburgh the name SITEE.

A query that joins these two tables would look like this:

```
SELECT SITEL.FNC_DEPT_TBL.DEPT_ID,
   SITEE.FNC_BRANCH_TBL.BRANCH_ID
FROM   SITEL.FNC_DEPT_TBL
   SITEE.FNC_BRANCH_TBL
WHERE
   SITEL.FNC_DEPT_TBL.DEPT_ID =
SITEE.FNC_BRANCH_TBL.DEPT_ID
```

This query has fully qualified each object name by preceding it with not only the table name but also its location. For sites that maintain more than one database the target database could also be included.

Assume that the London site database name is DBL and the Edinburgh site database is called DBE; our query would now look like this:

```
SELECT SITEL.DBL.FNC_DEPT_TBL.DEPT_ID,
   SITEE.DBE.FNC_BRANCH_TBL.BRANCH_ID
FROM    SITEL.DBL.FNC_DEPT_TBL
   SITEE.DBE.FNC_BRANCH_TBL
WHERE
   SITEL.DBL.FNC_DEPT_TBL.DEPT_ID =
SITEE.DBE.FNC_BRANCH_TBL.DEPT_ID
```

Two problems can immediately be seen. The first is that each database object name in the query is tediously long and the second is the JOIN predicate. How do you process a JOIN whose components reside in physically different locations? This problem is deferred to Part II.

Part of the first problem can be solved by using aliases:

```
SELECT A.DEPT_ID,B.BRANCH_ID
FROM    SITEL.DBL.FNC_DEPT_TBL A
     SITEE.DBE.FNC_BRANCH_TBL B
WHERE A.DEPT_ID = B.DEPT_ID
```

The query is much shorter, although the user still has to know where each object physically resides in order to build the query. We will see in Part II of the book how global data dictionaries are used to solve this locality problem. The second problem, processing distributed joins, is complex and requires a solid foundation in query optimization and scheduling. We will see in Chapter 5 how this is accomplished in a centralized environment. Part II will cover the optimization, scheduling, and execution of distributed queries in a distributed database environment. (That's when all the studying of relational algebra will pay off!)

The intent of this section was to raise these issues and make the reader aware of what a distributed SQL query might look like. Parts II and III of the book will address these and other issues that pertain to the processing of distributed queries. We will also see how global data dictionaries are used to solve the naming and location issues of distributed queries.

4.10 SUMMARY

The purpose of this chapter was to introduce the basic features of SQL to the reader. Although this is a book on distributed and multi-databases, SQL was included as it is the de facto standard for retrieving information from relational databases. SQL will be used throughout the book to assist us in the discussions on distributed query processing, optimization and scheduling of distributed queries, and transactions.

Section 4.9 was included to raise some issues that will be addressed in Parts II and III.

5

Concurrency and
Recovery

5.1 INTRODUCTION

Now that we have a fundamental understanding of relational algebra theory, databases, and SQL, we can begin to examine the concepts of concurrency and recovery of multiple concurrent transactions.

This chapter is dedicated to these issues as they apply to centralized database management systems. These discussions will be expanded to distributed systems in Part II of the book and to multiple database systems in Part III of the book.

This chapter begins by defining a transaction and introducing a simple model of a centralized DBMS that can process this transaction. For this database management system to be of any use, it must be able to process more than one of the transactions concurrently.

Section 5.4 discusses some issues involved in maintaining concurrency and introduces some solutions. These solutions are described in the following sections where serialization techniques, locking protocols, and deadlock management systems are discussed.

Sometimes transactions fail and it is necessary to implement a strategy that returns the database to the last consistent state prior to the execution of the transaction that failed. This is the topic of the last section of the chapter, where recovery management techniques are discussed. Let's begin by defining a transaction.

What Is a Transaction?

This section defines the basic concepts of a transaction. The reader is asked to pay specific attention to the following keywords and concepts:

1.   DATABASE CONSISTENCY (a concept)
2.   COMMIT
3.   ROLLBACK (ABORT)
4.   UNIT OF WORK (a concept)
5.   CONSISTENT DB STATE (a concept)
6.   UNCOMMITTED DB STATE (a concept)

Let's begin our discussions with database consistency. Figure 5.1 shows a database prior to execution of a transaction.

Here we see a database where two transactions are executed. The database begins in a consistent state "S1." Transaction 1 is executed and succeeds. The database management system makes the changes to the database permanent by issuing a "COMMIT" command. After the COMMIT is executed, the database is in a new consistent state "S2."

Transaction 2 is now submitted to the database management system. This time the transaction fails and a strategy has to be executed that returns the database to the state it was in prior to the execution of transaction S2. This strategy is called "ROLLBACK" and involves restoring old copies of any data that were changed during the execution of failed transaction S2.

The old data are usually kept in a log that is used to recover the database. On completion of the ROLLBACK the database is again in a consistent state: S3.

During the execution of a transaction and its subsequent COMMIT or ROLLBACK the database is in a period of inconsistency; that is, the data in the database are temporarily unreliable. Making the transaction permanent by issuing a COMMIT command or aborting the transaction with a ROLLBACK command returns the database to a consistent state.

A transaction can be defined as a process that contains either read commands, write commands, or both. Figure 5.2 shows some pseudocode that represents a transaction that is used to increase an employee's salary.

The transaction is implemented as a function called UP-DATE_SALARY(). It takes two parameters: a variable called EMP_ID, which contains an employee's identification number, and a variable called AMOUNT, which contains the amount of increase to the employee's current salary.

The transaction begins by executing a SQL query that reads the employee's current salary into a variable called EMP_SALARY. The WHERE clause specifies the search condition. That is, the query must return the employee's salary only if the employee record whose key matches the supplied employee identification number is found. If the employee ID is not found, the function fails and terminates the transaction by issuing a ROLLBACK command. The flag SUCCESS is set to FALSE and the function ends, notifying the calling program that the transaction failed.

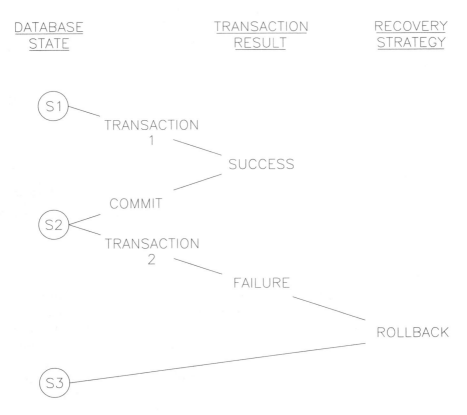

Figure 5.1 **Database state diagram**

```
BOOL UPDATE_SALARY(EMP,AMOUNT)
 {DECIMAL NEW_SALARY; BOOL SUCCESS;
  BEGIN SQL:
      SELECT, EMP_SALARY INTO :EMP_SALARY
      FROM TBL_SALARY
      WHERE EMP_ID = :EMP;
  END SQL;

  IF ( SQL_ERROR = NOT_FOUND)
      {PULLBACK WORK; SUCCESS = FALSE}
  ELSE
      {
      NEW_SALARY = EMP_SALARY + AMOUNT;

      UPDATE TBL_SALARY
         SET EMP_SALARY = :NEW_SALARY
      WHERE EMP_ID=EMP;

  IF (SQL_ERROR != SQL_SUCCESS)
      {ROLLBACK WORK; SUCCESS = FALSE}
  ELSE
      {COMMIT WORK; SUCCESS = TRUE;}
      }
  RETURN (SUCCESS);
  }
```

Figure 5.2 An update transaction

If the first query found the employee record, the function calcu-
lates the new salary and executes the following SQL query to update
the employee's salary:

```
UPDATE TBL_SALARY
SET EMP_SALARY = :NEW_SALARY
WHERE EMP_ID = EMP;
```

If this query fails, the function issues a **ROLLBACK** command,
which triggers the recovery mechanism (the recovery mechanism is
discussed in Section 5.13). If the function succeeds, the function
issues a COMMIT WORK command. We will see in later sections how
the "COMMIT WORK" is implemented.

Looking at this example at a higher level, we see a transaction that
involves a read, a mathematical operation, and a write. The above
transaction can be written as follows:

```
BEGIN TUPDATE_SALARY:
    R(:EMP_SALARY,EMP_SALARY);
    NEW_SALARY = EMP_SALARY + AMOUNT;
    W(EMP_SALARY,NEW_SALARY);
END TUPDATE_SALARY;
```

Although multiple operations have occurred, the DBMS considers them as one atomic operation. If any of the individual operations fail, the entire transaction fails. If all succeed, then the entire transaction succeeds. The series of operations between the BEGIN and END are considered a UNIT OF WORK. It is the job of the DBMS to execute multiple concurrent units of work and still guarantee that the database is not corrupted if any of these units of work fail.

5.2 A SIMPLE DBMS MODEL

Figure 5.3 shows a block diagram of a simple database management system.

This model basically follows the database model used in the literature and will be used throughout the book, as it represents the local version of systems used in a distributed database environment. Let's begin by discussing the role that each component plays at a conceptual level.

The first layer is called the query request monitor (QRM). Others call it the transaction monitor.[1] The role of this module is to offer users an interface and a queuing mechanism so that multiple transactions can be submitted—usually in a client/server architecture on a LAN. The QRM contains communications interface logic that allows queries to be read from the LAN and responses to be routed back to their original source.

Once a query is submitted to the QRM, it is placed in a queue so that the semantic analyzer module can retrieve it. The SA module checks it for correctness; that is, it must comply with the local language grammar of the host DBMS language and the database objects referred to by the query must exist. Checking database object existence is accomplished by referring to the database catalog, which contains a description of each object contained in the database.

If the query fails inspection, it is rejected by the SA and the database monitor informs the requester that the query failed. Usually,

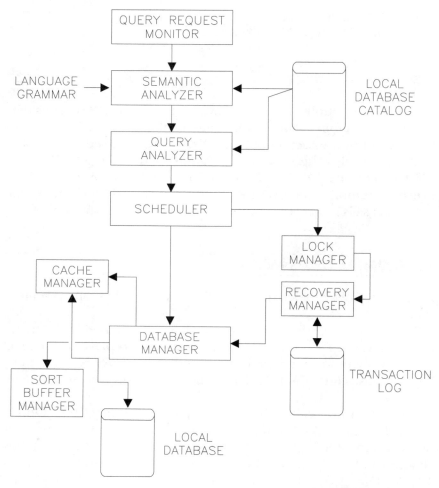

Figure 5.3 A centralized database management system (a very general model)

return codes together with explanations are returned to the user so that the query can be corrected.

If the query passes, it is passed to the next level, the query optimizer module (QOM). The QOM attempts to simplify the query and improve the order of the WHERE predicates so that system performance is improved. Let us see how this is accomplished.

Figure 5.4 shows a simple database catalog that contains statistics that will be used to optimize the query and generate an execution strategy plan to be submitted to the scheduler. This simple database

TNAME	NUM_ROWS
T1	10,000
T2	100,000
T3	1,000,000

CAT_TABLES

CNAME	TNAME	HKEY	LKEY
C1	T1	10,000	1
C2	T1	10,000	1
C3	T1	10,000	1
C1	T2	100,000	1
C2	T2	100,000	1
C3	T2	100,000	1
C1	T3	1,000,000	1
C2	T3	1,000,000	1

CAT_COLUMNS

Figure 5.4 A simple database catalog

catalog contains only two tables. Table CAT_TABLES contains the following columns:

TNAME   The table name
NUM_ROWS   Number of rows in the table. The values contained in this column are referred to as the table's cardinality.

Table CAT_COLUMNS contains the following columns:

CNAME   The column name
TNAME   Name of the table that owns the columns
HKEY   Highest key value in the columns domain
LKEY   Lowest key value in the columns domain

Let's assume the following query is submitted to the optimizer:

```
SELECT T1.C1, T3.C2
FROM T1, T3
WHERE T3.C1 = T1.C1
AND T3.C2 < 999,000
```

BAD STRATEGY
```
    SELECT T1.C1, T3.C2
    FROM T1,T3
    WHERE T3.C1 = T1.C1
        AND
            T3.C2 > 999,000
```

STEPS	NUM_ROWS
① JOIN TABLE T1 WITH T3 AND STORE RESULTS IN TEMPORARY TABLE TEMP. JOIN MUST COMPARE 10,000 ROWS AGAINST 1,000,000 ROWS	AT LEAST 10,000 TO 1,000,000 COMPARISONS IN JOIN, BAD JOIN ORDER
② SELECT ALL ROWS IN TEMPORARY TABLE WHERE VALUE OF C2 > 999,000	AT MOST 1000 ROWS RETURNED

GOOD STRATEGY	NUM_ROWS
① SELECT ALL ROWS IN TABLE T3 WHERE C2 VALUE IS GREATER THAN 999,000 AND STORE IN TEMPORARY TABLE TEMP.	AT MOST 1000 ROWS ARE GENERATED
② JOIN TEMP TABLE WITH TABLE T1. JOIN MUST COMPARE 1000 ROWS AGAINST 10,000 ROWS	AT MOST 1000 ROWS ARE GENERATED ONLY 1000 COMPARISONS REQUIRED BY THE JOIN

Figure 5.5 Two exception strategies

Figure 5.5 shows two strategies that can be used to execute the same query. Let us examine the "BAD STRATEGY" first. The query is executed verbatim. Table T3 is joined with table T1 over column C1. Table T3 is called the outer table. Assuming that the key values in column C1 are evenly distributed, we must check each of the keys in table T3 against the keys in table T1. Table T1 has one million rows; therefore, the DM must perform one million comparisons.

This operation is very costly in terms of computer resources such as CPU cycles and disk accesses. This join, once executed, generates a temporary result table that contains 10,000 rows. Once the result set is generated, the predicate in the WHERE clause that states that the values of C2 must be greater than 999,000 is applied. This can generate up to 1,000 rows in the final result set.

Now let's look at the "GOOD STRATEGY," which is generated by the optimizer. The optimizer decides to execute the predicate "C2 < 999,000" first. By doing this, it generates a temporary table with only

1,000 rows. Next, the optimizer performs the JOIN using the temporary table as the outer JOIN table and table T1 as the inner join table.
The optimizer is comparing 1,000 rows against 10,000 rows. The
optimizer has to perform only 1,000 comparisons if the key values
are evenly distributed among each of the tables involved in the JOIN.

Looking at the HKEY and LKEY values in the CAT_COLUMNS
database catalog table for column C1 in table T1, we see that LKEY =
1 and HKEY = 10,000. Chances are, the first 1,000 values in T1.C1
match the values in TEMP.C1. If this is the case, only 1,000 comparisons are performed in this strategy versus the 1,000,000 comparisons
in the first strategy. Obviously, system performance is greatly improved if the "GOOD STRATEGY" is used.

Let us see how the optimizer performs this improvement. Figure
5.6 shows the four basic steps that the optimizer takes to build an
opimized query. The four steps can be summarized as follows:

1. Translate a relational calculus query into a relational algebra
   query.
2. Generate a relational algebra tree from the query.
3. Optimize the relational algebra tree.
4. Generate the optimized relational algebra query.

In step one, the relational algebra query (SQL query) is transformed into the following relational algebra query:

$$\Pi_{PJA}(\sigma_{PF}(T1 \bowtie_{JF} T3))$$

where

   PJA = projection attributes C1,C2
   QF = qualifying predicate formula C2 < 999,000
   JF = join formula = T1.C1 = T3.C1

In step two, a relational algebra tree is constructed. This structure
takes the form of an inverted tree where the leaves contain the tables
that are to be joined. The trunk contains the WHERE clause qualifying the predicates and the root contains the SELECT clause. Step
three optimizes the tree by consulting statistical information in the
catalogs to improve the ordering of the JOINs. Any predicates that
reduce the size of the temporary tables are applied first.

This strategy reduces the cost of applying JOINs, as we saw earlier
when comparing the "GOOD STRATEGY" against the "BAD STRAT-

```
SELECT    T1.C1,  T3.C2
FROM      T1,T3
WHERE     T3.C1  =  T1.C1
AND       T3.C2  >  999.000
```

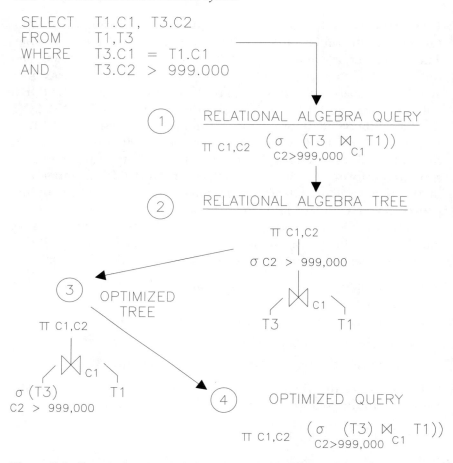

Figure 5.6 Generating a relational algebra tree from a relational calculus query

EGY." Finally, the fourth and last step takes this optimized relational algebra query tree and generates the optimized query:

$$\Pi_{PA}(\sigma_{PF}(\text{T3}) \bowtie_{JF} \text{T1})$$

where

PJA = projection attributes C1,C2
QF   = qualifying predicate formula T3.C2 < 999,000
JF   = join formula = (T3.C1 = T1.C1)

The SELECT predicate is applied first so that the JOIN performed with table T1 requires only 1,000 rows to be compared in the inner table with the 10,000 rows of the outer table. Additionally, if indexes are available for the columns referred to in the query, they will be used to further improve performance. For instance, if an index existed based on the C2 column, it could be used to retrieve the rows that fulfill the requirement that C2 be greater than 999,000. Let's see what the scheduler does with the optimized query.

The scheduler now accepts the optimized query and consults with the lock manager to see if the data objects that are required by the transaction can be locked or if they are already owned by some other transaction. If the locks are not available, the transaction is rescheduled for later execution. If all the lock requests are granted, the scheduler passes the transaction ID to the database manager module for execution.

The DM interacts with the cache manager module (CM) to retrieve and write rows to and from memory. To improve performance, parts of the database are always kept in a special area of system memory called cache memory. It is the responsibility of the cache manager to perform reads and writes between the database residing on disk and cache memory.

5.3 CONCURRENCY ISSUES AND SOLUTIONS

Centralized database managment systems must be able to run two or more transactions simultaneously. This ability is known as transaction concurrency. This ability poses a few problems. What if one of the transactions that is concurrently running with another transaction fails? Assume that both transactions are updating the same record in the database. The first transaction failed right after it wrote a value into the record. This value is now invalid! The second transaction reads this invalid value, performs some calculations, and updates several other records in the database based on the value that is now incorrect. The entire database is now corrupted and there is no way of recovering it!

A second problem (lost updates) is best illustrated by the classical banking example. Suppose two depositors simultaneously access the same bank account from different automatic teller machines in order to make deposits. The initial value in the bank account is £10,000. The first depositor performs the following transaction:

```
deposit = £500.00
transaction1 = read1(current_balance,balance);
               new_balance = current_balance + deposit;
               write2(balance,new_balance);
```

The second depositor performs the following transaction at the same time:

```
deposit = £15000.00
transaction2 = read2(current_balance,balance);
               new_balance = current_balance + deposit;
               write2(balance,new_balance);
```

Suppose the read/write operations are performed in the following order:

```
read1(current_balance,balance);
read2(current_balance,balance);
write2(balance,new_balance);
write1(balance,new_balance);
```

Notice what has happened. Transaction 1 reads the balance after which transaction 2 reads the same balance. So far so good! Now transaction 2 performs its operation and writes the new balance of £25,000 into the account. Next transaction 1 performs its operation and writes a balance of £10,500 into the same account. The correct bank balance should read £25,500. The actual balance is now £10,500. The £15,000 was lost!!!

This type of problem is solved by ordering each of the individual operations of a transaction in such a manner that they do not interfere with each other and cancel out each other's actions. There are two solutions for implementing this type of strategy:

- serialization techniques
- concurrency control algorithms

Serialization of concurrent transactions is defined in Section 5.4. Concurrency control algorithms are discussed in Section 5.5.

5.4 SERIALIZATION OF CONCURRENT TRANSACTIONS

In Section 5.1, a transaction was defined as a series of reads and writes on a database. These reads and writes were treated as one operation. Before we discuss serialization techniques, let's formally define a transaction in mathematical terms. A transaction[1,2] is defined as a partial order that takes the following form:

```
T = { E,< }
```

where E is the domain of elements that are being ordered and < is the set of binary operations shown in the required order.

In our case, the domain is the set of all the read, write, COMMIT, and ROLLBACK operations that constitute a transaction. The set of binary operations represents the execution order. Let's now examine the properties of a transaction.

End note 2 in this chapter defines the properties of transactions as follows:

1. E = ALL OPS, where OPS is all the possible operations belonging to the transaction, that is, all the reads, writes, COMMITS, or ROLLBACKS.

2. Given a database object X (a row or page for example), given two operations OP1(X) and OP2(X), with each operation belonging to a different transaction and each operation manipulating the same database object X, then either OP1(X) must precede OP2(X) or OP2(X) must precede OP1(X). This assumption holds if one operation is a write and the other is a read or if both operations are writes.

3. The last condition is that every series of operations must terminate either with a COMMIT or a ROLLBACK.

End note 1 in this chapter defines the properties of transactions as follows:

1. T = { R UNION W UNION [COMMIT OR ROLLBACK]}

    where R = all the read operations involved in the transaction, W = all the write operations involved in the transaction, COMMIT = the commit operation, and ROLLBACK = the abort operation if the transaction fails. As in number 1 above, this first property defines the possible operations that make up a transaction.

2. A transaction must terminate with either a COMMIT or a ROLLBACK. It cannot terminate with both.

3. Every operation on the database MUST terminate with either a COMMIT or an ABORT.

4. Given two operations OP1(X) and OP2(X), where X is the data object being accessed and one of the operations is a write and one of the operations is a read, then either OP1(X) precedes OP2(X) or OP2(X) precedes OP1(X).

This set of definitions differs from the second set of definitions in that an extra requirement is included; that is, the transaction must terminate with either a COMMIT or a ROLLBACK. It cannot terminate with both or none. Let's apply these definitions to the following three transactions:

```
T1 = r1(x),r1(y),w1(z),c1;
T2 = r2(x),w2(x),C2;
T3 = r3(x),r3(y),w3(x),c3);
```

Below are the partial orders used to define these transactions:

```
T1 = {E1,<1}
```

where

```
E1 = [r1(x),r1(y),w1(z),c1]
<1 = [(r1(x),r1(y),w1(z)),(r1(x),c1),(r1(y),c1),(w1(x),c1)];
```

```
T2 = {E2,<2}
```

where

```
E2 = [r2(x),w2(x),c2]
<2 = [(r2(x),w2(x)),(r2(x),c2),(w2(x),c2)];
T3 = {E3,<3}
```

where

```
E3 = [r3(x),r3(y),w3(x),c3]
<3 = [(r3(x),r3(y),w3(x)),(r3(x),c3),(r3(y),c3),(w3(x),c3)];
```

The scheduler accepts operations from each of the transactions and builds a stream of interleaved operations called a history. This history can then be executed by the database manager without fear of conflicting operations. The scheduler orders the operations in such a manner as to avoid conflicts but still maintain the integrity of the transactions; that is, after the history is executed, the effect is the same as if each transaction were executed serially.

Figure 5.7 shows a conceptual view of the transaction just discussed being submitted to the scheduler. The goal of the scheduler is to build a serial history that includes all the operations in T1, T2, and T3 by interleaving them into a serial stream of nonconflicting

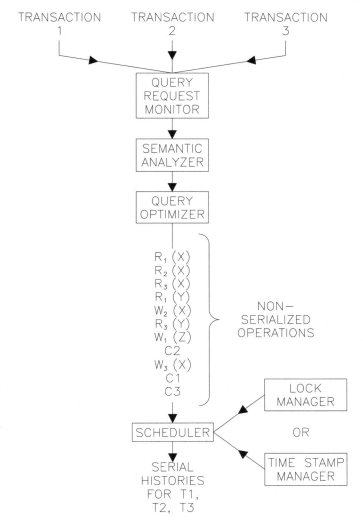

Figure 5.7 Transaction serialization

operations. Depending on the type of concurrency control algorithm used, the scheduler will assign locks or time stamps to implement this history.

Notice that the three transactions are accepted by the DM, analyzed by the semantic analyzer, and optimized by the optimizer. Each
transaction is then translated into a nonserialized stream of operations and submitted to the scheduler. It is the job of the scheduler to
produce the serial history of these transactions. Let's see how this is

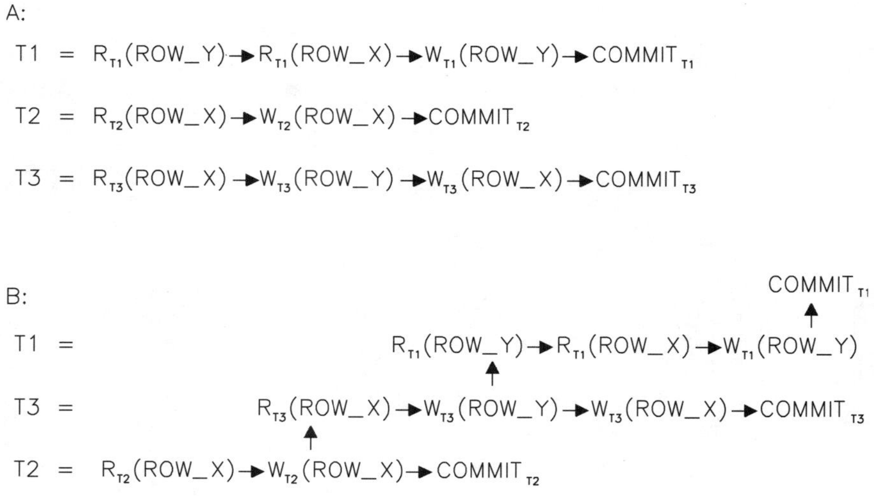

A:

$T1 \quad = \quad R_{T1}(ROW\_Y) \rightarrow R_{T1}(ROW\_X) \rightarrow W_{T1}(ROW\_Y) \rightarrow COMMIT_{T1}$

$T2 \quad = \quad R_{T2}(ROW\_X) \rightarrow W_{T2}(ROW\_X) \rightarrow COMMIT_{T2}$

$T3 \quad = \quad R_{T3}(ROW\_X) \rightarrow W_{T3}(ROW\_Y) \rightarrow W_{T3}(ROW\_X) \rightarrow COMMIT_{T3}$

B:

$COMMIT_{T1}$
$\uparrow$

$T1 \quad = \qquad\qquad\qquad\qquad R_{T1}(ROW\_Y) \rightarrow R_{T1}(ROW\_X) \rightarrow W_{T1}(ROW\_Y)$
$\uparrow$

$T3 \quad = \qquad\qquad R_{T3}(ROW\_X) \rightarrow W_{T3}(ROW\_Y) \rightarrow W_{T3}(ROW\_X) \rightarrow COMMIT_{T3}$
$\uparrow$

$T2 \quad = \quad R_{T2}(ROW\_X) \rightarrow W_{T2}(ROW\_X) \rightarrow COMMIT_{T2}$

Figure 5.8 Three serial transactions

accomplished. In the discussions that follow I use the same techniques and symbols that are presented in end notes 1 and 2.

Figures 5.8a and 5.8b show the individual histories of three new transactions. The arrows in the histories indicate that an operation precedes another operation. For example, transaction $T1 = r1(y) < r1(x) < w1(y) < c1$. This states that $r1(y)$ must precede $r1(x)$, which must precede $w1(y)$, which must precede the COMMIT command.

In Figure 5.8b, the vertical arrows indicate operation precedence between transactions. These operations can be executed in parallel. By starting at $r2(x)$ and working our way left to right, bottom to top, the scheduler produces the following serial history (SH):

```
SH(T1,T2,T3) =
  r2(x),w2(x),r3(x),c2,w3(y),r1(y),w3(x),r1(x),c3,w1(y),c1
```

The manner in which these arrows are assigned is the function of the concurrency control algorithms. Some of these algorithms are discussed in the next section.

5.5 CONCURRENCY CONTROL ALGORITHMS

One of the solutions to the transaction concurrency problem just described is to use a set of algorithms that enforce the serialization of transaction operations. This is accomplished by interleaving each of the operations in the transactions so that when they are executed they have the same effect as if they were executed one after the other. That is, given the following three transactions

```
T1 = r1(X), r1(Y), w1(Z), c1;
T2 = r2(X), r2(Y), w2(X), c2;
T3 = r3(X), w3(Z), c3;
```

each operation is interleaved so as to have the same effect as if the operations were executed in the following order:

```
r1(X), r1(Y), w1(Z), c1, r2(X), r2(Y), w2(X),
   c2,r3(X), w3(Z), c3;
```

If this is so desirable, why not just execute them in the above serial order and be done with it? If this were the case, the distributed database management system would be simple to implement, but the performance would be so poor as to render the entire system unusable! By interleaving the operations, the system's CPU is used more efficiently and the transactions are executed in such a manner as to appear as if they were being executed concurrently.

The literature identifies two categories of algorithms that are used to enforce this serialization strategy. The algorithms can be considered as either optimistic or pessimistic. Each algorithm enforces serialization by either placing some sort of a lock on the data object being manipulated or assigning a time stamp to place the operations in a serial order.

Pessimistic Concurrency Control Algorithms

Let's examine the pessimistic algorithms first. They are called pessimistic because they delay the execution of the transactions for fear of possible conflicts. The scheduler that implements this type of algorithm delays an operation to see if the subsequent operations that the QRM submits will conflict with the one that is currently being held. If there are no conflicts, both are scheduled. If a conflict exists, one is delayed while the other is permitted to execute. The delayed operation is placed in a holding queue for later processing.

This strategy risks that a delayed operation can be redelayed every time an attempt is made to schedule it. Priority indicators can be assigned to a transaction so that every time it is delayed its priority is increased. When the priority of the delayed transaction reaches a certain level, the transaction is permitted to be executed and the other conflicting transaction is now delayed.

Optimistic Concurrency Control Algorithms

This class of algorithm is the opposite of the pessimistic concurrency control algorithm. It never delays an operation. It assumes no conflicts will occur and the scheduler that implements this algorithm submits operations to the database manager as they come in. If a conflicting operation is found, the entire transaction is aborted and must be restarted.

Although these types of schedulers never delay an operation, they run the risk of aborting many transactions because conflicts are found at the last minute. We will concentrate on the "pessimistic" schedulers that use locks to enforce concurrency and data integrity. Let us now examine a protocol that "locks" data objects, thereby preventing conflicts between transactions.

5.6 TWO-PHASE LOCKING PROTOCOLS

Earlier we discussed how one of the solutions for maintaining transaction concurrency was to implement a scheme whereby locks are placed on data objects that are being manipulated by a transaction.

There are basically two types of locks, a read lock and a write lock. Certain locks are compatible. By this I mean that more than one transaction can place a lock on the same object.

A read lock is compatible with another read lock. If transaction T1 requests a read lock on object X and transaction T2 already has a read lock on object X, T1 is granted the lock anyway. If either or both of the transactions had requested a write lock on the object, then a conflict would have occurred and one of the transactions would have been denied the lock request. Figure 5.9 shows a simple table that indicates lock compatibilities and incompatibilities. Squares with check marks indicate compatibility. Squares with Xs indicate that the locks are incompatible.

A popular algorithm for implementing a locking strategy is called the "two-phase locking" algorithm. As the name implies, the protocol has two phases. The literature refers to these two phases as the growing phase and shrinking phase or the locking phase and unlock-

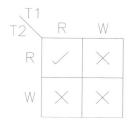

Figure 5.9 Simplified lock compatibility graph

ing phase. Figure 5.10 shows a diagram representing the two phases of the lock request strategy.

The first phase, the "growing phase," is where all the locks required by a transaction are obtained. The second phase is where all the locks that were previously obtained are released by the transaction. The two-phase rule states that once a transaction has released a lock, it cannot obtain another. It has been shown and proven in the literature that schedulers that follow the two-phase locking protocol always produce serial execution histories.[1,2]

There is a down side to using this protocol! It is possible to have two transactions request the same lock. Both of these transactions might also possess a lock on an object that the other transaction requires. Both transactions will not give up their current locks until they obtain locks on the objects each needs.

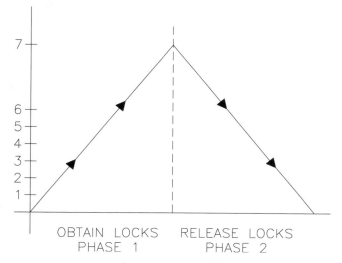

Figure 5.10 Two-phase locking graph

This situation is called deadlock and cannot be resolved unless terminated by an outside process. Figure 5.11a shows a table indicating three transactions that are currently deadlocked. Transaction T1 has a write lock on data object X. T1 needs a write lock on object Y and will not release the lock on X until it obtains it.

Transaction T2 has a write lock on Y and needs a write lock on object Z. It also will not release the write lock on Y until it gets its write lock on Z. Finally, transaction T3 has a write lock on object Z that transaction T2 requires. Transaction T3 needs a write lock on item X. Hey! Wait a minute! We are going around in circles! Transaction T1 has a write lock on object X and will not give it up. This is the classic deadlock situation. The transactions remain permanently blocked because of their greediness.

Figure 5.11b shows a graph called a WAIT-FOR-GRAPH. Notice the cycle that is produced in the graph. T1 waits for T2, which in turn waits for T3. Any histories that contain this type of cycle in their WAIT-FOR-GRAPH are deadlocked and the cycles must somehow be broken.

We will see in Section 5.9 how this graph is used by a background process called a deadlock detector to break the deadlock situations.

5.7 THE TIME STAMP ORDERING PROTOCOL

An alternate strategy to maintaining transaction concurrency is to assign time stamps to each of the operations in the transactions. The time stamp assigned to each operation is the same as the time stamp assigned to the entire transaction.

Operations with older time stamps are executed before operations with younger time stamps; that is, if $TS1(X)$ equals the time stamp of an operation belonging to transaction 1 and if $TS(2)$ equals the time stamp of an operation belonging to transaction T2, $OP1(X) < OP2(x)$ if $TS1(X) < TS2(X)$ else $OP2(X) < OP1(X)$ if $TS2(X) < TS1(X)$.

The time stamps are usually constructed from the transaction ID plus some counter value, such as the system clock or a value that is periodically incremented. This technique ensures that the time stamps generated for each transaction are unique.

Use of the time stamp ordering algorithms (TSO) eliminates deadlocks because operations are scheduled in increasing order due

A:

TID	HAS LOCK	NEEDS LOCK
T1	WL(ROW_X)	WL(ROW_Y)
T2	WL(ROW_Y)	WL(ROW_Z)
T3	WL(ROW_Z)	WL(ROW_X)

B:

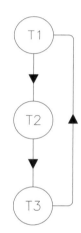

Figure 5.11 a) A simple lock list; b) WAIT-FOR-GRAPH for T1, T2, T3

to the increasing time stamp values. The down side to this strategy is that if a single operation of a transaction has a conflicting time stamp, the entire transaction is rejected. Therefore, TSO algorithms avoid deadlock by assigning time stamps but greatly increase the restarting of a transaction due to time stamp conflicts.

5.8 DEADLOCK AND DEADLOCK RESOLUTION

The concept of a deadlock was introduced in Section 5.6. Deadlocks occur when two or more histories contain cycles in their WAIT-FOR-GRAPHS. Deadlocks are inherent in locked in–based schedulers and can be broken using one of the following methods:

1. **Timeout intervals**

    If a transaction has been waiting around for a certain time period without any activity, the scheduler assumes that the transaction is deadlocked and aborts it. This method runs the risk of a transaction simply waiting for an object that is owned by another transaction that is taking a long time to finish.

2. **WAIT-FOR-GRAPHS**

    This method has a scheduler that maintains and monitors a data structure called a WAIT-FOR-GRAPH. This structure shows transactions waiting for data objects owned by other transactions. For instance, T1 waits for T2 and T4, which waits for T3 and T5. T3 waits for T5, T4 waits for T2, and T5 waits for T1. Figure 5.12a depicts this situation.

Deadlocked transactions are transactions that contain cycles in their WAIT-FOR-GRAPHS. These cycles are depicted as arcs in the WAIT-FOR-GRAPH. They are terminated by the deadlock detector for various reasons. For instance, the transaction that has the greatest number of cycles is terminated.

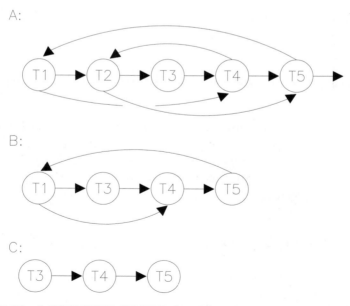

Figure 5.12 a) WAIT-FOR-GRAPH for five transactions; b) WAIT-FOR-GRAPH after T2 is terminated; c) WAIT-FOR-GRAPH after T1 is terminated

First, transaction T2 is involved in the cycle T1 < T2 < T3 < T4 < T5 and T1 < T2 < T5 < T1. Terminating transaction T2 in Figure 5.12a results in the WAIT-FOR-GRAPH shown in Figure 5.12b.

Terminating transaction T2 did not solve all the problems. The following cycles still remain:

```
T1 < T3 < T4 < T5 and T1 < T3 < T4 < T1
```

This time, T1 is a good candidate for rescheduling. Terminating this transaction results in the WAIT-FOR-GRAPH shown in Figure 5.12c.

Another approach for selecting a termination victim is to terminate the transaction that has performed the least amount of work. In any case, we see that locking-based algorithms provide serial histories but at the cost of rejecting transactions if they become involved in deadlocks.

Figure 5.13 shows a revised version of our database management system model that now includes a process called a deadlock detector.

The deadlock detector monitors its WAIT-FOR-GRAPH and notifies the scheduler of any cycles. On notification that a cycle exists, the scheduler aborts and restarts the most likely transaction that qualifies for postponement. Our discussions on deadlocks and deadlock resolution will be expanded for distributed environments in Chapter 10.

5.9 RECOVERY STRATEGIES

Any database management sysem must have the capability to recover from system crashes and application failures. It is the job of the recovery manager module to ensure that a database remain in a consistent state in spite of these diverse failures. Figure 5.14 shows a block diagram of a recovery manager together with the system resources it manipulates.

To improve performance, parts of the database are kept in volatile memory so as to reduce the number of physical disk accesses. This memory area is called the cache memory and is manipulated by a module called the cache manager (CM). The job of this module is to read and write portions of the database so that the database manager can execute the transactions and manipulate the data in memory rather than directly to disk. For our purposes, we assume that the cache manager loads only the required rows for each transaction

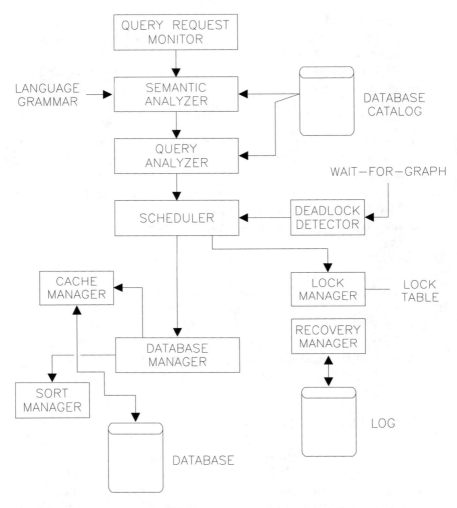

Figure 5.13 Modified database management system model

that it is currently processing. Associated with each row is a bit called a dirty bit, which indicates whether or not the rows in memory were used to update the database residing on the system disk. If the dirty bit is set to 0, it means the rows were not yet written to disk.

The next important resource manipulated by the recovery manager is the database log. The log is used to store a complete history of each transaction as it is executed. The log usually is made up of the following three data structures:

1. A COMMIT list

2. A ROLLBACK list

3. A DATA list

The COMMIT list contains a record for each transaction that successfully completes. It is necessary to maintain this list because the possibility exists that the system could fail prior to storing the "COMMITted" data back to disk; that is, changes could have been made to the row contained in the cache memory area but not yet recorded in the database residing on the stable disk storage. As committed transactions are stored first in the log, it is possible for a system to malfunction or fail before changes are recorded permanently in the database residing on the disk drive. We will see how this mechanism works after we describe the remaining components of the database log.

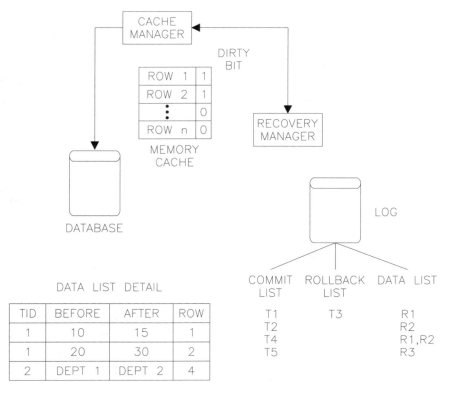

Figure 5.14 Recovery manager and transaction log detail

The ROLLBACK list contains a list of transactions that have failed. Some failures require that a transaction's actions be rolled back when a system is restarted after a failure. The ROLLBACK list is used to assist in identifying the transactions that may have corrupted the database and rendered it in an inconsistent state.

Finally, the DATA list component contains before and after images of each change to the database table rows. Togther with the lists described earlier, the data list can be used to either update rows that were not updated due to a system failure just after the transaction COMMITted or undo changes that were made permanent in the database from a transaction that issued a ROLLBACK just before the system crashed.

Let us see what happens when a transaction that runs to completion is interrupted by a system failure.

A transaction is submitted to the database manager for execution. The rows required by the transaction are loaded into memory by the cache manager. Next, the before images are recorded in the log. The required changes are made in memory, and the recovery manager then stores the after images to the log together with a "COMMIT" record in the COMMIT list for this transaction. Just as the cache manager is about to receive an instruction to record the changes permanently to the database, someone pulls the plug out of the wall socket and the system crashes.

On recovery, the recovery manager automatically scans its COMMIT list to see if any COMMITted transactions have to be reexecuted due to any failures. Since it finds a record for the transaction described above, it scans the before/after image list for that transaction, asks the cache manager to load it into cache memory, and then records it in the database residing on disk. In the literature, this is called "redo," as a transaction must be reexecuted to bring the database up-to-date. There are instances when an "UNDO" has to be executed to remove unwanted changes from a transaction that failed. Let's look at this case next.

Let's assume that the database manager module receives a transaction that changes 1,000 rows. The transaction successfully changes 990 rows in cache memory. Periodically, the cache manager makes the changes permanent by storing them to disk because the cache buffers are running out of space. Suddenly, the application aborts due to an application error.

The recovery manager is promptly notified and enters a record in the ROLLBACK list for this transaction. Just as the recovery manager is about to utilize the "before" images to restore the database to its original state (prior to the failure of the transaction) the same person who pulled the plug out of the wall socket before accidentally trips and does it again. The system crashes and now the database is left in an inconsistent state.

On recovery, the recovery manager can once again examine the ROLLBACK list to "undo" any transactions that failed by reading the before images of the data that were changed. This is how bad transactions are undone.

This was a high-level discussion on database recovery, but the reader can now see the importance of the database logs and the function that the recovery manager performs.

Various architectures exist for implementing recovery strategies. I've presented a simple general model that is based on the models currently discussed in the literature. Architectures exist that keep several copies of the logs to any point in the life of the database.

5.10 SUMMARY

We have now covered all of the information necessary for the understanding of how centralized database management systems work. The operation of a simple DBMS was discussed and the issues of maintaining concurrency and recovery were covered for a centralized environment. The reader now has sufficient ammunition to begin his or her study of distributed and multi-database systems. The next chapter concludes the first section of the book by identifying the various categories that constitute distributed and multi-database management systems.

5.11 END NOTES

1. Bernstein, P., V. Hadzilacos, and N. Goodman. *Concurrency Control and Recovery in Database Systems*, Reading, MA: Addison-Wesley, 1987.

2. Özsu, M. Tamer, and P. Valduriez. *Principles of Distributed Database Systems*, Englewood Cliffs, NJ: Prentice Hall, 1991.

6

Introduction to Distributed and Multi-Database Systems

6.1 INTRODUCTION

This is the last chapter in Part I of this book. It serves as a primer for the topics that will be covered in the remainder of the text. The chapter begins by classifying shared information systems and discusses fundamental design issues. Although this and other related topics will be covered in greater detail in succeeding chapters, I introduce the basic concepts here. Also included in this chapter are two sections explaining how expert systems can be used in a special case of a multi-database system called a federated database.

6.2 CLASSIFYING SHARED INFORMATION SYSTEMS

A shared information system can be considered as a series of computer systems interconnected by some sort of communications network. Residing on each computer is a data repository such as a relational database, a hierarchical or network database, a series of spreadsheets containing financial information, or a collection of flat files.

An added requirement for this type of system is that these diverse data repositories be somehow related. The goal of distributed and multi-database systems is to allow users to view this collection of data repositories as if they were a single entity.

121

To fulfill these requirements, some sort of software layer has to be built to interface all the data and allow the user access to the data. This section will classify the software layer as it is currently discussed in the literature. The classification will be at a slightly higher level, as various researchers have broken this layer into several subdivisions.

For example, in an article appearing in *IEEE Computer*,[1] global information systems were classified into these categories:

- Distributed databases
- Global schema multi-databases
- Federated databases
- Multi-database language systems
- Homogeneous multi-database language systems
- Interoperable systems

Figure 6.1 shows the simplified classification breakdown that will be used in this chapter. As can be seen, we will take a higher-level approach and concentrate on the following three layers:

- Distributed database systems
- Multi-database systems
- Federated database systems

A more detailed breakdown of shared information systems can be found in Özsu and Valduriez.[2] Let us continue by defining each system according to our simplified categorization scheme.

Distributed Database Systems

Better known as homogeneous distributed database systems, this type of distributed DBMS is characterized by similar access methods, optimization strategies, concurrent strategies, and data models. For instance, the data models at each of the distributed sites are relational. The concurrency control methods utilize locks and WAIT-FOR-GRAPHS. Designing a distributed database involves the fragmentation of the tables belonging to a central database. Each of the table fragments is distributed to a remote site according to some criteria (horizontal, vertical, or hybrid table fragments).

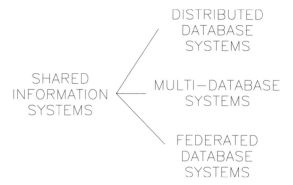

Figure 6.1 Simple classification of shared information systems

These design methods will be introduced in Section 6.3 and discussed in Chapter 8.

Multi-Database Systems

Better known as heterogeneous multi-database systems, this type of global DBMS is characterized by dissimilar data models, concurrency and optimization strategies, and access methods. Unlike its cousin, the homogeneous distributed database, the data models that compose the global database could be based on the relational, hierarchical, or network model. Access methods and concurrency control algorithms would utilize locking mechanisms at one site and time stamp strategies at another site. I will expand on features of this type of system in Section 6.5 of this chapter. Part III of this book will be dedicated to multi-database systems.

Federated Database Systems

Distributed and multi-database systems have at least one feature in common. They both utilize a global data dictionary or schema to allow users access to the data objects at each remote site. Federated database systems do not use a global schema. At each site, an export and import schema are used. Export schema identify the data that each site is willing to share with other sites. The import schema identify the remote data that a site can access. This type of DBMS is discussed in Section 6.7 of this chapter.

6.3 DISTRIBUTED DATABASE SYSTEMS

Let us now take a closer look at a distributed database system from an architectural point of view. (We will study distributed database systems from a schematic point of view in Part II of this book.) Figure 6.2a shows a simple architecture composed of IBM hardware and software products.

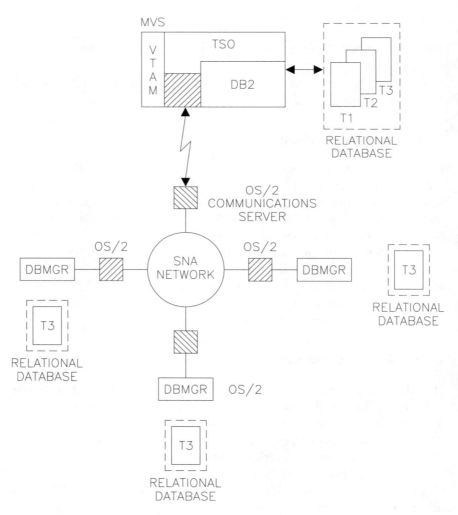

Figure 6.2a A distributed database

The distributed database is composed of a host system running MVS as its operating system. On board is IBM's relational database management system DB2, a communications manager called VTAM, and interface software to DB2 called TSO. The relational database managed by DB2 is made up of three tables: T1, T2, and T3. The cross-hatched box represents the top layer of the distributed database management system.

Attached to the host system via an IBM SNA network are three servers, each running IBM's OS/2 as the operating system. On board each server is IBM's OS/2 relational database management system called Database Manager. The cross-hatched boxes represent the local server components of the distributed database management system.

In this particular case, the distributed database will be implemented by loading each server site with one of the tables from the original database. Table T1 will be assigned to site 1, table T2 will be assigned to site 2, and table T3 will be assigned to site 3. This is a fairly simplistic and unrealistic approach for distributing data, but for now it will suffice. Section 6.3 will discuss a more realistic approach called horizontal and vertical fragmentation. Chapter 8 will go into the topic of distributed database design in greater detail. For now let us be satisfied with the technique of downloading a table to each site in the distributed environment. The original database on the DB2 system is kept as a backup in case of failures at each site.

Earlier we mentioned that the cross-hatched boxes represent the distributed software layer for our system. User queries are submitted to the top-level layer of this software and then fragmented to each of the sites involved in the query. Each site executes its fragment and returns the results to the host software layer so any joins can be performed. The final results are passed to the user who requested the translation.

Referring back to the diagram, notice why this is a homogeneous distributed database system. The database model is the same at all sites. (It's relational.) The software components are also the same; that is, IBM's DB2 executes transactions and maintains concurrency in a fashion similar to IBM's OS/2 Database Manager residing on a local server. All of the software components are compatible. The distributed database management system (the cross-hatched boxes) could be a set of custom software modules or a vendor architecture such as IBM's DRDA (Distributed Relational Database Architecture).

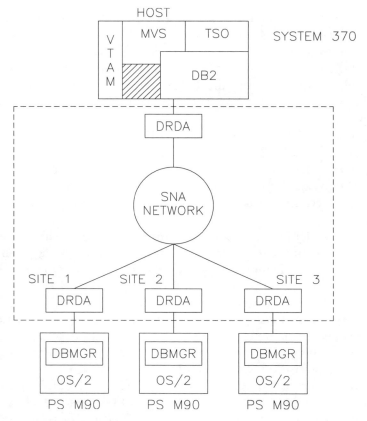

Figure 6.2b IBM's DRDA

Figure 6.2b shows IBM's DRDA architecture as the distributed DBMS
for our model.

6.4 DESIGN ISSUES

In the previous section we were confronted with a DB2 database that
was made up of three tables. A distributed database was implemented by loading each of the tables at a remote site. This is not a
realistic approach, as it does not take into account any factors such as
the application that will access the distributed database or the hardware platforms that they will run on.

In this section we introduce two techniques of distributed database
design. The first technique is called vertical table fragmentation.[2-4]

The second technique is called horizontal table fragmentation.[2,3] A third technique called hybrid fragmentation[2] is a combination of the above two techniques.

Horizontal Fragmentation

Figure 6.3 shows a relational database table and three fragment tables that were derived from it. The table is composed of four attributes:

EMP_ID   employee identification number
LNAME   employee last name
DEPT   employee department
SALARY   employee yearly salary

EMP_TABLE

EMP_ID	LNAME	DEPT	SALARY
E1	SMYTHE	D1	50000
E2	BILLINGS	D1	40000
E3	WILLIAMS	D2	80000
E4	JONES	D3	90000

EMP_TABLE_FRAGMENT 1

EMP_ID	LNAME	DEPT	SALARY
E1	SMYTHE	D1	50000
E2	BILLINGS	D1	40000

EMP_TABLE_FRAGMENT 2

EMP_ID	LNAME	DEPT	SALARY
E3	WILLIAMS	D2	80000

EMP_TABLE_FRAGMENT 3

EMP_ID	LNAME	DEPT	SALARY
E4	JONES	D3	90000

Figure 6.3 Horizontal table fragmentation

Horizontal fragmentation implies the division of relations along its tuples. For this we use the relational algebra SELECT operation to fragment the table into three smaller fragments. In this case, our procedure is to allocate a department to each site. Therefore, our three relational algebra operations to perform this task are

1. EMP_TABLE_FRAGMENT_1 = SELECT(EMP_TABLE)
    WHERE DEPT = D1

2. EMP_TABLE_FRAGMENT_2 = SELECT(EMP_TABLE)
    WHERE DEPT = D2

3. EMP_TABLE_FRAGMENT_3 = SELECT(EMP_TABLE)
    WHERE DEPT = D3

Executing the above three formulas results in three table fragments:

EMP_TABLE_FRAGMENT_1 (contains 2 tuples)
EMP_TABLE_FRAGMENT_2 (contains 1 tuple)
EMP_TABLE_FRAGMENT_3 (contains 1 tuple)

We have now succeeded in fragmenting the table by departments so that each site contains only information relevant to the department it represents. The design steps required to implement horizontal fragmentation will be discussed in greater detail in Chapter 8. Next, we examine vertical fragmentation.

Vertical Table Fragmentation

It stands to reason that vertical fragmentation works by splitting a table between attributes. For this method, the relational PROJECT operation is used. Figure 6.4 shows the same table that was horizontally fragmented in the previous section. An extra attribute (SKILL) was added to make things more interesting.

This time our criteria for fragmentation are that site 1 is to contain only skills data and site 2 is to contain payroll data. For this reason, we want site 2 to have access to the employee's salary. Site 1 will not have access to salary information but it will have access to SKILLs information. The following two relational algebra queries satisfy this requirement:

```
EMP_TABLE_FRAGMENT_1 = PROJECT(EMP_TABLE)
     EMP_ID,DEPT,LNAME,SKILL
```

```
EMP_TABLE_FRAGMENT_2 = PROJECT(EMP_TABLE)
     EMP_ID,SALARY
```

There is one important point to highlight at this time. Notice that the EMP_ID attribute was duplicated at both sites. This is necessary, as this attribute is used as the key index for the original table. This attribute must be duplicated at each site so that JOINs can be performed between the two tables. An example distributed SQL query against these two fragments would be

```
SELECT EMP_TABLE_FRAGMENT_1.EMP_ID,
           EMP_TABLE_FRAGMENT_1.SKILL,
           EMP_TABLE_FRAGMENT_2.SALARY,
     FROM   EMP_TABLE_FRAGMENT_1,EMP_TABLE FRAGMENT_2
     WHERE  EMP_TABLE_FRAGMENT_1.EMP_ID =
               EMP_TABLE_FRAGMENT_2.EMP_ID
     AND    EMP_TABLE_FRAGMENT_2.SALARY > 80000
```

Execution of this query yields the following results:

```
EMP_ID    SKILL        SALARY
E4        MANAGER      90000
```

Chapter 8 will discuss the steps required to implement vertical fragmentation in a distributed database design.

EMP_TABLE

EMP_ID	LNAME	DEPT	SALARY	SKILL
E1	SMYTHE	D1	50000	PROG
E2	BILLINGS	D1	40000	ANALYST
E3	WILLIAMS	D2	80000	DESIGNER
E4	JONES	D3	90000	MANAGER

EMP_TABLE_FRAGMENT_1

EMP_ID	LNAME	DEPT	SKILL
E1	SMYTHE	D1	PROG
E2	BILLINGS	D1	ANALYST
E3	WILLIAMS	D2	DESIGNER
E4	JONES	D3	MANAGER

EMP_TABLE_FRAGMENT_2

EMP_ID	SALARY
E1	50000
E2	40000
E3	80000
E4	90000

Figure 6.4 Vertical table fragmentation

6.5 MULTI-DATABASE SYSTEMS

Unlike homogeneous distributed database systems, multi-database systems are heterogeneous; that is, their components and data models are dissimilar. Figure 6.5 shows an example of a multi-database architecture. It is composed of a central global location and two distributed sites. The central global access site contains the global access layer and the global data dictionary. Another name for the global data dictionary is the global database schema. This term is currently used in the literature.

The local sites each contain a local access layer, a local database management system, and a database. The local access layers, together with the global access layer, make up the multi-database sys-

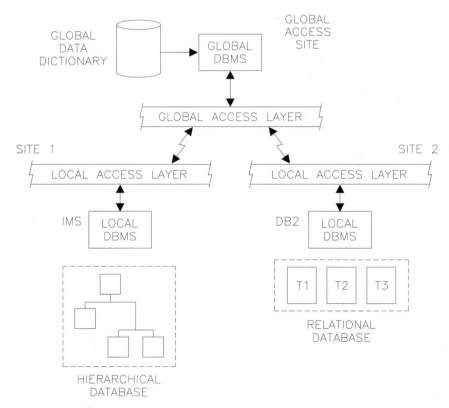

Figure 6.5 Multi-database architecture

tem. I will cover the components of the multi-database system in Part III, Chapter 13 of this book.

Notice that site A's local DBMS is IMS and site B's local DBMS is DB2. This is what we mean by a heterogeneous multi-database system. The local components are based on two different database management systems and data models.

The global data dictionary contains information that makes these two databases appear to the user as if they were one large database. When a user submits a distributed query to the global access layer, the query is decomposed and transformed to the appropriate data retrieval language for each site. To the user, it appears that the entire distributed database is based on the relational model (assuming the global data dictionary is based on the relational model). Let us examine two design approaches for multi-database systems.

6.6 DESIGN ISSUES

There are two types of multi-database systems. The first is based on a global schema;[2] the second is based on the multi-database languages.[1] Since in this book we will concentrate on the global schema approach, I will only briefly discuss multi-database systems based on the multi-database language approach.

Global Schema Approach

Figure 6.6 shows a model of a multi-database architecture based on the ANSI/SPARC model. This model is the same model introduced in Özsu and Valduriez.[2]

Notice that both local and global external schemas exist. The global multi-database schema (GMDBS) is the UNION of all local conceptual schemas. Global users can access distributed data via information contained in the GMDBS. Notice that local site autonomy is preserved to a degree, since the local external schemas represent applications unique to the local site.

Multi-Database Language Approach

This approach does not rely on a centralized global schema. The retrieval language contains primitives that route queries and per-

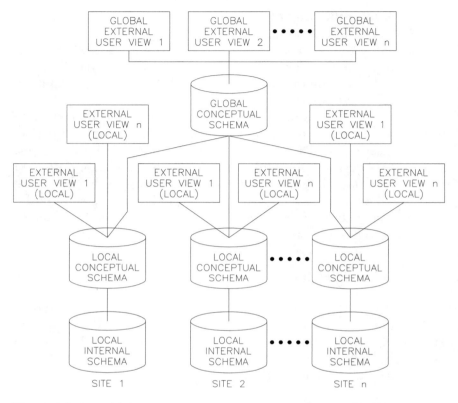

Figure 6.6 A multi-database architecture based on the ANSI/SPARC data model

form any data translation between different database models. Functions and tools are supplied to the user to create distributed queries embedded with these primitives.

Although this method greatly increases site autonomy, it greatly increases the complexity of generating distributed queries, as it leaves the responsibilites of data localization and translation to the programmer.

6.7 FEDERATED DISTRIBUTED DATABASE SYSTEMS

Federated distributed database systems are a special case of multi-database systems. They are completely autonomous, do not rely on the global data dictionary to process distributed queries, and each

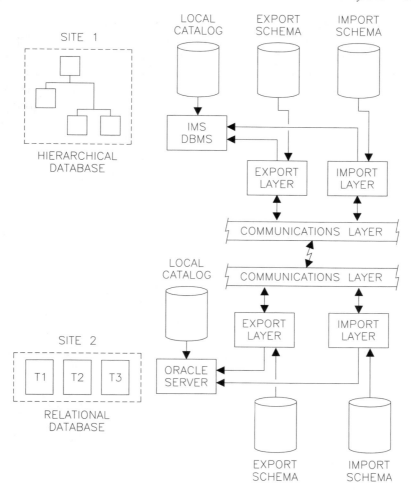

Figure 6.7 A federated database

site can join or leave the multi-database system at will without affect-
ing the other members. Figure 6.7 shows an example of a simple
federated database system made up of two nodes. This particular
system has an IMS DBMS residing at site 1. Site 2 contains an OR-
ACLE relational DBMS. (*Note:* The IMS system data model is hierarchical; the ORACLE data model is relational.)

As stated earlier, federated databases do not rely on global data
dictionaries to assist them in processing distributed queries. Each
node in the federation has an export schema and an import schema.

The export schema is used to identify the data objects that the node is willing to share with other nodes in the federation. The import schema contains data object description of information that the other nodes in the federation are willing to share with this node. Therefore, the distributed queries generated at each node are defined according to the information present in the local import schema. The members of the federation agree on general communication protocols and methods for routing queries and data.

Before concluding this discussion on federated databases, let's take a closer look at the import and export schemas. Figure 6.8 shows an export schema based on portions of a local node database catalog.

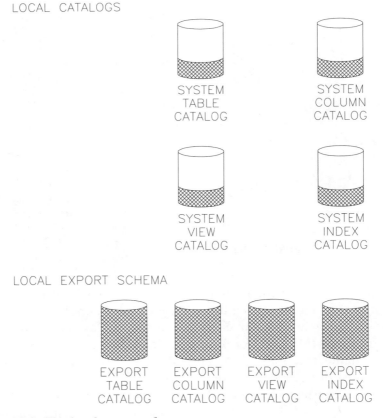

Figure 6.8 The local export schema

The local catalog is made up of four tables: the system table, column, view, and index catalogs. The cross-hatched areas in each table represent the descriptions of the database objects that the node is willing to share with other members of the federation. As can be seen by the diagram, the local export schema is made up of the cross-hatched portions of the local database catalogs.

The local import schema is just the union of the export schemas of all the other members. Further discussions on these types of databases are deferred to Chapter 15. There we will discuss a federated multi-database system that negotiates transaction requests via "contracts"[5] with other sites.

6.8 THE ROLE OF EXPERT SYSTEMS

In this section we briefly examine the role that expert systems can play in a federated database environment.

Processing distributed query requests in this type of environment is especially difficult, as we are dealing with multiple independent databases with their own rules for query optimization, deadlock detection, and concurrency (just to name a few!). An added handicap is the absence of a global schema and global mapping algorithms to aid in the construction of a global access plan.

Expert systems could play a role in this type of environment by supplying a knowledge base that contains rules for data object conversion, rules for resolving naming conflicts, and rules for exchanging data. The expert system would take as its input rules, the distributed query and the export/import schema information to generate a "result transfer plan." This plan would be used to convert the data to any required format acceptable to the requesting site. Additionally, any communications protocol requirements could be included in this plan to facilitate the physical transfer of the data.

Figure 6.9 shows a simplified block diagram of such an expert system.

These expert systems are called agents.[5] Agents work together in a cooperative manner so as to solve problems that they could not individually solve on their own. In this case, the problem is to execute a distributed query in a federated database environment. Each agent has a knowledge base that has rules that are used to generate a result transfer plan.

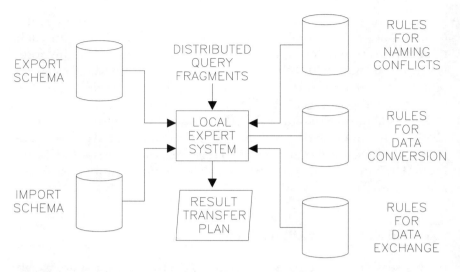

Figure 6.9 Using expert systems in federated databases

6.9 AGENTS AND FEDERATED DISTRIBUTED DATABASE SYSTEMS

Figure 6.10 shows a typical member site of a federated distributed database system. The federated system software components are:

LRRM	local response router module
LDBMS	local database management system
AGENT	local expert system
LTM	local transaction monitor

The query is received by a component called the LTM. It submits the query to the AGENT, which consults its knowledge base and import/export schema so as to generate a response plan. Any modifications to the query are done at this time so that they are compatible with the syntax and requirements of the LDBMS. For instance, the query just received may be a SQL query, but the required data reside in a series of spreadsheets. It is the job of the AGENT to translate the SQL query into equivalent spreadsheet macro language commands to retrieve the required data.

Next, the query is executed by the LDBMS and the results are returned to the LRRM. Together with the results, the LRRM uses the response plan generated by the AGENT to generate and route the

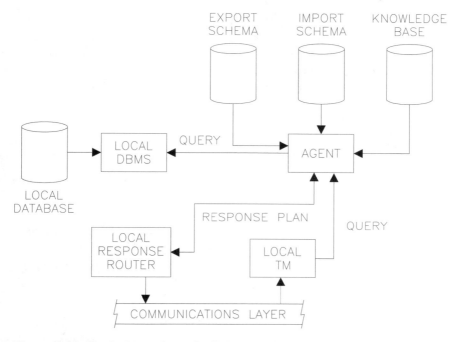

Figure 6.10 Typical member of a federated database system

packets that contain the required data back to the originator of the query.

6.10 SUMMARY

The purpose of this chapter was to categorize the different types of shared information systems that come under the title "Distributed Databases." By now the reader should have not only a fundamental understanding of each type of distributed database system but also a strong knowledge of how centralized database systems optimize and schedule queries.

The brief discussion on federated database systems was based on concepts described in Deen.[5] I will expand on one concept, "the negotiation of contracts" between federated sites in Chapter 15. This discussion will be based on one of the papers in Deen.[5]

In this first part of the book we also reviewed fundamental relational theory, relational algebra, and SQL. The reader is now ready to apply these disciplines to the discussions in the remainder of the book.

In Part II we will examine how distributed databases process, optimize, schedule, and execute distributed transactions. We will also extend the discussions on centralized database recovery methods to distributed environments. Along the way, I will introduce some pitfalls and some solutions recognized by the distributed database community.

6.11 END NOTES

1. Bright, M. W., A. R. Hurson, and Simin H. Pakzad. "A Taxonomy and Current Issues in Multidatabase Systems," *IEEE Computer* (March 1992): pp. 50, 59.

2. Özsu, M. Tamer, and P. Valduriez. *Principles of Distributed Database Systems*, Englewood Cliffs, NJ: Prentice Hall, 1991.

3. Ceri, S., and G. Pelagatti. *Distributed Databases: Principles and Systems*, New York: McGraw-Hill, 1984.

4. Navathe, S., S. Ceri, G. Wiederhold, and J. Dou. "Vertical Partitioning Algorithms for Database Design," *ACM Transactions on Database Systems*, vol. 9, no. 4 (December 1984): pp. 680–710.

5. Deen, S. M., ed. *Cooperating Knowledge-Based Systems*, New York: Springer-Verlag, 1991.

P A R T II

Distributed Database Architectures

7

Introduction to Distributed Database Systems

7.1 INTRODUCTION

This is the first chapter in Part II of the book, which is dedicated to homogeneous distributed database systems. The main components of a DDBMS will be identified and their functions will be explained. This will be performed at a very high level, as the operational details will be discussed in subsequent chapters.

We begin by examining the data model used by a distributed system. It is based on an extended version of the ANSI/SPARC data model described in Özsu and Valduriez.[1] Modifications include components such as a global database schema. In this book I will be referring to a component called a global database catalog. This is just another name for the global schema. I do this so the reader can see the correspondence to the database catalogs used in centralized database systems.

After discussing the global data model, a brief analysis of the global catalog, fragment catalog, and local database catalogs follows. A simple example of each component will be built. Next, a review of the physical schema of centralized databases is included so the reader can understand the mapping that occurs between the local conceptual schema and the physical schema.

Having covered all the components of the data model of a distributed database architecture, we move to the software components that make up a general distributed system. I have deviated slightly from the other literature by including some of the more low-level modules and communications components that might be found in actual vendor implementations of distributed systems. This was done so that the reader gets a broader picture of the sequence of operation. During the course of this chapter the reader will be introduced to a fictitious distributed database system. We will assume that the software components were designed from scratch and are being used to interconnect an IBM DB2 database situated at a central host such as an IBM S/370. This host contains the global components of the distributed database. The remote sites will be made up of servers running IBM's OS/2 and OS/2 Database Manager plus the local components of a distributed database.

7.2 THE DATA MODEL

Let us begin by reviewing the database model developed by a committee of the American National Standards Institue. The committee was called "Standards Planning and Requirements Committee," hence the model is called the ANSI/X3/SPARC database model.[2,3]

Figure 7.1 shows a simple block diagram of this architecture. As can be seen, it is divided into three layers. The top layer is called the external schema. It represents the view of the database that users and/or applications might see. Recall the definition of a SQL view: A user sees the portion of the database that he or she is allowed to see. This view is usually defined by the systems administrator.

The second layer is called the conceptual schema. This is similar to the database catalog of a relational database system that was explained in Chapter 2. At this level the database objects such as tables, columns, views, and indexes are defined. These definitions provide mappings to the next level of the model, which is where the physical layout of the database is defined.

Last but not least is the internal schema layer. As mentioned earlier, this is where the actual layout of the records and fields is defined. Let us look at a simple example of the three layers:

External Schema

```
CREATE VIEW V1 (CV1,CV2,CV3)
AS
```

```
SELECT C1,C2
FROM T1
```

Conceptual Schema

```
CREATE TABLE   T1
      (COL1 CHAR[10] NOT NULL,
       COL2 DECIMAL NOT NULL,
       COL3 DATE NOT NULL);
```

Internal Schema

```
struct TABLE T1
      {
      CHAR col1[10];  // 10 bytes
      FLOAT col2;     // used to store decimal values
      CHAR col3[8];
      };
```

The first layer, the external schema, uses a SQL "CREATE VIEW" statement to create a view composed of two columns from table T1. The user of the view sees only the two columns although the base table used to create this table contains three columns.

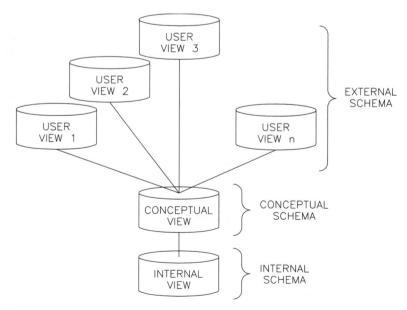

Figure 7.1 ANSI/X3/SPARC database architecture

The conceptual schema is implemented via a SQL CREATE table statement. The database administrator uses this command to create a table composed of three columns.

The final layer, the internal schema, is implemented as a C language structure used to describe the physical byte layout of the record that is used to store one row of information for the table.

Let us now extend this model to make it compatible with a distributed database environment. Figure 7.2 shows a block diagram of the ANSI/SPARC model extended to include some global access components. The model I describe follows the model introduced in Özsu and Valduriez.[1]

We now see a distributed model with n remote sites. As can be seen, the model is extended by including a global conceptual schema that is used to integrate all of the local conceptual schemas. At each site the two lower levels of the original ANSI/SPARC model are still preserved. The local internal schema and the local conceptual schema remain. At the central site, a new component called the

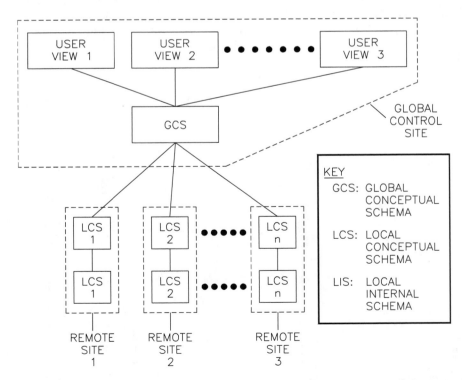

Figure 7.2 Simple extension of ANSI/X3/SPARC framework for a DDBMS

global conceptual schema is introduced. This component is the UNION of all the local conceptual schemas at each remote site:

```
GCS = UNION(LCS1,LCS2,...,LCSn)
```

The user external views have now been altered so as to refer to the global conceptual schema. The external views now have access to any of the local conceptual schemas in each of the remote sites. Let us examine the global conceptual schema in more detail. As stated earlier, we will refer to it as the global database catalog.

Note: The model of the distributed database architecture used in this book is identical to the model used in Özsu and Valduriez.[1]

7.3 THE GLOBAL DATABASE CATALOG

Figure 7.3 shows a simple schema that can be used to implement a global database catalog. (We will assume that the global database catalog is based on the relational model because of its popularity.) The catalog is divided into two schemas:

1. The global schema
2. The fragment schema

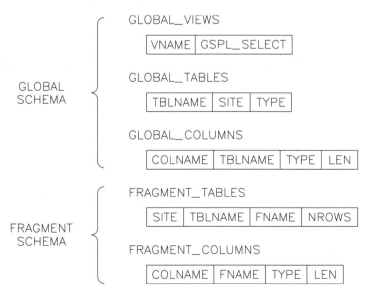

Figure 7.3 A generic global database catalog

The global schema contains the definitions of the global relations used to create the global user views. This portion of the catalog defines the global view of the distributed database.

The fragment schema includes tables that contain localization information that is used when the distributed query is broken down to subqueries; that is, it identifies the location of all the table fragments that make up each global relation. Let us examine the contents of each table in the global catalog starting with the global schema.

The global schema is made up of the following three tables:

1. Global views
2. Global tables
3. Global columns

The global views table contains the following columns:

VNAME	Name of the user external view
GSQL-SELECT	The SQL SELECT statement used to construct the view

The global tables table contains three columns:

TBL NAME	Name of the global relation
SITE	Name of the site where the table is distributed
TYPE	Type of table, view, or actual base table

Note: If a table is distributed to multiple sites, as is usually the case in a distributed database, it will contain multiple row entries. For example, if global relation GT1 is distributed among sites S1, S2, and S3, the entries in this catalog table would be as follows:

```
TBL NAME       SITE       TYPE (T = table, V = view)
GT1            S1         T
GT2            S2         T
GT3            S3         T
```

The global columns catalog table contains the following attributes:

COL NAME	Name of the column
TBL NAME	Table that owns the column
TYPE	Data type of the column
LEN	Length in bytes of the column

Let us now turn our attention to the fragment schema. As stated earlier, the fragment schema portion of the global database catalog contains localization information used for fragmenting the distributed query into subqueries that can run at each site involved with the query.

This portion of the catalog is divided into the following two tables:

1. FRAGMENT TABLES
2. FRAGMENT COLUMNS

The FRAGMENT TABLES table contains the following columns:

SITE	Name of the site that contains the table fragment
TBL NAME	Name of the global table from which this fragment was derived
FNAME	Name of this table fragment
NROWS	Number of rows contained in the table fragment. This statistic is used to optimize the distributed query.

The FRAGMENT COLUMNS table contains information describing the columns contained in the table fragment. It is made up of the following columns:

COL NAME	Name of the column
FNAME	Name of the table fragment that owns this column
TYPE	Data type of the column
LEN	Length of the column (see note below)

Note: This information is important when calculating the size of temporary tables that are transmitted between sites in order to perfrom distributed joins.

7.4 THE GLOBAL APPLICATION VIEWS

Figure 7.4 shows the schematic of the global views table. As stated earlier, this table is used to store the external user views that are used

GLOBAL_VIEWS

VNAME	GSQL_SELECT

GV1   SELECT GC1, GC2, GC3 FROM GT1
      WHERE GC3>1000

GV2   SELECT GC1, GC2, GC4
 •   FROM GT1, GT2
 •   WHERE GT1.COL1 = GT2.COL1
 •   AND GC4>1000

Figure 7.4 The global application views

to access the distributed tables. Recall that this table is composed of
the following two attributes:

V NAME   Name of the external view
GSQL SELECT   The attribute that stores the global dis-
                tributed SQL query used to create the global
                view

Let's look at some examples. External view GV1 is derived from
the following SQL select query:

Column	Alias
DOM1.T1.C1	GC1
DOM1.T1.C2	GC2
DOM1.T1.C3	GC3
DOM2.T1.C4	GC4

Table	Alias
DOM1.T1	GT1
DOM2.T1	GT2

Here the view is based on one remote table and is fairly simple to
process. External view GV2 is based on two tables and must execute
a distributed JOIN:

```
SELECT DOM1.T1.C1,DOM1.T1.C2,DOM2.T1.C4
    FROM    DOM1.T1,DOM2.T1
    WHERE   DOM1.T1.C1 = DOM2.T1.C1
    AND     DOM2.T1.C4 > 1000
```

This second query must perform a distributed join between remote sites DOM1 and DOM2. Distributed JOIN execution will be covered in Chapter 9.

Below are the actual SQL CREATE DCL language commands used to create the above views:

```
CREATE VIEW GV1 AS
SELECT DOM1.T1.C1,DOM1.T1.C2,DOM1.T1.C3
     FROM    DOM1.T1
     WHERE   DOM1.T1.C3 > 1000

CREATE VIEW GV2 AS
SELECT DOM1.T1.C1,DOM1.T1.C2,DOM2.T1.C4
     FROM    DOM1.T1,DOM2.T1
     WHERE   DOM1.T1.C1 = DOM2.T1.C1
     AND     DOM2.T1.C4 > 1000
```

We will see in Chapter 9 how the information contained in the global database catalog is used to take a distributed query (such as GV2), optimize it, fragment it, and simplify it for execution at the local sites. Let us now examine the local database catalogs.

7.5 THE LOCAL DATABASE CATALOGS

The local database catalogs are similar to the global database catalogs with some minor differences. Again, we assume that the catalogs are implemented with the relational database model. Figure 7.5 shows a schematic of the local database catalog tables.

The catalog is made up of the following four tables: LCAT_TABLES, LCAT_VIEWS, LCAT_COLUMNS, and LCAT_INDEXES. (This last table is not present in the global database catalogs.)

The table LCAT TABLE stores definitions for the tables that are included in the local database. It is made up of the following attributes:

TABLE_NAME	Name of the table
TYPE	Table type, T = table, V = VIEW
NUM_ROWS	Number of rows contained in the tables. This is usually referred to as the tables' cardinality.

LCAT_TABLES

TBL_NAME	TYPE	NUM_ROWS

LCAT_VIEWS

VIEW_NAME	LSQL_QUERY

LCAT_COLUMNS

COL_NAME	TABLE	TYPE	LEN	HKEY	LKEY

LCAT_INDEXES

INDEX_NAME	KEY_COLS	SORT	PCT_UNIQUE

Figure 7.5   The local database

The LCAT_VIEWS table is similar to its global counterpart. It contains definitions for all of the views that can be found in the database. It is made up of the following columns:

VIEW_NAME	Name of the view
LSQL_QUERY	SQL query used to define the view

The LCAT_COLUMNS table is used to define all of the columns that can be found in the tables that make up the local database. It is also similar to its global counterpart except that two new attributes have been added: HKEY and LKEY. Below are the attributes that make up this table:

COL_NAME	Name of the column
TABLE	Table that owns this column
TYPE	Data type of the column
LEN	Length of the column in bytes
HKEY	High key value of the column
LKEY	Low key value of the column

The HKEY and LKEY attributes are used when building an access plan for a query that requires this column in its WHERE clause. These two attributes are used in a formula that roughly determines the number of rows that will be returned from a table. As an example, assume that table T2 has 1,000 rows. The following query is issued against this table:

```
SELECT * from T2 WHERE C2 > 700
```

Assume that the values in attribute C2 are evenly distributed among each of the tuples in T2. The optimizer would use the following formula to determine how many rows would be returned when this query is executed:

```
(HKEY - 700) / (HKEY - LKEY)
```

If HKEY = 1,000 and LOWKEY = 0, the formula would return: $(1,000 - 700)/(1,000 - 0) = 300/1,000$ or .333. This means that .333 times 1,000 tuples or about 333 tuples would be returned by this query. This optimization technique will be discussed in greater detail in Chapter 9. (This formula is one of many formulas used in RDBMS today that allow optimizers to estimate the cardinality of temporary tables when a qualifying SQL predicate is used.)

Finally, the LCAT_INDEXES table contains information describing each index stored in the database. It contins the following columns:

INDEX_NAME	Name of the index
KEY_COLS	Column names that make up the index
SORT	Sort order
PCT_UNIQUE	Percentage of unique values

7.6 THE LOCAL PHYSICAL DATABASE SCHEMA

The local physical database schema is used to define the actual files that will store the records on disk. It is derived from the local conceptual schema. Below are the SQL CREATE commands used to create the relational tables together with equivalent C language structures used as templates for each physical table record:

```
CREATE TABLE FNCDEPTTBL (
        DEPTID          CHAR(4)        NOT NULL,
        DEPTMGRID       CHAR(4)        NOT NULL,
        DEPTLOCATION    CHAR(20)       NOT NULL,
        DEPTNAME        CHAR(20)       NOT NULL,
        NUMEMP          INTEGER,
        PRIMARY KEY     (DEPTID))
```

```
struct FNCDEPTTBL {
    CHAR DEPTID[4];
    CHAR DEPTMGRID[4];
    CHAR DEPTLOCATION[20];
    CHAR DEPTNAME[20];
    INTEGER NUMEMP;
    struct INDEX_LIST *pIndexList;
};

CREATE TABLE   FNCEMPTABLE (
    EMPID           CHAR(5)         NOT NULL,
    EMPNAME         CHAR(20)        NOT NULL,
    EMPDEPT         CHAR(4)         NOT NULL,
    EMPTITLE        CHAR(20)        NOT NULL,
    EMPSALARY       DECIMAL         NOT NULL,
    EMPHIREDATE     DATE            NOT NULL,
    PRIMARY KEY     (EMPID),
    FOREIGN KEY     (EMPDEPT) REFERENCES   FNCDEPTTBL)

struct   FNCEMPTABLE {
    CHAR EMPID[5];
    CHAR EMPNAME[20];
    CHAR EMPDEPT[4];
    CHAR EMPTITLE[20];
    FLOAT EMPSALARY;
    CHAR EMPHIREDATE[8];
    struct INDEX_LIST *pIndexList;
};

CREATE TABLE FNCBRANCH (
    BRANCHID        CHAR(4)         NOT NULL,
    DEPTID          CHAR(4)         NOT NULL,
    BRANCHNAME      CHAR(20)        NOT NULL,
    BRANCHLOCATION  CHAR(20)        NOT NULL,
    PROFITSTODATE   DECIMAL         NOT NULL,
    BRANCHMANAGER   CHAR(5)         NOT NULL,
    PRIMARY KEY         (BRANCHID),
    FOREIGN KEY (DEPTID) REFERENCES FNCDEPTTBL,
    FOREIGN KEY (BRANCHMANAGER) REFERENCES FNCBMGRTBL)

struct FNCBRANCH {
    CHAR BRANCHID[4];
    CHAR DEPTID[4];
    CHAR BRANCHNAME[20];
    CHAR BRANCHLOCATION[20];
    FLOAT PROFITSTODATE;
    CHAR BRANCHMANAGER[5];
    struct INDEX_LIST *pIndexList;
};
```

```
CREATE TABLE FNCBMGRTBL (
      BRANCHMGRID       CHAR(5)        NOT NULL,
      DEPTID            CHAR(4)        NOT NULL,
      EMPID             CHAR(5)        NOT NULL,
      BRANCHID          CHAR(4)        NOT NULL,
      PRIMARY KEY (BRANCHMGRID),
      FOREIGN KEY (DEPTID) REFERENCES FNCDEPTTBL,
      FOREIGN KEY (EMPID) REFERENCES FNCEMPTBL,
      FOREIGN KEY (BRANCHID) REFERENCES FNCBRANCHTBL)

struct FNCBMGRTBL {
      CHAR BRANCHMGRID[5];
      CHAR DEPTID[4];
      CHAR EMPID[5];
      CHAR BRANCHID[4];
      struct INDEX_LIST *pIndexList;
};

struct INDEX_LIST {
      struct INDEX_LIST *pNextNode;
      CHAR IndexName[8];
      INT SortOrder; // 1 = ascending, 2 = descending
      struct KEY COLUMN *pKeyColumnList;
};

struct KEY_COLUMN {
      struct Key Column *pNextColumn;
      CHAR Column Name;
      INT Col Len;
      INT ColType;
};
```

Notice that each structure that contains the definitions for each of the columns that makes up a table also has a structure called IN-DEX_LIST. This structure points to a linked list of nodes that defines each index created for the table. The INDEX_LIST structure contains the index name, the sort order, and another structure that points to another linked list. This second list contains definitions for each of the columns that is used to define the index. This structure contains the column name, its length, and data type.

7.7 THE SYSTEM COMPONENT ARCHITECTURE

We are now ready to leave the data model side of the architecture and examine the software components that make up a distributed homogeneous database system. We will first examine the architecture at a high level and then look at each component in greater detail. Figure 7.6 shows a high-level block diagram of a distributed database system

This architecture follows the one introduced in Özsu and Valduriez[1] with some minor extensions. Notice the global transaction monitor; it takes as input user queries and global database

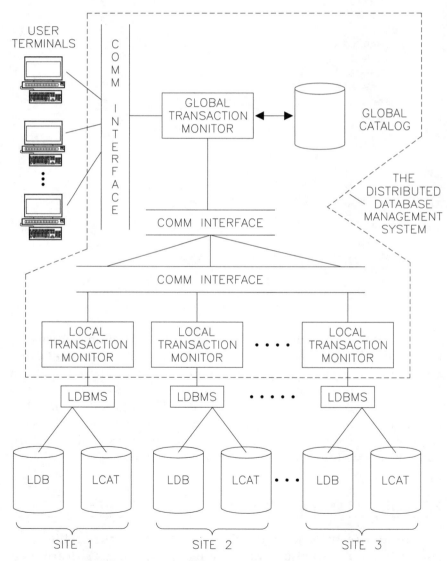

Figure 7.6 Distributed system components

catalog information to build access plans and schedules used to execute distributed queries. The communications interface components include software for routing the distributed queries and temporary result sets between sites.

Once the distributed queries are checked for correct syntax and semantics, they are decomposed into query fragments. The site where each query fragment is to be executed is identified and a schedule similar to the centralized database schedules that was discussed in Chapter 5 is built. Each query is then sent to its respective site via the communications interface software, where it is read by the local transaction monitor. The local transaction monitor logs some information and then passes the query to the local database manager. The local database manager does its own syntax checking, optimization, and scheduling. If everything goes well, the query is executed and the results are sent back to the global transaction monitor so that any global distributed joins can be executed.

It is the responsibility of the local transaction monitors to communicate with the global transaction monitors to identify any potential problems such as deadlocks due to lock conflicts or aborted transactions at any of the local sites. The global transaction monitor together with all of the local transaction monitors form the distributed database management system. An example of such a system is IBM's DRDA or ASK-Ingres's INGRES-STAR.

Let us look at the global transaction monitor in more detail.

7.8 THE GLOBAL TRANSACTION MONITOR

Figure 7.7 shows a simplified block diagram of the global transaction monitor. It is made up of the following nine components:

- The Global Transaction Request Module
- The Global Request Semantic Analyzer Module
- The Global Query Decomposer Module
- The Global Query Object Localizer Module
- The Global Query Optimizer Module
- The Global Transaction Scheduler Module
- The Global Recovery Manager Module
- The Global Lock Manager Module
- The Transaction Dispatcher Module

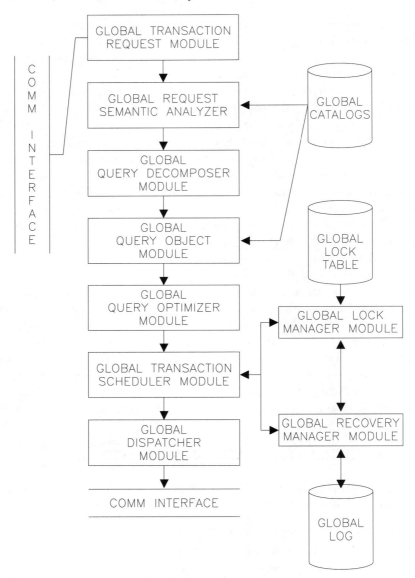

Figure 7.7 The global transaction monitor

The global request semantic analyzer module and the query object localizer module must both consult the global catalogs when processing a distributed query.

The global recovery manager maintains a global transaction log and interfaces with the global lock manager and global scheduler to maintain global concurrency.

The global lock manager maintains a global lock list to check for any global deadlock situations. Let us examine the functions that each of these components executes in order to process a distributed query.

The Global Transaction Request Module

Looking back at Figure 7.7, the first module in the architecture is the global transaction request module (GTR). This is the global software component that interfaces with the communications network to accept distributed transactions from users. This component includes logic that polls all the workstations for requests, accepts transactions, and puts them in a queue for processing. (It also handles logging on and off functions.)

The queue contains information such as the requesting site ID, user ID, password, date and time of the request, and the request itself. A C language structure for implementing a typical record for this queue is shown below:

```
struct DIST_REQUEST
    {
    CHAR req_site[10];   // requesting site ID
    CHAR date[8];        // date of request
    CHAR time[8];        // time of request
    CHAR user_id[8];     // user id
    CHAR password[8];    // password
    CHAR request[1024];  // distributed query
    };
```

This is a simplified version of a typical structure, but it illustrates the basic information required to process a distributed query.

The req_site member is used to identify the workstation that issued the request. An internal table is accessed by the communicatons software to identify the network address of the workstation. For instance, it could be implemented as follows:

```
SITE ID       NETWORK ADDRESS
S1            0X000000001000
S2            0X000000001001
S3            0X000000001002
*                  *
*                  *
```

The date and time members are used to record the time the request was received. The user ID and password are used for security purposes, and the request member contains a SQL transaction. The size was arbitrarily set to 1,024 bytes. A more sophisticated system would not place a restriction on a transaction's size. The global transaction request module also uses this information to build a response packet that the dispatcher module will use to route results back to the requesting user. It takes the form of the following C structures:

```
struct DIST_REQUEST
    {
    CHAR req_site[10]; // requesting site ID
    CHAR date[8];      // date of request
    CHAR time[8];      // time of request
    CHAR processing code; // 1 = failure
                          // 0 = success
    struct RESPONSE *RESP LIST; // pointer to
                                // response data
    long num respnodes;         // number of
                                // responses
    };

struct RESPONSE
    {
    struct RESPONSE *pNext; // pointer to next node
    long row index;    // index of row this column
                       // belongs to
    short col index;   // column index
    short type code;   // column data type
    char data[256];    // column data
    };
```

The global dispatcher module uses these structures to build a string of data packets to route responses back to the requesting user.

The Global Request Semantic Analyzer

After the transaction is placed in the global request queue, it is read by the global semantic analyzer so that its syntax and objects can be checked for correctness. Input to this module is the query language grammar and information contained in the global catalogs. The semantic analyzer checks all the data objects that are referenced in the transaction to see that they exist in the catalogs. If the query is correct, it is passed on to the next module. If the query is not correct, it is rejected at this time, the global dispatcher module is notified,

and the user is notified of the rejected transaction. The semantic
analyzer could include detailed information so that the user can
correct the mistake; for instance:

```
SELECT LAST NAME,SALARY
FROM T1 ←──────── no such table!
WHERE SALARY = 'New York' ←──┐
                             │
           incompatible data types!
```

The above query was rejected because table T1 was not found in the
global catalog. It was also rejected because the attribute SALARY is
defined as a decimal data type and it is being compared to a string.
Distributed semantic analyzers will be discussed in greater detail in
Chapter 9.

The Global Query Decomposer

The query decomposition module (QDM) takes a distributed query
and begins to break it down into subqueries so that they can be sent
to the remote sites where the table fragments involved in the transaction physically exist. The query decomposition module works together with the query object localizer to build a simple relational
algebra query that contains communication primitives that will aid in
moving around the intermediate table relations used to solve the
transaction. Recall that the original distributed query was written in
a relational calculus language such as SQL. The job of the query
decomposer and query object localizer is to perform this translation
by transforming the distributed relational calculus query into its
equivalent relational algebra query. This module uses the information in the global catalogs to perform the transformation.

This module cooperates and feeds information to the global query
object localizer module so that the location of the table fragments
can be determined. Global query decomposition will be examined in
Chapter 9. Let us continue with the role of the global query object
localizer module.

The Global Query Object Localizer Module

As stated earlier, this module modifies the relational algebra query
that was produced from the original distributed query by replacing
the names of the global relations with the names of the relation

fragments located at the distributed sites. Once this transformation occurs, the relational algebra query is ready to be optimized. Communication primitives are added at this layer so that the query fragments can be routed to their respective sites. Recall that the global transaction request module used a table that contained the network addresses of the nodes in the communications network. This table contained the following fields:

```
SITE          NETWORK ADDRESS
S1            0x000000001001
S2            0x000000001002
S3            0x000000001003
*                  *
*                  *
*                  *
```

The global query localizer module is also discussed in Chapter 9.

The Global Query Optimizer Module

The global query optimizer takes the simplified relational algebra query and optimizes it by removing redundant predicates that do not produce any intermediate table relations that help in solving the query. The optimizer also reorganizes the order of any other qualifying predicates in the query so that the intermediate relations produced by the predicates are as small as possible. Information in the global database catalogs such as fragment table cardinality is used to make this determination. The smaller the intermediate results, the less communications time is required to solve the query. Remember, data must be routed between sites in order to perform distributed joins. This module and the distributed optimization techniques will be covered in Chapter 9.

The Global Transaction Scheduler

Once the original relational calculus distributed query has been transformed into a relational algebra query, simplified, and optimized, it is passed to the global scheduler so that global locks can be assigned and a global serialization access plan can be built. The job of the scheduler is to maintain global concurrency as multiple concurrent transactions are submitted from users of the system.

This module works with the global recovery manager to maintain global transaction concurrency. The local sites communicate with the global recovery manager to inform it of progress or about situations for the fragments of the distributed query that they are processing. We will see in Chapter 11 how the global recovery manager maintains a global serialization graph to monitor any incidents of global deadlocks. We will also see in Chapter 10 how the two-phase COMMIT protocol is used in distributed systems to COMMIT or ABORT local transactions.

The Global Recovery Manager

The global recovery manager(GRM) maintains the global transaction log and interfaces with the global scheduler and global lock manager to maintain global transaction concurrency and recovery as the system attempts to process each distributed transaction submitted by its users. Here we are assuming a system that uses a global locking scheme to maintain serial access to the distributed data objects. A system that uses some sort of time ordering scheme could be used as well.

Recall from Chapter 5 that the transaction log contains information such as before/after images and commit/abort lists that can be used to recover the system in case of a system failure or aborted transaction. The global transaction log contains similar information but at a global level. We will examine how this component works in Chapter 11.

The Global Lock Manager

This component maintains a global list of all the data objects that have been locked for transactions submitted by the global scheduler. It is this component that checks for global deadlocks and advises the global transaction monitor when a deadlock has occurred. Information such as which sites are involved is supplied so that transactions can be aborted and restarted.

The global lock manager takes as its input the transaction ID, a list of required objects that are to be read and/or written. This information is stored in the global lock table.

On receipt of the above information, the global lock manager consults the global lock table to see if any of the required locks are taken. If this is the case, the transaction is postponed. Otherwise the global lock manager consults the scheduler, which then passes the transaction to the global dispatcher module.

The Transaction Dispatcher

The last module in the global component of the distributed system is the communication module, which sends the query fragments to the distributed sites. Recall that the query fragments have been enhanced with communications primitives that optimize the way in which temporary result relations are sent back to the central site to be processed and joined.

This module accepts back the results from the distributed site so that the last stages of processing can be completed. It also accepts messages from the distributed sites that indicate whether a transaction is committed or rolled back. Either type of message is passed back up to the global scheduler so that any appropriate action can be taken.

7.9 THE LOCAL TRANSACTION MONITOR

We now change the focus of our attention from the global components to the local components situated at a typical remote site. We will begin our discussion with the local transaction monitor. A simple block diagram of this component can be seen in Figure 7.8. This component has a function similar to its global counterpart, the global transaction monitor. It accepts the query fragment that was generated from the distributed query submitted by one of the users of the system.

The figure shows a software layer labeled "local comm interface." This layer interfaces at a local level with the communications network to accept query fragments and send back intermediate result relations. This module maintains two queues, a request queue and a response queue. Once a query fragment is received, it is placed in the request queue. While it is receiving a request, this module can concurrently check its response queue for any data items that have to be routed back to the central site. If any are found, they are read off of the queue and passed to the communications interface module so that they can be dispatched.

If a query fragment is found in the request queue, it is read off of the queue and passed to the local database management system via the local database interface layer.

This layer is usually made up of a series of APIs that are supplied by the vendor of the database system. These APIs come in the form of a library that the user can link to with an external software module

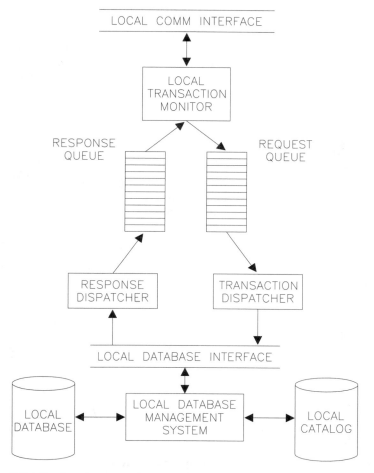

Figure 7.8 The local transaction monitor

such as our transaction monitor. These APIs access low-level database system functions such as execute SQL, fetch rows, and log off the database. We will identify some of these APIs when we discuss the database interface in the next section.

7.10 THE LOCAL DATABASE MANAGEMENT SYSTEM

The local database management system is discussed next. Figure 7.9 shows the components that make up a generic centralized relational database management system. The first layer is the vendor database interface layer. This layer contains entry points for applications such

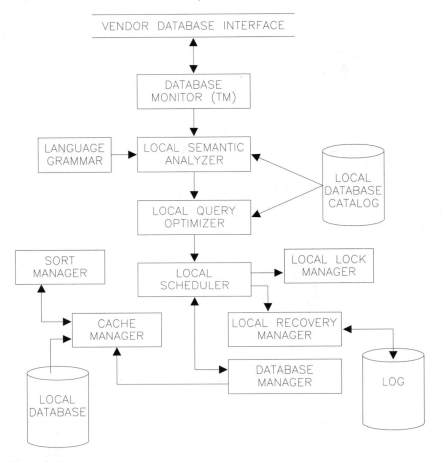

Figure 7.9 The local database management system

as the transaction monitor to use for submitting queries. The queries are received and processed by the database monitor. Let us examine the functions performed by each layer as a distributed query fragment is processed.

The Database Interface (APIs and Services)

As stated earlier, the database interface layer contains entry points in the form of APIs (application program interface functions) contained in a library. Below is a partial list of some of the functions that a typical library contains:

```
db_logon();
db_logoff();
submit_sql();
open_cursor();
fetch_row();
close_cursor();
commit();
abort();
```

The names of the functions are self-explanatory. The transaction monitor would use these functions to submit a query fragment to the database engine and to retrieve the resulting rows by opening a cursor, fetching the rows, and closing the cursor. The transaction monitor would then commit or abort the transaction depending on instructions from the global transaction monitor or return codes from the local database engine. Queries could also be update or insert row queries.

The Database Request Monitor (Some Call It TM)

The first layer of the local database engine is the database monitor. Its function is to accept the query fragments that were submitted by the local transaction monitor. It places them in a queue so that the local semantic analyzer can retrieve them. (This layer is also called the transaction monitor in the literature.)

Once the query is in the queue, it can be retrieved by the next layer of the database management system for further processing.

The Local Semantic Analyzer

The local semantic analyzer retrieves the query fragment and submits it to a syntax and semantic check just like its global counterpart, the global semantic analyzer. It consults the local query language grammar and the local database catalog to make sure the query is correct. If the query is not correct, it is rejected and the transaction is aborted at this time. If it is correct, it is passed on to the next model, the local query optimizer.

The Local Query Optimizer Module

The local query optimizer module (LQOM) takes as its input the local query fragment that has just been checked and attempts to optimize it for increased performance. It can now take advantage of statistical information in the local database catalog that was not available to the global optimizer. Once any optimization is performed, the query is passed to the local scheduler. Recall from Chapter 5 how database catalog statistics are used to restructure the query so that the predicates that return the smallest temporary relations are executed first. The query optimizer then decides the order of the joins and if any intermediate sorts are required. If indexes exist that can be used to optimize the query they are used. Sometimes indexes are available but the tables involved are so small that they are loaded entirely into memory and scanned sequentially.

Once the query is optimized it is passed to the local scheduler.

The Local Scheduler

Like the global transaction monitor, the local database engine can execute more than one query at the same time. The function of the local scheduler is to assign any required locks (if a locking-based scheduling algorithm is used) via instructions to the lock manager and to generate a serial execution history. The discussions of Chapter 5 apply at this level.

The local scheduler interacts with the local recovery manager, the lock manager, and the database manager. Once a schedule is generated, it is passed to the local database manager for execution.

If the transaction COMMITs, the database manager notifies the scheduler, which notifies the local lock manager to release all the locks. The local recovery manager is also notified that the transaction has committed and the logs are updated accordingly. The cache manager is notified so that any pages in memory that are required to update the stable database on disk can be flushed.

If the transaction rolls back, a similar series of actions are taken but the recovery strategy is executed, which causes old information in the log to be read and rewritten to the database so that the earlier stable state is restored. Please refer back to Chapter 5 for the exact steps in the recovery routine.

The Local Recovery Manager

The local recovery manager maintains a local transaction log that is conceptually similar to the global transaction log kept by the global recovery manager. It works with the cache manager and database manager to execute the query fragment. By maintaining before images of each transaction in the log, the recovery manager can recover a database to a consistent state should a local failure or aborted transaction occur. If a transaction commits, the cache manager is notified so that the updated database pages can be rewritten back into the stable version of the database.

The Local Buffer (Cache) Manager

The local buffer manager is responsible for reading and writing portions of the database to and from stable storage. As mentioned in Chapter 5, maintaining part of the database in system memory increases system performance as access times for system memory are faster than access times for disk storage. The discussions in Chapter 5 on how the cache manager fetches and flushes data pages to and from the database and the transaction log apply here.

The Sort Manager

The sort manager is the module that performs any sorting of intermediate relations as required by the transaction. If any sorting is required due to joins between tables, it is the job of the sort manager to perform this task. If the optimizer located a suitable index, the sort manager can omit this extra sort. Sorts are also induced by the ORDER BY clause and the GROUP BY clause of a SQL statement. It is a good idea to create indexes for queries that are executed frequently and contain ORDER BY or GROUP BY clauses so that the sort manager does not have to perform these extra sorts.

We have now finished examining the functions of each of the layers in a simple model of a local database management system. The roles of these components will be expanded in the chapters that follow.

7.11 SUMMARY

We have now finished examining the distributed database management system from a very high level point of view. The purpose of this chapter was not to go into every detail of how each component works but to introduce each module to the reader. Basic interface and functional specifications were discussed. The remainder of Part II of the book will cover these layers at a detailed level. The topics covered in Chapter 5 will now be expanded so as to be applicable in a distributed database environment.

7.12 END NOTES

1. Özsu, M. Tamer, and P. Valduriez. *Principles of Distributed Database Systems,* Englewood Cliffs, NJ: Prentice Hall, 1991.

2. ANSI/X3/SPARC Study Group on Database Management Systems. Interim Report, *ACM FDT Bulletin* (1975).

3. Tsichritzis, D. C., and A. Klug, "The ANSI/X3/SPARC DBMS Framework Report of the Study Group on Database Management Systems," *Information Systems* (1978): pp. 173–191.

8

Homogeneous Distributed Database Design

8.1 INTRODUCTION

This chapter is dedicated to the techniques that a designer must use to properly design a distributed database. I will follow the same steps that are discussed in Özsu and Valduriez.[1] These steps were first introduced in a paper by Navathe et al.[2]

The chapter begins with a comparison of database partitioning versus database replication at distributed sites. Database partitioning involves the fragmentation of table relations according to some specified requirement among the sites. This requirement is usually derived from the applications that will be executed against the distributed database.

Database replication involves the duplication of tables that make up a database among one or more of the distributed sites. This chapter will concentrate on the database partitioning strategy.

Following the discussion on database partitioning and replication I discuss the two primary methods of partitioning a database. The first method is horizontal table fragmentation; the second method is vertical table fragmentation.

Horizontal table fragmentation involves the splitting of the relation along the tuples (rows). There are two types of horizontal fragmentation: primary and derived. These techniques will be discussed

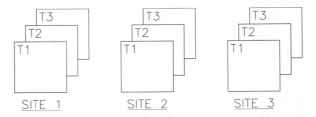

Figure 8.1 Full table replication

in detail in Section 8.3 and are the same as those discussed in Özsu and Valduriez.[1]

Vertical table fragmentation involves the partitioning of tables along the attributes, or columns. Without further ado, let's begin by investigating database partitioning and replication.

8.2 PARTITIONING VERSUS REPLICATION

In this section we examine the merits of two methods of data distribution among tables located at remote database sites in a distributed database system. The first method, table replication, involves the duplication of tables at each of the distributed sites. Each table can be fully replicated, as illustrated in Figure 8.1.

Alternatively, some schemes require that only portions of the tables are duplicated at each site. This technique is illustrated in Figure 8.2.

Although these methods guarantee the safety of the data by redundant copies, they are expensive to maintain because of the cost incurred in performing synchronized inserts, updates, and deletes on each of the table copies. One possible implementation of partial table replication duplicates the indexes only, to improve query execution time (in relational databases). Each table is updated at the distributed site, including all of the duplicate indexes.

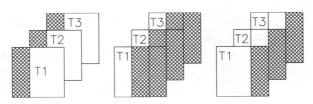

Figure 8.2 Partial table replication

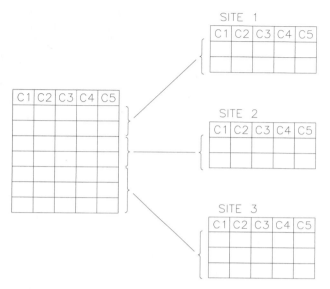

Figure 8.3 Horizontal table fragmentation

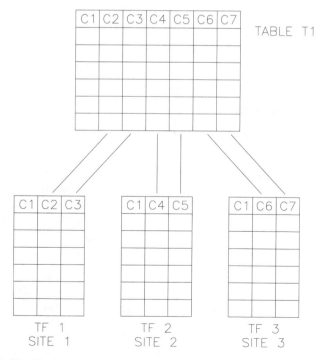

Figure 8.4 Vertical table fragmentation

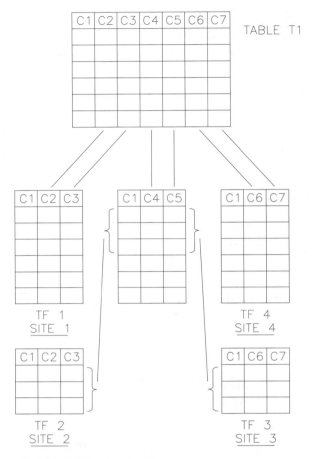

Figure 8.5 Hybrid table fragmentation

An alternative method involves the partitioning of the tables along either the columns or the rows. The former method is vertical table fragmentation; the latter is horizontal table fragmentation. Figure 8.3 shows three tables that are fragmented and distributed to three remote sites via the horizontal table fragmentation method. Figure 8.4 shows three tables that are fragmented and distributed to three remote sites via the vertical table fragmentation method.

A third partitioning technique, hybrid table fragmentation, involves the combination of vertical and horizontal fragmentation methods. Figure 8.5 shows a single table database that is distributed to remote sites using the hybrid fragmentation method.

This chapter will concentrate on horizontal and vertical table fragmentation and will briefly discuss hybrid table fragmentation in Section 8.5.

8.3 HORIZONTAL FRAGMENTATION

In this section we examine the two primary methods for creating horizontal table fragments for distribution to remote database sites on a multinode communications network. The first method, primary horizontal fragmentation, involves splitting the base tables along the rows according to some simple predicate or minterm predicate in an application.

The second method, derived horizontal fragmentation, involves semi-joins of the base tables with tables that were created by using the primary horizontal fragmentation method. The techniques discussed in this section follow the methods and logic that are explained in Özsu and Valduriez.[1]

Primary Horizontal Fragmentation

We now examine the steps that a designer must perform to fragment a database table according to the primary horizontal fragmentation techniques.

1. Given a set of simple predicates, extract the minimal and complete set of predicates by applying the MC_RULE. (The MC_RULE is explained below.)

2. From the same set of simple predicates, derive a set of implications that can be used to eliminate contradictory predicates. These types of predicates generate table fragments that contain zero rows and are therefore useless.

3. From the minimal and complete predicates derive a set of minterm predicates that can be used to generate table fragments. Recall that the minterm predicates are the conjunctions of simple predicates. For example, given two simple predicates:

        P1 = LOCATION = 'London'
        P2 = PROFITS_TO_DATE >> 1,000,000.00

A minterm predicate using P1 and P2 is (P1 AND P2) or:

```
(LOCATION = 'London') AND (PROFITS_TO_DATE >>
1,000,000.00)
```

4. To the set of minterm predicates, apply the implications derived in step 2, thereby eliminating the minterm predicates that generate empty table fragments.

We now introduce the MC_RULE as discussed in Özsu and Valduriez.[1]

MC_RULE for Ensuring MINIMALITY and COMPLETENESS

1. Requirement for Minimality

   Each of the table fragments must be accessed by a unique process in a unique manner; otherwise, the existence of the table fragment is redundant.

2. Requirements for Completeness

   (a) An equal probability must exist that any two rows of a table fragment can be accessed by every process defined for the table fragments.

   (b) The table fragment must have been generated by a minterm fragment.

In what follows, each step is applied to a simple example. We then derive an engine that generates table fragments by applying the horizontal table fragmentation techniques.

Horizontal Fragmentation Engine

We wish to fragment the FNC_BRANCH_TABLE by tuples whose PROFITS_TO_DATE attribute values are less than £1,000,000. These tuples are placed in a fragment table called FNC_BRANCH_A at site SITE_A. Tuples whose PROFITS_TO_DATE attribute values are greater than £1,000,000 are placed in a fragment table called FNC_BRANCH_B at site SITE_B. The following simple predicates fulfill these design requirements:

```
SP1 = PROFITS_TO_DATE << 1,000,000
SP2 = PROFITS_TO_DATE >> 1,000,000
SPS = {SP1,SP2}
```

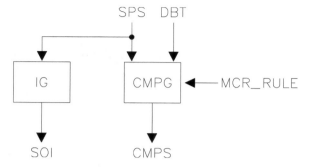

Figure 8.6 The first two components of the horizontal fragmentation engine

Figure 8.6 shows the first components of our horizontal fragmentation engine (HFE), which are:

1. CMPG—Complete and Minimal Predicate Generator module.
2. IG—Implication Generator module.

The inputs to the above components are:

1. SPS—Simple Predicate Set composed of simple predicates SP1 and SP2.
2. DBT—Database Table schema as described in the database catalogs or global schema.
3. MC_RULE—The Minimal and Complete Rule discussed earlier in this section.

The outputs are:

1. SOI—Set of Implications that are to be used to eliminate contradictory minterm predicates.
2. CMPS—Minimal and Complete Predicate set.

Let's see what happens when we apply the inputs to the first part of our fragmentation engine.

The complete and minimal predicates generated from the simple predicates after the MC_RULE is applied happen to be the original predicates, as they satisfied the requirements of the MC_RULE:

```
CMPS = SPS = {SP1,SP2}
```

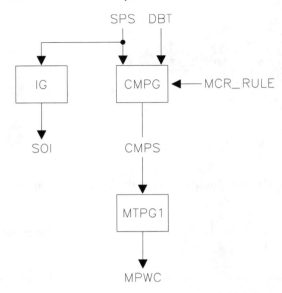

Figure 8.7 The horizontal fragmentation engine with MTPG1 component

The implications generated from the SOI module are:

I1   (PROFITS_TO_DATE << 1,000,000) implies
        NOT(PROFITS_TO_DATE >>= 1,000,000)

I2   NOT(PROFITS_TO_DATE << 1,000,000) implies
        (PROFITS_TO_DATE >>= 1,000,000)

I3   NOT(PROFITS_TO_DATE >>= 1,000,000) implies
        (PROFITS_TO_DATE << 1,000,000)

I4   (PROFITS_TO_DATE >>= 1,000,000) implies
        NOT(PROFITS_TO_DATE << 1,000,000)

The next step is to take the minimal and complete predicate set
CMPS and feed it to the next component of our engine. Figure 8.7
shows the engine revised to include the new component.

Input to the minterm predicate generator MTPG1 is the complete
and minimal predicates generated by the CMPG module. Below are
the minterm predicates:

MTP1 =   (PROFITS_TO_DATE << 1,000,000) AND
         (PROFITS_TO_DATE >>= 1,000,000)

MTP2 =   NOT(PROFITS_TO_DATE << 1,000,000) AND
         NOT(PROFITS_TO_DATE >>= 1,000,000)

MTP3 =   (PROFITS_TO_DATE << 1,000,000) AND
NOT(PROFITS_TO_DATE >>= 1,000,000)

MTP4 =   NOT(PROFITS_TO_DATE << 1,000,000) AND
(PROFITS_TO_DATE >>= 1,000,000)

The output of MTPG1, DMP (dirty minterm predicates) is the set {MTP1,MTP2,MTP3,MTP4}. By inspecting these minterm predicates, we can visually determine that two of them are contradictory and generate empty tables—hence, the name dirty minterm predicates. The final phase of the engine eliminates these contradictory predicates.

Figure 8.8 shows the complete horizontal fragmentation engine. The final fragment generator (FFG) takes as input the set of implications (SOI) and the dirty minterm predicates (DMP). The FFG applies each implication to the dirty minterm predicates to generate the table shown below.

Implication	MTP	Rejected	Accepted
I1	MTP1	X	
I1	MTP2	X	
I1	MTP3		X
I1	MTP4	X	
I2	MTP1	X	
I2	MTP2	X	
I2	MTP3	X	
I2	MTP4		X
I3	MTP1	X	
I3	MTP2	X	
I3	MTP3		X
I3	MTP4	X	
I4	MTP1	X	
I4	MTP2	X	
I4	MTP3	X	
I4	MTP4		X

We can see from this table that the FFG accepted MTP3 by applying implications I1 and I3. MTP4 was accepted by the application of implication I4. All the other minterm predicates were rejected!

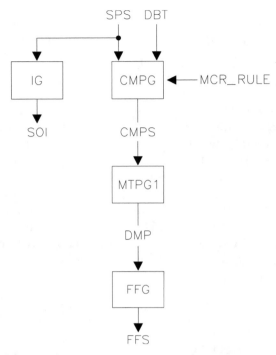

Figure 8.8 The complete horizontal fragmentation engine

The final fragment generator creates four SQL commands, two to create each fragment and two to fill the fragments with information from the original table. The SQL statements are shown below.

```
CREATE TABLE FNC_BRANCH_A
      (
      BRANCH_ID             CHAR(4)              NOT NULL,
      DEPT_ID               CHAR(4)              NOT NULL,
      BRANCH_NAME           CHAR(4)              NOT NULL,
      BRANCH_LOCATION       CHAR(20)             NOT NULL,
      PROFITS_TO_DATE       DECIMAL              NOT NULL,
      BRANCH_MANAGER        CHAR(5)              NOT NULL,
      PRIMARY KEY      x1  (BRANCH_ID)
      );

CREATE TABLE FNC_BRANCH_B
      (
      BRANCH_ID             CHAR(4)              NOT NULL,
      DEPT_ID               CHAR(4)              NOT NULL,
      BRANCH_NAME           CHAR(4)              NOT NULL,
```

```
BRANCH_LOCATION      CHAR(20)              NOT NULL,
PROFITS_TO_DATE      DECIMAL               NOT NULL,
BRANCH_MANAGER       CHAR(5)               NOT NULL,
PRIMARY KEY      x1 (BRANCH_ID)
);
```

The next two SQL commands are used to initialize the new table fragments.

```
INSERT INTO TABLE FNC_BRANCH_A
SELECT * FROM FNC_BRANCH_TABLE
WHERE PROFITS_TO_DATE << 1,000,000

INSERT INTO TABLE FNC_BRANCH_B
SELECT * FROM FNC_BRANCH_TABLE
WHERE PROFITS_TO_DATE >>= 1,000,000
```

Derived Horizontal Fragmentation

Primary horizontal fragmentation created new tables by fragmenting the original base tables along the rows according to some selected predicate. For example, let's create three new table fragments by splitting the FNC_DEPT_TBL according to the contents of the DEPT_LOCATION column:

```
DFRAG1 = PROJECT(SELECT(FNC_DEPT_TBL))
            ALL     DEPT_LOCATION = 'London'

DFRAG2 = PROJECT(SELECT(FNC_DEPT_TBL))
            ALL     DEPT_LOCATION = 'Edinburgh'

DFRAG1 = PROJECT(SELECT(FNC_DEPT_TBL))
            ALL     DEPT_LOCATION = 'Cirencester'
```

These three relational algebra queries translated into SQL are:

```
INSERT INTO DFRAG1
SELECT * FROM FNC_DEPT_TBL
WHERE DEPT_LOCATION = 'London'

INSERT INTO DFRAG2
SELECT * FROM FNC_DEPT_TBL
WHERE DEPT_LOCATION = 'Edinburgh'

INSERT INTO DFRAG3
```

```
SELECT * FROM FNC_DEPT_TBL
WHERE DEPT_LOCATION = 'Cirencester'
```

Let's call these new tables the horizontal fragment tables. We will use Derived Horizontal Fragmentation to create new fragments that have the same schema as the FNC_EMP_TABLE. Let's call these three fragments EFRAG1, EFRAG2, and EFRAG3. The specifications are that EFRAG1 is to contain only employees whose departments are located in London, EFRAG2 is to contain only employees whose departments are in Edinburgh, and EFRAG3 is to contain only employees whose departments are located in Cirencester. Performing a semi-join on the FNC_EMP_TBL base table to each of the horizontal table fragments produces the desired result:

```
EFRAG1 = PROJECT(DFRAG1 SEMI_JOIN FNC_EMP_TBL)
            ALL              DEPT_ID,EMP_ID

EFRAG2 = PROJECT(DFRAG2 SEMI_JOIN FNC_EMP_TBL)
            ALL              DEPT_ID,EMP_ID

EFRAG3 = PROJECT(DFRAG3 SEMI_JOIN FNC_EMP_TBL)
            ALL              DEPT_ID,EMP_ID
```

The above relational algebra operations can be executed with the following procedures containing embedded SQL commands:

```
PROC CREATE_DERIVED_FRAGMENT_EFRAG1
EXEC SQL
    CREATE TABLE DFRAG1
        (
        DEPT_ID         CHAR(4)         NOT NULL,
        DEPT_MGR_ID     CHAR(4)         NOT NULL,
        DEPT_LOCATION   CHAR(20)        NOT NULL,
        DEPT_NAME       CHAR(20)        NOT NULL,
        NUM_EMP         INT
        );
EXEC SQL
    CREATE TABLE EFRAG1
        (
        EMP_ID          CHAR(5)         NOT NULL,
        EMP_NAME        CHAR(20)        NOT NULL,
        EMP_DEPT        CHAR(4)         NOT NULL,
        EMP_SALARY      DECIMAL         NOT NULL,
        EMP_HIRE_DATE   DATE            NOT NULL
        );
```

```
// Perform Primary Horizontal Fragmentation
EXEC SQL
INSERT INTO DFRAG1
SELECT * FROM FNC_DEPT_TBL
WHERE DEPT_LOCATION = 'London';
IF(SQL_ERROR == 0)
    EXEC SQL COMMIT WORK;
ELSE
    {
    EXEC SQL ROLLBACK WORK
    EXIT
    }

// Perform Derived Horizontal Fragmentation
EXEC SQL
INSERT INTO EFRAG1
SELECT EMP_ID, EMP_NAME, DEPT_ID, EMP_TITLE, EMP_SALARY,
    EMP_HIRE_DATE
FROM FNC_EMP_TBL, DFRAG1
WHERE
    FNC_EMP_TBL.EMP_DEPT = DRAG1.DEPT_ID;
IF(SQL_ERROR == 0)
    EXEC SQL COMMIT WORK;
ELSE
    {
    EXEC SQL ROLLBACK WORK
    EXIT
    }
END PROC CREATE_DERIVED_FRAGMENT_EFRAG1
PROC CREATE_DERIVED_FRAGMENT_EFRAG2
EXEC SQL
    CREATE TABLE DFRAG2
        (
        DEPT_ID         CHAR(4)         NOT NULL,
        DEPT_MGR_ID     CHAR(4)         NOT NULL,
        DEPT_LOCATION   CHAR(20)        NOT NULL,
        DEPT_NAME       CHAR(20)        NOT NULL,
        NUM_EMP         INTEGER
        );
IF(SQL_ERROR == 0)
    EXEC SQL COMMIT WORK;
ELSE
    {
    EXEC SQL ROLLBACK WORK
    EXIT
```

```
        }
EXEC SQL
    CREATE TABLE EFRAG2
        (
            EMP_ID          CHAR(5)         NOT NULL,
            EMP_NAME        CHAR(20)        NOT NULL,
            EMP_DEPT        CHAR(4)         NOT NULL,
            EMP_SALARY      DECIMAL         NOT NULL,
            EMP_HIRE_DATE   DATE            NOT NULL
        );
IF(SQL_ERROR == 0)
    EXEC SQL COMMIT WORK;
ELSE
    {
    EXEC SQL ROLLBACK WORK
    EXIT
    }

// Perform Primary Horizontal Fragmentation
EXEC SQL
INSERT INTO DFRAG2
SELECT * FROM FNC_DEPT_TBL
WHERE DEPT_LOCATION = 'Edinburgh';
IF(SQL_ERROR == 0)
    EXEC SQL COMMIT WORK;
ELSE
    {
    EXEC SQL ROLLBACK WORK
    EXIT
    }

// Perform Derived Horizontal Fragmentation
EXEC SQL
INSERT INTO EFRAG2
SELECT EMP_ID,EMP_NAME,DEPT_ID,EMP_TITLE,EMP_SALARY,
        EMP_HIRE_DATE
FROM FNC_EMP_TBL,DFRAG2
WHERE
    FNC_EMP_TBL.EMP_DEPT = DRAG2.DEPT_ID;
IF(SQL_ERROR == 0)
    EXEC SQL COMMIT WORK;
ELSE
    {
    EXEC SQL ROLLBACK WORK
```

```
        EXIT
        }
END PROC CREATE_DERIVED_FRAGMENT_EFRAG2

PROC CREATE_DERIVED_FRAGMENT_EFRAG3
EXEC SQL
    CREATE TABLE DFRAG3
          (
          DEPT_ID          CHAR(4)        NOT NULL,
          DEPT_MGR_ID      CHAR(4)        NOT NULL,
          DEPT_LOCATION    CHAR(20)       NOT NULL,
          DEPT_NAME        CHAR(20)       NOT NULL,
          NUM_EMP          INT
          );
IF(SQL_ERROR == 0)
    EXEC SQL COMMIT WORK;
ELSE
    {
    EXEC SQL ROLLBACK WORK
    EXIT
    }
EXEC SQL
    CREATE TABLE EFRAG3
          (
          EMP_ID           CHAR(5)        NOT NULL,
          EMP_NAME         CHAR(20)       NOT NULL,
          EMP_DEPT         CHAR(4)        NOT NULL,
          EMP_SALARY       DECIMAL        NOT NULL,
          EMP_HIRE_DATE    DATE           NOT NULL
          );
IF(SQL_ERROR == 0)
    EXEC SQL COMMIT WORK;
ELSE
    {
    EXEC SQL ROLLBACK WORK
    EXIT
    }

// Perform Primary Horizontal Fragmentation
EXEC SQL
INSERT INTO DFRAG3
SELECT * FROM FNC_DEPT_TBL
WHERE DEPT_LOCATION = 'Cirencester';
IF(SQL_ERROR == 0)
```

```
        EXEC SQL COMMIT WORK;
ELSE
        {
        EXEC SQL ROLLBACK WORK
        EXIT
        }
// Perform Derived Horizontal Fragmentation
EXEC SQL
INSERT INTO EFRAG3
SELECT EMP_ID,EMP_NAME,DEPT_ID,EMP_TITLE,EMP_SALARY,
        EMP_HIRE_DATE
FROM FNC_EMP_TBL,DFRAG3
WHERE
        FNC_EMP_TBL.EMP_DEPT = DRAG3.DEPT_ID;
IF(SQL_ERROR == 0)
        EXEC SQL COMMIT WORK;
ELSE
        {
        EXEC SQL ROLLBACK WORK
        EXIT
        }
END PROC CREATE_DERIVED_FRAGMENT_EFRAG3
```

Each procedure began by creating an empty table for each of the primary horizontal tables and the derived horizontal tables. Each procedure then initialized the fragments with the SQL INSERT commands. The first INSERT used the simple predicate to initialize the primary horizontal table fragment:

```
WHERE DEPT_LOCATION = <City Name>
```

Since the procedures use SQL, the second INSERT command used a JOIN instead of the SEMI_JOIN operation to initialize the derived horizontal table fragments (most vendor implementations do not support semi-join operations).

```
WHERE FNC_EMP_TBL.EMP_DEPT = DFRAG1.DEPT_ID
WHERE FNC_EMP_TBL.EMP_DEPT = DFRAG2.DEPT_ID
WHERE FNC_EMP_TBL.EMP_DEPT = DFRAG3.DEPT_ID
```

Primary and derived horizontal fragmentation are fairly simple techniques. The next section will show vertical fragmentation to be more difficult, as the designer must take into account the applications that will run against the table fragments and the number of times the applications are run at a given time.

8.4 VERTICAL FRAGMENTATION

In this section we examine the steps required to design a distributed database by fragmenting relations along the attributes. As mentioned in the introductory section of this chapter, the steps I will follow were first introduced in a paper by Navathe et al.[2] and illustrated in Özsu and Valduriez.[1]

Design Steps

Vertical fragmentation splits tables along the attribute (columns) to create table fragments that can be distributed to remote sites. The goal of this technique is to minimize the amount of distributed joins that have to be performed when a set of applications or processes are executed against the distributed table fragments. Below are the four primary steps that a designer must follow:

Step 1: Define the attribute usage matrix.
Step 2: Build the clustered affinity matrix.
Step 3: Partition the clustered affinity matrix.
Step 4: Assign the generated table fragments to the remote sites.

Step 1 involves the identification of the processes that will run against the distributed database. A two-dimensional matrix is constructed for each of the tables in the database. The horizontal axis of the matrix contains each of the columns that make up the table. The vertical axis shows all of the processes that will access the columns in the table.

Once all the attribute usage matrices are identified, access frequencies have to be assigned to the application that will run against the table fragments.For example, if a distributed database is composed of three sites and process P1 runs at each site, we must identify how many times the process will access its assigned tables during a specified period of time.

To illustrate this point further, process P1 accesses table fragment TF1. Process P1 is executed at sites S1, S2, and S3 on a weekly basis. The access frequencies of each process at each site would be

Process	Site	Runs/Week
P1	S1	5
P1	S2	10
P1	S3	2

Shorthand notation for the above table would be:

```
ACC(P1) = 5       ACC(P1) = 10      ACC(P1) = 2
SITE = S1         SITE = S2         SITE = S3
```

Once each process is identified and the attribute usage matrix is created for each table, the "affinity," or how closely the attributes are related during process execution, must be identified. This identification process is performed in step 2.

Step 2 involves the creation of the clustered affinity matrix. This matrix shows the clustering of attributes that have the highest probability of being accessed together. The partitioning of these clusters defines the fragmentation scheme that will be used to derive the distributed table fragments. This is accomplished in step 3.

Step 3 takes the clustered affinity matrix and applies some cost formulas to locate the coordinates that define the ideal splitting point for the matrix. (The splitting point identifies the table fragments that are to be distributed to the remote sites.) Finally, the assignment of the fragments is accomplished in step 4.

To illustrate these concepts we will use the FNC_DEPT_TBL table from our Traditional Fish 'n' Chips enterprise database. Let us begin by identifying the processes that will run against the table and ther construct the attribute usage matrix from this information.

Defining the Attribute Usage Matrix

Below is a simplified schema for the FNC_DEPT_TBL base table:

Attribute	Alias
DEPT_ID	C1
DEPT_MGR_ID	C2
DEPT_LOCATION	C3
DEPT_NAME	C4
DEPT_NUM_EMP	C5

The processes that will run against this table are defined below:

```
/* process 1 */
EXEC SQL // declare host variables
    BEGIN DECLARE SECTION
    char DEPTID[4];
    char DEPTNAME[20];
```

```
EXEC SQL
     END DECLARE SECTION;
main()
     {
     EXEC SQL // declare the cursor
          DECLARE CURSOR CP1 FOR
          SELECT DEPT_ID,DEPT_NAME
          INTO :DEPTID,:DEPTNAME
          FROM DEPT

     EXEC SQL // open the cursor
          OPEN CP1;

     do
          { // fetch all rows
          EXEC SQL
               FETCH CP1;
          printf("DEPT: %s NAME: %s\n",DEPTID,DEPTNAME);
          }while(SQL_ERROR == 0)

     EXEC SQL // close the cursor
          CLOSE CP1;
     exit(0);
}
/* process 2 */
EXEC SQL // declare host variables
     BEGIN DECLARE SECTION
     char DEPTMGRID[4];
     CHAR NUMEMP[5];
EXEC SQL
     END DECLARE SECTION;
main()
     {
     EXEC SQL // declare the cursor
          DECLARE CURSOR CP2 FOR
          SELECT DEPT_MGR_ID
          INTO :DEPTMGRID
          FROM DEPT
          WHERE DEPT_NUM_EMP  :NUMEMP;
     printf("Enter number of employees: ");
     gets(NUMEMP);
     EXEC SQL // open the cursor
          OPEN CP2;
     do
          { // fetch all the rows
          EXEC SQL
               FETCH CP2;
```

```
                 printf("DEPT MANAGER: %s\n",DEPTMGRID);
                 }while(SQL_ERROR == 0)

      EXEC SQL // close the cursor
           CLOSE CP2;
      exit(0);
}
/* process 3 */
EXEC SQL // declare the host variables
      BEGIN DECLARE SECTION
      char LOCATION[4];
      char NAME[20];
EXEC SQL
      END DECLARE SECTION;
main()
      {
      EXEC SQL // declare the cursor
           DECLARE CURSOR CP3 FOR
           SELECT DEPT_LOCATION,DEPT_NAME
           INTO :LOCATION,:NAME
           FROM DEPT

      EXEC SQL // open the cursor
           OPEN CP3;

      do
           { // fetch all rows
           EXEC SQL
                FETCH CP3;
           printf("LOCATION: %s NAME %s\n",LOCATION,NAME);
           }while(SQL_ERROR == 0)

      EXEC SQL // close the cursor
           CLOSE CP3;
      exit(0);
}
/* process 4 */
EXEC SQL // declare the host variables
      BEGIN DECLARE SECTION
      char DEPTID[4];
      char DEPTLOC[20];
EXEC SQL
      END DECLARE SECTION;
main()
      {
      EXEC SQL // declare the cursor
```

```
            DECLARE CURSOR CP4 FOR
            SELECT DEPT_ID,DEPT_LOCATION
            INTO :DEPTID,:DEPTLOC
            FROM DEPT

      EXEC SQL // open the cursor
            OPEN CP4;
      do
            { // fetch all rows
            EXEC SQL
                FETCH CP4;
            printf("DEPT ID: %s LOCATION: %s\n",
                ,DEPTID,DEPTNAME);
            }while(SQL_ERROR == 0)
      EXEC SQL // close the cursor
            CLOSE CP4;
      exit(0);
}
/* process 5 */
EXEC SQL // declare all host variables
      BEGIN DECLARE SECTION
      char LOCATION[20];
      int NUMEMP;
EXEC SQL
      END DECLARE SECTION;
main()
      {
      EXEC SQL // declare the cursor
            DECLARE CURSOR CP5 FOR
            SELECT DEPT_LOCATION,DEPT_NUM_EMP
            INTO :LOCATION,:NUMEMP
            FROM DEPT;

      EXEC SQL // open the cursor
            OPEN CP5;
      do
            { // fetch all rows
            EXEC SQL
                FETCH CP5;
            printf("LOCATION: %s NUM EMP: %d\n",
                ,LOCATION,NUMEMP);
            }while(SQL_ERROR == 0)
      EXEC SQL // close the cursor
            CLOSE CP5;
      exit(0);
}
```

	C1	C2	C3	C4	C5
P1	X			X	
P2		X			X
P3			X	X	
P4	X		X		
P5			X		X

Figure 8.9 The attribute usage matrix

Using the aliases for each of the columns, let's identify the columns that are used by each process.

Process	Column Aliases
P1	C1, C4
P2	C2, C5
P3	C3, C4
P4	C1, C3
P5	C3, C5

The attribute usage matrix is shown in Figure 8.9. Let's assume that these processes can be run on a weekly basis at four sites: SITE1, SITE2, SITE3, and SITE4. The access frequencies for each process can be represented by the following simplified formula:

```
ACC(Pj) = VALUE
Site = i
```

where P represents the process, j is the number of processes, and i is the number of sites. VALUE represents (in our case) the number of times this process is run at a site on a weekly basis. The more complicated formula used in Özsu and Valduriez[1] is

```
AF = REF(Pj) * ACC(Pj)
```

where REF is the number of references an application makes to the table.

As in Özsu and Valduriez,[1] we will assume this value is 1. The process could be run daily, hourly, or any time interval the designer picks. The table below shows the access frequencies for the processes at each site:

Process Application Frequencies

Site1	Site2	Site3	Site4	Sum
ACC(P1) = 2 S = 1	ACC(P1) = 0 S = 2	ACC(P1) = 2 S = 3	ACC(P1) = 0 S = 4	4
ACC(P2) = 0 S = 1	ACC(P2) = 4 S = 2	ACC(P2) = 3 S = 3	ACC(P2) = 0 S = 4	7
ACC(P3) = 0 S = 1	ACC(P3) = 0 S = 2	ACC(P3) = 5 S = 3	ACC(P3) = 0 S = 4	5
ACC(P4) = 5 S = 1	ACC(P4) = 0 S = 2	ACC(P4) = 0 S = 3	ACC(P4) = 0 S = 4	5
ACC(P5) = 1 S = 1	ACC(P5) = 0 S = 2	ACC(P5) = 3 S = 3	ACC(P5) = 0 S = 4	4

The row-wise sum calculated for the access frequencies of each process will be used to create the clustered affinity matrix. This matrix will show the "affinity" or closeness that each column has to the other columns in the table. The affinity is related to the process that runs against each column. The affinities are defined below:

Process Attribute Affinity Table

Process	Attributes	Affinity
P1	C1, C4	4
P2	C2, C5	7
P3	C3, C4	5
P4	C1, C3	5
P5	C3, C5	4

The clustered affinity matrix is shown in Figure 8.10a.

The diagonal values, calculated and shown in Figure 8.10b, will be used by the algorithms that cluster the attributes according to usage.

Note: The diagonal values are calculated by taking the row-wise sums of each attribute. For example, the value at C2, C2 = 7 was calculated by adding $0 + 0 + 0 + 7$. The value at C4, C4 = 9 was calculated by adding $4 + 0 + 0 + 5 + 0$.

Now that the clustered affinity matrix is defined, it must be rearranged so that the highest contribution values are clustered to-

	C1	C2	C3	C4	C5
C1	0	0	0	4	0
C2	0	0	0	0	7
C3	0	0	0	5	4
C4	4	0	5	0	0
C5	0	7	4	0	0

Figure 8.10a The clustered affinity matrix

gether. The contribution values are calculated by the following formula:[1-3]

```
CONT(X,Y,Z) = 2 * BOND(X,Y) + 2 * BOND(Y,Z) - 2 * BOND(X,Z)
```

X, Y, and Z are the columns involved in the contributions. For instance, given columns C1, C2, and C3 in the clustered affinity matrix, we wish to find the column ordering that yields the highest value when the contribution formula is applied. The possible ordering of the columns is C1, C2, C3 or C2, C1, C3 or C1, C3, C2. The contribution algorithm uses a formula called the BOND energy algorithm,[4] which is simply the row-wise sum of the product of the values of two columns in the clustered affinity matrix. For example,

	C1	**C3**	**Product**
C1	0	0	0
C2	0	0	0
C3	0	0	0
C4	4	5	20
C5	0	4	0
BOND =			20

	C1	C2	C3	C4	C5
C1	4	0	0	4	0
C2	0	7	0	0	7
C3	0	0	9	5	4
C4	4	0	5	9	0
C5	0	7	4	0	11

Figure 8.10b The clustered affinity matrix with calculated diagonal values

	C1	C2	C3
C1	4	0	0
C2	0	7	0
C3	0	0	9
C4	4	0	5
C5	0	7	4

Figure 8.11 Positioning column C3

Each of the attributes in the clustered affinity matrix must be tested for every possible position combination. An arbitrary starting point is selected and the algorithms are applied. The attribute ordering that yields the highest contribution value is kept and the next column is picked. Let's illustrate these concepts by starting at the leftmost column, C1 in our matrix. We begin by finding which attribute order yields the highest contribution when the algorithms are applied.

Figure 8.11 shows C3 about to be placed inside the clustered affinity matrix. We want to test every possible column-ordering combination.

```
C0,       C3,       C1
C1,       C3,       C2
C2,       C3,       C4
```

We will begin with the contributions for the first combination C0, C3, C1:

```
CONT(C0,C3,C1) = 2 X BOND(C0,C3) + 2 X BOND(C3,C1) -
                 2 X BOND(C0,C1)
BOND(C0,C3) = BOND(C0,C1) = 0
BOND(C3,C1) = 5 X 4 = 20
CONT(C0,C3,C1) = 2 X 20 = 40

CONT(C1,C3,C2) = 2 X BOND(C1,C3) + 2 X BOND(C3,C2) -
                 2 X BOND(C1,C2)
BOND(C1,C3) = 40
BOND(C3,C2) = 7 X 4 = 28
BOND(C1,C2) = 0
CONT(C1,C3,C2) = (2 X 40) + (2 X 28) - (2 X 0) = 136

CONT(C2,C3,C4) = 2 X BOND(C2,C3) + 2 X BOND(C3,C4) -
                 2 X BOND(C2,C4)
```

	C1	C3	C2		
C1	4	0	0		
C2	0	0	7		
C3	0	9	0		
C4	4	5	0		
C5	0	4	7		

Figure 8.12   Column C3 positioned between C1 and C2

```
BOND(C2,C3) = 28
BOND(C3,C4) = 0
BOND(C2,C4) = 0
CONT(C2,C3,C4) = (2 X 28) + (2 X 0) - (2 X 0) = 56
```

Since CONT(C1,C3,C2) yields the highest value, the order C1, C3, C2 is used in the clustered affinity matrix. Figure 8.12 shows the revised matrix.

Next, we want to find the best possible position for inserting column C4 into the clustered affinity matrix. Figure 8.13 shows the next column ready for positioning. The combinations to check are

C0	C4	C1
C1	C4	C3
C3	C4	C2
C2	C4	C5

The border conditions are calculated first:

```
CONT(C0,C4,C1) = 2 X BOND(C0,C4) + 2 X BOND(C4,C1) -
                 2 X BOND(C0,C1)
BOND(C0,C4) = BOND(C0,C1) = 0
BOND(C4,C1) = (4 X 4) + (9 X 4) = 52
CONT(C0,C4,C1) = (2 X 52) + (2 X 0) + (2 X 0) = 104

CONT(C2,C4,C5) = 2 X BOND(C2,C4) + 2 X BOND(C4,C5) -
                 2 X BOND(C2,C5)
BOND(C2,C4) = 0
BOND(C4,C5) = 0
BOND(C2,C5) = 0
CONT(C2,C4,C5) = (2 X 0) + (2 X 0) - (2 X 0) = 0

CONT(C1,C4,C3) = 2 X BOND(C1,C4) + 2 X BOND(C4,C3) -
                 2 X BOND(C1,C3)
```

	C1	C3	C2		C4
C1	4	0	0		4
C2	0	0	7		0
C3	0	9	0		5
C4	4	5	0		9
C5	0	4	7		0

Figure 8.13 Positioning column C4

Note: To determine border conditions, the position of the column to be inserted must be tested in either the first position or last position of the current matrix. This means that imaginary columns such as C0 are included. Calculations involving these imaginary columns always yield a result of 0.

```
BOND(C1,C4) = 52
BOND(C4,C3) = (9 X 5) + (5 X 9) = 90
BOND(C1,C3) = 40
CONT(C1,C4,C3) = (2 X 52) + (2 X 90) - (2 X 40) = 204

CONT(C3,C4,C2) = 2 X BOND(C3,C4) + 2 X BOND(C4,C2) -
                 2 X BOND(C3,C2)
BOND(C3,C4) = 90
BOND(C4,C2) = 0
BOND(C3,C2) = 28
CONT(C3,C4,C2) = (2 X 90) + (2 X 0) - (2 X 28) = 124
```

Since CONT(C1,C4,C3) yields the highest value, column C4 is placed between column C1 and C3 in the clustered affinity matrix. Figure 8.14 shows the revised matrix.

	C1	C4	C3	C2		C5
C1	4	4	0	0		0
C2	0	0	0	7		7
C3	0	5	9	0		4
C4	4	9	5	0		0
C5	0	0	4	7		11

Figure 8.14 Positioning column C5

We next calculate the final contribution value so as to insert column C5 in the optimal position in the clustered affinity matrix. We now have five possible orderings:

```
C0        C5        C1
C1        C5        C4
C4        C5        C3
C3        C5        C2
C2        C5        C6
```

The border conditions are calculated first:

```
CONT(C0,C5,C1) = 2 X BOND(C0,C5) + 2 X BOND(C5,C1) -
                 2 X BOND(C0,C1)
BOND(C0,C5) = BOND(C0,C1) = 0
BOND(C5,C1) = 0
CONT(C0,C5,C1) = (2 X 0) + (2 X 0) - (2 X 0) = 0

CONT(C2,C5,C6) = 2 X BOND(C2,C5) + 2 X BOND(C5,C6) -
                 2 X BOND(C2,C6)
BOND(C5,C6) = 0
BOND(C2,C6) = 0
BOND(C2,C5) = (7 X 7) + (7 X 11) = 126
CONT(C2,C5,C6) = (2 X 126) + (2 X 0) - (2 X 0) = 252

CONT(C1,C5,C4) = 2 X BOND(C1,C5) + 2 X BOND(C5,C4) -
                 2 X BOND(C1,C4)
BOND(C1,C5) = 0
BOND(C5,C4) = (5 X 4) = 20
BOND(C1,C4) = 52
CONT(C1,C5,C4) = (2 X 0) + (2 X 20) - (2 X 52) = -64

CONT(C4,C5,C3) = 2 X BOND(C4,C5) + 2 X BOND(C5,C3) -
                 2 X BOND(C4,C3)
BOND(C4,C5) = 20
BOND(C5,C3) = (9 X 4) + (4 X 11) = 80
BOND(C4,C3) = 90
CONT(C4,C5,C3) = (2 X 20) + (2 X 80) - (2 X 90) = 20

CONT(C3,C5,C2) = 2 X BOND(C3,C5) + 2 X BOND(C5,C2) -
                 2 X BOND(C3,C2)
```

Calculating the three BOND values yields:

```
BOND(C3,C5) = 80
BOND(C5,C2) = 126
```

	C1	C4	C3	C5	C2
C1	4	4	0	0	0
C2	0	0	0	7	7
C3	0	5	9	4	0
C4	4	9	5	0	0
C5	0	0	4	11	7

Figure 8.15a The final clustered affinity matrix

```
BOND(C3,C2) = 28
CONT(C3,C5,C2) = (2 X 80) + (2 X 126) - (2 X 28) = 356
```

The order C3, C5, C2 yields the highest contribution value, so column C5 is inserted after column C3 and before column C2 in the clustered affinity matrix. Figure 8.15a shows the final matrix.

Now that the columns in the clustered affinity matrix have been reordered, the horizontal rows must be in the same order as the columns. The final clustered affinity matrix can be seen in Figure 8.15b.

Intuitively we can see that the fragmentation point is somewhere in the middle of the matrix—we do not know exactly where it is! By applying some cost calculations and maximizing them, we can locate the exact X,Y coordinates in the matrix that yield the optimal fragmentation point. This process is given in the next step.

The partitioning phase of the vertical design process involves splitting the clustered affinity matrix into a top part and a bottom part. This is accomplished by selecting a starting point in the matrix. At each phase of the partitioning process, we must identify which of the processes access columns that are either located in the top half, the

	C1	C4	C3	C5	C2
C1	4	4	0	0	0
C4	4	9	5	0	0
C3	0	5	9	4	0
C5	0	0	4	11	7
C2	0	0	0	7	7

Figure 8.15b Reordering the rows

bottom half, or both. The following variables are used to identify these categories:

CTQ: Applications that access columns in the top half only.

CBQ: Applications that access columns in the bottom half only.

CTBQ: Applications that access columns in the top and bottom parts only.

These variables represent the sum of the affinities for each of the applications involved in the above categories. They are repeated below for the convenience of the reader:

```
AFF(P1) = AFF(C1,C4) = 4
AFF(P2) = AFF(C2,C5) = 7
AFF(P3) = AFF(C3,C4) = 5
AFF(P4) = AFF(C1,C3) = 5
AFF(P5) = AFF(C3,C5) = 4
```

We will begin the partitioning process by starting at the lower right-hand side of the matrix at coordinates C2, C2. At each phase the process names and the columns they access in the matrix will be repeated for ease of reference. Figure 8.16 shows the selected point at coordinate C2, C2. The processes and their associated columns are

P1 accesses columns C1, C4

P2 accesses columns C2, C5

P3 accesses columns C3, C4

P4 accesses columns C1, C3

P5 accesses columns C3, C5

```
PCTQ (Process Columns top half) = P1,P3,P4,P5
PCBQ (Process Columns bottom half) = none
PCTBQ (Process Columns top and bottom) = P2

Cost of PCTQ = 4 + 5 + 5 + 4 = 18
Cost of PCBQ = 0
Cost of PCTBQ = 7
```

The maximized value for the above costs is

```
MAXVAL_OF_COSTS = 18 * 0 - (7^2) = -49
```

Figure 8.17 shows the next selection point at coordinates C5, C5. Notice the arrows originating from row C2 and column C1. This means that in the next selection-point phase we must shift the last row to the first row position and shift the first column to the last

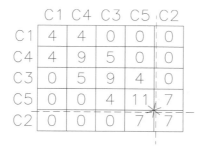

Figure 8.16 Selecting the first splitting point

column position. This process is repeated for each selection-point phase until the upper left-hand selection coordinate is reached.

The processes and their associated columns are

P1 accesses columns C1, C4
P2 accesses columns C2, C5
P3 accesses columns C3, C4
P4 accesses columns C1, C3
P5 accesses columns C3, C5

```
PCTQ (Process Columns top half) = P1,P3,P4
PCBQ (Process Columns bottom half) = P2
PCTBQ (Process Columns top and bottom) = P5

Cost of PCTQ = 4 +5 + 5 = 14
Cost of PCBQ = 7
Cost of PCTBQ = 4
```

The maximized value for the above costs is

```
MAXVAL_OF_COSTS = 14 X 7 - (4^2) = 82
```

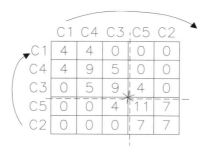

Figure 8.17 Selecting the second splitting point

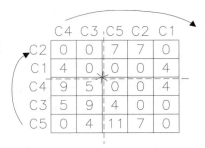

Figure 8.18 Selecting the third splitting point (after shift)

Figure 8.18 shows the next selection point at coordinates C4, C5. Notice that the last row and first column have shifted positions!
The processes and their associated columns are

P1 accesses columns C1,C4
P2 accesses columns C2, C5
P3 accesses columns C3, C4
P4 accesses columns C1, C3
P5 accesses columns C3, C5

```
PCTQ (Process Columns top half) = P3
PCBQ (Process Columns bottom half) = P2
PCTBQ (Process Columns top and bottom) = P1,P4,P5

Cost of PCTQ = 5
Cost of PCBQ = 7
Cost of PCTBQ = 4 + 5 + 4 = 13
```

The maximized value for the above costs is

```
MAXVAL_OF_COSTS = 5 X 7 - (13^2) = -134
```

Figure 8.19 shows the selected point at coordinates C2, C5. Again, notice that the last row and first column have shifted positions!
The processes and their associated columns are

P1 accesses columns C1, C4
P2 accesses columns C2, C5
P3 accesses columns C3, C4
P4 accesses columns C1, C3
P5 accesses columns C3, C5

```
PCTQ (Process Columns Top Quadrant) = none
PCBQ (Process Columns Bottom Quadrant) = P1,P2
```

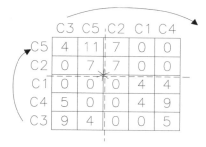

Figure 8.19 Selecting the fourth splitting point

```
PCTBQ (Process Columns Top and Bottom Quadrant) =
P3,P4,P5

Cost of PCTQ = 4 + 7 = 11
Cost of PCBQ = 5 + 5 + 4 = 14
Cost of PCTBQ = 5 + 5 + 4 = 14
```

The maximized value for the above costs is

```
MAXVAL_OF_COSTS = 0 X 11 - (14^2) = -196
```

Coordinates C3, C3 represent the splitting point that yields the highest maximized value for the costs.

The partitioning scheme that yielded the highest maximum value of 82 is shown in Figure 8.20. This partitioning arrangement will be used and yields the following schemas for the fragments:

Fragment	Columns	Site
DF1	C1, C4, C3	S1
DF2	C1, C5, C2	S2

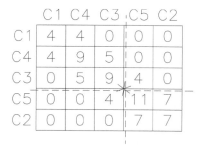

Figure 8.20 C5, C5 as the fragmentation point

Notice that the primary key attribute C1 was included in the fragment DF2; it is required to uniquely identify each row of the fragment. This concludes our discussion on vertical table fragmentation.

8.5 HYBRID FRAGMENTATION

Hybrid fragmentation creates new fragments by using a combination of the methods discussed in the last two sections. Figure 8.21 is a diagram containing table fragments located at five distributed sites that were derived with the hybrid fragmentation approach.

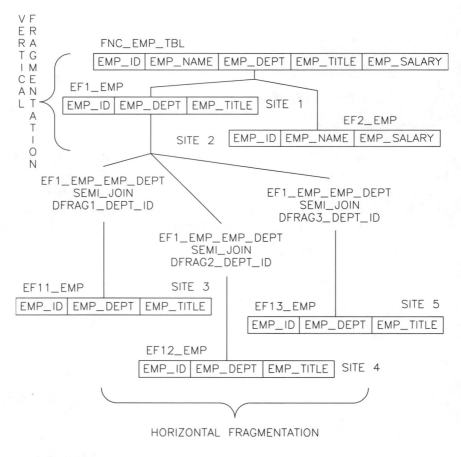

Figure 8.21 Hybrid fragmentation

The global table FNC_EMP_TBL is first vertically fragmented by projecting the columns EMP_ID, EMP_DEPT, and EMP_TITLE to SITE_1. Next, columns EMP_ID, EMP_NAME, and EMP_SALARY are projected to create the vertical fragment for SITE_2. Derived horizontal fragmentation is used to horizontally fragment the vertically fragmented table at site 1 to sites SITE_3, SITE_4, and SITE_5. The primary horizontal fragments on table FNC_DEPT_TBL were used to derive the new fragments. Tables DFRAG1, DFRAG2, and DFRAG3 were SEMI_JOINed with table EF1_EMP over the EMP_DEPT and DEPT_ID columns to produce the new tables.

8.6 SUMMARY

The discussions on horizontal and vertical fragmentation and hybrid fragmentation in this chapter were greatly simplified to illustrate the key design steps required to implement each of the fragmentation schemes. The discussions in Sections 8.3 and 8.5 follow the steps and methods introduced in Özsu and Valduriez[1] and the discussions in Section 8.4 follow the methods, steps, and formulas discussed in Özsu and Valduriez[1] and introduced in Navathe et al.[2]

8.7 END NOTES

1. Özsu, M. Tamer, and P. Valduriez. *Principles of Distributed Database Systems*, Englewood Cliffs, NJ: Prentice Hall, 1991.

2. Navathe, S., S. Ceri, G. Wiederhold, and J. Dou. "Vertical Partitioning Algorithms for Database Design," *ACM Transactions on Database Systems*, vol. 9, no. 4 (December 1984): pp. 680–710.

3. Hoffer, H. A., and D. G. Severance. "The Use of Cluster Analysis in Physical Database Design," *Proceedings of the First International Conference on Very Large Databases*, Framingham, MA (September 1975): pp. 69–86.

4. McCormick, W. T., P. J. Schweitzer, and T. W. White. "Problem Decomposition and Data Reorganization by a Clustering Technique," *Operations Research*, vol. 20, no. 5 (1972): pp. 993–1009.

9

Distributed Query Processing

9.1 INTRODUCTION

We are now ready to examine how a distributed database management system processes a distributed query submitted by a user at a remote workstation. An example query, together with a global and fragment schema, is introduced to demonstrate the steps necessary to process and route the global query to its final local sites. At each of these sites, the queries are processed and optimized one more time by the local query optimizer before they are submitted to the local scheduler for execution.

The chapter begins with a description of the components and inputs that make up the distributed database management system. A simple model similar to the one described in Özsu and Valduriez[1] is introduced together with the global query and schemas required to process the query. The chapter continues with a section dedicated to each of the major components of the model:

- The Syntax Analyzer
- The Query Decomposer
- The Query Object Localizer
- The Query Optimizer
- The Local Query Processers

Some of these components are further broken down into subcomponents so that we can discuss each of the steps that are taken at each stage of the processing of the query. For example, the query decomposer model is broken down into the following subcomponents:

- The Normalization Module
- The Semantic Analyzer
- The Query Simplifier
- The Relational Algebra Query Generator

Certain components require several inputs such as database statistics, communication cost models, and cardinality estimation formulas. These statistics, models, and rules are introduced and explained as required.

Let us proceed by introducing the generic model of our distributed database management system. This model is similar to the general model discussed in the literature. It follows the steps described in Özsu and Valduriez.[1]

9.2 THE DDBMS MODEL

In this section we will examine the general details and functions of the distributed database management system that will be used for the Traditional Fish 'n' Chips company. It is based on the model used in Özsu and Valduriez[1] with some added components. Figure 9.1 shows a block diagram of the system.

User queries are generated at a remote workstation and submitted over a communications network, where they are received at the communications interface component labeled 1. This component is responsible for returning any results to the original remote workstation that submitted the query.

Once the query is received at the central distributed management site it is read by the syntax analyzer (labeled 2) so that it can be checked for correctness. At this stage the syntax analyzer uses as input the rules of the language grammar. In our case we assume that they are the grammar rules for the Structured Query Language (SQL).

Assuming the query is correct, it passes to the next level, the query decomposition stage. This function is performed by the query decomposer module (labeled 3). At this stage, various rules and information from the global database dictionary are used to translate the relational calculus query (the SQL query) to a relational algebra query.

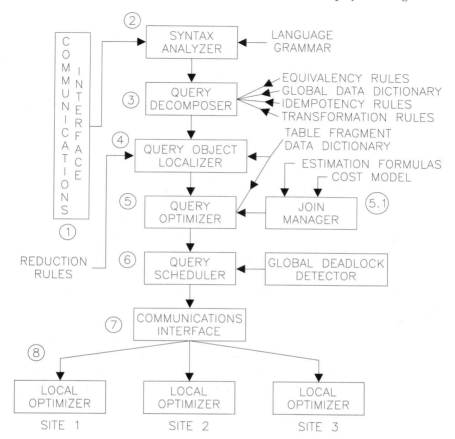

Figure 9.1 Distributed database management system model

The next phase of the processing requires that the global relations that are members of the distributed query be transformed into the equivalent fragment relations that are distributed at the various sites. This is the job of the query object localizer module (labeled 4).

This module uses information contained in the table fragment dictionaries and reduction rules to modify the query so that it refers to the actual distributed table fragments. The reduction rules are used to simplify the query and eliminate contradictory or unnecessary qualifying predicates in the query.

We are not finished yet! Now that the query has been translated from a relational calculus query into a relational algebra query it must be optimized. Up to this point our distributed database management system has not used any of the really important database statistics contained in the global or fragment data dictionaries. The optimization phase is performed at the query optimizer module (labeled 5). This module works in tandem with the join manager module to improve the order in which the joins are performed. At this stage, a communications cost model and several estimation formulas are used to rewrite the query. The modified query can be rewritten to utilize system resources so as to yield optimal performance. At this stage, the query is also modified to include communications primitives that will be used to route temporary result sets between sites to perform the joins.

Once the query has been modified, it is passed to the query scheduler module for execution. This module works with the global deadlock detector to properly schedule transactions that might have conflicting requests. This processing occurs at level 6 of our diagram.

At this stage the query has been translated to several relational algebra fragment queries. These fragment queries can now be distributed to the sites involved in generating a solution to the query. This distribution and transfer is performed at level 7, another communications interface module.

Each of the fragment queries is transferred to each of the local sites where they are optimized one more time by the local DBMS to take advantage of the information available in the local data dictionaries. This phase is performed at level 8 of our diagram. We will now proceed to discuss the functions performed at each level in detail.

9.3 AN EXAMPLE

Let us now introduce the distributed query that we will use to illustrate the stages required to process it. Additionally, we will examine the global data dictionary, the reconstruction rules used to rebuild the global relation schemes from the fragment schemes, and the local data dictionaries. Below is the distributed query that will be processed:

```
SELECT DEPT.DEPT_ID,BMGR.BRANCH_MGR,
          BRANCH.BRANCH_ID,BRANCH.BRANCH_LOCATION,
          EMP.EMP_NAME,EMP.EMP_SALARY
     FROM DEPT,EMP,BMGR,BRANCH
     WHERE DEPT.DEPT_ID = BMGR.DEPT_ID
     AND   BMGR.BRANCH_ID = BRANCH.BRANCH_ID
     AND   BMGR.BRANCH_MGR = EMP.EMP_ID
     AND   BRANCH.PROFITS_TO_DATE > 2,000,000.00
```

```
AND     BRANCH.BRANCH_LOCATION = 'LONDON'
AND     EMP.EMP_SALARY > 50,000
```

As can be seen, the query contains three joins over the global relations and has three qualifying predicates. It will be interesting to see how our distributed database management system processes this rather complicated query.

Figure 9.2 shows the global database dictionary for our distributed database. The primary keys are identified by the asterisk (*) in the key column of each table, the foreign keys by the double asterisks (**). Below are the relational algebra formulas used to fragment the global relations into the distributed fragments.

Table DEPT is fragmented as follows:

```
DEPT1 = SELECT(DEPT) WHERE DEPT_LOCATION = 'LONDON'
DEPT2 = SELECT(DEPT) WHERE DEPT_LOCATION = 'EDINBURGH'
DEPT3 = SELECT(DEPT) WHERE DEPT_LOCATION = 'CIRENCESTER'
```

Table EMP is fragmented as follows:

```
EMP1 = SELECT(EMP) WHERE EMP_TITLE = 'MGR'
EMP2 = SELECT(EMP) WHERE EMP_TITLE = 'CHEF'
EMP3 = SELECT(EMP) WHERE EMP_TITLE = 'WAITER'
```

Table BRANCH is fragmented as follows:

```
BRANCH1 = SELECT(BRANCH) WHERE BRANCH_ID < B10
BRANCH2 = SELECT(BRANCH) WHERE B10 <= BRANCH_ID <= B20
BRANCH3 = SELECT(BRANCH) WHERE BRANCH_ID > B20
```

Table BMGR is fragmented as follows:

```
BMGR1 = SELECT(BMGR) WHERE BRANCH_ID < B10
BMGR2 = SELECT(BMGR) WHERE B10 <= BRANCH_ID <= B20
BMGR3 = SELECT(BMGR) WHERE BRANCH_ID > B20
```

Recall that these formulas can also be used to reconstruct the original global relations:

```
DEPT = UNION DEPT1 UNION DEPT2 UNION DEPT3
EMP = UNION EMP1 UNION EMP2 UNION EMP3
BRANCH = UNION BRANCH1 UNION BRANCH2 UNION BRANCH3
BMGR = BMGR1 UNION BMGR2 UNION BMGR3
```

We will see how these reconstruction formulas are used to localize the data in the localization step performed by the query object localizer module.

ENTITY	ATTRIBUTES	DATA TYPE	KEY
DEPT	DEPT_ID	CHAR	✳
	DEPT_MGR_ID	CHAR	
	DEPT_LOCATION	CHAR	
	DEPT_NAME	CHAR	
	DEPT_NUM_EMP	INTEGER	

ENTITY	ATTRIBUTES	DATA TYPE	KEY
EMP	EMP_ID	CHAR	✳
	EMP_NAME	CHAR	
	EMP_DEPT	CHAR	✳✳
	EMP_TITLE	CHAR	
	EMP_SALARY	DECIMAL	
	EMP_HIRE_DATE	DATE	

ENTITY	ATTRIBUTES	DATA TYPE	KEY
BRANCH	BRANCH_ID	CHAR	✳
	DEPT_ID	CHAR	✳✳
	BRANCH_NAME	CHAR	
	BRANCH_LOCATION	CHAR	
	PROFITS_TO_DATE	CURRENCY	
	BRANCH_MGR	CHAR	✳✳

ENTITY	ATTRIBUTES	DATA TYPE	KEY
BMGR	BRANCH_MGR	CHAR	✳
	DEPT_ID	CHAR	✳✳
	EMP_ID	CHAR	✳✳
	BRANCH_ID	CHAR	✳✳

KEY:
✳ = ATTRIBUTE USED AS A PRIMARY KEY
✳✳ = ATTRIBUTE USED AS A FOREIGN KEY

Figure 9.2 Global data dictionary

Figure 9.3 shows a diagram of how the table fragments are distributed. The database will be distributed among the following sites:

Site 1: table DEPT1, BRANCH1
Site 2: table DEPT2, BRANCH2
Site 3: table DEPT3, BRANCH3
Site 4: table EMP1, BMGR1, BMGR2, BMGR3
Site 5: table EMP2, EMP3

Finally, Figure 9.4 shows the table fragment data dictionary that shows important locality information used for query localization.

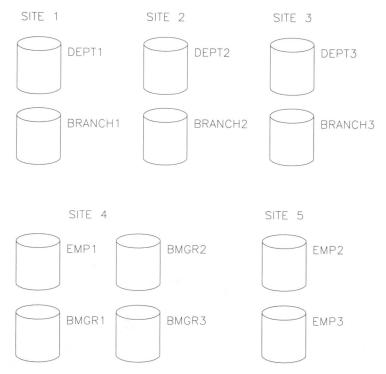

Figure 9.3 Fragment table distribution

TBL_NAME	FRAGMENT_NAME	SITE
DEPT	DEPT1	SITE1
DEPT	DEPT2	SITE2
DEPT	DEPT3	SITE3
BRANCH	BRANCH1	SITE1
BRANCH	BRANCH2	SITE2
BRANCH	BRANCH3	SITE3
EMP	EMP1	SITE4
EMP	EMP2	SITE5
EMP	EMP3	SITE5
BMGR	BMGR1	SITE4
BMGR	BMGR2	SITE4
BMGR	BMGR3	SITE4

Figure 9.4 Table fragment data dictionary

211

```
QUERY := SELECT_CLAUSE + FROM_CLAUSE + WHERE_CLAUSE

SELECT_CLAUSE := 'SELECT' + <COLUMN_LIST>

FROM_CLAUSE := 'FROM' + <TABLE_LIST>

WHERE_CLAUSE := 'WHERE' + VALUE1 OP VALUE2

VALUE1 := VALUE/COLUMN_NAME

VALUE2 := VALUE/COLUMN_NAME

OP := +/-///*/=
```

Figure 9.5 Simple SQL grammar

9.4 THE SYNTAX ANALYZER

The syntax analyzer takes the distributed query, parses it into tokens, and analyzes the tokens and their order to make sure they comply with the rules of the language grammar. Figure 9.5 shows a very simple version of a grammar that could be used to implement a SQL statement. This grammar could be used to implement a SQL query such as the one shown here:

```
SELECT  col1, col2, col3, col4
FROM    t1
WHERE   col2 > 10000
AND     col3 = 'LONDON'
AND     col4 between 1000 and 50000
```

If an error is found in the query submitted by the user, it is rejected and an error code together with an explanation of why the query was rejected is returned to the user.

9.5 THE QUERY DECOMPOSER

We now proceed by examining the process that occurs at the first stage of the distributed query processing. The query submitted by the user at the remote workstation is structured as a relational calculus query (SQL). This query must be translated into a relational algebra query so that it can be simplified and optimized. The query decomposer goes through four stages of processing to accomplish

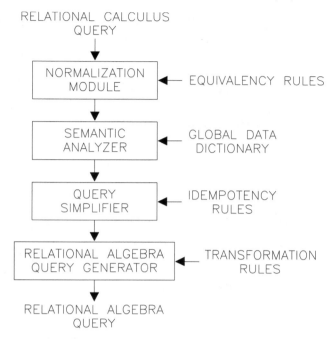

Figure 9.6 Query decomposer detail

this translation. Figure 9.6 shows the details of our query decomposer module.

The query decomposer module contains four submodules, one to perform each phase of the decomposition and translation process:

1. Normalization phase
2. Semantic analysis phase
3. Query simplification phase
4. Relational algebra query generation phase

Let us examine what's involved in the normalization phase.

The Normalization Module

The primary goal of the normalization module is to apply a set of rules called "equivalency transformation rules"[1,2] so that the projection and selection operations included in the query are simplified to avoid redundancy. Additionally, the order in which the selection predicates are processed is optimized. The projection operation corresponds to the SELECT clause in a SQL query; the selection operations correspond to the predicates found in the WHERE clause. Below are the equivalency transformation rules that are applied to each distributed query—where UNARYOP means a UNARY operation, BINOP = a BINARY operation, and REL1, REL2, and REL3 are relations.

1. **Commutativity of UNARY operations**

   ```
   UNARYOP1 UNARYOP2 REL <-> UNARYOP2 UNARYOP1 REL
   ```

2. **Commutativity of BINARY operations**

   ```
   REL1 BINOP (REL2 BINOP REL3)
           <-> (REL1 BINOP REL2) BINOP REL3
   ```

3. **Idempotency of UNARY operations**

   ```
   UNARYOP REL <-> UNARYOP1 UNARYOP2 REL
   ```

4. **Distributivity of UNARY operations with respect to BINARY operations**

   ```
   UNARYOP(REL1 BINOP REL2)
           <-> UNARYOP(REL1) BINOP UNARYOP(REL2)
   ```

5. **Factorization of UNARY operations**

   ```
   UNARYOP(REL1) BINOP UNARYOP(REL2)
           <-> UNARYOP(REL1 BINOP REL2)
   ```

The Semantic Analyzer

The purpose of this component is to examine the relational calculus query to make sure it contains only data objects that are defined in the distributed database catalog. By data objects, I mean tables, columns, views, and indexes that are part of the database. Additionally, the SA makes sure that each object in the query is referenced correctly according to its data type.

Below is a simple database catalog that contains information about a distributed database that contains only two relations:

```
DIST-TABLES:              DIST COLUMNS
TABLE NAME    SITE     COL NAME    TABLE     TYPE
T1            S1       C1          T1        CHAR
T2            S2       C2          T1        INT
                       C1          T2        CHAR
                       C2          T2        INT
                       C3          T2        CHAR
```

Below is a distributed SQL query submitted to the semantic analyzer for examination:

```
SELECT C1,C2,C3
FROM T1,T3
WHERE     T1.C1 = T2.C1
AND       C2 > 'London'
```

The FROM clause contains an error—table T3 is not in the DIST TABLES catalog; therefore, the query is referencing an object that does not exist. The WHERE clause also contains an error—the predicate C2 > 'London' contains a column defined as an integer data type. The predicate is attempting to test it against a character string value. The semantic analyzer will reject the query and return an error together with an explanation message.

The Query Simplifier

Assuming that the semantic analyzer did not reject the query, the next phase in the processing of the query is to submit it to the query simplifier module so that any redundant clauses in the distributed relational calculus query can be eliminated. This step is implemented by applying the following 10 rules, called idempotency rules:[1,2]

1. PRED AND PRED <—> PRED
2. PRED OR PRED <—> PRED
3. PRED AND TRUE <—> PRED
4. PRED OR FALSE <—> PRED
5. PRED AND FALSE <—> FALSE
6. PRED OR TRUE <—> TRUE
7. PRED AND NOT(PRED) <—> FALSE

8. PRED OR NOT(PRED) <—> TRUE
9. PRED1 AND (PRED1 OR PRED2) <—> PRED1
10. PRED1 OR (PRED1 AND PRED2) <—> PRED1

Let's modify our global distributed query introduced in Section 9.2 by applying some extra predicates:

```
SELECT DEPT.DEPT_ID,BMGR.BRANCH_MGR,
       BRANCH.BRANCH_ID,BRANCH.BRANCH_LOCATION,
       EMP.EMP_NAME,EMP.EMP_SALARY
FROM DEPT,EMP,BMGR,BRANCH
WHERE     DEPT.DEPT_ID = BMGR.DEPT_ID
      AND     BMGR.BRANCH_ID = BRANCH.BRANCH_ID
      AND     BMGR.BRANCH_MGR = EMP.EMP_ID
      AND     BRANCH.BRANCH_LOCATION = 'Cirencester' ———-+
      AND NOT(BRANCH.BRANCH_LOCATION = 'Cirencester'          +—- 1
              AND BRANCH.BRANCH_LOCATION = 'Edinburgh')   —+
      AND BRANCH.PROFITS_TO_DATE > 2,000,000.00
      AND EMP.EMP_SALARY > 50,000.00
      AND NOT(BRANCH.BRANCH_LOCATION = 'Edinburgh')
      AND DEPT.DEPT_LOCATION = 'London')
```

Let's examine the qualification predicate labeled 1 in closer detail:

```
      AND     BRANCH.BRANCH_LOCATION = 'Cirencester'
      AND NOT(BRANCH.BRANCH_LOCATION = 'Cirencester' AND
              BRANCH.BRANCH_LOCATION = 'Edinburgh')
```

Let BRANCH.BRANCH_LOCATION = 'Cirencester' = PRED1
Let BRANCH.BRANCH_LOCATION = 'Cirencester' = PRED2
Let BRANCH.BRANCH_LOCATION = 'Edinburgh' = PRED3

Our query now looks like this:

```
PRED1 AND NOT(PRED2 AND PRED3)
```

The normalizer module receives these predicates and applies rule 2 of the equivalency rules to obtain the following form:

```
(PRED1 AND (NOT(PRED1)) AND NOT(PRED3)
```

The normalizer module now applies rule 7 of the idempotency rules and obtains this next form:

```
FALSE AND NOT(PRED3)
```

The above form is equivalent to:

```
NOT(PRED3)
```

Translating the WHERE predicate into SQL, our WHERE clause (without the JOINS) looks like this:

```
NOT(BRANCH.BRANCH_LOCATION = 'Edinburgh')
AND BRANCH.PROFITS_TO_DATE > 2,000,000.00
AND EMP.EMP_SALARY > 50,000.00
AND NOT(BRANCH.BRANCH_LOCATION = 'Edinburgh')
```

But predicates 1 and 4 are identical! The simplifier module applies idempotency rule 1 to obtain the following form:

```
NOT(BRANCH.BRANCH_LOCATION = 'Edinburgh')
AND BRANCH.PROFITS_TO_DATE > 2,000,000.00
AND EMP.EMP_SALARY > 50,000.00
```

Notice how the application of the idempotency rules and the equivalency rules (in the normalization step) greatly simplifies the query. The final form of the SQL query looks like this:

```
SELECT DEPT.DEPT_ID,BMGR.BRANCH_MGR,
       BRANCH.BRANCH_ID,BRANCH.BRANCH_LOCATION,
       EMP.EMP_NAME,EMP.EMP_SALARY
FROM DEPT,EMP,BMGR,BRANCH
WHERE     DEPT.DEPT_ID = BMGR.DEPT_ID
    AND       BMGR.BRANCH_ID = BRANCH.BRANCH_ID
    AND       BMGR.BRANCH_MGR = EMP.EMP_ID
    AND NOT(BRANCH.BRANCH_LOCATION = 'Edinburgh')
    AND BRANCH.PROFITS_TO_DATE > 2,000,000.00
    AND EMP.EMP_SALARY > 50,000.00
    AND DEPT.DEPT_LOCATION = 'London'
```

This section was meant to illustrate how the simplifier module (with help from the normalizer module) improved a query that was submitted by a naive user. The query contained many redundant predicates that were eliminated without changing the semantics of the query.

Let us now proceed to see how the relational calculus query is transformed into a relational algebra query.

Relational Algebra Query Generator

At this phase we must recall that we are still processing a relational calculus query that refers to the global relations. The steps required to generate a relational algebra version of the query that will be used are the same as those in Özsu and Valduriez.[1] At the end of this process we will have generated a relational algebra query from the relational calculus query. *Note:* This query will still be referring to the global relations.

Basically, two steps are involved in this process. The first is to translate the relational calculus query into a structure called a relational algebra tree.[1] Several trees can be generated in this step.

The second step of this process is to apply six transformation rules to the set of generated relational algebra trees so as to pick the best one. Below are these transformation rules.[1,2]

Transformation Rules

Given three relations REL1, REL2, and REL3, CP = Cartesian product.

Rule 1   Commutativity of binary operations

```
REL1 CP REL2 <-> REL2 CP REL1
REL1 JOIN REL2 <-> REL2 JOIN REL1
REL1 UNION REL2 <-> REL2 UNION REL1
```

Rule 2   Associativity of binary operations

```
(REL1 CP REL2) CP REL3 <-> REL1 CP (REL2 CP REL3)
(REL1 JOIN REL2) JOIN REL3 <-> REL1 JOIN (REL2 JOIN REL3)
```

Rule 3   Idempotency of unary operation

Assume a relation REL with attributes C1, C2, Cn; that is, REL = {C1,C2, . . . ,Cn}. Also assume that the set of attributes C' are a subset of C and the set of attributes C'' are also a subset of C and a subset of C'. Rule 3 states:

```
SELECT C' (SELECT C'' (REL)) <-> SELECT C'(REL)
```

Rule 4   Commuting selection with projection

```
PROJECT_C1,Cn(SELECT_PRED(Attr)(REL)) <->
PROJECT_C1,Cn(SELECT_PRED(Attr)(PROJECT_C1,Cn(REL)))
```

Rule 5   Commuting selection operations with binary operations

5.1   Commuting selection with Cartesian products

```
SELECT_PRED(Attri)( REL1 CP REL2 ) <->
 (SELECT_PRED(Attri)(REL1)) CP REL2
```

5.2 Commuting selection with Join

```
SELECT_PRED(Attri)(REL1 JOIN_JPRED(Attrj,Attrk) REL2)  <->
SELECT_PRED(Attri)(REL1) JOIN_JPRED(Attrj,Attrk) REL2
```

5.3 Commuting selection with Union operations

```
SELECT_PRED(Attri)(REL1 UNION REL2) <->
SELECT_PRED(Attri)(REL1) UNION SELECT_PRED(Attri)(REL2)
```

5.4 Commuting selection with Difference operation

```
SELECT_PRED(Attri)(REL1 DIFF REL2)  <->
SELECT_PRED(Attri)(REL1) DIFF SELECT_PRED(Attri)(REL2)
```

Rule 6   Commuting project with binary operations

For this final rule, let us assume the following:

1. REL1 AND REL2 are relations.
2. REL1 contains attributes REL1.C1,REL1.C2, . . . REL1,C3.
3. REL2 contains attributes REL2.C1,REL2.C2, . . . REL2,C3.
4. The set of attributes CREL1$'$ is a subset of relation REL1's attributes.
5. The set of attributes CREL2$'$ is a subset of relation REL2's attributes.
6. The set of attributes CREL = CREL1$'$ UNION CREL2$'$.

6.1 Projection and Cartesian product

```
PROJECT_CREL(REL1 CP REL2) <-> PROJECT_CREL1'(REL1) CP
PROJECT_CREL2'(REL2)
```

6.2 Projection and Join

```
PROJECT_CREL(REL1 JOIN_JPRED(REL1.Ci,REL2.Cj) REL2)  <->
PROJECT_CREL1'(REL1) JOIN_JPRED(REL1.Ci,REL2.Cj) PROJECT(REL2)
```

6.3 Projection and Union

```
PROJECT_CREL(REL1 UNION REL2)  <->  PROJECT_CREL(REL1)
UNION PROJECT_CREL(REL2)
```

With the introduction of these rules completed, let us generate two relational algebra query trees from our relational calculus query and then proceed to pick the best one. Figure 9.7 shows one of several possible trees that can be generated from our original SQL query.

The query tree shows that a Cartesian product is being executed between the EMP relation and the BRANCH relation. If the EMP relation contains 10,000 employees and the BRANCH relation contains 100 rows, this results in a temporary table with 100 by 10,000 or 1 million rows. This is clearly not a good strategy.

A second relational algebra query tree is shown in Figure 9.8. The query tree has replaced the Cartesian product operation with a join. It also pushed down the selection operations so that the intermediate result sets are reduced.

Application of the transformation rules allows the relational algebra trees to be restructured so that the "best" ones can be picked and

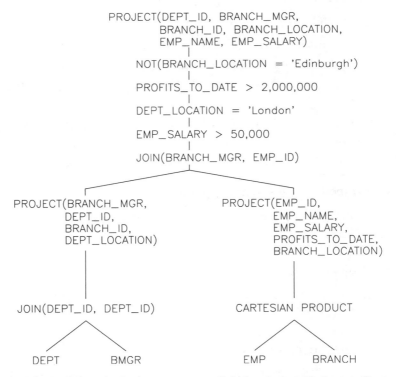

Figure 9.7 Relational algebra tree on global relations using a Cartesian product

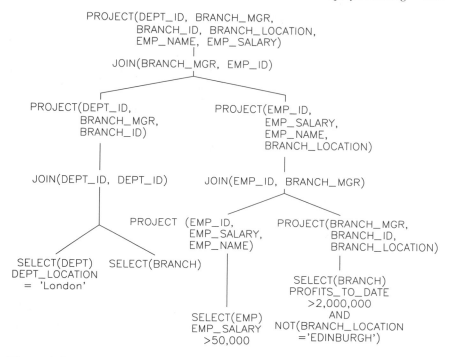

Figure 9.8 Relational algebra tree on global relations using JOINs

passed to the localizer module. We examine the functions performed at this component next.

9.6 THE QUERY OBJECT LOCALIZER

Figure 9.9 shows a block diagram of the query object localizer.

Recall that the first steps of the decomposition phase of a distributed query all take place on the relational calculus version of the query. The output of the third phase is the "best" version of a translated relational algebra tree.

We now want to localize the query by replacing the global relations with the relevant fragment relations that reside at each of the remote sites involved in the distributed query. One way of accomplishing this replacement is by simply substituting the reconstruction rules for each of the global relations. Below are the reconstruction rules for our distributed database that were introduced earlier in the chapter.

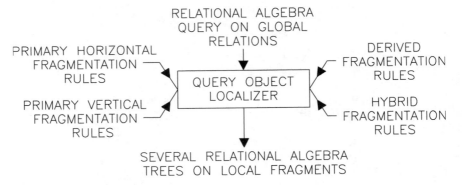

Figure 9.9 Query object localizer detail

Global Relation DEPT: (DEPT1,DEPT2,DEPT3)

```
DEPT1 = SELECT(DEPT) WHERE DEPT_LOCATION = 'London'
DEPT2 = SELECT(DEPT) WHERE DEPT_LOCATION = 'Edinburgh'
DEPT3 = SELECT(DEPT) WHERE DEPT_LOCATION = 'Cirencester'
```

The reconstruction formula for this global relation is DEPT = DEPT1 UNION DEPT2 UNION DEPT3. (Recall that horizontal fragmentation was used.)

Global Relation EMP: (EMP1,EMP2,EMP3)

```
EMP1 = SELECT(EMP) WHERE EMP_SALARY < 30,000.00
EMP2 = SELECT(EMP) WHERE 30,000.00 <= EMP_SALARY <= 50,000.00
EMP3 = SELECT(EMP) WHERE EMP_SALARY > 50,000.00
```

Global Relation BRANCH: (BRANCH1,BRANCH2,BRANCH3)

```
BRANCH1 = SELECT(BRANCH) WHERE PROFITS_TO_DATE < 1000000
BRANCH2 = SELECT(BRANCH)
               WHERE 1000000 <= PROFITS_TO_DATE <= 2000000
BRANCH3 = SELECT(BRANCH) WHERE PROFITS_TO_DATE > 2000000
```

Global Relation BMGR: (BMGR1,BMGR2,BMGR3)

```
BMGR1 = SELECT(BMGR) WHERE BRANCH_ID < 'B10'
BMGR2 = SELECT(BMGR) WHERE 'B10'<= BRANCH_ID <= 'B20'
BMGR3 = SELECT(BMGR) WHERE BRANCH_ID > 'B20'
```

Figure 9.10 shows the "best" relational algebra query tree with the global relations substituted with the required reconstruction formulas.

This version of the query is called the general or generalized version of the relational algebra query.[1] It is a naive approach in that

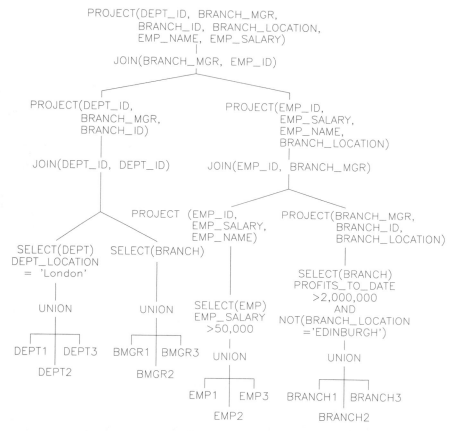

Figure 9.10 Relational algebra tree on local fragments (generalized tree)

there was a straight substitution of the global relations with the reconstruction formulas. In some situtations this is acceptable because the alternative is to perfrom several distributed joins, which is costly in terms of communication costs.

The localizer attempts to simplify the query by removing portions of the reconstruction formulas that contain contradictory predicates. Contradictory predicates are useless, as they produce no results. Figure 9.11 shows a simplified version of the query tree after the useless predicates have been removed.

Starting from left to right at the bottom of the tree we see the predicate "DEPT_LOCATION = 'London'." This predicate is equivalent to the predicate that was used to build the table fragment at site1, DEPT1. This is the predicate that is kept, as the other two fragments were built with predicates contrary to the predicate in our

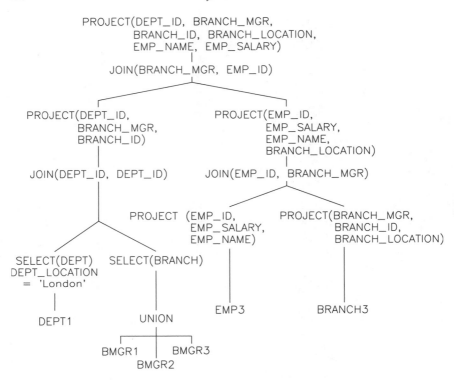

Figure 9.11 Optimized relational algebra query tree

tree. (Actually, this predicate is now unnecessary as table DEPT1 contains only rows with DEPT_LOCATION = 'LONDON'.)

Next, we see that the global relation BMGR was replaced with a UNION of the three table fragments BMGR1, BMGR2, and BMGR3. Since their reconstruction formulas are based on predicates that fragment BMGR horizontally via the values of the branch ID attribute, there is not much the localizer can do.

The third branch in the relational algebra tree involves the UNION of the table fragments EMP1, EMP2, EMP3. The reconstruction formulas are repeated below:

```
EMP1 = SELECT(EMP) WHERE EMP_SALARY < 30,000
EMP2 = SELECT(EMP) WHERE 30000 <= EMP_SALARY < 50000
EMP3 = SELECT(EMP) WHERE EMP_SALARY > 50000
```

Well, we must be lucky as a predicate exists in the relational algebra tree that states we want to process only rows whose EMP_SALARY attribute values are greater than 50,000. It just so happens that this predicate exactly matches the reconstruction formula for fragment EMP3. The other two fragments are eliminated from the algebra tree. The fourth and final subtree is made up of the reconstruction formula of the global relation BRANCH. Eliminating the contradictory predicates leaves us with fragment BRANCH3.

Notice how three of the four subtrees were simplified by the localizer. The only subtree that could not be simplified was the subtree that involved the BMGR fragments.

We now move on to the query optimizer. Although only one simplified relational algebra tree was generated in our example, several trees are usually generated. It is the job of the next module to select the best tree and submit it to the global scheduler.

9.7 THE QUERY OPTIMIZER

The last phase of processing prior to scheduling the global query is the optimization phase. Figure 9.12 shows a detailed block diagram of the query optimizer. There are four inputs to this module:

1. Several simplified relational algebra query trees generated by the simplifier module
2. Statistical data from the fragment database catalog
3. Estimation formulas used to determine the cardinality of the intermediate result tables
4. A communications cost model

Two outputs are generated by this module:

1. The optimized relational algebra query
2. A communications strategy for routing intermediate result sets and for processing distributed queries

Before discussing the process, let's examine each of the required inputs beginning with the communications cost model. Basically, the model involves the cost of initializing communications between the sites involved in the processing of the distributed query, transferring data to the sites, and terminating communications. For our purposes, the formulas we will use are

```
T(TOTAL COST) = T(LOGON) + T(TRANSMIT) + T(LOGOFF)
```

T = Total cost of the transmission
T(LOGON) = the cost of log on and initialization
T(TRANSMIT) = T(UNIT) * 10,000 bytes
T(UNIT) = cost per unit of transmission, assume 1
T(LOGOFF) = cost of logging off and ending communications

Assume that T(LOGON) and T(LOGOFF) each cost .5 units.

This is a very simple model but it suffices for our purposes; it is based on the model described in Özsu and Valduriez.[1]

Next, we concern ourselves with the estimation rules used for approximating the number of rows returned by qualifying predicates.[1-3] Associated with each predicate is a selectivity factor (SF for short) which, when multiplied by the number of rows in a table (its cardinality), gives an approximate value of the rows generated when the query is executed. The selectivity factor is a value between 0 and 1 and is defined as follows:

```
SF(FORMULA) = SELECT_FORMULA(RELATION)/CARD(RELATION)
Note: (if Attr = key)
     CARD(SELECT(RELATION)) = CARD(RELATION)
     CARD(SELECT_Attr(RELATION) = number of unique values
if Attr is not a key.
```

MAX(Attr) = largest attribute value in the attribute.
MIN(Attr) = smallest value found in the attribute.

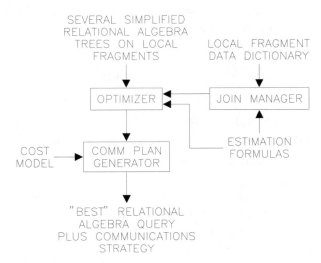

Figure 9.12 Query optimizer detail

Below are the formulas used for SELECTIVITY predicates:

```
SF(Attr = Value) = 1/(CARD(SELECTAttr(RELATION)))

SF(Attr > Value) = (MAX(Attr) - Value) /
                   (MAX(Attr) - MIN(Attr))

SF(Attr < Value) = (Value - MIN(Attr)) /
                   (MAX(Attr) - MIN(Attr))

SF(PRED(Attri) AND PRED(Attrj) =
 SF(PRED(attri)) * SF(PRED(Attrj))

SF(PRED(Attri) OR PRED(Attrj) =
 (SF(PRED(attri))+SF(PRED(Attrj))) - (SF(PRED(attri)) *
 SF(PRED(Attrj)))

SF( Attr IN(List of values)) =
 (SF(Attr = Value)) X (CARD([list of values]))
```

Selectivity factors for JOINs[1] use the following approximations:

```
CARD(R JOINAttr1 = Attr2 S) = CARD(R)

CARD(R JOIN S) = SF(JOIN) * CARD(R) * CARD(S)
```

Additionally, there are estimation formulas for Cartesian products and differences but we will not be concerned with them here. The reader is directed to one of the end notes in this section for further details.

Let us now continue by seeing how the optimizer applies the estimation formulas, cost model, and fragment statistics to our original "best" relational algebra tree and an optional but equivalent (in terms of semantics) relational algebra tree. Figure 9.13 shows the table fragment catalogs we will use.

For each table, the row cardinality is displayed; for each attribute in the table fragment the following information is displayed:

ATTRIBUTE	Name of the attribute
%UNIQUE	Percentage of unique values
LEN	Length of attribute in bytes
HKEY	The highest value in the attribute
LKEY	The lowest value in the attribute

ENTITY	CARD	ATTRIBUTES	%UNIQUE	LEN	HKEY	LKEY
DEPT 1	100	DEPT_ID	100	4	D100	D1
		DEPT_MGR	100	20	E100	E1
		DEPT_LOCATION	90	20	GLASGOW	ABERFELDY
		DEPT_NAME	100	20	DEPT100	DEPT01
		DEPT_NUM_EMP	100	2	100	2

ENTITY	CARD	ATTRIBUTES	%UNIQUE	LEN	HKEY	LKEY
EMP 3	10000	EMP_ID	100	4	E10000	E1
		EMP_NAME	95	20	ZELDA	ALLEN
		EMP_DEPT	80	4	D100	D1
		EMP_TITLE	20	20	MGR	COOK
		EMP_SALARY	90	12	80000	20000
		EMP_HIRE_DATE	70	8	12/01/92	01/01/80

ENTITY	CARD	ATTRIBUTES	%UNIQUE	LEN	HKEY	LKEY
BRANCH 3	500	BRANCH_ID	100	4	B500	B1
		DEPT_ID	20	4	D100	D1
		BRANCH_NAME	65	20	BR500	BR001
		BRANCH_LOCATION	50	20	GLASGOW	ABERFELDY
		PROFITS_TO_DATE	80	12	300000	20000
		BRANCH_MGR	100	4	E601	E101

ENTITY	CARD	ATTRIBUTES	%UNIQUE	LEN	HKEY	LKEY
BMGR 1	200	BRANCH_MGR	100	4	E300	E100
		DEPT_ID	20	4	D30	D1
		BRANCH_ID	100	4	B200	B1

ENTITY	CARD	ATTRIBUTES	%UNIQUE	LEN	HKEY	LKEY
BMGR 2	200	BRANCH_MGR	100	4	E501	E301
		DEPT_ID	20	4	D50	D31
		BRANCH_ID	100	4	B401	B201

ENTITY	CARD	ATTRIBUTES	%UNIQUE	LEN	HKEY	LKEY
BMGR 3	200	BRANCH_MGR	100	4	E702	E502
		DEPT_ID	20	4	D71	D51
		BRANCH_ID	100	4	B602	B102

Figure 9.13 Global fragment data dictionary

Furthermore, assume the following distribution of fragments: (->
means "distributed to")

```
DEPT1->SITE1     BMGR1->SITE4     EMP1->SITE3     BRANCH1->SITE4
DEPT2->SITE2     BMGR2->SITE5     EMP2->SITE1     BRANCH2->SITE2
DEPT3->SITE3     BMGR3->SITE6     EMP3->SITE2     BRANCH3->SITE3
```

Assume that the strategy implemented by the optimizer is to per-form the JOIN at the central global site. Let's calculate the cost for each fragment:

```
FROM/TO          # ROWS
DEPT1->GS        1/90*100 or about 2 rows.
TRANSMISSION COST
```

(2 * 66 bytes) = 132 bytes, cost is about 1 unit to log on and off. Total cost for this transmission is about 1 unit.

```
FROM/TO          # ROWS
BMGR1->GS        200 rows
TRANSMISSION COST
```

(200 * 16) = 3,200 bytes, approx .33 units + 1 unit = 1.3 units.

```
FROM/TO          # ROWS
BMGR2->GS        200 rows
TRANSMISSION COST
```

(200 * 16) = 3,200 bytes, approx .33 units + 1 unit = 1.3 units.

```
FROM/TO          # ROWS
BMGR3->GS        200 rows
TRANSMISSION COST
```

(200 * 16) = 3,200 bytes, approx .33 units + 1 unit = 1.3 units.
Note: Total cost is about 3 * 1.3 = 3.9 or about 4 units.

```
FROM/TO          #ROWS
EMP1->G2         10,000 rows
TRANSMISSION COST
```

(10,000 * 16 bytes) = 160,000 bytes = 10 units, 16 units + 1 unit = 17 units. (Watch out for this one!)

```
FROM/TO          # ROWS
BRANCH3->GS      500 rows
TRANSMISSION COST
```

(500 * (4 + 12 + 20)) = 18,000 bytes. About 2 units plus 1 unit = 3 units.

Let's assume that the communications network can transfer infor-mation at the rate of 10,000 bits/sec. We will call this unit a Transfer Time Unit (TTU). Therefore, to transmit 1 unit (10,000 bytes), the time delay is 10,000 bytes * 8 bits/byte = 80,000 bits; 80,000/10,000 = 8 sec.

It will take 8 seconds to transmit 10,000 bytes or 1 unit. The table below shows the elapsed times for each of the transfer rates calculated by our optimizer:

FROM/TO	# Units	# TTU's(sec)
DEPT1->GS	1	8
EMP1->GS	17	136
BRANCH3->GS	3	24
BMGR1->GS	1.3	8
BMGR2->GS	1.3	8
BMGR3->GS	1.3	8

Total approx. cost = 31 units, 136 sec (see note).

Note: Since these operations all occur in parallel, the largest elapsed time is 136 sec or about two minutes. The bottleneck in our strategy seems to be at site 2. Transmitting 10,000 rows takes two minutes. That means the query will take two minutes to process plus whatever local CPU time (which we have ignored). Also, 17 units is a fairly high transmission cost. (I warned you to look out for this!)

Figure 9.14 shows a portion of a relational algebra tree that represents an alternate strategy. This time, site 3 transfers table fragment BRANCH3 to SITE2 where a join is performed with fragment EMP3. Let's look at the statistics generated by this new strategy:

FROM/TO	# ROWS
BRANCH3->SITE2	500
TRANSMISSION COST	

(500 * 64 bytes) = 32,000 bytes. This equals 3 units + 1 unit = 4 units.

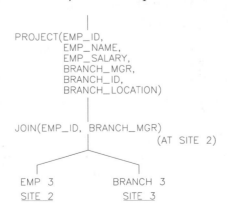

```
                        |
        PROJECT(EMP_ID,
                EMP_NAME,
                EMP_SALARY,
                BRANCH_MGR,
                BRANCH_ID,
                BRANCH_LOCATION)
                        |
        JOIN(EMP_ID, BRANCH_MGR)
                        |                (AT SITE 2)
                _____|_____
               |                 |
           EMP 3             BRANCH 3
           SITE 2             SITE 3
```

Figure 9.14 Optimized branch

```
FROM/TO            # ROWS
TEMP->GS           500  (see note)
TRANSMISSION COST
```

500 * (4+12+12+20) = 500 * 48 or 24,000 bytes. This comes to about 4 units.

```
FROM/TO            # UNITS      TTU (sec)
BRANCH3->SITE2     4            4 * 8 = 32 sec
TEMP->GS           2.5          2.5 * 8 = 20 sec
Total              6.5          42 sec
```

Look at this! This strategy reduces the cost from 17 units to 6.5 units, a savings of 10.5 units. Let's look at the elapsed time, as the data transfer had to be performed in two sequential operations.

Note 1:

```
CARD(BRANCH3 JOIN_EMP_ID = BRANCH_MGR EMP3) =
CARD(BRANCH3) = 500 rows.
```

Note 2:

The JOIN at site 3 produces 500 rows. This strategy not only proves to be cheaper in terms of transmission unit cost but also in elapsed time. The time was reduced by two-thirds.

The optimizer would have received this strategy as one of the several relational algebra trees. After applying the cost model formulas, estimation formulas, and fragment statistics it would have chosen this strategy as the best—not the one we thought was the best earlier! The communication and execution strategies for the query are as follows:

1. At SITE1, TDEPT = SELECT(DEPT1) WHERE DEPT_LOCA-TION = 'London'.

2. Transfer TDEPT1 to global site GS.

3. Transfer BMGR1 to GS.

4. Transfer BMGR2 to GS.

5. Transfer BMGR3 to GS.

6. At GS, perform TBMGR = BMGR1 UNION BMGR2 UNION BMGR3.

7. Transfer BRANCH3 to site 3.

8. Perform BRANCH3 JOIN EMP3 at SITE3.

9. At site 3, TEMP3 = PROJECT(EMP_ID,EMP_SALARY,PROF-ITS_TO_DATE,BRANCH_LOCATION).

10. Send TEMP3 to global site GS.

11. At GS, JOIN TDEPT1 with TBMGR and produce TEMP1.

12. At GS, JOIN TEMP1 with TEMP3 and produce TEMP.

13. PROJECT from TEMP, EMP_ID,DEPT_LOCATION, EMP_SALARY,BRANCH_ID,PROFITS_TO_DATE, and BRANCH_LOCATION.

14. Send results to user.

15. Erase all temporary tables.

Let's now look at the last phase of a distributed query process, the local optimization phase.

9.8 THE LOCAL QUERY OPTIMIZER

Optimization not only occurs in the central site of the distributed database management system but also occurs at each of the local sites involved in the distributed query. At this phase, information such as index availability and local database statistics can be used to optimize the query fragments.

Figure 9.15 shows a detailed block diagram of the final component of our model, the local optimizer. Input to this module is the simplified, optimized relational algebra query that is based on one or more of the fragment relations at the local site. Two other inputs, the

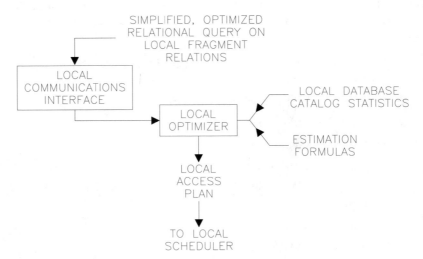

Figure 9.15 Local optimizer detail

estimation formulas and the local database catalog statistics, are used to optimize the query. From these inputs the local optimizer generates an access plan that is submitted to the local scheduler for processing. At this stage the techniques described in Chapter 5 are used to generate a local optimized query. The reader is referred back to that chapter for the details.

9.9 SUMMARY

This chapter showed how a generic distributed database system processed a query on multiple distributed fragment relations. The model used was similar to the model described in Özsu and Valduriez.[1] The queries were submitted to a central site where they were checked for syntax, simplified, and optimized to include communication primitives based on a specific cost model. The queries were read-only and did not involve updating of any relations at the remote sites. Since today's distributed systems allow transactions that update one or more distributed tables, we need to expand our model to allow for this capability. This is the topic of Chapter 10, where we discuss distributed transaction processing.

9.10 END NOTES

1. Özsu, M. Tamer, and P. Valduriez. *Principles of Distributed Database Systems*, Englewood Cliffs, NJ: Prentice Hall, 1991.

2. Ceri, S., and G. Pelagatti. *Distributed Databases: Principles and Systems*, New York: McGraw-Hill, 1984.

3. Selinger, P. G., M. M. Astrahan, D. D. Chamberlin, R. A. Lorie, and T. G. Price. "Access Path Selection in a Relational Database Management System," *Proceedings of the ACM SIGMOD International Conference on Management of Data*, Boston, MA (May 1979): pp. 23–24.

10

Transaction Processing, Concurrency, and Deadlocks in Distributed Architectures

10.1 INTRODUCTION

Now that we have studied the basics of distributed database design and have examined the components of a distributed database management system, it is time to discuss how distributed transactions are processed in this architecture.

This chapter is dedicated to the topics of transaction processing, concurrency in distributed systems, and the detection and resolution of deadlocks in distributed environments. Recall that concurrency was examined in centralized database management systems in Chapter 5. I will expand on those discussions so as to make them applicable in a distributed environment.

The chapter begins with a review of general transaction concepts—that is, what is a transaction? What are the general properties of a transaction? Next, two distributed transactions are shown and translated to their primitive read and write operations so that concurrent execution strategies can be studied. The reader will see how the primitive operations are manipulated by schedulers to generate what the literature calls schedules or histories.

Next, concurrency issues are covered. This includes the necessary conditions for local and then global transaction serialization. The two-phase locking protocol is reviewed again, as it is a mechanism that guarantees the correctness of local and global serializable executions. We will see how the use of the two-phase locking protocol leads to local and distributed deadlock conditions.

Deadlock resolution in a centralized database management system was discussed in Chapter 5. In this chapter we examine how distributed deadlocks are resolved by discussing several strategies that are currently popular in the literature.

The chapter concludes with a study of the two-phase and three-phase commit protocols viewed from the transaction's point of reference. A general architecture is introduced in Section 10.9 that is similar to distributed architectures in the literature.The role of each component will be examined. Chapter 11 will concentrate on the recovery components of this architecture and the strategies that will be used to ensure that distributed transactions maintain database serializability. Let us proceed by reviewing the general properties of transactions.

10.2 REVIEW OF CLASSICAL TRANSACTION PROCESSING

Recall from the earlier discussions that a transaction is a collection of read and write operations treated as a single atomic action. For the transaction to commit, all of the operations must complete successfully. If only one operation fails, the entire transaction fails. Below is a transaction that updates columns in several table rows by incrementing their values by 100:

```
BEGIN_TRANSACTION T1:
READ(TABLE = T1,ROW = 10, OBJECT = COL1);
:COL1 = COL1 + 100;
WRITE(TABLE = T1, ROW = 10, OBJECT = COL1, VALUE = :COL1);

READ(TABLE = T2,ROW = 10, OBJECT = COL2);
:COL2 = COL2 + 100;
WRITE(TABLE = T2, ROW = 20, OBJECT = COL2, VALUE = :COL2);

READ(TABLE = T3,ROW = 30, OBJECT = COL3);
:COL3 = COL3 + 100;
WRITE(TABLE = T3, ROW = 30, OBJECT = COL3, VALUE = :COL3);
END_OF_TRANSACTION1;
```

Note: The variables :COLx store data in memory. This convention of prefixing the variable name with a colon is similar to the convention used in languages that support embedded SQL.

Basically, the transaction is divided into three pairs of read and write operations; each reads a column's value from a table, increments it by a given amount, and proceeds to write the new value back into the column before proceeding to the next table. Let's examine the properties that a transaction should have to ensure that a database remains in a stable state after the transaction is executed.

The literature lists the following four poperties that a transaction must have to guarantee the above requirements:

1. ATOMICITY Property

   A transaction must execute and complete each operation in its logic before it commits its changes. As stated earlier, the transaction behaves as if it were one operation, even if it includes multiple reads, writes, and other operations.

2. CONSISTENCY Property

   Execution of a transaction must leave a database in either its prior stable state or a new stable state that reflects the new modifications made by the transaction. In other words, if the transaction fails, the database must be returned to the state it was in prior to the execution of the failed transaction. If the transaction commits, the database must reflect the new changes.

3. ISOLATION Property

   The transaction must act as if it is the only one running against the database. It acts as if it owned its own copy and could not affect other transactions executing against their own copies of the database. No other transaction is allowed to see the changes made by a transaction until the transaction safely terminates and returns the database to a new stable or prior stable state. (This depends on whether or not the transaction committed or aborted its changes.)

4. DURABILITY Property

   This last property states that the changes made by a transaction are permanent. They cannot be lost by either a system failure or by the erroneous operation of a faulty transaction.

The literature refers to these four properties as the ACID properties or the ACIDITY of a transaction.

Let us continue by formally defining a transaction. I will follow the notation used in the literature to denote the individual operations of a transaction.

Ti = some transaction; i is the current number of the transaction.

Ri = read operation belonging to transaction i.

Wi = write operation belonging to transaction i.

x, y, and z are objects manipulated by a transaction operation (i.e., rows, columns, and so on).

$Ri(x)$ = read operation performed on object x.

$Wi(x)$ = write operation performed on object x.

$WLi(x)$ = transaction i requests a write lock on object x.

$RLi(x)$ = transaction i requests a read lock on object x.

Ceri and Pelagatti[1] define a transaction as the union of the read set and write set that make up the operations of the transaction. With this notation and Ceri and Pelagatti's definition in mind, let's introduce two transactions, T1 and T2:

```
T1 = R1(x),W1(x),R1(y),W1(z)
T2 = R2(x),R2(y),R2(z),W2(x)
```

The read and write set (denoted by SETR, SETW) of transaction T1 is

```
SETR(T1) = {R1(x),R1(y)}
SETW(T1) = {W1(x),W1(z)}
```

Therefore, using Ceri and Pelagatti's[1] definition, a transaction Ti = SETR(i) UNION SETW(i). In our case, T1 = SETR(1) UNION SETW(1). Quickly looking at transaction T2, the read and write sets are as follows:

```
SETR(T2) = {R2(x),R2(y),R2(z)}
SETW(T2) = {W2(x)}
```

Formally, T2 = SETR(T2) UNION SETW(T2). Although this exercise is fairly obvious, it sets the stage for the definitions and requirements for ensuring local and then global serializability, which is required to ensure correct concurrent execution of multiple transactions. Let's continue by examining some more definitions and terminology used in the literature to prove concurrent execution strategies. Recall our two simple transactions T1 and T2. If operations are collected together as a set, that set is called a schedule:

```
S = {R1(x),W1(x),R1(y),W1(z),R2(x),R2(y),R2(z),W2(x)}
```

The above is a serial schedule because the transaction will execute one after the other. As can be seen, all the operations of transaction T1 precede the operations of transaction T2. They are not interleaved and, therefore, they do not conflict with each other. In our case, transaction T2 executes immediately after transaction T1. Although this execution schedule is correct, it does not take advantage of concurrency and leads to poor performance if multiple transactions are received at any site.

Concurrency control mechanisms attempt to interleave read and write operations of multiple transactions so that the interleaved execution yields results that are identical to the results of a serial schedule execution. (This interleaving creates the impression that the transactions are executing concurrently.)

Now that these basic concepts have been introduced, let's examine the issues and solutions that surround concurrency in local and distributed systems.

10.3 CONCURRENCY ISSUES

In this section we will examine the conditions necessary for ensuring correct execution of transaction schedules, the conditions necessary to ensure correctness for both local and global serializability transaction schedules, and the role that the two-phase locking protocol plays in enforcing the correctness requirements. We saw in Chapter 5 how the use of two-phase locking leads to a phenomenon called deadlock. This phenomenon is also experienced in distributed architectures and its detection and resolution will be discussed in Section 10.6.

Let us introduce another definition that is used in the literature. Recall that a serial schedule is an ordering of operations belonging to multiple transactions that appear one after the other. Recall from the prior section, schedule S:

```
S = {R1(x),W1(x),R1(y),W1(z),R2(x),R2(y),R2(z),W2(x)}
```

Another way to denote this sequence of executions is by the execution order T1,T2. Ceri and Pelagatti[1] refer to this series as SERIAL(S). In our case SERIAL(S) = T1,T2. This definition is used by Ceri and Pelagatti to define the correctness requirements for a schedule. Recall that the execution of a serial execution does not exploit concurrency in a system.

As we want to exploit concurrency, we want a mechanism that produces a schedule that permits concurrent executions of the individual transaction operations. For this concurrent execution to be correct, it must be equivalent to a serial execution. (Let us denote this schedule as Sc for a concurrent schedule.) Therefore, we want Sc = SERIAL(S). This is the requirement stated in Ceri and Pelagatti. A schedule that permits concurrent operations must have the same effect as if those operations were executed in a serial schedule!

With this in mind, let us introduce what the literature calls conflicting operations. Two operations conflict if

1. They operate on the same data object.
2. Either or both of the operations is a write operation.
3. Each operation belongs to a different transaction.

Below are some examples of conflicting operations for two transactions, T1 and T2:

1. W1(x),W2(x) (Two writes on same data object by different transactions)
2. W1(x),R2(x) (A write and a read on same data item by different transactions)
3. R1(x),W2(x) (A read and a write on same data item by different transactions)

Let's recall our original serial schedule and identify the conflicting operations:

```
S = {R1(x),W1(x),R1(y),W1(z),R2(x),R2(y),R2(z),W2(x)}
```

The conflicting operations are:

```
R1(x),W2(x)
W1(x),R2(x)
W1(x),W2(x)
W1(z),R2(z)
```

Assume that transaction 1 performs the following actions:

```
Transaction 1
R1(x)
x = x + 5;
W1(x);
R1(y);
z = x + y;
W1(z);
```

Assume that transaction 2 performs these actions:

```
Transaction 2
R2(x);
R2(y)
R2(z);
x = x + y + z;
W2(x);
```

In the case of the serial schedule, the conflicting operations pose no problem because the two transactions execute serially; that is, all the operations of T1 precede all the operations of T2. This is great but as stated earlier, it does not exploit concurrent execution!

Recall that concurrent execution strategies attempt to generate nonserial execution schedules that are equivalent to serial schedules. The criterion required for this goal is that the order of conflicting operations be equivalent in both the serial schedule and the nonserial concurrent schedule. Below is a schedule that exploits concurrency:

```
S = R1(x),W1(x),R1(y),R2(x),W1(z),R2(y),R2(z),W2(x)
```

The asterisks show which operations can be executed in parallel:

```
T1 = R1(x),W1(x),R1(y)*,W1(z)*
T2 =                 R2(x)*,R2(y)*,R2(z),W2(x)
```

That is, R1(y) and R2(x) can be executed concurrently and so can W1(z) and R2(y).

Recall the conflicting operations:

```
R1(x),W2(x)
W1(x),R2(x)
W1(x),W2(x)
W1(z),R2(z)
```

Is the order of conflicting operations maintained in the schedule? Let's introduce another common notation used in the literature to show that an operation precedes another operation:

```
Rm(x) < Wn(x)
```

Here, the read operation for a transaction *m* precedes the write operation for transaction *n* on the same object.

In our example, $R1(x) < W2(x)$ in the new schedule; and $W1(x) < R2(x)$. $W1(x)$ precedes $W2(x)$ and $W1(z)$ precedes $R2(z)$. We were able to exploit concurrency by executing operations $R1(y)$ and $R2(x)$ and $W1(z)$ and $R2(y)$ concurrently. The example proves that the order of the conflicting operations in the new schedule follows the order of the conflicting operations in the serial schedule. Since this condition is satisfied, the nonserial schedule is equivalent to the serial schedule; that is, when both schedules are executed they produce the same results on the database.

The literature states that a schedule is correct if it is serializable; that is, the order of its conflicting operations is the same as the order of the same operations if they appear in a serial schedule. Is this criterion sufficient for a distributed architecture? As luck would have it, no! Fortunately, there is only one additional requirement and I discuss it as it appears in Ceri and Pelagatti.[1]

Criteria to Ensure Serializability of Transactions

Ceri and Pelagatti discuss another term called a TOTAL ORDERING. The total ordering of transactions is simply the listing of the order of the distributed transactions that are to execute at the distributed sites (I will refer to this definition as "TO").

For example, if we have four distributed transactions and each of the four has operations that execute at three sites, the total ordering for these transactions is

```
TO = T1,T2,T3,T4
```

Each of the three sites has a schedule that exploits concurrent execution of the operations belonging to T1, T2, T3, and T4. We will refer to the schedules as S1, S2, and S3.

Recall that for the execution of the schedules that exploit concurrency to be correct, they must be equivalent to a serial schedule. In our case, we define three serial schedules: S1′, S2′, S3′. Assume the following conditions are true:

```
S1' = SERIAL(S1)
S2' = SERIAL(S2)
S3' = SERIAL(S2)
```

The requirement that guarantees serial execution of distributed transactions states that the order of the conflicting operations in the serial schedules S1′, S2′, and S3′ must be in the same order as the operations that belong to the transactions in the total order TO that was specified earlier. That is, if operation OP1(X) precedes OP2(x) in the total order, then this same order must appear in any of the serial schedules at the sites that execute transactions T1 and T2.

To ensure this ordering in systems that execute nonconflicting operations in parallel, locking mechanisms are used to ensure that transactions that attempt to access data objects currently being accessed by another transaction are forced to wait. Let us briefly review the two-phase locking protocol from Chapter 5 and show how it can lead to deadlock when executing distributed transactions.

10.4 REVIEW OF THE TWO-PHASE LOCKING PROTOCOL

In Chapter 5 we saw how one of the solutions for maintaining transaction concurrency was to implement a scheme whereby locks are placed on data objects that are to be manipulated by a transaction.

Recall that two types of locks were identified: a read lock and a write lock. Certain locks are compatible. This means that more than one transaction can place a lock on the same object.

A read lock is compatible with another read lock. If transaction T1 requests a read lock on object X and transaction T2 already has a read lock on object X, T1 is granted the lock anyway. If either or both of the transactions have requested a write lock on the object, a conflict occurs and one of the transactions is denied the lock request. (This is how the ordering of conflicting operations is enforced.)

The literature states that concurrent algorithms that use the two-phase locking protocol guarantee correct and serial execution of concurrent transactions. Recall that there are two phases to this protocol: the growing phase and the shrinking phase.

The first, the "growing phase," is where all the locks required by a transaction are obtained. The second phase is where all the locks that were previously obtained are released by the transaction. The two-phase rule states that once a transaction has released a lock, it cannot obtain another. Furthermore, it has been shown and proven in the literature that schedulers that follow the two-phase locking protocol always produce serial execution histories.

Situations arise where two transactions request the same lock. Both of these transactions might also possess a lock on a data object that the other transaction requires. Neither transaction will give up its current lock until it obtains a lock on the object it needs.

This situation is called deadlock and cannot be resolved unless it is terminated by an outside process.

Recall the example in Chapter 5 where transaction T1 had a write lock on data object X. T1 needed a write lock on object Y and would not release the lock on X until it had obtained it.

Transaction T2 had a write lock on Y and needed a write lock on object Z. It also would not release the write lock on Y until it got its write lock on Z. Finally, transaction T3 had a write lock on object Z that transaction T2 required. Transaction T3 needed a write lock on item X. Transaction T1 had a write lock on object X and would not give it up. The transactions remained permanently blocked because of their greediness. An outside process had to be introduced to break the deadlock cycle.

The remedy to the above deadlock scenario was a background process called a deadlock detector. It used a data structure called a WAIT-FOR-GRAPH that enabled it to spot transactions involved in deadlocks. By spotting cycles in the graph, it was able to detect which transactions generated the cycles. It then aborted one or more of the transactions to eliminate the cycles and, therefore, the deadlocks.

Section 10.6 will examine the detection and resolution of deadlocks in a distributed database environment. We will see that the two-phase locking protocol is not powerful enough to resolve deadlocks in a distributed environment. A way of building global WAIT-FOR-GRAPHS or letting each site involved in a distributed transaction know about its potential participation in a distributed deadlock is required.

10.5 DISTRIBUTED CONCURRENCY CONTROL STRATEGIES

Now that we have reviewed the two-phase locking protocol, let's see what effect its use has on transactions executing in a distributed environment. For our discussions, let us assume the following scenario is about to transpire at the Traditional Fish 'n' Chips enterprise described earlier.

Two of the branch sites in the company usually lend each other cases of frozen chips when one or the other's inventory supply runs low. Assume that site 1 has just received a request from site 2 for 100 cases of frozen chips. Site 1 must find out how much inventory is in stock, deduct 100 cases from it, and update its database to reflect the transfer. (The initial stock level is at 500 cases.) The transaction must then update site 2's database to reflect the transfer of the stock. The following transaction has been coded by one of the programmers at site 1 to perform this task:

```
// Update Inventory Transaction executed at Site 1
// Transaction UIT1
// Initial Inventory level = 500 cases
UIT1(XFER_AMT = 100)
READ(S1_INV_AMT);
S1_INV_AMT = S1_INV_AMT - 100;
WRITE(S1_INV_AMT);
READ(S2_INV_AMT); // READ INVENTORY AMOUNT AT SITE 2
S2_INV_AMT = S2_INV_AMT + XFER_AMT; // LOAN SITE 2
                                    // 100 CASES
WRITE(S2_INV_AMT);
EOT UIT1;
```

The transaction begins by reading its current stock level, decreases it by 100 cases, and updates the local stock level to reflect the transfer of the cases. Site 1 now has 400 cases left in its inventory. Next, transaction 1 reads the inventory level at site 2, increases the level by the 100 cases it has loaned its partner site, and updates the remote site's database. Site 2 originally had 400 cases in its inventory. It now has 500 cases! Let's simplify transaction T1 by using the notation currently popular in the literature.

Assume:

```
READ(S1_INV_AMT)  = R1(x)
WRITE(S1_INV_AMT) = W1(x)
READ(S2_INV_AMT)  = R1(y)
WRITE(S2_INV_AMT) = W1(y)
```

Transaction UIT1 now reads as follows:

```
UIT1 = R1(x),W1(x),R1(y),W2(y)
```

If the lock request operations are included, transaction UIT1 looks like this:

```
UIT1=RL1(x),R1(x),WL1(x),W1(x),RL1(y),R1(y),WL1(y),WL1(y),C
```

[Recall that RL*i*(x) means transaction *i* requests a read lock on object x; WL*i*(x) means transaction *i* requests a write lock on object (x). A read or write lock requested before each operation and each transaction must end with a commit operation (C).]

Let's further complicate our scenario by adding the following events. At the same time site 1 is transferring the 100 cases to site 2, a diligent manager at site 2 decides to pay back site 1 the 50 cases that were borrowed last month!

A programmer at site 2 builds the following program to accomplish the transaction:

```
// Update Inventory Transaction executed at Site 2
// Transaction UIT2
// Initial Inventory level = 400 cases
UIT2(XFER_AMT = 50)
READ(S2_INV_AMT);
S2_INV_AMT = S2_INV_AMT - 50;
WRITE(S2_INV_AMT);
READ(S1_INV_AMT); // READ INVENTORY AMOUNT AT SITE 1
S1_INV_AMT = S1_INV_AMT + XFER_AMT; // LOAN SITE 1
50 CASES
WRITE(S1_INV_AMT);
EOT UIT2;
```

This transaction operates in exactly the same logic as the one that is about to be executed at site 1. The transaction begins by reading its current inventory level. From this it deducts 50 cases and writes the new lower inventory amount back to the database. Next, it reads the inventory level at site 1, increases it by the 50 cases, and writes the new amount back into site 1's database. Using the simplifed notation, transaction UIT2 looks like this:

```
UIT2 = R2(y),W2(y),R2(x),W2(x)
```

If the lock request operations are included, transaction UIT2 reads as follows:

```
UIT2=RL2(y),R2(y),WL2(y),W2(y),RL2(x),R2(x),WL2(x),W2(x),C
```

Notice what is happening. Each site is simultaneously updating its own database and each other's database. Assume the following operations occur in parallel:

	Site 1	Site 2
1.	R1(x)	R2(y)
2.	W1(x)	W2(y)
3.	R2(x)	R1(y)
4.	W2(x)	W1(y)

Recall that the two-phase locking protocol is being used. The first two operations at sites 1 and 2, respectively, request a read lock and a write lock on the objects that each owns. Site 1 now has a read lock and a write lock on object x. It will need to obtain a read lock and a write lock on object y at site 2. Concurrently at site 2, the transaction has successfully obtained a read and write lock on object y. It now proceeds to request a read lock on object x at site 1. The request is denied as the transaction at site 1 now owns a read lock and a write lock on object x. The transaction at site 2 is now suspended and cannot proceed until the transaction at site 1 releases the locks it has acquired on object x. The transaction at site 1 now requests a read lock and a write lock on object y at site 2 but is denied because transaction 2 at site 2 already owns a read and write lock on object y.

Both transactions are deadlocked, as neither can release its original locks without violating the two-phase locking rule: "No transaction can release a lock until all required locks have been obtained!"

Let's take a look at a WAIT-FOR-GRAPH that illustrates the scenario that has just unfolded. (See Figure 10.1a.) Notice that at site 1 transaction UIT2 is waiting for UIT1 and at site 2 UIT1 is waiting patiently for transaction UIT2 to complete. This seems innocent enough but the dashed lines show that there is a cycle between site 1 and site 2. Figure 10.1b shows this cycle.

Notice that each site is blissfully unaware of the deadlock cycle. As far as each site is concerned, there is no deadlock in each of the local WAIT-FOR-GRAPHS, so they just happily sit there waiting for each other to release their locks so that they can acquire the locks on the other objects they need. An external force or some strategy is required to break this deadly deadlock stalemate!

We will examine some strategies to remedy this situation in the next section of this chapter. Let's discuss this scenario a bit further.

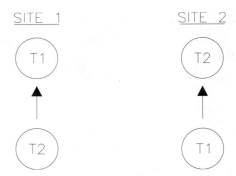

Figure 10.1a Local view of the WAIT-FOR-GRAPHS

If two-phase locking were not being used, the following two sequences of events could have occurred at each site:

Sequence 1

Site 1	Site 2
x = 500	y = 400
R1 (x)	R2 (y)
x = x − 100	y = y − 50
W1 (x)	W2 (y)
R2 (x)	R1 (y)
x = x + 50	y = y + 100
W2 (x)	W1 (y)

x now equals 500 − 100 + 50 = 450
y now equals 400 − 50 + 100 = 450

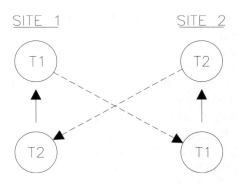

Figure 10.1b WAIT-FOR-GRAPHS showing deadlock

Sequence 2

Site 1	Site 2
x = 500	y = 400
R2(x)	R1(y)
x = x + 50	y = y − 100
W2(x)	W1(y)
R1(x)	R2(y)
x = x − 100	y = y − 50
W1(x)	W2(y)

x now equals 500 + 50 − 100 = 450
y now equals 400 + 100 − 50 = 450

Notice that both execution orders yield the same results when the transactions complete. In this situation, two-phase locking is unnecessary! As a matter of fact, it hampers the execution of the transactions by causing them to go into deadlock.

We cannot completely forget about using the two-phase locking protocol; there are many situations in which its omission could cause incorrect execution of transactions, resulting in database corruption. However, as the reader saw in our example, there are times when the two-phase locking protocol is unnecessary. Notice that our two transactions used similar operations; that is, they both performed decrement and increment operations on the database. Since these operations commute, it doesn't matter in what order they are executed. Even though their primitive read and write operations might conflict as far as the two-phase locking protocol is concerned, the higher-level operations that we just saw can be performed in any order without danger of corrupting the database. Knowing whether or not these types of operations are present in the transaction can assist in the execution of distributed transactions by selectively relaxing the two-phase locking protocol restrictions. The literature recognizes this as the "semantics" of a transaction. In our example, the transactions can be rewritten as follows:

```
UIT1 = R1(x),DECR(x by 100),W1(x)
       R1(y),INCR(y by 100),W1(y)

UIT2 = R2(y),DECR(y by 50),W2(y)
       R1( y),INCR(x by 50),W2(x)
```

Many sources and papers exist that discuss the use of the semantic knowledge of a transaction in a distributed environment for the purpose of increasing the concurrent execution of subtransactions and their interleaved operations at distributed sites. I refer the reader to a paper by Garcia-Molina[2] for further information on this topic. Let us now proceed to see how distributed deadlocks are detected and resolved.

10.6 DISTRIBUTED DEADLOCK DETECTION AND RESOLUTION

In the previous section we discovered how the two-phase locking protocol led to deadlocked transactions in a distributed environment. In this section we will briefly examine a technique whereby sites pass along their WAIT-FOR-GRAPHS to neighboring sites so that potential deadlock situations can be discovered and resolved. I will describe a technique that was introduced in a paper by Obermarck.[3] My description will be at a very high level and the reader is referred to the original paper for the finer points and details. The local WAIT-FOR-GRAPH for two sites involved in a distributed deadlock situation is shown in Figure 10.2a.

Site 1 is executing transactions T1, T2, T5, and T4. The WAIT-FOR-GRAPH shows a cycle between transaction T2 and T5 that can be resolved by the local deadlock resolution strategy used at the site. Site 2 is in the process of executing transactions T1, T2, and T3. We can see that the sites are involved in a global cycle, as transaction T4 at site 1 is waiting for T3 at site 2. T3 at site 2 is waiting for transaction T2, which in turn is waiting for transaction T1. Transaction T1 at site 2 is waiting for its counterpart at site 1, which is waiting for transaction T2. Earlier we mentioned that transaction T2 is involved in a local deadlock situation with T5. Therefore, all five transactions are in a suspended state because they are now all involved in a deadlock situation. I call the reader's attention to the triangular figures in the diagram. Obermarck[3] refers to these figures as external nodes or inputs. They are used to refer to transactions at remote sites that a local transaction is waiting for. These external nodes are used to identify potential deadlock situations. Obermarck uses these nodes to construct special messages that represent the local WAIT-FOR-GRAPHS of a site that might be involved in a distributed deadlock. Let us see how these messages are used to spot and resolve distributed deadlocks, using Obermarck's strategy.

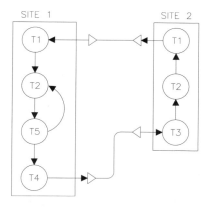

Figure 10.2a Site 1 terminates T2

At the first phase of the deadlock resolution process, site 1 decides to terminate process T2, which is involved in a local deadlock with transaction T5. As T2 has performed only 40 operations versus the 90 of transaction T5, it is selected as the victim. (Some deadlock resolution algorithms use this criterion to select potential deadlock victims.) Site 2 notices that it has an incoming node at transaction T3 and an outgoing node at T1. Obermarck's algorithm states that if the ID of the transaction with an incoming node is higher than the ID of a transaction with an outgoing node, that site must prepare the message that describes the WAIT-FOR-GRAPH of the site and pass it on to the site pointed to by the outgoing node.

In our case, site 2 prepares the following message for transfer to site 1:

$MSG_{S2->S1}$ = ExNode,T3,T1,ExNode

On receiving this message, site 1 modifies its own local WAIT-FOR-GRAPH to reflect the new information. This can be seen in Figure 10.2b. It is clear that transactions T3 and T1 are involved in cycles, so one of them must be terminated. Since transaction T3 is executing at a remote site, site 1 gallantly volunteers to abort transaction T1. Transaction T1 is rescheduled and the deadlock situation is broken.

In this example, two transactions, T2 and T1, had to be terminated to let the other three transactions run to completion.

Other strategies used to resolve deadlock in distributed systems involve a central deadlock resolution process that collects all the local WAIT-FOR-GRAPHS, interconnects them to a global WAIT-FOR-GRAPH, and selects a likely candidate for termination to break

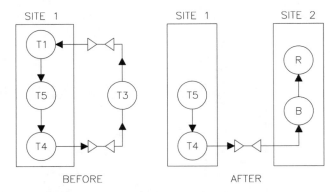

SITE 1   SITE 1   SITE 2

BEFORE   AFTER

Figure 10.2b Site 1 terminates T1 breaking the global deadlock

the global deadlocks. In this strategy, the local sites still have the responsibility to resolve local deadlocks. The Obermarck strategy is more efficient because the local sites not only resolve their local deadlocks but the sites involved in distributed deadlocks resolve their own problems, thereby reducing transmission costs (since it is not necessary for the local sites to transmit their WAIT-FOR-GRAPHS to a centralized detector).

10.7 TWO-PHASE COMMIT PROTOCOL

In this and the next section we will examine the two-phase and three-phase commit protocols from a conceptual point of view. These two sections serve as an introduction; the algorithms used by these protocols will be examined in greater detail in Chapter 11.

The two-phase commit protocol is a coordination strategy that controls the unified commit or abort of distributed transactions across multiple sites. The literature divides the members involved in the execution of a distributed transaction into "participants" and "coordinator." We will follow this convention and introduce a modifed conceptual architecture of the components involved in this strategy. Figure 10.3 shows the global and local components of the participant-coordinator architecture.

At the global level, we have the by now familiar global scheduler and recovery manager. Attached to the recovery manager is another component called the global recovery coordinator. Its function is to collect the termination states of subtransactions that have executed at remote participating sites. (Recall that these subtransactions are

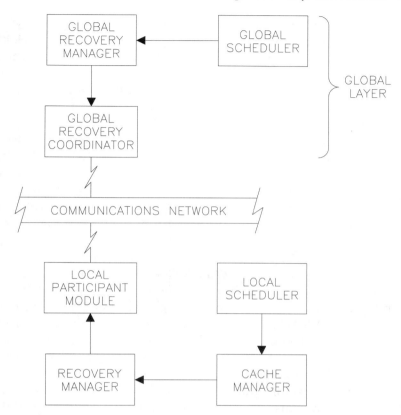

Figure 10.3 Participant–coordinator architecture

all part of a global distributed transaction.) As votes of each of the termination states arrive from the remote sites, the global recovery coordinator collects them, tallies the results, and makes a global decision as to the outcome of the transaction.

If all the local members voted to commit their portion of the transaction, the global recovery coodinator decides to globally commit the transaction. If even one of the sites decided to abort its portion of the transaction, the global recovery coordinator has no choice but to globally abort the transaction. It then sends all of the sites participating in the transaction a command to abort the transaction. The global recovery coordinator updates its transaction log and continues to process the next distributed transaction waiting in the queue.

At the local level, we see that the components are similar. The local scheduler communicates with the recovery manager, which in turn communicates with the cache manager to load and unload data to and from the database and database logs. Attached to the local recovery manager is the local participant module. Its role is to submit its vote to the global recovery coordinator whenever its site has executed a subtransaction that is part of a global distributed transaction. If all goes well, the participant votes to locally commit its subtransaction. If the subtransaction fails, it votes to locally abort the transaction. In either case, its next task is to wait for the global decision from the global recovery coordinator at the central site. On receiving the decision from the global recovery coordinator, the participant informs the local recovery manager that it can go ahead and commit or abort the local transaction. Figure 10.4 is a state transition diagram for both the global recovery coordinator and the local participant modules.

Let's examine the coordinator's state transition diagram. Its first state is the BEGINNING_OF_TRANSACTION_STATE. This is where the start of the distributed transaction is recorded in the global transaction log. At this state, the global recovery coordinator sends a PREPARE_TO_VOTE message to all the participants of the current distributed transactions. On receiving this message the participants move from their BEGINNING_OF_TRANSACTION_STATE to a READY_TO_VOTE state.

During this transition they decide whether or not to locally commit or abort their transaction. (At this time the coordinator is in the WAIT_FOR_VOTE state.) As each participant votes by sending a LOCAL_COMMIT_VOTE or a LOCAL_ABORT_VOTE, the coordinator tallies the results and keeps waiting until all the participants have voted. Once all the participants have voted it sends its global decision to each participant so that they can terminate the transaction by updating their local databases and logs. At this stage of the protocol each of the participants leaves the ready state and proceeds to enter either the LOCAL_COMMIT state or the LOCAL_ABORT state and then terminate the transaction.

There is one problem with this protocol. Although very elegant and simple, it is possible for the coordinator to fail before it sends out its global instruction. If this were to happen, the participants would be left waiting in their READY_TO_VOTE state and could not proceed to either commit or abort—waiting for instructions from the coordinator that will never arrive (at least until the coordinator is brought back up by the global systems administration staff!). This

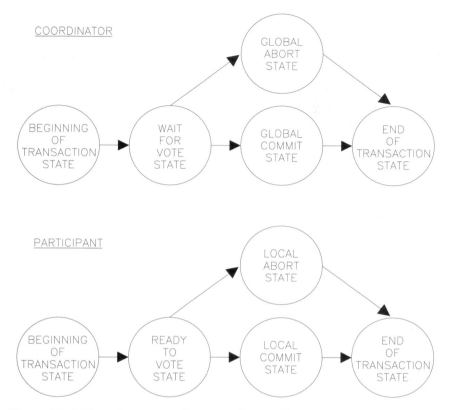

Figure 10.4 Two-phase commit protocol state diagram

is why the literature calls the two-phase commit protocol a blocking protocol. The participants are blocked in the READY_STATE should the coordinator fail while in the WAIT_STATE. The three-phase commit protocol was introduced to alleviate this problem.

10.8 THREE-PHASE COMMIT PROTOCOL

Figure 10.5 is the state transition diagram for the states that make up the three-phase commit protocol for both the coordinator and the participants.

The diagram is identical to that of the two-phase commit protocol except for the inclusion of an additional state called the PRE_COMMIT state and a state transition for this new state to the abort state.

The logic is the same as that of the two-phase commit protocol except that the participant enters into the PRE_COMMIT state and waits for global instructions from the coordinator. In this state, the participant waits for a predetermined period of time. If the time interval expires, the participant assumes that the coordinator has failed, changes state to the LOCAL_ABORT state, and aborts the transaction. On recovery, the coordinator sees that the participating sites have decided to abort the transaction, and it updates its own

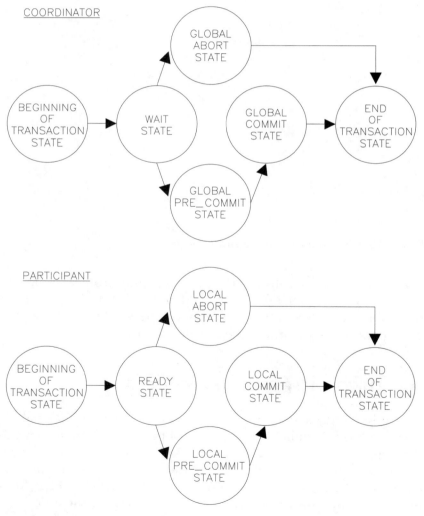

Figure 10.5 Three-phase commit state diagram

global transaction logs to reflect their decisions. If the coordinator does not fail, it issues a GLOBAL_COMMIT instruction to the participants to go ahead and commit. Each site then leaves the LOCAL_PRE_COMMIT state, enters the LOCAL_COMMIT state, and ends the transaction.

We have just seen that adding the PRE_COMMIT state and the path from the LOCAL_PRE_COMMIT state to the LOCAL_ABORT state eliminates the blocking problem. That is why the literature calls the three-phase commit protocol a nonblocking protocol.

We have examined these two protocols at a very high level to introduce the reader to the basic features of each. We will discuss them again in Chapter 11 in greater detail.

10.9 GENERAL ARCHITECTURE REVIEWED

Now that we have discussed distributed transaction processing and covered the detection and resolution of distributed deadlocks, let's review the architecture of a distributed database management system. Figure 10.6 is a block diagram of the global components of the distributed database management system.

The first component is the user interface layer. This is where users or user applications submit transactions to the distributed database management system. The transaction is passed to the global semantic analyzer module, where its syntax is checked. The data objects that are referred to in the transaction are also checked against the global schema to see if they actually exist. (Input to this layer is the system query language grammar and the global schema.)

If the transaction passes inspection, it is submitted to the global localizer layer. Here, the referenced data objects are identified by their locations in the distributed sites. The transaction is modified to include the location references and is passed on to the global optimizer layer.

At the global optimizer layer, models are applied to the transactions to optimize communication costs.

Recall from Chapter 9 that the transaction has now been translated to a relational algebra formula.

The transaction is now passed to the next layer for scheduling against any other transactions that might have been submitted to the system. The global scheduler communicates with the global deadlock detector and the global recovery layer to ensure that distributed

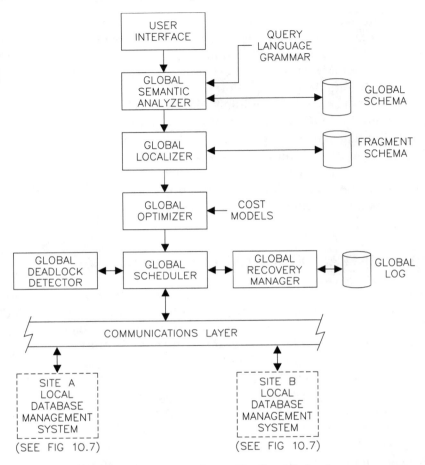

Figure 10.6 General architecture for a distributed database management system

deadlocks are resolved and that system failures or transaction errors do not damage the distributed database.

The transaction is submitted to the communications layer, which interconnects all the sites in the distributed system. Let us take a look at a typical local site and examine its architecture components.

Figure 10.7 shows two sites, SITE A and SITE B, that are linked to the distributed system via the communications layer. Assume that a distributed transaction DTSQL was split into two subtransactions: STSQL1 and STSQL2. Let's follow the process of STSQL1 as it passes down the layers that make up SITE A.

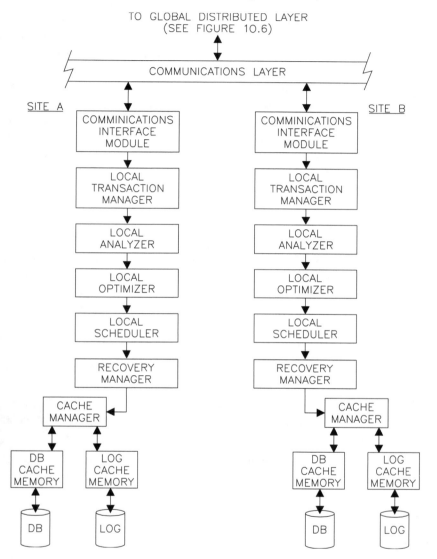

Figure 10.7 Local distributed management layer

The local communications interface module retrieves the sub-transaction and passes it on to the local transaction manager. Recall that this subtransaction also contains instructions on how to transfer intermediate data that might be required by other sites to resolve a distributed join or to meet a qualifying predicate requirement.

The local transaction manager analyzes these transfer instructions, sets up an execution strategy, and passes the subtransaction to the local analyzer. At this layer, the local syntax and semantic checks are performed to make sure the transaction can be executed.

Next, the local transaction is passed to the local optimizer so that the local statistics can be used to further optimize the subtransaction. Recall that these statistics were not available to the global transaction manager. The optimized subtransaction is now passed to the local scheduler, which passes it on to the recovery manager for execution. Local recovery manager strategies were discussed in Chapter 5 and are discussed in Chapter 11 in greater detail.

10.10 SUMMARY

This chapter concludes our discussions on distributed transaction processing and deadlock detection in a distributed homogeneous database architecture.

10.11 END NOTES

1. Ceri, S., and G. Pelagatti. *Distributed Databases: Principles and Systems*, New York: McGraw-Hill, 1984.

2. Garcia-Molina, H. "Using Semantic Knowledge for Transaction Processing in a Distributed Database," *ACM Transactions on Database Systems*, vol. 8, no. 2 (June 1983): pp. 186–213.

3. Obermarck, R. "Distributed Deadlock Detection Algorithm," *ACM Transactions on Database Systems*, vol. 7, no. 2 (June 1982): pp. 187–208.

11

Distributed and Local Recovery Strategies

11.1 INTRODUCTION

This chapter is dedicated to distributed and local recovery methods that are required to guarantee the stability of a distributed database. Distributed recovery is concerned with the coordination of the activities that occur at the local sites when a transaction fails. For this reason, one half of this chapter deals with the different algorithms available for local recovery architectures. The second half of the chapter deals with the protocols used to coordinate the recovery activities. The two-phase and three-phase commit protocols will be included in our discussions, as they are the most popular methods used in systems today. Recall that the two-phase and three-phase commit protocols were discussed in Chapter 10 from the point of view of distributed transaction processing.

The chapter begins with a general introduction on the different types of failures that can occur in a distributed and local database system. I follow with an example of a generic recovery architecture that is currently popular in the literature. Next, the different logging methods are introduced, after which the strategies are classified into four general groups or classes.

The remaining sections of this chapter concentrate on two-phase commit and three-phase commit protocols that are used to coordinate the local recovery strategies. We will see that three architectures can be implemented that use the above protocols. Without further ado, let's examine the four types of failures that can occur in a distributed database transaction system.

11.2 FAILURE CATEGORIES

There are basically two categories of failures that we must examine: local and distributed. The first concerns failures that can occur at a centralized database system site. There are three types of local failures:

1. Transaction Failures
2. System Failures
3. Media Failures

Transaction failures usually occur because a user has entered incorrect data or the application terminates because an internal error has occurred. This error could be due to a programming bug or some built-in error recovery algorithm that causes the transaction to abort.

System failures occur when all or part of the computer's memory fails. The internal memory is currently referred to as "volatile memory" in the literature. This is opposed to "stable memory" or "stable storage," by which the literature refers to disk drives.

The third type, media failures, occur when one or more of the disk drives on the system fail due to some physical damage such as a head crash. The only way to deal with this type of failure is to use an architecture that writes transaction updates to two or more parallel disk drives. This ensures that the availability of at least one copy of the database will always be on line should another fail.

Another strategy is to use a tape backup system to make a copy of the database at regular intervals. This ensures that a recent copy of the database will be available should a physical media failure occur.

Distributed failures are the same as those that occur at local sites except that we must now contend with a fourth type of failure, namely, communication failures. Two-phase and three-phase commit protocols are used to ensure database recovery should some sort of communication failure occur.

In this chapter we deal with system and communication failures only; that is, we wish to examine how local systems (and distributed systems) recover when some or all of the "volatile memory" fails at one or more of the local sites. Let's examine a generic architecture that is currently popular in the literature, for example Özsu and Valduriez[1] and Bernstein et al.[2]

11.3 A GENERIC RECOVERY SYSTEM

Figure 11.1 shows a simple architecture that can be used at local sites of a distributed system to ensure database recovery in case of loss of "volatile memory" or a transaction failure. The recovery system is composed of the following general components:

1. Recovery Manager (RM)
2. Cache Memory Manager (CMM or CM)
3. Cache Volatile Memory (CVM)
4. Log Volatile Memory (LVM)

The recovery manager interfaces with the scheduler to accept atomic read and write operations that make up a transaction. These reads and writes are translated to fetch and flush operations that are

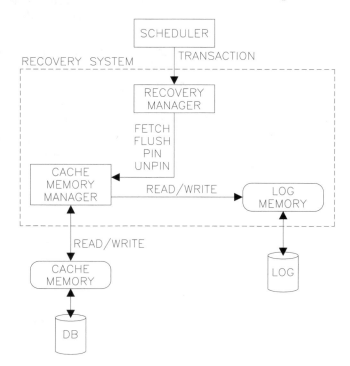

Figure 11.1 Generic recovery architecture

given to the cache memory manager, which in turn executes the corresponding read and write primitives to load or unload page buffers to and from disk storage. The pages are loaded into the CMM's cache volatile memory where they are then updated by the transaction. The CMM will write these pages back at its own discretion, usually when it runs out of cache volatile memory space. This strategy improves execution performance but runs the risk of losing updates should some sort of system failure occur. It is for this reason that part of the recovery system is another volatile memory area, called the log volatile memory, and a stable storage area called the database log.

Before any updates occur to the stable copy of the database, they are stored in the database log. The literature refers to this as "write-ahead logging." It will be discussed in greater detail later on. This strategy ensures that no updates are lost if a system failure occurs. We will examine the strategies used to safely update logs and the database in Section 11.5 when recovery systems are categorized as one of four types currently discussed in the literature.

Let us examine the details of how cache memory and the database log are implemented in a simple architecture that will be used throughout this chapter. This architecture is a generalization of architectures used in systems today. Figure 11.2a shows the cache volatile memory implemented as a linked list.

Real systems use the "page" as the atomic unit for reading and writing data between stable storage and volatile storage. To simplify our discussions, we will use a table row as the unit of data transfer.

The linked list in the figure stores the row identifiers, pointers to the next node in the linked list, and pointers to the data stored in the row. Figure 11.2b is a more detailed example of this implementation.

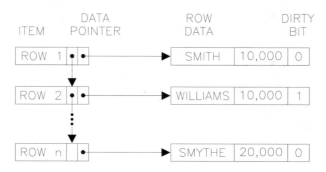

Figure 11.2a Cache memory as a linked list

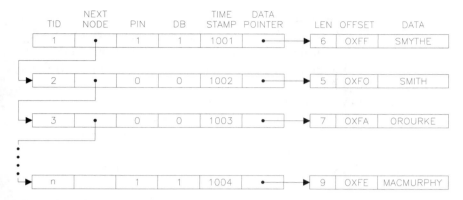

Figure 11.2b   Cache memory architecture

Notice that there is extra information in the nodes assigned to each row. Let us examine a C language structure that can be used to implement each component of the linked list:

```
struct CACHE_ROW
    {
    short TID;       // Transaction ID
    struct CACHE_ROW *pNext; // pointer to next node
    BOOL fPinned;   // flag indicating that row is pinned
    BOOL fDirtyBit; // dirty bit flag
    unsigned long Time stamp; // time stamp used by FIFO
                              // algorithm for flushing
    struct ROW_DATA *pRow;    // pointer to row data
    };

struct ROW_DATA
    {
    short len;               // length of the data
    unsigned long offset;   // offset used for disk storage
    DATA *pData;             // pointer to data
    };
```

Let us identify the members of each structure. The TID member of the CACHE_ROW structure is used to store the transaction's identification number. The next member is a pointer to the next node in the linked list. The Boolean fPinned member is used to indicate whether or not the data page and row node are pinned or unpinned. (Setting fPinned = TRUE means that the row is pinned; setting fPinned = FALSE means that the row is unpinned.) This simply shows whether or not the cache memory manager can write the row information to disk and out of stable storage. (Setting this structure member to TRUE indicates that the data have changed.) The Boolean fDirtyBit flag is used to indicate whether or not the row data have been changed since they were last retrieved (fetched) from the database in stable storage.

The time stamp member is used to store the time when the row data were read from disk storage. This information is used by the FIFO algorithm to remove nodes should the cache memory manager run out of space. Should this ever occur, the node or nodes with the oldest time stamps will be written back to disk storage to make room for new data.

Last but not least is the member structure ROW_DATA *pRow. This is a pointer to the structure that contains the actual row database information required by a transaction. Let's examine this structure next.

This structure contains three members. Member len stores the length of the row. Member offset stores the address offset, where the row data are stored on disk. Member DATA *pData is a pointer to the row data. Its length is specified by the len member. Let's continue by taking a look at the different log architectures that can be used by a typical database recovery system.

11.4 POPULAR LOGGING STRATEGIES

Currently, two types of logging methods are discussed in the literature:

1. In-place logging
2. Out-of-place logging

In-Place Logging

The term "in-place logging" is used to identify systems that update the logs directly on a single copy of the log. When the log runs out of space, the system deletes obsolete transaction entries and starts at the beginning of the log.

Figure 11.3 is a simple diagram of a data structure that can be used to implement this type of log. It is composed of a master record that contains pointers to four linked lists. The first linked list is made up of nodes that contain the transaction ID and the before-and-after

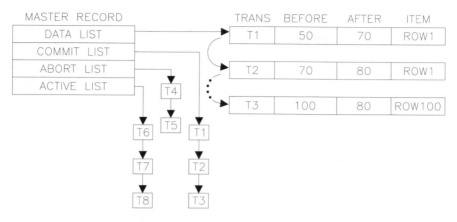

Figure 11.3 General log components

images of the changed database object. Again, for the sake of simplicity, we will consider the table row as the object; real systems use a page or the portion of the page that was changed. In addition to the above information, the identifier of the row being changed is kept in this node.

The remaining three linked lists are used to store the IDs of the transactions that have committed, aborted, and were active during a particular state of the system. Below are four C language structures that can be used to implement the log architecture in volatile memory:

```
struct MASTER_LOG_RECORD
    {
    struct TDATALIST *pTData;
        // pointer to data linked list
    struct COMMIT_LIST *pCommitTID
        // pointer to committed transaction list
    struct ABORT_LIST *pAbortTID
        // pointer to list of aborted transactions
    struct ACTIVE_LIST *pActiveTID;
        // pointer to list of active transactions
    unsigned long DataDiskAddress;
        // address of start of data list on disk
    unsigned long CommitDataAddress;
        // address of start of committed TID list on disk
    unsigned long AbortDataAddress;
        // address of start of aborted TID list on disk
    unsigned long ActiveDataAddress;
        // address of active TID list on disk
    }
```

The restart algorithm will load this structure as part of any recovery event so that the linked lists can be built in memory. The restart algorithm will use the last four members of the structure to find the disk address where each of the four lists is stored. Each list is then loaded into memory so that the recovery algorithms can restore the database to a stable state.

These algorithms will be covered in Section 11.5. The remaining structures used in the log are:

```
struct TDATALIST
    {
    short TID;         // transaction ID
    void *pBeforeImage; // pointer to row before image
    void *pAfterImage;  // pointer to row after image
    short RowID;        // row identifier
    struct TDATALIST *pNext;    // pointer to next node
    };

struct COMMIT_LIST
    {
    short TID;              // transaction ID
    struct COMMIT_LIST *pNext; // pointer to next node
    };

struct ABORT_LIST
    {
    short TID;              // transaction ID
    struct ABORT_LIST *pNext; // pointer to next node
    };

struct ACTIVE_LIST
    {
    short TID;              // transaction ID
    struct ACTIVE_LIST *pNext; // pointer to next node
    };
```

The members of each structure are self-explanatory. Let us examine the details of out-of-place logging next.

Out-of-Place Logging

This term is used to identify architectures and recovery strategies that maintain copies of the database as a logging technique. Should the transaction fail, the recovery system goes back to the copy that represented the last stable state of the database prior to the failure of the transaction. We will briefly examine the following types of out-of-place logging architectures:

1. Shadow Logging Implementations
2. Differential File Logging Implementations

Shadow Logging

Figure 11.4 shows a database composed of four pages. The cross-hatched areas in the pages represent the current stable state of the

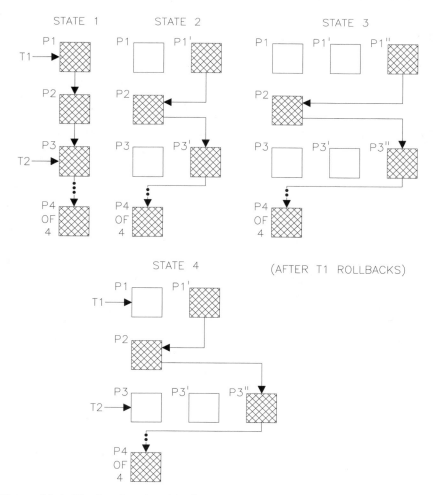

Figure 11.4 Shadow logging (paging)

database. Let's see what happens when two transactions are executed against the database. Initially, in state 1, the database is stable. Transactions T1 and T2 are executed. T1 changes page P1 to P1′, and T2 changes page P3 to P3′. In the figure, state 2 shows the new stable version of the database. It is composed of pages P1′, P2, P3′, and P4.

Transactions T1 and T2 execute again and state 3 represents the new database state. This time, transaction T1 fails. Page P1″ is not stable and must be discarded.

The recovery system restores the database to a stable state by discarding this "bad" page but keeps page P3″, which was successfully altered by transaction T3. The new stable state is labeled state 4.

Differential File Logging

Figure 11.5 illustrates the recovery techniques that are used in differential file logging. Three types of files are kept: a read-only file that represents the database in its latest stable state, a write file used to maintain inserts and updates to the database, and a delete file used to record the rows of the file that were deleted by a transaction.

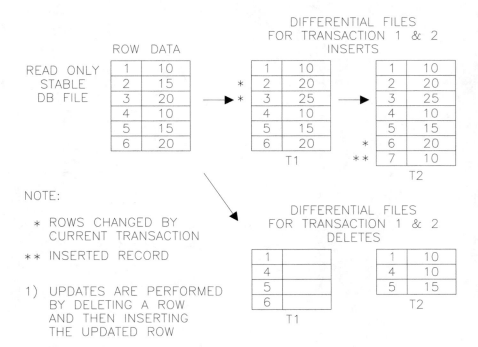

Figure 11.5 Differential file logging

Note that updates are performed by first deleting the target row and then inserting the update value as if it were a new row. Periodically, the insert and delete files are merged by the system with the read-only file so that it represents the new stable database.

11.5 CLASSIFYING RECOVERY SYSTEMS

Let's wrap up our investigation of recovery systems by classifying them and then examining some algorithms that are used to implement each category.

Basic Design Rules

Two basic "rules" are followed by recovery systems:

1. The REDO rule
2. The UNDO rule

The REDO rule simply states that any transaction that successfully completed but its changes were not recorded in stable storage must be redone to reflect the new changes.

The UNDO rule states that any transaction that aborted but actually changed portions of the stable database must be undone; that is, the changes must be undone so that the affected information is restored to the state it was in prior to the execution of the failed transaction.

Let's apply these two rules to a simple database that contains only three rows. Three transactions will be executed against the database. Two will run to successful completion and commit the changes they performed, and one transaction will fail. Figure 11.6 illustrates the scenario for our example.

As stated earlier, the database contains one table with only three rows, each row containing one column called DATA. The volatile cache memory area contains space for only two rows and the log grows as transactions are executed. Below are the three transactions that will run against the database:

```
T1 = Write(row = 1, value = 20 ) + other processing
T2 = Write(row = 2, value = 30)
T3 = Write(row = 3, value = 40)
```

Recovery Manager and Cache Manager Operations

Transactions T1 and T2 are received by the scheduler first, which in turn informs the recovery manager of their presence and intentions. The recovery manager promptly informs the cache manager to read rows 1 and 2 into cache memory. Next, the data in each row are updated and the before-and-after images of the two transactions are stored in the log. Keep in mind that the stable database has not yet been updated and transaction T1 is still running, doing some other miscellaneous processing. The top portion of Figure 11.6 reflects the changes that we have discussed so far.

Now, transaction T3 comes along, announces its intentions, and the cache memory manager is requested by the recovery manager to load row 3 into volatile cache memory so that it can be processed by transaction T3.

Let's pay close attention to what happens next. The cache memory manager has no room in volatile cache memory, so it must flush one of its buffers. It writes back transaction T1's changes to stable storage and hopes nothing goes wrong. Next, it loads row 3 into the newly freed slot in the cache memory area and allows transaction 3 to update the data.

The before-and-after images of row 3 are stored in the log. Keep in mind that only transaction T1's changes are reflected in the stable database. So far, only the log reflects all the changes. Remember that transaction T1 is still running, doing some other mysterious processing! Well, as luck has it, transaction T1 fails and causes the whole system to fail.

The system must now recover the database by undoing T1's changes. It must also REDO T2 and T3, as they successfully committed but their changes were not yet reflected in the stable database. The recovery manager does this by examining the status column of the log. (This is a primitive version of the active, abort, and commit lists of a real log.) The recovery manager sees that transaction T1 failed so it loads the before image of row 1 into the cache memory. It also sees that transactions T2 and T3 ran to completion, so it loads their after images into cache memory.

The recovery manager isn't really doing the loading—it's instructing its partner, the cache memory manager, to perform reads and writes on its behalf. By fetch commands, the cache manager is instructed to perform the reads from the database log in stable storage. Now that all of the after images and before images are loaded, the

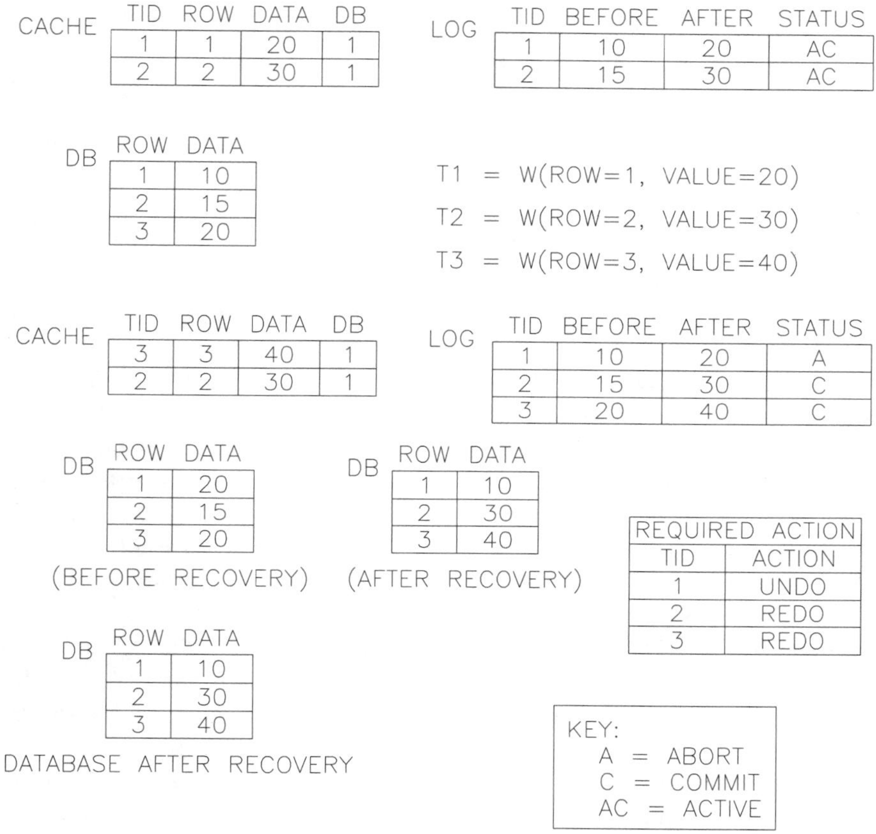

CACHE

TID	ROW	DATA	DB
1	1	20	1
2	2	30	1

LOG

TID	BEFORE	AFTER	STATUS
1	10	20	AC
2	15	30	AC

DB

ROW	DATA
1	10
2	15
3	20

T1 = W(ROW=1, VALUE=20)

T2 = W(ROW=2, VALUE=30)

T3 = W(ROW=3, VALUE=40)

CACHE

TID	ROW	DATA	DB
3	3	40	1
2	2	30	1

LOG

TID	BEFORE	AFTER	STATUS
1	10	20	A
2	15	30	C
3	20	40	C

DB

ROW	DATA
1	20
2	15
3	20

(BEFORE RECOVERY)

DB

ROW	DATA
1	10
2	30
3	40

(AFTER RECOVERY)

REQUIRED ACTION	
TID	ACTION
1	UNDO
2	REDO
3	REDO

DB

ROW	DATA
1	10
2	30
3	40

DATABASE AFTER RECOVERY

KEY:
  A = ABORT
  C = COMMIT
  AC = ACTIVE

Figure 11.6 Fundamental operations of REDO/UNDO

recovery manager issues a flush instruction and the cache memory manager writes all of the data in the volatile cache buffers in cache memory to the stable database residing on the disk drive of the database server. These events are reflected in the bottom portion of Figure 11.6.

This simple example has illustrated what is meant by recovering a database by following a redo/undo protocol. Since things are rarely this simple, the academicians and researchers in this field have defined four basic categories of recovery systems that use the redo and undo strategies:

1. REDO/UNDO recovery strategy
2. REDO/NO-UNDO recovery strategy

3. NO-REDO/UNDO recovery strategy

4. NO-REDO/NO-UNDO recovery strategy

REDO/UNDO systems, as we have just described, require that committed transactions whose changes are not reflected in the stable database be reexecuted or actually redone. They require that aborted transactions whose changes are reflected in stable storage be undone.

REDO/NO-UNDO systems require that the REDO portion of the strategy be executed. UNDO is not required, as changes made by bad transactions are never stored in stable storage.

NO-REDO/UNDO is the converse of REDO/NO-UNDO. This strategy is used on optimistic recovery systems that assume all transactions executed will commit. Whenever one transaction commits, all the changes in the cache memory buffers are flushed into stable database storage. This includes changes made by uncommitted transactions. Therefore, if any of the uncommitted transactions fail, their changes must be undone whenever the system recovers.

The last type of recovery strategy that we are interested in is the NO-REDO/NO-UNDO strategy. It is called NO-REDO/NO-UNDO, as the only time a transaction's changes are written to the stable database is when the transaction commits. Its changes, and only its changes, are written to the database. Any other data are kept in cache memory until its transaction commits. Therefore, no redo or undo is necessary. Obviously, this is the simplest type of recovery system, but it suffers from potential performance problems as transaction updates to stable storage are performed only one at a time. Let's look at each method more closely by examining the algorithms each system uses.

One additional note, the literature discusses five basic operations or functions that are used by typical systems:

```
RMGR_READ();
RMGR_WRITE();
RMGR_ABORT();
RMGR_COMMIT();
RMGR_RESTART():
```

I will follow the same basic logic used in Özsu and Valduriez[1] and Bernstein et al.[2] I will embellish each algorithm by adding some extra detail and support functions.

The REDO/UNDO Algorithm

We will begin by discussing the generic read, write, and cache slot update algorithms that will be used by all four of the recovery manager categories. Figure 11.7a shows a flow chart for a generic read algorithm called RMGR_READ(TID,OBJNAME).

The algorithm based on the flow chart is passed the transaction ID and the name of the object to be updated. Recall that for our discussions we consider an object to be a table row. In real systems, the object is usually a database page, which is 512 bytes or multiples of 512 bytes.

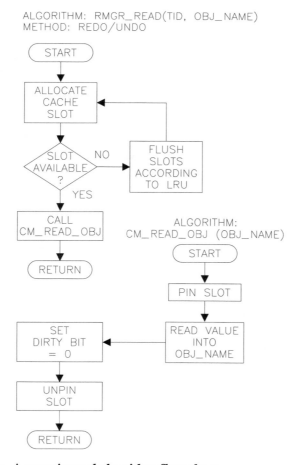

Figure 11.7a A generic read algorithm flow chart

The flow chart begins by checking if any free slots are available in cache memory. If none are available, the cache is flushed via the FIFO algorithm that was previously discussed. Once a slot is available, the object's value is read into the slot by placing a call to the CM_READ_OBJ function. This function is passed the name of the object as a parameter. This function pins the slot, reads in the value of the row, sets the dirty bit to 0, and unpins the slot. Figure 11.7b shows the flow chart for the generic write algorithm.

The algorithm based on this flow chart is passed the transaction's ID, the object name, and the new value of the object as its parame-

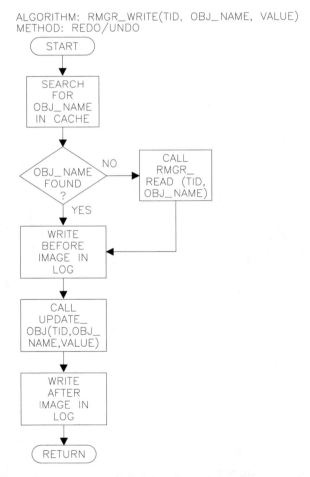

Figure 11.7b A generic write algorithm flow chart

ters. The algorithm first searches the cache memory slots; if the object is not found, a call is placed to RMGR_READ() (which we have just discussed), which will read in the previous value of the object in cache memory.

Once the object is located or read into cache memory, the before image of the object is stored in the log to aid in any future recovery efforts. Next, a call is made to the generic algorithm called UP-DATE_OBJ(). The transaction's ID, object name, and the new value for the object are passed to this routine. The after image of the object is written into the log to be available for any future REDO recovery actions. Figure 11.7c shows the flow chart for the generic update object algorithm.

The algorithm used by this flow chart begins by pinning the slot that belongs to the object. Once the slot is pinned, the new value is written into the slot, the dirty bit is set to 1, and the slot is unpinned.

ALGORITHM: UPDATE_OBJ(TID, OBJ_NAME, VALUE)
METHOD: GENERIC

Figure 11.7c Generic update object flow chart

Recall the C language structure that was used to depict a cache memory slot as if it were a node in a linked list:

```
struct CACHE_ROW
    {
    short TID; // transaction ID
    struct CACHE_ROW *pNext; // pointer to next node
    BOOL fPinned; // flag indicating pinned/unpinned slot
    BOOL fDirtyBit; // dirty bit flag
    unsigned long Time stamp; // time stamp for FIFO
    struct ROW_DATA *pRow; // pointer to row data
    };
```

Recall that pinning a slot prevents the cache manager from flushing it during any subsequent buffer flushing activity. Setting structure member fPinned to TRUE pins the slot. Setting the structure member fDirtyBit to TRUE indicates that the value in the slot is now different from the value stored in the stable database.

Figure 11.7d shows the flow chart that could be used to build a simple algorithm that commits a transaction.

An algorithm based on this flow chart executes three simple tasks: It adds the transaction ID to the log's commit list; it signals the

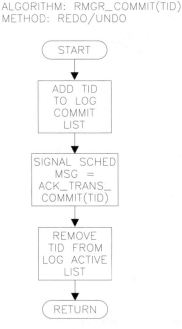

Figure 11.7d Commit transaction algorithm flow chart

scheduler that the transaction committed; and, finally, it removes the ID of the transaction from the active list. The active list simply shows transactions that have not yet committed or aborted.

Next, we examine the flow chart that can be used to develop an algorithm to abort transactions according to the REDO/UNDO strategy, Figure 11.7e. The algorithm based on this flow chart begins by placing the ID of the failed transaction in the abort list.

Next, it searches the log for any updates performed by the transaction. If none are found, it simply notifies the scheduler that the abort routine for the failing transaction successfully completed and then proceeds to remove the ID of the failed transaction from the active list of the log.

Let's see what happens if updates are found! If updates of a failed transaction are found, a check is made to see if the first object for the failed transaction is in cache memory. If it is not, a slot is allocated for the object, the before image of the object is read from the log, and a call to the UPDATE_OBJ routine is made. A search is then made for the next object updated by the failed transaction. This logic continues until no more objects remain unprocessed.

The logic for the restart algorithm is discussed next. Because it is a fairly complex algorithm, it is treated as three separate routines:

1. RMGR_RESTART()
2. CHECK_ALL_LOG_ENTRIES()
3. UPDATE_ACTIVE_LIST()

The algorithm begins by checking if there are any slots allocated in cache memory. If there are, they are all freed. Next, space is allocated in memory for two linked lists. The first will be a list that contains the IDs of all the transactions that have been processed by the REDO algorithm. The second linked list will contain all the IDs of transactions that were undone.

When all the entries in the log are either in one or the other list, the recovery session is considered completed. Now that the lists are allocated, a call is made to the CHECK_ALL_LOG_ENTRIES() algorithm (Figure 11.7f). Once all the log entries are checked, all the committed transactions are removed from the active list and the scheduler is notified that the restart session has successfully completed.

Figure 11.7g shows the flow chart that can be used to implement an algorithm that processes all the log entries by executing either

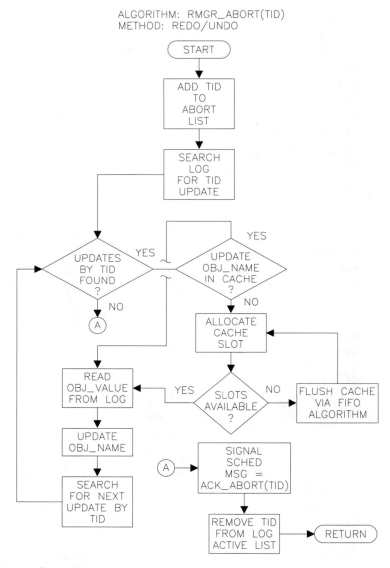

ALGORITHM: RMGR_ABORT(TID)
METHOD: REDO/UNDO

Figure 11.7e Abort transaction flow chart

REDO or UNDO as required by the transaction termination condition.

The algorithm begins by allocating a REDO and UNDO list and then reading the last record in the log (it will work from the end of the log to the beginning). For each record read, the name of the object belonging to the transaction is checked via a call to

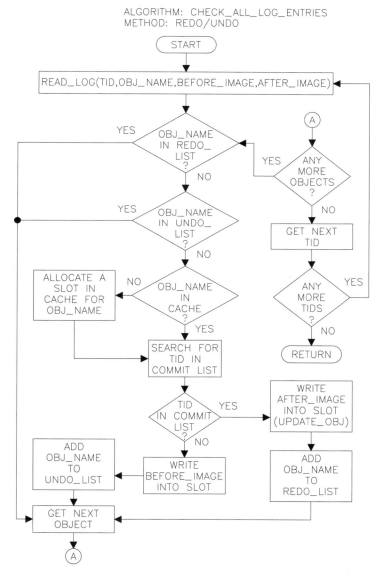

ALGORITHM: CHECK_ALL_LOG_ENTRIES
METHOD: REDO/UNDO

Figure 11.7f Flow chart for CHECK_ALL_LOG_ENTRIES

CHECK_ALL_LOG_ENTRIES. This algorithm is shown in Figure 11.7f to see if it is in either or both the REDO or UNDO list. If either or both of these conditions are TRUE, the next object belonging to the transaction is fetched. If both of these conditions are FALSE, a check is made to see if the object is in one of the slots in the cache memory. If the object is not present, a slot is allocated.

ALGORITHM: RMGR_ RESTART
METHOD: REDO/UNDO

```
                    ┌──────────────┐
                    (    START     )
                    └──────────────┘
                           │
                           ▼
                       ╱CACHE ╲           ┌──────────┐
                      ╱ SLOTS  ╲   YES    │  GO  TO  │
                     ⟨ ALLOCATED⟩ ──────▶ │  FIRST   │
                      ╲   ?    ╱          │  SLOT    │
                       ╲     ╱            └──────────┘
                         │ NO                  │
                         ▼                     ▼
                   ┌──────────┐           ┌──────────┐
                   │ ALLOCATE │           │  STORE   │
                   │    A     │ ◀──────   │ REFERENCE│ ◀──┐
                   │ REDO LIST│       │   │ TO NEXT  │    │
                   └──────────┘       │   │  SLOT    │    │
                         │            │   └──────────┘    │
                         ▼            │        │          │
                   ┌──────────┐       │        ▼          │
                   │ ALLOCATE │       │   ┌──────────┐    │
                   │   AN     │       │   │  FREE    │    │
                   │ UNDO LIST│       │   │ CURRENT  │    │
                   └──────────┘       │   │  SLOT    │    │
                         │            │   └──────────┘    │
                         ▼            │        │          │
                   ┌──────────┐       │        ▼          │
                   │ START AT │    NO │    ╱ NEXT ╲        │
                   │ TAIL OF  │       │   ╱  SLOT  ╲       │
                   │   LOG    │       └──⟨ ALLOCATED⟩      │
                   └──────────┘          ╲   ?   ╱        │
                         │                ╲     ╱         │
                         ▼                   │ YES         │
                   ┌──────────┐              ▼             │
                   │  CALL    │         ┌──────────┐       │
                   │ CHECK_ALL│         │ MAKE NEXT│       │
                   │LOG_ENTRIES         │  SLOT    │       │
                   └──────────┘         │ CURRENT  │ ──────┘
                         │              │  SLOT    │
                         ▼              └──────────┘
                   ┌──────────┐
                   │  CALL    │
                   │ UPDATE_  │
                   │ACTIVE_LIST
                   └──────────┘
                         │
                         ▼
                   ┌──────────┐
                   │ SIGNAL   │
                   │ SCHED    │
                   │ MSG=     │
                   │ACK_RESTART
                   └──────────┘
                         │
                         ▼
                    ┌──────────────┐
                    (   RETURN     )
                    └──────────────┘
```

Figure 11.7g   Restart algorithm flow chart

Next, the transaction is checked to see if its ID is in the commit list or the abort list. If it is in the COMMIT list, the after image of the object belonging to the transaction is loaded into cache memory. If the transaction ID is in the abort list, the object before image is loaded in cache memory. Both steps accomplish their task by placing a call to the generic update object algorithm. If the transaction is in the commit list, the name of the object is placed in the REDO list. If the transaction ID is in the ABORT list, the name of the object just processed is placed in the UNDO list. If there are more objects belonging to the transaction, this logic that was just discussed is repeated. If not, a check is made to see if there are any more transactions in the log. If there are, the algorithm repeats itself; otherwise, it terminates. Finally, we examine the flow chart used for the UP-DATE_ACTIVE_LIST() algorithm. This flow chart is shown in Figure 11.7h.

An algorithm based on this flow chart is passed a pointer to the head of the commit list. The algorithm starts at the head of the list and deletes any transactions in the active list that have the same transaction ID as the IDs of the transactions in the commit list. This logic iterates in a loop until all the transactions in the commit list have been examined.

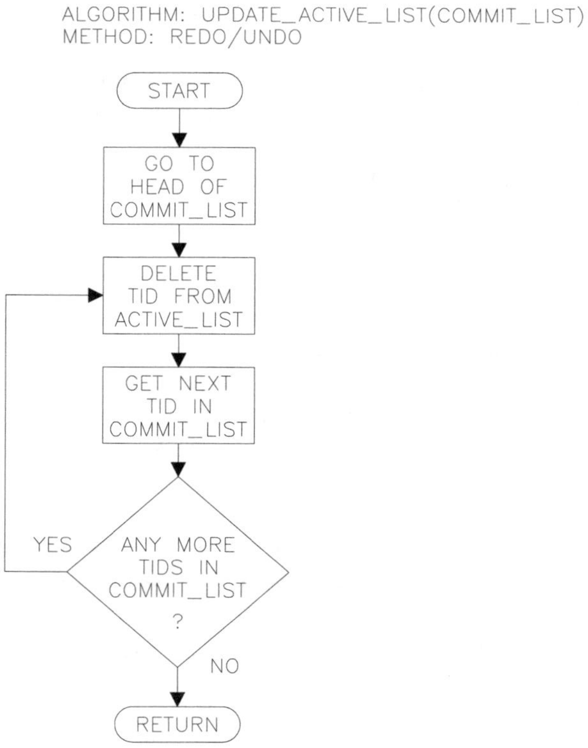

ALGORITHM: UPDATE_ACTIVE_LIST(COMMIT_LIST)
METHOD: REDO/UNDO

Figure 11.7h Flow chart for UPDATE_ACTIVE_LIST

Before we conclude our discussions of the REDO/UNDO recovery strategy, let's discuss why REDO and UNDO are required.

Note that the cache manager indiscriminately flushes the slots in cache memory whenever it needs space to read in new row data. This action writes updates made by transactions that might abort to the stable database. The use of the UNDO algorithm is then required if the system fails due to an aborting transaction.

Alternatively, committed updates might still be in cache memory but not in the stable database. This condition requires that the REDO action be executed whenever system recovery is required. Fortunately, the changes are always written to the log before they are recorded in stable storage. Recall that this technique is called write-ahead logging (WAL for short). This technique is a critical feature of the UNDO/REDO recovery strategy. Let's now examine systems that require only REDO.

REDO/NO-UNDO Algorithm

Figure 11.8a is the flow chart that can be used to implement the restart algorithm for a recovery system that uses the REDO/NO-UNDO strategy. It is similar to the restart flow chart described for the REDO/UNDO algorithm discussed earlier except that no facilities are included for the UNDO transaction list—none are required. The corresponding CHECK_ALL_LOG entries flow chart has also been modified to reflect the absence of any logic that supports UNDO algorithms.

The algorithm begins by checking for the presence of any occupied cache slots. If any are found, they are freed. Next, the REDO_TRANS list is allocated; all the log entries are checked by placing a call to the modified CHECK_ALL_LOG_ENTRIES algorithm (which is described next); and, finally, the scheduler is notified that the restart process has completed successfully.

Figure 11.8b is the flow chart that can be used to implement the CHECK_ALL_LOG_ENTRIES algorithm. The algorithm behaves similarly to its REDO/UNDO counterpart except that before images are not processed or required—they are unnecessary with this strategy.

Figure 11.8c is the flow chart that can be used to implement the algorithm for the RMGR_COMMIT function of the REDO/NO_UNDO recovery system.

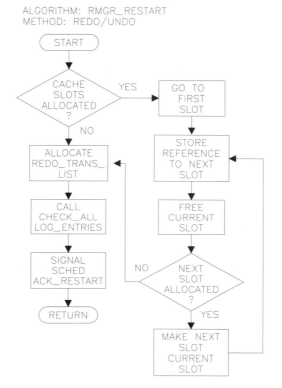

ALGORITHM: RMGR_RESTART
METHOD: REDO/UNDO

Figure 11.8a The RMGR_RESTART algorithm flow chart

The recovery manager passes the ID of the transaction that is about to commit to this algorithm. The transaction ID is then entered into the commit list, and all the slots in the cache memory belonging to the transaction are unpinned and written to stable storage. The scheduler is then notified that the transaction has committed. (This notification allows the scheduler to release any locks it had obtained on data objects on behalf of the transaction.)

Figure 11.8d is the flow chart used for implementing the RMGR_ABORT algorithm.

The transaction's ID is passed to the algorithm; all slots belonging to the failed transaction are unpinned and freed. The TID is added to the abort list and the algorithm terminates.

The RMGR_READ and RMGR_WRITE algorithms are the same as the ones used in the REDO/NO-UNDO algorithm. Notice that it is possible for the system to fail just prior to committed transactions

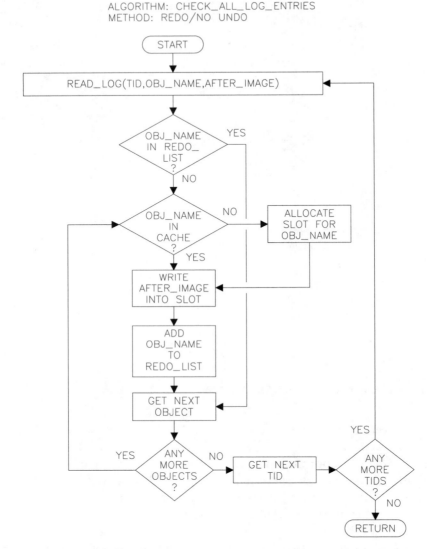

Figure 11.8b The CHECK_ALL_LOG_ENTRIES algorithm flow chart

being flushed to stable storage. That's why the REDO algorithm is necessary.

In the flushing stage, only transactions that are committed are written back to stable storage. Uncommitted transactions are never written to stable storage; the necessity for any UNDO strategy is

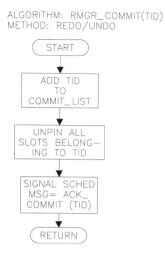

Figure 11.8c The RMGR_COMMIT algorithm flow chart

thereby avoided. Let us now examine recovery systems that require UNDO but never require REDO.

The UNDO/NO-REDO Algorithm

This strategy is very optimistic. It assumes that all transactions will commit. Consequently, it ends up flushing slots that belong to un-committed transactions. This is why the UNDO strategy is required. Transactions that commit are immediately written to stable storage,

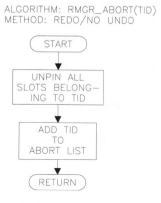

Figure 11.8d The RMGR_ABORT algorithm flow chart

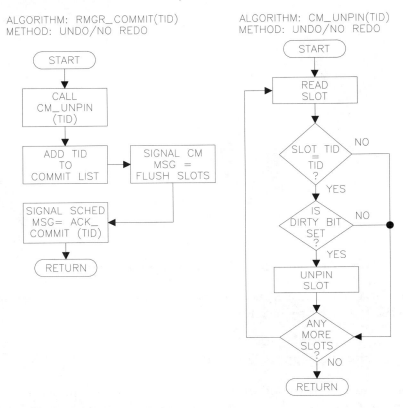

Figure 11.9a   The RMGR_COMMIT flow chart

thereby eliminating the need for the REDO logic. Figure 11.9a shows the flow charts for the RMGR_COMMIT and CM_FLUSH algorithms.

Let's examine the RMGR_COMMIT flow chart first. The transaction's ID is passed to the algorithm and a call is made to the CM_UNPIN function to unpin all the slots that belong to the transaction that's about to commit. Keep in mind that some of the slots belonging to the transaction may have been flushed to stable storage earlier.

The ID of the transaction is added to the commit list, and the recovery system notifies the cache manager to flush its slots. Finally, the scheduler is signaled that the commit for the transaction was successful.

The CM_FLUSH flow chart is fairly straightforward. It keeps looping until all slots have been checked. Slots belonging to the committed transaction are unpinned so that they can be flushed.

ALGORITHM: RMGR_ABORT(TID)
METHOD: UNDO/NO REDO

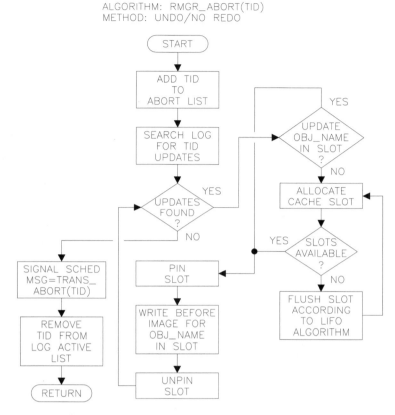

Figure 11.9b   The RMGR_ABORT flow chart

The flow chart for the RMGR_ABORT algorithm is shown in Figure 11.9b. The algorithm begins by adding the ID of the aborted transaction to the abort list. It then searches the log for the updates belonging to this transaction. If updates are found, a slot is allocated for them, the slot is pinned, and the before image of the update is written into the cache slot. Once this is accomplished, the slot is unpinned and the algorithm goes back and keeps searching for more updates until all the updates are found. Once all updates are found, the scheduler is notified that the transaction was successfully aborted. The ID of the transaction is removed from the abort list.

The flow chart for the RMGR_RESTART algorithm is shown in Figure 11.9c. As was the case with the other methods, if any cache slots were allocated, they are freed at this time. A list is allocated for the transactions that will require UNDO and a call is placed to the UNDO_ABORT_LIST function. (This function will be described

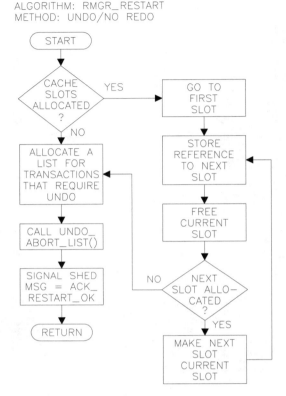

ALGORITHM: RMGR_RESTART
METHOD: UNDO/NO REDO

Figure 11.9c The RMGR_RESTART flow chart

next.) On completion of all UNDOs the scheduler is notified that the restart process has completed.

Figure 11.9d shows the flow chart that can be used to implement the UNDO_ABORT_LIST algorithm. The algorithm begins by reading the end of the abort list and working its way backwards. As it reads each record it checks if the object name (i.e., row ID) is already in the UNDO list. If it is, it ignores it and proceeds to obtain the next object for the transaction. If the object is not in the undo list, it checks if the object is already in a cache slot. If it isn't, it loads it into cache memory, writes the before image of the data object into the slot, and adds the name of the transaction to the UNDO list. This logic is repeated until all transactions in the abort list have been processed. Let's examine the last strategy, a recovery system that does not require REDO or UNDO.

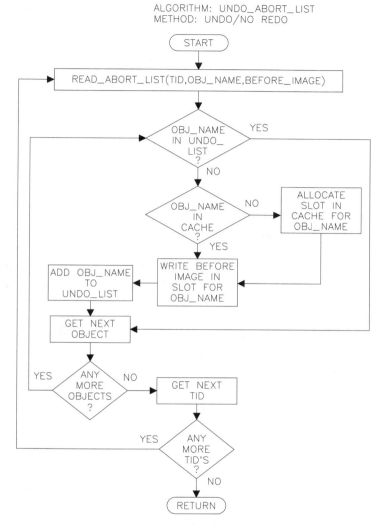

Figure 11.9d The UNDO_ABORT_LIST flow chart

NO-UNDO/NO-REDO Algorithm

This strategy does not require UNDO—the transactions that abort never had a chance to write data to stable storage. They were simply ignored and the results in cache memory discarded. This strategy does not require REDO because transactions are written to stable storage only at commit time.

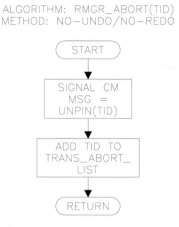

Figure 11.10a The RMGR_ABORT flow chart

Figure 11.10a is the flow chart for the **RMGR_ABORT** algorithm. The algorithm simply notifies the cache manager to unpin all the slots belonging to the transaction that has aborted; the ID of the transaction is then added to the abort list.

Figure 11.10b is the flow chart that can be used to implement the **RMGR_COMMIT** algorithm. The cache manager is instructed to unpin all the slots belonging to the transaction that is about to

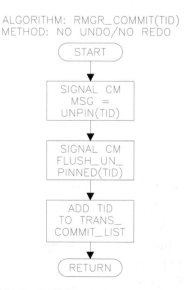

Figure 11.10b The RMGR_COMMIT flow chart

commit. Next, the cache manager is instructed to flush all slots belonging to the transaction that has just committed. Finally, the ID of the successful transaction is added to the commit list.

The UNPIN and FLUSH_UNPINNED algorithms are shown in Figures 11.10c and 11.10d. The algorithms are straightforward so I will not elaborate on them any further.

The algorithms that we have just studied suffer from bad perform-ance during execution of the recovery strategies, as they must exam-

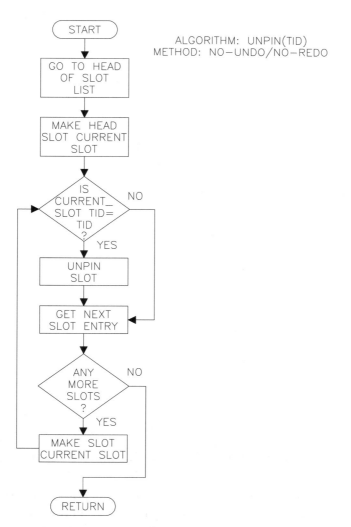

Figure 11.10c The UNPIN algorithm flow chart

ALGORITHM: FLUSH_UNPINNED(TID)
METHOD: NO UNDO/NO REDO

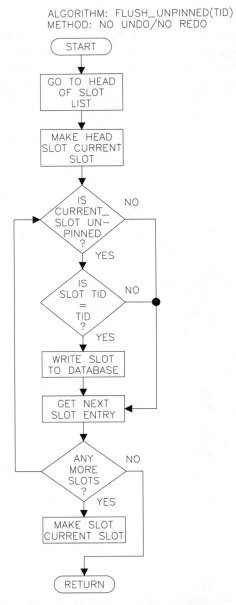

Figure 11.10d The FLUSH_UNPINNED algorithm flow chart

ine every entry in the log. This could be a very costly process if there are thousands of entries to be processed. The literature discusses a solution to this problem called checkpointing. We briefly examine it now.

Checkpointing

The algorithms we have just examined are seriously lacking in that the restart procedures can take a long time if the points between failures are far and few between! This causes the recovery log to grow very large. For this reason, recovery systems will insert checkpoint records in the log that indicate that all commits and aborts have been processed during normal operation of the system.

At the interval prior to the point when the checkpoint record is to be inserted, the recovery manager will suspend the scheduler so that no new transactions can be processed. It will then instruct the cache memory manager to flush all slots and update all of the log records. On completion of these tasks, the checkpoint record is inserted into the log. Any subsequent system crash will require that restart procedures process the log only from the tail of the log to the last checkpoint record.

This concludes our examination of local recovery strategies. We will now examine the protocols used to coordinate these recovery strategies in a distributed database environment.

11.6 DISTRIBUTED RECOVERY COORDINATION PROTOCOLS

In this section we will examine the strategies used in distributed systems to ensure that local sites can recover from failures in a uniform manner. Centralized sites depend on local logs and recovery strategies to return the database to a consistent state after a system failure such as loss of volatile memory. Since distributed transactions involve multiple sites, either all sites successfully commit their portion of the distributed transaction or all sites abort their portion of the distributed transaction. If even one site fails, all sites must abort their transactions.

Two popular protocols, the two-phase and three-phase commit protocols, will be examined. Both involve intercommunications dialog to determine the outcome of a transaction. Our discussions will examine three types of communication architectures discussed in the literature that implement two- or three-phase commit protocols. The architectures are

1. Centralized
2. Linear
3. Distributed

Centralized architectures involve communications between two entities that the literature likes to call the "coordinator" and the "participants." The role of the coordinator is to collect the termination conditions of transactions that have executed at each of the sites. (Keep in mind that the local site transactions are actually subtransactions of a global distributed transaction submitted to some central coordinating site.)

The role of the coordinator is to collect the termination conditions at each site. Each participating site votes to commit or abort the local subtransaction and informs the coordinator of the decision. The coordinator collects all the decisions and then makes a final decision called the global termination condition. If all the sites have decided to commit, the coordinator updates its own log (the global transaction log) and then informs all the participating sites that they can go ahead and commit their portions of the transactions. If even one site had decided to abort its local subtransaction, the coordinator would have decided to globally abort the distributed transaction by informing all the sites to abort their subtransactions.

This centralized architecture leads to problems if the coor-dinator's site fails. We will see that the second protocol discussed in this section, the three-phase commit protocol, attempts to alleviate the problems caused by centralized two-phase commit strategies.

The linear architecture has no centralized coordinator. The participants pass their decisions along to their adjacent neighbor in a predetermined order. As each site makes a decision, it passes it along to the next site until the last site involved in the distributed transaction is reached. The last site in the chain then returns the decision down the line. This last decision is the one that all the sites abide by.

Notice that if one of the sites somewhere in the middle of the chain aborts, its next neighbor is informed of the failure and the vote changes from commit to abort. The remaining sites now get an abort vote for the transaction. The last site returns the abort vote back up the chain. Eventually, any site that had originally voted to commit is now informed that it must abort. Each site changes its vote until the first site is reached, whereby the global distributed transaction is now aborted.

The distributed architecture approach allows all sites in the network to communicate with each other. In this approach, each site receives the decisions of all the other sites involved in the transaction. Each local site makes its own decision by collecting the votes from the other sites. If one or more of the other sites vote to abort, the site aborts its subtransaction. With this strategy, each site acts as its own coordinator.

All three of these architectures will be discussed later on in this section. Let us now examine the logic of the two-phase and three-phase commit protocols. After our discussions, we will see that the two-phase protocol is called a blocking protocol by the literature. This means that if the coordinator fails, it is possible that one or more of the participants are left in a blocked state because they are waiting for an instruction from the coordinator that will never arrive. The three-phase commit protocol was devised to correct this serious condition.

Two-Phase Commit Protocol

As the name implies, this protocol has two phases or stages that it goes through to terminate a distributed transaction. The coordinator enters a "WAIT" phase while it polls the participants for their decision as to the fate of the distributed transaction. On receiving all of the participants' votes, the coordinator enters either a global commit or global abort phase. The participants enter a ready phase after they inform the coordinator of their termination condition. This "READY" phase is where each participant waits for the coordinator's final decision on the outcome of the global transactions. On receiving the coordinator's decision, each participant enters either a local commit or a local abort phase, after which the transaction ends at each of the sites.

Figure 11.11 shows a simplistic but effective scenario of how the protocol would work if it were implemented between silly stick figures that have the ability to communicate with each other for the purpose of executing global distributed transactions!

In step 1, the coordinator stick figure sends out a prepared message to both participants and immediately enters a WAITING state. In step 3, both participants respond with a COMMIT decision and enter a READY state. The stick figure finishes its coffee, collects both commit responses from the participants, and issues a global commit response to the two participants.

On receiving this response from the coordinator, both the participants locally commit their subtransaction and the dialog ends.

The scenario could have been such that participant number 2 at site 2 decided to abort the transaction while the participant at site 1

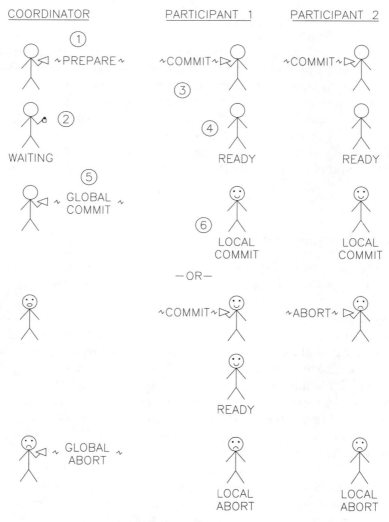

Figure 11.11 Two-phase commit protocol

decided to commit its portion of the transaction. The coordinator
stick figure received one positive response and one negative response, so it decided to abort the transaction globally. It now sends
out a global abort message, and the disappointment can be seen in
the faces of the participants.

Let us now look at this dialog in a more formal, scientific manner.
Figure 11.12 is a state transition diagram for the coordinator process
and the two participating processes in a distributed system. The

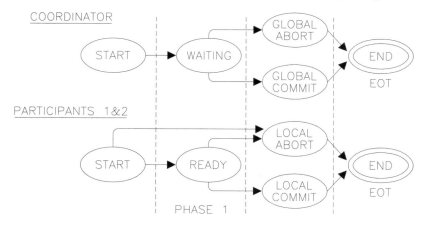

Figure 11.12 Two-phase commit state diagrams

coordinator enters a START state by issuing a PREPARE command
to the participants of the distributed transaction. The coordinator
goes immediately to its next state, the WAITING state.

The participants, on receiving the PREPARE instruction from the
coordinator, send a reply to the coordinator in the form of a local
abort or local commit vote. If the local site aborts, it immediately
goes to the local abort state and waits for the coordinator's response.
If the local site's response was a commit, it enters a READY state and
waits for the coordinator's final global decision. Let's return to the
coordinator state transition diagram (Figure 11.12) and see what
happens next. If both of the participants vote LOCAL COMMIT, the
coordinator leaves the WAITING state and transmits a global COM-
MIT instruction.

Back at each site that is participating in the distributed transaction, the local recovery manager receives the global instruction and
leaves the READY state. Since the coordinator voted to GLOBAL
COMMIT the transaction, both local sites take the appropriate meas-
ures to successfully conclude the execution of their subtransactions.
Each site then acknowledges the local commit so that the coordinator can end the global transaction.

Had one of the participants decided to abort just prior to entering
the READY state, it would have sent a LOCAL ABORT vote to the
coordinator. On tallying all the votes, the coordinator would have
seen that there was one ABORT vote and would have proceeded to
issue a GLOBAL ABORT instruction to all the participants of the
distributed transaction. Notice that the participating site that had

originally voted to COMMIT can now leave the READY state and change its mind by entering the abort state. From these discussions and state diagrams, we can design algorithms for the following three conditions:

1. COMMIT/ABORT decisions
2. Termination processing
3. Recovery processing

(This is left as an excercise for the reader!)

Reliability Protocols

These algorithms work fine if all the sites remain in communication throughout the life of a distributed transaction and no network failures occur. Should a failure occur at one of the sites, the other sites could remain in a WAIT state or READY state, waiting for instuctions from the coordinator that will never come, at least not until the communicatons failure is corrected.

One remedy to this situation is to include a timeout condition for each of the states wherein both the coordinator and the participants are vulnerable to failures. With this timer process, if a response is not received in a certain period of time, the participants or coordinator assume that the other site has failed and it can begin to abort the transaction at its site. Let's see how the coordinator handles this situation.

The coordinator can first implement the timer in the WAITING state of the state transition diagram. If the timer period terminates and all the participants have not returned their decisions, the coordinator decides to terminate the global transaction by sending a GLOBAL ABORT instruction to all the sites participating in the distributed transaction.

Next, the coordinator can time out in either the GLOBAL ABORT or GLOBAL COMMIT state. If all the participants have not acknowledged the global instruction after the coordinator has timed out, the coordinator keeps sending it until the offending site or sites respond.

Once this occurs, it means that the remote failing site(s) has recovered and implemented its local recovery routines. It can now process the global instruction sent by the coordinator and acknowledge it.

Let's take a look at the two states where a participant can time out—either in the INITIAL state or in the READY state. If the participant times out in the INITIAL state, it locally aborts the subtransaction and terminates. A timeout condition in this participant state indicates that the coordinator has failed. When the coordinator recovers, it will wait for a response from the site. Since this site is already finished it will not respond. The coordinator will time out and globally abort the transaction.

If the participant times out in the READY state, it's in a real dilemma. It has already decided to commit the transaction and requires a decision from the coordinator (which is probably down) so it can proceed to the next state. It cannot decide on its own what action to take next as it has no way of knowing the decisions of the other participants involved in the distributed transaction. The three-phase commit protocol takes this condition into account and is discussed next.

Three-Phase Commit Protocol

We have just seen that the two-phase commit protocol is a blocking protocol because coordinator site failures can occur that can cause participants to be blocked in the READY state. The three-phase commit protocol attempts to alleviate this problem by introducing a third phase, the precommit phase. Figure 11.13 shows our old stick figure coordinator and participant friends reenacting the previous COMMIT conversation, this time with the precommit instruction.

The dialog continues as in the two-phase commit protocol up to the WAITING and READY phases, respectively, in the coordinator and participant states. Once the coordinator has received all the votes it enters a precommit state and issues a global precommit message to the participants. The participants receive the global precommit message and proceed to enter a precommit state at each site. Following the precommit message, the coordinator issues the global commit command and both participants happily issue a commit vote as usual.

How does this new state prevent blocking? Let's take a look at a modified version of the two-phase commit protocol so that it now includes the global and local precommit states (Figure 11.14).

Notice that the precommit state has a path to the local abort state in the participant's state transition diagram. Now, if the participant times out at the local precommit state, it can proceed to locally abort

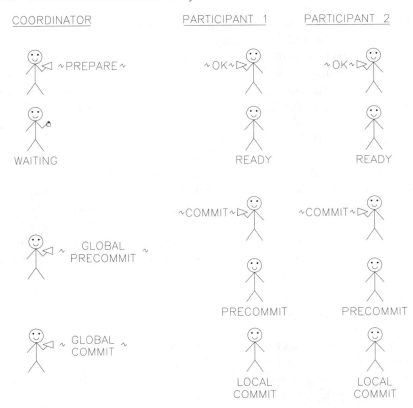

Figure 11.13 Three-phase commit protocol

the transaction, even though it had decided to precommit and eventually commit the local subtransaction.

Recall that in the two-phase commit protocol, once the participant decided to commit the transaction, it could not change its mind. Therefore, we can plainly see that the three-phase commit protocol is a nonblocking protocol. This is because it allows each participant in the distributed transaction a handy escape route from the precommit state if it should time out due to a coordinator site failure or a communication failure that causes the participating site to lose communication contact with the coordinator.

In addition to this feature, some versions of this protocol allow participants to act as a stand-by coordinator should the main coordinator fail. Should this situation occur, the stand-by coordinator assumes its new role and guides the remaining participants to a logical termination of the currently executing distributed transaction. Let

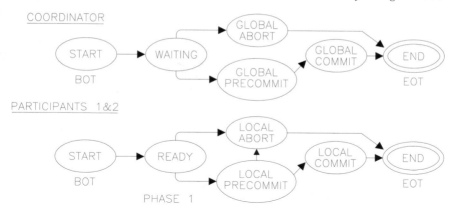

Figure 11.14 Three-phase commit state diagrams

us now briefly examine the three architectures that can be used to implement distributed recovery systems, mentioned earlier in the chapter:

1. The centralized commit architecture
2. The distributed commit architecture
3. The linear commit architecture

Figure 11.15 is a stick figure version of the centralized architecture. As we have just reviewed the functionality of this strategy, I will simply summarize its features by stating that the coordinator is in charge of successfully guiding each participant of the distributed transaction to a termination condition. All of the participants agree to commit the transaction. If even one participant decides to abort the transaction, the coordinator has to instruct all the other participants to abort their portion of the distributed transaction by issuing a global abort message.

Figure 11.16 shows the distributed approach to recovery systems. In this version of the recovery architecture, all participants communicate with each other to find out what each site involved in the transaction has decided to do. The coordinator's role is to inform the local sites that they are involved in the transaction.

In other words, all sites are not necessarily involved in all transactions; therefore, they have to be notified individually as to their participation status. Additionally, the coordinator informs each site as to which other sites are participants in the transaction so that they can initiate conversations with each other to vote on the outcome of

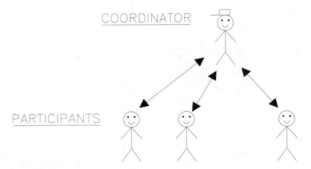

Figure 11.15 Centralized commit architecture

the transaction. With this strategy, each participant knows what the other participants have decided in terms of termination conditions for the transaction. If any participant fails to inform the others as to the decision (because it experienced a site failure), the remaining participants time out while waiting for its decision and each site decides to abort their portion of the distributed subtransaction.

Finally, let's examine the linear approach to recovery architectures. Figure 11.17 shows the stick figures passing a note from left to right.

The note represents the transaction termination condition of each site. The coordinator is the first participant and is there to inform the other participants that they are members of the distributed transaction. The coordinator votes and passes its decision to its right-hand neighbor. The neighbor first examines the vote. If it is a commit vote, and if the current participant decides to commit its portion of the distributed transaction, it passes the commit vote to its neighbor.

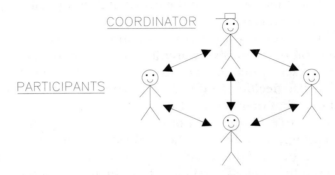

Figure 11.16 Distributed commit architecture

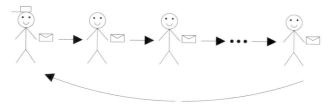

Figure 11.17 Linear commit architecture

If either the coordinator or the participant votes to abort, the next neighbor would receive an abort vote. Once the last participant receives the vote, it sends it back up the chain so that each participant can reexamine the decision. If some participant in the line aborted the transaction, the remaining participants can still change their decisions from commit to abort.

11.7 SUMMARY

This chapter concludes Part II of the book. We have examined distributed design, distributed architecture components, distributed transaction processing, and recovery methods. We were first introduced to the two-phase and three-phase commit protocols in Chapter 10, where they were analyzed in terms of transaction processing in a distributed environment. In this chapter they were examined from the point of view of distributed recovery strategies. We now forge ahead to Part III, where we examine the difficulties that a heterogeneous environment introduces to distributed database architectures.

11.8 END NOTES

1. Özsu, M. Tamer, and P. Valduriez. *Principles of Distributed Database Systems*, Englewood Cliffs, NJ: Prentice Hall, 1991.

2. Bernstein, P. A., V. Hadzilacos, and N. Goodman. *Concurrency Control and Recovery*, Reading, MA: Addison-Wesley, 1987.

P A R T   I I I

Multi-Database
Architectures

12

Introduction to Multi-Database Architectures

12.1 INTRODUCTION

Congratulations, you have made it to the third part of the book. This first chapter is a detailed introduction to the data and component architecture of multi-database management systems. Recall the main characteristic of this architecture: Individual local systems that make up the multi-database system are heterogeneous; that is, each has its own strategy for implementing concurrency, deadlock resolution, and recovery. Additionally, each local system may be based on a different data model.

This chapter will begin by reviewing the three most popular data models. Next, we will design an inventory multi-database for the Traditional Fish 'n' Chips enterprise. The multi-database will span three sites, each site based on one of the models previously discussed.

Once we've derived the schemas, we will design a multi-database model based on the ANSI/SPARC architecture that was discussed in Chapter 3. This approach is taken in Özsu and Valduriez,[1] so we will follow it here. From this model we will design a multi-database management system (MDBMS) and the various layers that make up its query processing strategy.

A critical component of the MDBMS is the global transaction manager. It will be described in Section 12.6. The local component of the multi-database system will also be described in Section 12.6.

12.2 REVIEW OF DATABASE SCHEMAS

A review of the three principal data models is necessary, as we will base our local multi-database schemas on these data models. Figure 12.1 shows a simple relational database containing three relational tables.

Recall that this model requires no pointers or special records to implement the relationships among the tables. These relationships are defined by primary key to primary or foreign key links. These links are called joins and are defined during table creation by specifying which columns act as primary and foreign keys.

Figure 12.1 shows table 1 linked to table 2 over the common column C1 in each table. Table 2 is linked to table 3 via the foreign key C2 belonging to each table; that is, column C1 is the primary key of table T1, and column C2 is a foreign key in tables T2 and T3. A typical query joining these three tables is

```
SELECT T1.C1,T1.C2,T2.C2,T3.C3
FROM T1,T2,T3
WHERE T1.C1 = T2.C1
AND
      T2.C2 = T3.C2
```

The Hierarchical Model

Figure 12.2 shows a database based on the hierarchical data model. This database contains four files and implements the following relationships via special pointers embedded in the files' records:

File 1 is parent to file 2 and file 3.
File 2 is parent to file 4.

Notice that a child entity can have only one parent. A child entity can also be a parent to another child entity. Relationships are defined by including pointers between related records of different files. Programmers must write a new program every time a different view of the data is required. Navigation among records is accomplished by

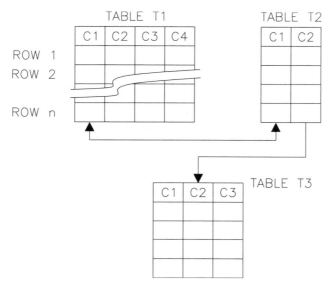

Figure 12.1 A relational database

loading the required address pointers to memory variables and following the links to the related records.

The Network Model

Figure 12.3 is a block diagram of a database based on the CODASYL model. Relationships among network database files are implemented via special data objects called DBTG (database task group) sets. These records contain pointers that link related records in files, permitting one-way or two-way navigation. An application program

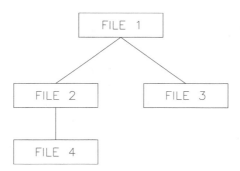

Figure 12.2 A hierarchical data model

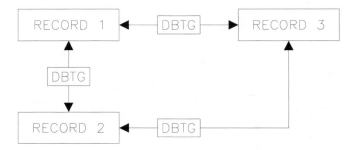

Figure 12.3 The network (CODASYL) model

reads these DBTG sets and navigates through the links. Unlike the hierarchical model, a child can have more than one parent, thereby increasing the modeling power by allowing designers to define complex relationships among files.

This has been a brief review of the three data models for anyone needing a quick refresher. The reader may refer back to Chapter 3 if a more in-depth review is required. Let us now create three inventory databases for our Traditional Fish 'n' Chips enterprise. Each of the inventory databases will be situated in a different city and based on a different data model, as shown by the following table:

Site	DB Model
Edinburgh	Relational
Aberdeen	Hierarchical
Liverpool	Network

12.3 THE TRADITIONAL FISH 'N' CHIPS MULTI-DATABASE SCHEMAS

We will begin the design process in this chapter by creating an entity relationship diagram for each of the three databases. This exercise serves two purposes: First, it shows the relationships among entities so that the proper DBTG sets, pointer records, and primary–foreign key combinations can be derived for each data model. Second, we will integrate these diagrams to create a global multi-database schema when design issues are discussed in Chapter 13. Let's begin by examining the E-R diagram for the Edinburgh site database. Figure 12.4 is an entity-relationship diagram for this site that contains three entities.

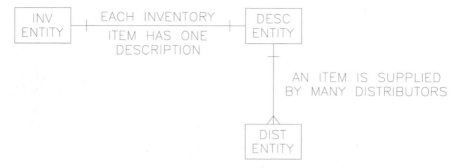

Figure 12.4 E-R diagram for Edinburgh site database

This diagram is used to build a database containing three relational tables. The first entity, inventory (INV), is used to store the inventory levels for each of the food items sold at a typical Traditional Fish 'n' Chips restaurant. It is linked to another entity, item description entity (DESC), by a one-to-one relationship link. This link states:

"For every inventory item there is one description."

The item description entity will contain two attributes, an item code and a description attribute.

The item description entity is linked to another entity, distributor (DIST), over a one-to-many relationship. The relationship states:

"An item is supplied by more than one supplier."

Below is a table showing the attributes of each entity:

Entity	Attribute Name	Description Name
INV	icode	item identification code
	qty	item inventory level
	site	restaurant site
DESC	icode	item identification code
	desc	item description
DIST	icode	item identification code
	dname	distributor's name
	price	item price (per case)
	tel	distributor's telephone

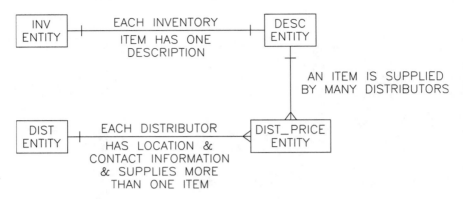

Figure 12.5 E-R diagram for Aberdeen site database

Next, let's examine the E-R diagram for the database situated in Aberdeen, Scotland. Figure 12.5 is an E-R diagram depicting a database that contains four entities.

Before describing the relationship between each entity, let us define each entity's role and the attributes that it contains. The inventory and item entities are similar to the same entities in the previous diagram. They contain the following attributes:

Entity	Attribute Name	Description Name
INV	ucode	unit code
	qty	quantity on hand
	site	restaurant site
DESC	ucode	unit code
	desc	description

A third entity is DIST_PRICE. Its purpose is to show the distributor for each item together with the item's price. This entity contains the following attributes:

Entity	Attribute Name	Description Name
DIST_PRICE	ucode	item code
	price	item price
	dcode	distributor code

The last entity is distributor information, used to contain distributor-related information such as name and address. It contains the following attributes:

Entity	Attribute Name	Description Name
DIST	dcode	distributor code
	dname	distributor name
	address	distributor address
	tel	distributor telephone

Now let's define the relationships among the entities. The first three entities have identical relationships as described in the E-R diagram for the Edinburgh site, so they will not be repeated. The third entity, DIST_PRICE, is related to the DIST entity via the following relationship:

```
"Each distributor has location and contact information."
```

Additionally,

```
"Each distributor supplies more than one item."
```

We can see that the relationship is a one-to-many relationship!

Let us examine the last E-R diagram for the inventory database that will be situated at the Liverpool site. Figure 12.6 shows an entity relationship diagram containing five entities. As with the prior two cases, the first two entities serve identical functions, so I will list only the attributes:

Entity	Attribute Name	Description Name
INV	icode	item code
	qty	item inventory level
	olvl	order level
	dcode	distributor code
	rname	restaurant name
DESC	icode	item code
	desc	description
PRICE	icode	item code
	dcode	distributor code
	price	item price
DIST	dcode	distributor code
	name	name of distributor
	acode	distributor address code
	tel	distributor telephone

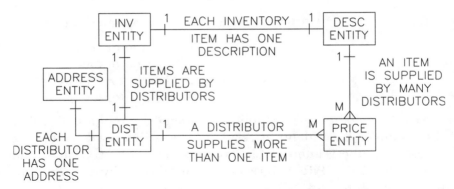

Figure 12.6 E-R diagram for Liverpool site database

Entity	Attribute Name	Description Name
ADDRESS	acode	distributor address code
	city	city name
	street	address

Notice the slight difference in the number and domain of the attributes in each of the entity-relationship diagrams? These discrepancies will have to be resolved when a global schema is designed for the multi-database. (This topic will be discussed in Chapter 13.)

Now that the E-R diagrams for the databases for each site have been defined, let us build the actual database schema for each location. Figure 12.7 shows the three tables that make up the relational database at the Edinburgh site. The following three SQL DDL statements can be used to create the three tables:

```
EXEC SQL
CREATE TABLE INV_TBL
        (
        ICODE    CHAR(4)     NOT NULL,
        QTY      INTEGER     NOT NULL,
        SITE     CHAR(20)    NOT NULL,
        PRIMARY KEY(CODE));

EXEC SQL
CREATE TABLE INV_DESC
        (
        ICODE    CHAR(4)     NOT NULL,
        DESC     CHAR(40)    NOT NULL,
        PRIMARY KEY(CODE));
```

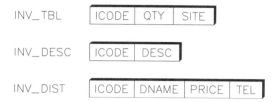

Figure 12.7 Relational schema for Edinburgh site

```
EXEC SQL
CREATE TABLE INV_DIST
        (
        ICODE    CHAR(4)    NOT NULL,
        DNAME    CHAR(20)   NOT NULL,
        DECIMAL  PRICE      NOT NULL // (PER CASE PRICE)
        CHAR     TEL(7)     NOT NULL,
        PRIMARY KEY(ICODE));
```

Not a complicated schema, but notice the absence of an address field in all of the tables. This will be a problem when schema integration takes place in the design process. The reader can plainly see that only the primary keys are used to implement relationships—no foreign keys are required.

Let's take a look at the database schema for the hierarchical database at the Aberdeen site. This schema can be seen in Figure 12.8.

The reader should immediately notice three things. First, the fields used as keys for the item codes have different names than the ones used in the relational database situated in Edinburgh. Second, four files are required to implement the same basic information that took only three tables in the relational model. Third, there are two new fields, an address and a telephone number, that were not present in the relational schema for the Edinburgh site. Keep these facts

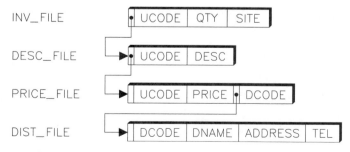

Figure 12.8 Hierarchical model for Aberdeen site

in mind—they will pose significant problems when we design the global schema in Chapter 13.

Below is the schema implemented as a pseudo C language data structure:

```
struct INV_FILE
     {
     char ucode[5]; // inventory code
     long quantity  // inventory level quantity
     char site[20]; // restaurant site
     struct ITEM_FILE *pItemRec;
     }inv_tblbuf;

#define PRIMARY_INV_FILE_KEY inv_tblbuf.ucode

struct DESC_FILE
     {
     char ucode[5]; // inventory code
     char desc[80]; // item description
     struct ITEM_DIST *pItemDist;
     }item_tblbuf;

#define PRIMARY_ITEM_FILE_KEY item_tblbuf.ucode

struct PRICE_FILE
     {
     char ucode[5];  // inventory code
     double price;   // item price for one case
     char dcode[8];  // distributor code
     struct DIST_INFO *pDistInfo;
     } dist_tblbuf;

// primary key for the file
#define PRIMARY_DIST_KEY dist_tblbuf.ucode;

// foreign key used to link to dist-info file
#define FOREIGN_DIST_KEY dist_tblbuf.dcode
```

Last but not least is the C structure used for defining a record in the dist_info file:

```
struct DIST_FILE
     {
     char dcode[8]; // distributor code
     char dname[20]; // distributor name
     char address[80]; // distributor address
     char tel[8]; // distributor telephone
     }dinfo_buf;

// primary key definition
#define PRIMARY_DISTINFO_KEY dinfo_buf.dcode
```

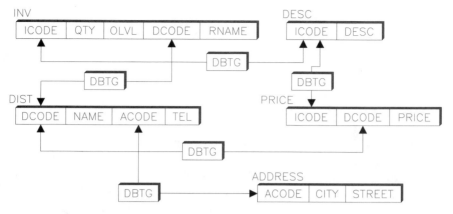

Figure 12.9 Network model for Liverpool site

The reader should have noticed that each structure (except for the last one) has an embedded structure as its member. These embedded structures are used to hold the address pointers when an application builds the links required for navigation from one related record to the next. These pointers take the place of the primary key definitions of the relational model.

Let us create our final database schema. This schema is used at the Liverpool site to create a database based on the CODASYL network model. Figure 12.9 is a block diagram of the schema together with the DBTG sets used to implement the relationships among the files. Below is a pseudocode that defines the schema for this database.

```
DECLARE RECORD INV_FILE:
     ICODE   CHAR(5);    // inventory code
     QTY     INTEGER;    // inventory level
     OLVL    INTEGER;    // order level
     DCODE   CHAR(5);    // distributor code
     RNAME   CHAR(20);   // restaurant name

PRIMARY KEY IS ICODE;    // declare field ICODE as primary key
FOREIGN KEY IS DCODE;    // declare field DCODE as foreign key
END DECLARE RECORD INV_FILE;

DECLARE RECORD DESC_FILE:
     ICODE   CHAR(5);    // inventory code
     DESC    CHAR(40);   // description field

PRIMARY KEY IS ICODE;
END DECLARE RECORD DESC_FILE;
```

```
DECLARE RECORD PRICE_FILE:
     ICODE   CHAR(5);    // inventory code
     DCODE   CHAR(5);    // distributor code
     PRICE   DECIMAL;    // item price per 10 cases !!!

PRIMARY KEY IS ICODE;
FOREIGN KEY IS DCODE;
END DECLARE RECORD PRICE_FILE;
```

The reader should notice that in this database the price is for 10 cases per unit order. In the other two schemas each price was on a per-case unit order quantity. Does the reader think this difference will be a problem when the global schema is created? YES!!! Let's define the remaining records and DBTG sets for this database.

```
DECLARE RECORD DIST_FILE:
     DCODE   CHAR(5);    // distributor code
     NAME    CHAR(40);   // distributor name
     ACODE   CHAR(5);    // distributor address code
     TEL     CHAR(11);   // distributor telephone number

PRIMARY KEY IS DCODE;
FOREIGN KEY IS ACODE;
END DECLARE RECORD DIST_FILE;

DECLARE RECORD ADDR_FILE:
     ACODE   CHAR(5);    // address code
     CITY    CHAR(20);   // city name
     STREET  CHAR(40);   // distributor street address

PRIMARY KEY IS ACODE;
END DECLARE RECORD ADDR_FILE;
```

Now let's introduce some more pseudocode to create the DBTG sets for this database.

```
DECLARE DBTG RECORD INV_TO_DESC:
PRIMARY KEY INV_FILE.ICODE LINKS TO
     PRIMARY KEY DESC_FILE.ICODE:
     INV_ICODE_ADDRESS LONG; // pointer to INV_FILE record
     DESC_ICODE_ADDRESS LONG; // pointer to DESC_FILE record
END DECLARE DBTG RECORD INV_TO_DESC;

DECLARE DBTG_RECORD DESC_TO_PRICE:
PRIMARY KEY DESC_FILE.ICODE LINKS TO
     PRIMARY KEY PRICE_FILE.ICODE;
     DESC_ICODE_ADDRESS LONG; // pointer to DESC_FILE record
```

```
      PRICE_ICODE_ADDRESS LONG; // pointer to PRICE_FILE record
END DECLARE DBTG RECORD DESC_TO_PRICE;

DECLARE DBTG RECORD PRICE_TO_DIST:
    FOREIGN KEY PRICE_FILE.DCODE LINKS TO
        PRIMARY KEY DIST_FILE.DCODE;
    PRICE_DCODE_ADDRESS LONG; // pointer to PRICE record
    DIST_DCODE_ADDRESS LONG;  // pointer to DIST record
END DECLARE DBTG RECORD PRICE_TO_LIST;

DECLARE DBTG RECORD DIST_TO_ADDRESS:
    FOREIGN KEY DIST_FILE.ACODE LINKS TO
        PRIMARY KEY ADDR_FILE.ACODE;
    DIST_ACODE_ADDRESS LONG; // pointer to DIST record
    ADDR_ACODE_ADDRESS LONG; // pointer to ADDRESS record
END DECLARE DBTG RECORD DIST_TO_ADDRESS;

DECLARE DBTG RECORD DIST_TO_INV:
    PRIMARY KEY DIST_FILE.DCODE LINKS TO
        FOREIGN KEY INV_FILE.DCODE;
    DIST_DCODE_ADDRESS LONG; // address to DIST record
    INV_DCODE_ADDRESS LONG;  // address to INV record
END DECLARE DBTG RECORD DIST_TO_INV;
```

What did this exercise accomplish? The reader should notice that although each site requires the same type of data to be stored in its database, each site has implemented the data model in a drastically different way. First, the data models are different (relational versus hierarchical versus network). Second, Edinburgh needed only three table files to model the information, Aberdeen needed four, and Liverpool needed five files. Third, the reader should have noticed slight semantic differences (like the price attribute semantic). In the first two sites, the price refers to the price each vendor quotes for one case. In the Liverpool database, the price refers to 10-case shipments.

Finally, the reader should have noticed that the Edinburgh site failed to include address information. The database at Aberdeen includes address information as a field in the dist-info file record. In the Liverpool database, the address information is implemented as a new entity called ADDR_FILE. The actual address information is broken up into a city field and a street address field.

We can plainly see that conflicts occur in the following general areas:

1. Attribute names (synonyms and homonyms)
2. Attribute semantics

3. Data object structure representation

4. Units of measure (i.e., price for 1 case versus price for 10 cases)

I hope I have succeeded in making the reader aware of these issues. Chapter 13 will show how the literature attempts to address these problems and what type of design steps are required to integrate diverse database schemas to generate a global schema that can be used by a multi-database system. Let's continue by examining the components of a simple multi-database system.

12.4 MULTI-DATABASE ARCHITECTURE BASED ON THE ANSI/SPARC MODEL

In this section we briefly review a multi-database model that is based on the ANSI/SPARC model. As others have done in the literature, we will discuss an architecture for multi-databases derived from this model. Figure 12.10 shows the three layers of the model.

The lowest level (internal schema) represents the physical file layouts of the database table records. This is where the table lengths, field sizes, and disk offsets are defined for each of the files that

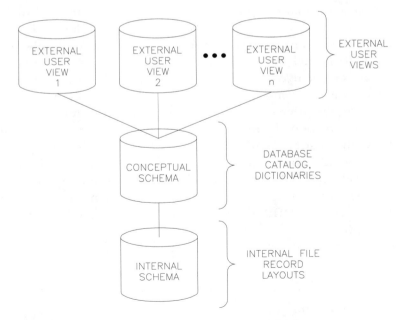

Figure 12.10 The ANSI/SPARC data model revisited

compose a typical database. The next level is the conceptual schema. This is where the objects that make up the database are defined. This level is typically seen by the database administrator and is implemented as either database catalogs or data dictionaries. The third and final layer is the external user view layer. This level is seen and accessed by the users or application programs at each local site. If a relational model is used, the "view" object is used to represent this level. For example, the following SQL DDL command can be used to create an external user view called PAYROLL:

```
CREATE VIEW PAYROLL
      (
      EMP_NAME CHAR(20) NOT NULL,
      SALARY   DECIMAL NOT NULL)
AS SELECT ENAME,SAL FROM EMP_PAY;
```

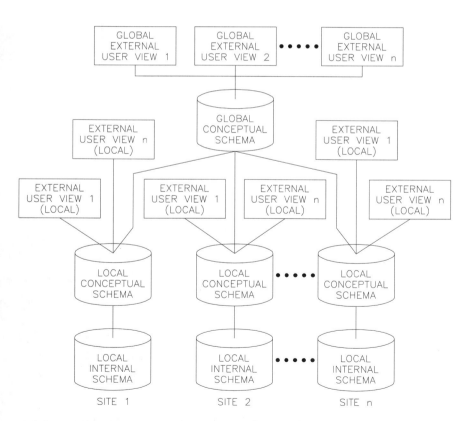

Figure 12.11a A multi-database architecture based on the ANSI/SPARC data model

External views are based on all or portions of relations that are defined in the conceptual schema. Figure 12.11a shows a multi-database model that is derived by integrating all of the local conceptual schemas into one global conceptual schema. New global external user views are created to allow users of the multi-database access to the system.

The reader should notice that the local external user views still exist at the local site, preserving local user autonomy. An alternate approach is to integrate all or some of the local external user views to create the global conceptual schema. This approach is shown in Figure 12.11b.

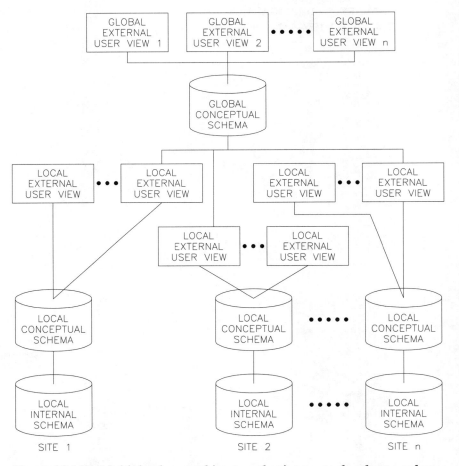

Figure 12.11b Multi-database architecture that integrates local external user views

Throughout our discussions we will utilize the approach depicted by the first data model. Let us now examine the software components used to implement a multi-database system.

12.5 TWO EXAMPLE MDBMS ARCHITECTURES

In this section, two architectures are presented that are discussed in the literature. The first model is described in Özsu and Valduriez[1] and represents a general model that describes the behavior of a typical multi-database management system. The second system is modeled after the PEGASUS system that was created at Hewlett-Packard. The reader is referred to an article by Ahmed et al.,[2] for complete details on the sequence of operation and architecture of the modules that make up the system. I will use concepts from both of these architectures to derive a simple MDBMS that will be used by our Traditional Fish 'n' Chips enterprise to connect the three inventory databases described earlier in this chapter.

Let us now continue by examining the general model described in Özsu and Valduriez.[1] A high-level block diagram of this architecture can be seen in Figure 12.12a.

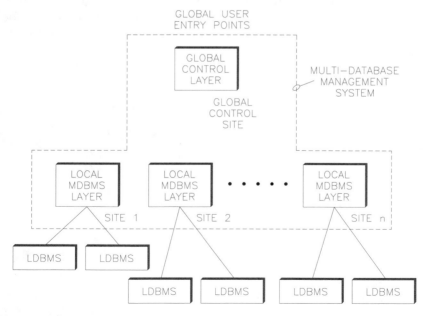

Figure 12.12a Multi-database architecture

The central architecture is composed of a central global control layer situated at a dedicated control site. Its main functions are to accept global user queries, fragment them according to the sites where the data reside, dispatch the query fragments, and coordinate all activities among sites involved in the query so as to generate a final result for the user.

At each local MDBMS site there is a local layer that interacts with the global layer to process each query fragment that was routed to each site involved in the global query. Each site contains one or more local DBMS; it is the function of the local MDBMS to further decompose the global query fragments into subfragments, perform any required translation from the global query language to the local query language, and route the translated fragment to the appropriate local DBMS. Let's examine each of the two layers in greater detail.

Figure 12.12b shows a detailed view of the general components that make up the global control layer. The fragmentor component accepts queries submitted by the global user. It consults a directory for location information and fragments the query into global fragments to be routed to the sites where the desired data are located. The global query fragments are passed to an optimizer/router layer so that an execution strategy can be generated. This execution strategy contains information as to how intermediate result sets are to be generated, joined, and routed to sites that will perform the distributed joins.

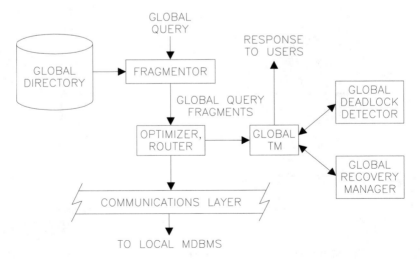

Figure 12.12b The global control layer detail

Once the strategy is created, it is passed to the local MDBMS (via the communications layer software) and to the global transaction manager. Connected to the global transaction manager are the global deadlock detector and global recovery manager, whose functions we are already familiar with.

Figure 12.12c shows details of the local MDBMS and the local DBMS. The global query fragments plus the execution instructions

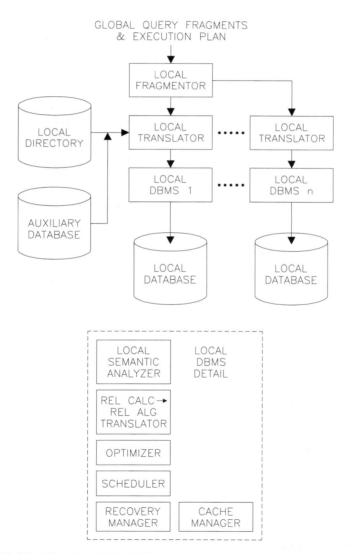

Figure 12.12c The local MDBMS detail global query fragments and execution plan

are received by the LMDBMS and the query fragment is passed on to the local fragmentor. Input to the local fragmentor are the query fragment and information from a local directory. The local directory contains information about the databases that reside at the site.

The fragmentor splits the query into more subfragments, which are then passed to local translator modules. Each module translates the query fragments (whose syntax is already based on the global query language) to the syntax that is used by the local DBMS. An auxiliary database is used for this database. (Auxiliary databases are discussed in Chapter 13.) The auxiliary database contains the mapping and grammar conversion rules required to perform the translation.

Once this translation is performed, the query fragment is passed to the appropriate local DBMS. For example, let's assume that a query fragment for a local site was received by the local MDBMS. The query fragment accesses two databases at this site. The first database is implemented with IBM's DB2 and uses SQL as the query language. The second database is implemented with the INGRES DBMS and uses QUEL as the query language. Further assume that the global query language is also SQL. The following query is generated and submitted to the global site:

```
SELECT T1.C1,T1.C2,T2.C3
FROM T1,T2
WHERE T1.C1 = T2.C1
AND T3.C3 = 'London'
```

Assume table T1 is located in the DB2 database and table T2 is located in the INGRES database. The fragmentor generates the following two subfragments:

```
// DB2 syntax
     SELECT T1.C1,T1.C2
     FROM T1

// QUEL syntax
RANGE OF TVT2 is T2
RETRIEVE (TVT2.C1,TVT2.C3)
WHERE TVT2.C3 = 'London'
```

Each of these fragments is passed on to its respective database management system for final processing.

The boxed-in area of Figure 12.12c shows the main components of a typical local DBMS. The subquery is accepted for analysis by the local semantic analyzer. Once it passes inspection, it is translated from a relational calculus query to a relational algebra formula so

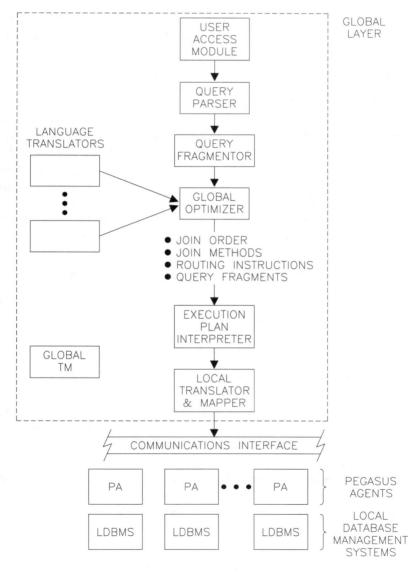

Figure 12.13 The PEGASUS MDBMS architecture

that it can be optimized and finally passed to the scheduler for execution.

These last steps were discussed in Chapter 5, where centralized database management systems are examined. I refer the reader to that chapter for further details. Let's see how the PEGASUS system fits in with this general model.

Figure 12.13 is a simplified block diagram of the PEGASUS architecture. This architecture is also split into a global layer and various local layers. A global layer submits a query to the global access module, which in turn passes it on to the parser and query fragmentor. The query fragmentor generates fragments that are translated and optimized by the global optimizer. The optimizer generates a plan that includes global join ordering, join strategies, and routing instructions for the temporary result sets generated by the subqueries. This information is passed on to the execution plan interpreter for routing and processing. The local translator and mapper provide further translation functions that might not be included in the global optimizer step discussed earlier.

The translated query fragments are now passed on via the communications interface to the local site where processes called query agents make sure that the transaction is submitted to their local DBMS for execution. The PEGASUS agents pass back any temporary result information for final processing at the central site.

Let's derive a multi-database architecture for our Traditional Fish 'n' Chips enterprise based on the features of the two architectures just discussed.

12.6 THE TRADITIONAL FISH 'N' CHIPS MDBMS

Now that we have examined a generic architecture and an actual architecture of an MDBMS, let's derive a simple system that combines the important features of both. Figure 12.14 is a block diagram of our architecture.

This architecture is also divided into a global software component and multiple local components. The global component of Figure 12.14 is divided into the following four layers:

1.   The global fragmentation layer
2.   The localizer layer
3.   The translation layer
4.   The strategy generation layer

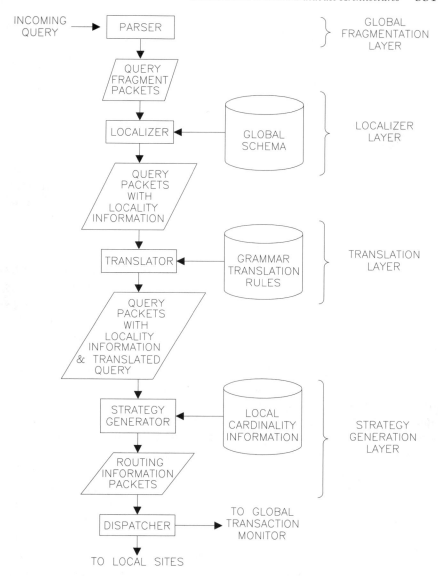

Figure 12.14 MDBMS architecture for the Traditional Fish 'n' Chips enterprise

The Global Layers

Let us begin with the global fragmentation layer. This layer is composed of one module called the parser. Its function is to accept incoming queries from global users, parse them, and generate specialized packets called query fragment packets. The query packets contain lists that describe the major database objects referenced by the query:

1. All relations referred to by the query
2. Attributes for each relation
3. All qualifying predicates in each query
4. Sites involved in the query

The query fragment packets are passed to the localizer module, whose function is to add location information. In our simple model, the localizer consults the global schema and adds site location names to each of the packets that identify the relations referenced by the query.

Next, the query packets (which now contain location information) are passed to the translator module. The translator module consults its grammar translation database, identifies each site involved in the query, and translates each query fragment to the appropriate syntax supported by each local site. As part of this information, the query packets retain the original global syntax version of the query and the new translated version.

The query packets are now passed on to the strategy generator. This module consults the global schema for local relation cardinality information so as to generate a strategy for routing temporary result sets and performing global joins. It applies some of the cost functions discussed in Chapter 9 to optimize the join order of tables located at remote sites.

Now that an execution strategy has been generated, the entire series of packets and instructions are sent to the dispatcher for routing. The combination of the query packets and strategy instructions is bundled into a series of packets called routing information packets. These packets are routed to the local sites involved in the processing of global queries and also to the global transaction monitor.

Let's examine the subarchitecture of the global transaction monitor next. Figure 12.15 shows this architecture.

Notice the by now familiar global deadlock detector and the global recovery manager. In our case, input to the global deadlock detector is a WAIT-FOR-GRAPH that contains information used to identify global deadlocks. It is the responsibility of the local MDBMS components to submit local WAIT-FOR-GRAPHS (at predetermined intervals) to the global deadlock detector (GDD). The GDD then

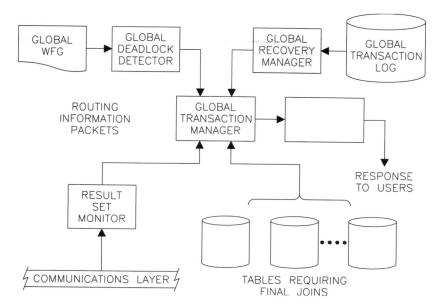

Figure 12.15 The global transaction manager

assembles them into a global WAIT-FOR-GRAPH and proceeds to look for deadlocks.

The global recovery manager maintains a global transaction log to monitor the success or failure of global transactions. Inputs for the global transaction manager are the routing information packets generated by the strategy generator module. The global transaction manager receives packets that instruct it on how to perform any joins of temporary result sets generated by the local sites involved in the query.

It is the responsibility of the result set monitor to accept any result sets transmitted by the local sites and place them in temporary work areas so that they can be processed by the global transaction manager.

As these results are received, the result set monitor notifies the GTM of their availability. When all required result sets are in the temporary work area, the GTM performs any joins and notifies the response router module to send the results to the requesting user site.

The Local MDB Interface Layer

Figure 12.16 shows the architecture of a typical site. The local MDB interface layer retrieves query fragments that are routed over the

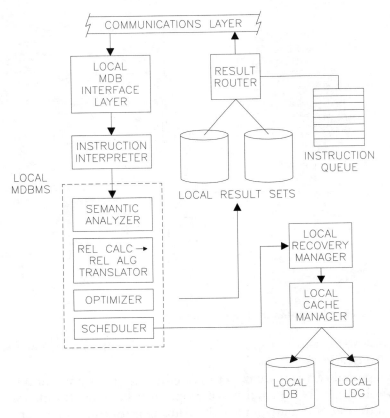

Figure 12.16 The local DBMS layer architecture

communications network. It submits the fragments together with the processing instructions to the local instruction interpreter module. At this level, the query is submitted to the local DBMS and the instructions are placed in a queue belonging to the result router module.

The result router monitors this queue and builds a list of temporary result set names together with their destinations. As each result is created by the DBMS, the result router reads it and transmits it to its destination site. It then removes the names from its holding list and proceeds to process the next items in its list.

The local MDBMS architecture follows the architecture that is currently described in the literature; that is, upon receiving a query fragment, it proceeds to analyze it in the semantic analyzer module, and translates the calculus form of the query to its relational algebra equivalent in the decomposition module. The relational algebra formula is optimized in the optimizer and finally submitted to the scheduler.

The architecture just described has been greatly simplified. It combines the components of the model described in Özsu and Valduriez[1] and the components of the PEGASUS architecture.[2] Each site supports only one database management system and one database. Distributed joins are processed at either the global control site or the local designated sites, as specified by the execution strategy plan. Global optimization consists of simply reordering the join requirements according to the sizes of the intermediate result sets. Global statistics are limited to table cardinalities, used by cost formulas to determine the sizes of the intermediate result sets after qualifying predicates are applied.

12.7 SUMMARY

Now that we have reviewed the schema of the Traditional Fish 'n' Chips enterprise, we can explore various design techniques currently popular in the literature. Chapter 13 introduces these design methodologies so that we can create a global schema out of the local schemas for each site just reviewed.

12.8 END NOTES

1.   Özsu, M. Tamer, and P. Valduriez. *Principles of Distributed Database Systems*, Englewood Cliffs, NJ: Prentice Hall, 1991.

2.   Ahmed, R. et al. "The PEGASUS Heterogeneous Multidatabase System," *IEEE Computer*, vol. 24, no. 12 (December 1991): pp. 19–27.

13

Multi-Database Design Issues

13.1 INTRODUCTION

Chapter 8 in Part II of this book discussed design strategies for distributed databases. We saw that the design process was "top-down"; that is, none of the local site schemas existed, so the designer had to start from an existing global schema and generate each of the table fragments in the distributed database by applying the techniques of horizontal, vertical, or hybrid fragmentation.

This chapter deals with the issues and methodology that a designer must be familiar with in order to implement a multi-database system. We will see that the design protocol is "bottom-up." The designer is given a set of database schemas; possibly the data models are heterogeneous. The designer must somehow integrate them to generate a global schema that contains all the mappings, translations, and locality information for the components of each local database.

The chapter begins by introducing some simple steps that are basically intuitive. These steps are explained as we integrate the three schemas of the Traditional Fish 'n' Chips enterprise that were created in Chapter 12.

Next, Section 13.3 translates each schema to an intermediate schema common to all the sites involved in the integration process. To accomplish this task, we will select the entity-relationship method for schema representation.

Section 13.4 reviews some of the integration techniques that are currently discussed in the literature.

In Section 13.5, we proceed to apply simple design steps to generate an intermediate global schema that integrates all three of the local schemas.

In Section 13.6, the intermediate global schema is converted to a relational schema and the SQL commands for creating each of the tables in the schema are introduced.

The simplified steps discussed in this chapter are a subset of the more formal design phases that are currently popular in the literature. Özsu and Valduriez[1] have integrated these steps and we conclude the chapter by discussing their approach. The reader will see that the simplified approach discussed in the chapter is merely a subset of the approach discussed in Özsu and Valduriez.

13.2 SIMPLIFIED DESIGN STEPS

Figure 13.1 illustrates the three principal steps together with the subtasks that make up the simplified design methodology.

The first two steps, schema translation and schema integration, are the same steps discussed in the literature. Step 3, generation, involves the creation of the templates for each relation that is a member of the global schema. Let's briefly discuss each of the main steps and then analyze the subtasks for each step.

The schema translation step is where each of the local data models is translated to a common data model to facilitate the integration procedure that occurs in step 2. Usually, the following translation occurs:

1. Hierarchical-to-entity relationship
2. Network-to-entity relationship
3. Relational-to-entity relationship

This translation step has the following subtasks:

1. Select the global schema model.
2. Select the schema integration method.

Subtask 1 requires that the designer select the data model that will be used to implement the global schema. Subtask 2 is discussed in Section 13.4, where we examine the various schema integration techniques discussed in the literature. For our purposes, we will select the

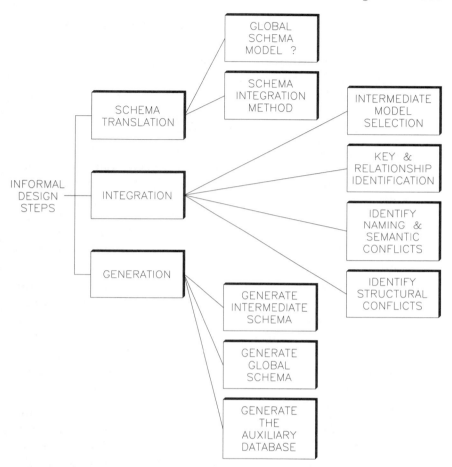

Figure 13.1 Informal, intuitive design steps

relational model for the global schema because of its current popularity and versatility.

The second design step, integration, involves the application of a set of techniques that integrate the local schemas into one large, common schema that contains the attributes and characteristics of all the local schemas. As the integration process progresses, the following four subtasks must be performed:

1. Intermediate model selection. This is when the designer selects a data model that can be used to integrate all the local schemas. We will translate the local schemas to the entity-rela-

tionship model, and we will retain that model as the intermediate global schema representation.

2. Key and relationship identification. As the design process progresses, the primary and foreign keys in each table are identified. The relationships between the tables are also identified. This will facilitate the selection of primary and foreign keys when the final global schema is created.

3. Identification of naming and semantic conflicts. In this phase the designer must isolate the data objects that have either different names but refer to the same object domain or objects with identical names that refer to completely different domains. Additionally, the designer must isolate objects that are semantically different. In our case we saw that the price of an item was given on a per-case basis in two of the databases but in the third database the price reflected a 10-case shipment.

4. Identifying structural conflicts. During this phase of the design process, the designer must isolate objects that are represented differently from one schema to the other. Case in point, the address object in one of the relations in the Aberdeen database is represented as an attribute of a relation. In the Liverpool database it is represented as a relation with fields that include an address code, city name, and street address.

The third step in our simplified design methodology is schema generation. The intermediate schema is generated after all the information in step 2 has been identified and documented. The designer then proceeds to implement the global schema by defining the relation definitions that will be used to create each relation in the global schema.

The generation step will be discussed in Section 13.6. The relational model will be selected as the representation for our global schema. Let's now proceed to translate each of the local schemas of the Traditional Fish 'n' Chips inventory database. Recall that the Edinburgh site implements the relational model, the Aberdeen site implements the hierarchical model, and the Liverpool site implements the network model.

The steps we will follow begin with the translation of each local model to the entity-relationship model. Once we have the three E-R models, we will integrate them into one large E-R representation and then convert it to a relational model. Let's proceed!

13.3 SCHEMA TRANSLATION

Usually, database schemas are derived from an entity-relationship diagram. This step requires us to perform the inverse of this traditional method. Given a database schema, we must

1. Identify the target model.
2. Identify the keys.
3. Derive the relationship from the keys. For this step we must seek the assistance of the local administrator to find out the semantics of each relationship.

We will begin by analyzing the Edinburgh site. Figure 13.2a shows the schema together with the derived entity-relationship diagram for the local schema.

We will see that the data model for this database is the relational model. Tables are linked by joining over the primary key ICODE that

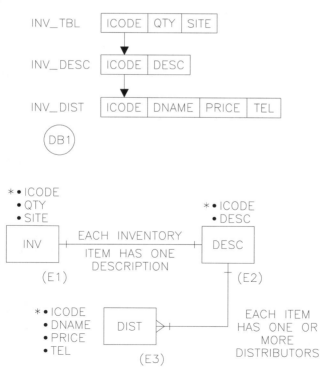

Figure 13.2a Edinburgh site schema

appears in each table. The following relationships are supplied by the local administrator in Edinburgh.

The inventory table contains supply levels for each item sold in a local restaurant. Each item must be described by a record in the DESC entity. Therefore, the relationship between the INV entity and the DESC entity is one to one.

Each item described in the DESC entity can be supplied by one or more distributors. Hence, the relationship between the DESC entity and the DIST entity is one to many.

The database schema and entity-relationship diagram for the Aberdeen site are shown in Figure 13.2b. Here we see a hierarchical database composed of four files. The records in the first three files

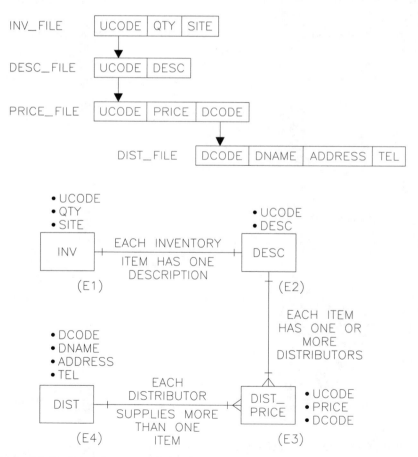

Figure 13.2b Aberdeen site schema

are related by the following pointers supplied in the unit code (UCODE) field. The record in the fourth file is related to the third file via a pointer identified by the distributor code (DCODE) field.

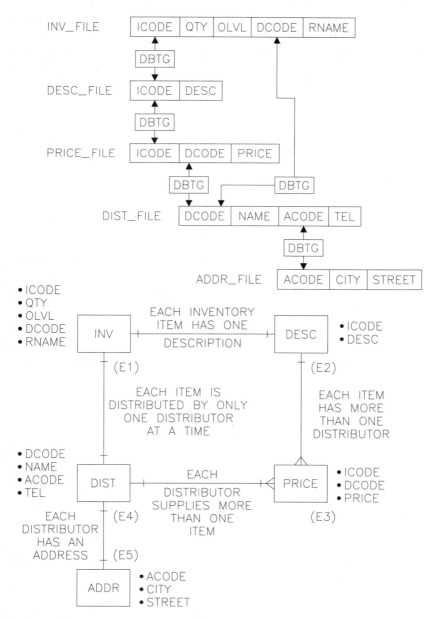

Figure 13.2c Liverpool site schema

Comparing this schema with the Edinburgh schema, we see that the latter is a subset of the former. Some extra attributes have been added to implement the relationship with the new distributor entity.

Figure 13.2c shows the schema and entity-relationship diagram for the database situated in Liverpool. This is a much more complicated schema. Recall that the data model is the CODASYL network model.

There are five entities; each defines relationships with the other entities via one or more DBTG sets. Below is a summary of the relationships supplied by the local administrator at the Liverpool site:

- Relationship between INV and DESC entities. Each inventory item has one description.

- Relationship between DESC and PRICE entities. Each item described can be supplied by one or more vendors. (Some vendor prices are less than the others.)

- Relationship between PRICE and DIST entities. Each distributor has one address record in the ADDR entity.

Again, we see that the schemas of the Edinburgh site and the Aberdeen site are subsets of this schema. The one important point to be aware of is that another entity has been added, namely, the ADDR address information entity. The Aberdeen site implemented this data object as an attribute of the DIST entity. In the Liverpool site, it is implemented as a new relation.

Let's continue by introducing three basic integration techniques before actually integrating our three E-R diagrams. We will select one of the integration methods after analyzing each technique.

13.4 INTEGRATION TECHNIQUES

Now that the local schemas have been generated, we must merge them to create one intermediate schema that will be used to create the global schema. Below are the three methods that we will discuss together with the references to the researchers that discussed or authored the methods:

1. Pure Binary Schema Integration (Batini and Lenzirini[2] and Dayal and Hwang[3])

2. Ladder Binary Schema Integration (Pu[4])

3. Nary Integration Techniques (Batini et al.[5])

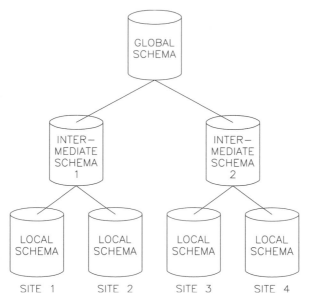

Figure 13.3 Pure binary schema integration

Figure 13.3 shows the pure binary schema integration technique. At the bottom of the figure, we see four local schemas. The schema at site 1 is integrated with the schema at site 2 to generate the intermediate schema 1. The schema at site 3 is integrated with the schema at site 4 to generate the intermediate schema 2. Finally, the two intermediate schemas are integrated to create the final global schema.

This technique has the benefit of simplicity. The designer can choose to select the two simplest schemas, integrate them, and then select the next two simplest schemas, integrate them, and so on until the final global schema is generated.

By simplest, I mean the two schemas that have the fewest naming, semantic, and structural conflicts. We also wish to integrate schemas that are almost identical in appearance as to attribute count, type, and domain.

Figure 13.4 is a block diagram depicting the binary ladder schema integration method. This method is similar to the pure binary technique in that two schemas are integrated at a time. This retains the simplicity benefit. Figure 13.4 shows *n* local schemas that require integration. The schema at site 1 is integrated with the schema at site 2 to generate the first intermediate schema.

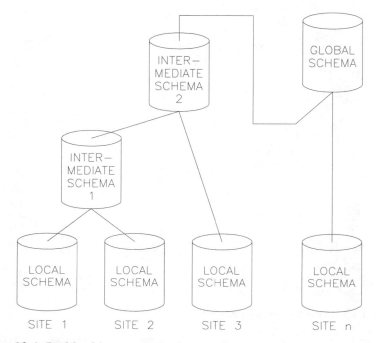

Figure 13.4 Ladder binary schema integration

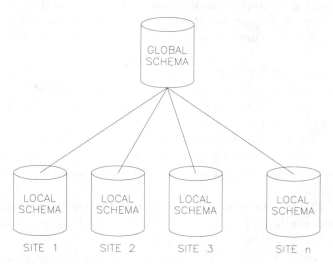

Figure 13.5 Nary schema integration

The first intermediate schema is integrated with the third local schema to generate intermediate schema 2. Each intermediate schema is then integrated with the next local schema in line until the last local schema is absorbed. At this point, the resulting intermediate schema represents the intermediate global schema that can be transformed to the selected target model for the global schema.

Figure 13.5 is a block diagram for the Nary integration technique. This is a one-shot strategy. The information for all sites is collected and all the local schemas are integrated at one time. Although this is a faster technique, it is much more complicated to implement. We will select the binary ladder technique to integrate the three entity-relationship diagrams that were created earlier in the chapter.

13.5 SCHEMA INTEGRATION

We are now ready to integrate our local schemas to generate a global intermediate schema that will be located at the global control site of the global layer of a multi-database system. We will follow the steps and subtasks identified in Figure 13.1 for this phase of the design process. I've selected the binary ladder technique and define the integration order of the local schemas as follows:

1. Integrate the Edinburgh schema with the Aberdeen schema to generate an intermediate schema called IGS1.

2. Integrate the intermediate schema IGS1 with the local Liverpool schema to generate the final intermediate schema.

The final intermediate schema will be converted to the relational model in Section 13.6. As we proceed with this phase of the design process, we will keep an eye out for the following anomalies:

1. Attribute or relation naming conflicts

2. Semantic conflicts

3. Structural conflicts

4. Relationship conflicts (i.e., many-to-one relationships in a local database schema represented as one to many in another local schema)

In addition, we will identify the key combinations used to implement the relationships among the entities. Figure 13.6 shows the first

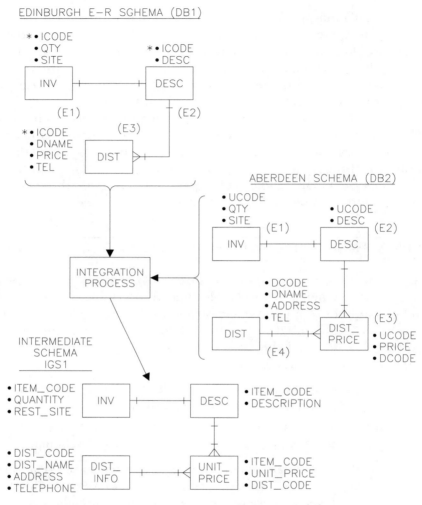

Figure 13.6 Integrating Edinburgh and Aberdeen schemas

integration step. The Edinburgh schema is being integrated with the Aberdeen schema to generate the first intermediate schema, IGBS1.

Notice that we have compensated for the extra entity that appears in the Aberdeen schema. The following anomalies were detected:

1. Attribute naming conflicts — The key attributes are named differently: The name ICODE is used at the Edinburgh site, and the name UCODE is used at the Aberdeen site.

2. Semantic conflicts   Fortunately, none.

3. Structural conflicts   A new entity DIST_PRICE has been introduced. It now contains pricing information together with a new attribute key that links it with the DIST entity that contains attributes common to both schemas. Some new attributes are introduced, like the address field.

4. Relationship conflicts   No conflicts except for the introduction of the new entity DIST_PRICE linked to the DIST entity.

The first intermediate schema reflects the inclusion of the new entity in the integration process. The relationships between the inventory, desc, and unit-price entities are specified by the item-code attribute included in each entity. Additionally, a key called DIST_CODE is used to specify the link between the DIST_INFO and UNIT_PRICE entities in the intermediate schemas.

To resolve the naming conflicts, we must keep track of the original attribute names that map to the new names in the intermediate schema. These mappings will be stored in a separate database called an auxiliary database.[6] (More on this in the next section.) For now, here is the mapping information that must be retained. (Assume the Edinburgh database is DB1 and the Aberdeen database is DB2.)

Attribute Mapping Table

ENTITY:INVENTORY

Attribute	Maps To
item_code	db1.e1.icode,db2.e1.ucode
quantity	db1.e1.qty,db2.e1.qty
rest_site	db1.e1.site,db2.e1.site

A brief note at this stage: Assume the following global query is submitted to an MDBMS with the global schema we have derived so far:

```
SELECT ITEM_CODE,QUANTITY,REST_SITE
FROM INVENTORY
```

Our MDBMS software would have to accomplish the following query translation to process the query:

```
SELECT DB1.E1.ICODE,DB1.E1.QTY,DB1.E1.SITE
FROM DB1.E1
UNION
SELECT DB2.E1.UCODE.DB2.E1.QTY,DB2.E1.SITE
FROM DB2.E1
```

It is for this reason that we must keep track of the mapping information and eventually store it in some sort of catalog to facilitate the query translation process. Let's document the remaining three entities and the mapping information.

Attribute Mapping Table

ENTITY:DESC

Attribute	Maps To
item_code	db1.e2.icode,db2.e2.ucode
description	db1.e2.desc,db2.e2.desc

ENTITY:UNIT_PRICE

Attribute	Maps To
item_code	db1.e3.icode,db2.e3.ucode
unit_price	db1.e3.price,db2.e3.price
dist_code	db2.e3.dcode

ENTITY:DIST_INFO

Attribute	Maps To
dist_code	db2.e4.dcode
dist_name	db1.e3.dname,db2.e4.dname
address	db2.e4.address
telephone	db1.e3.tel,db2.e4.tel

Let's proceed to integrate the first intermediate schema with the local schema of the Liverpool site. Figure 13.7 depicts the integration of the final two schemas. We identify and resolve our naming conflicts by updating the attribute mapping table.

Attribute Mapping Table

ENTITY:INVENTORY

Attribute	Maps To
item_code	db1.e1.icode,db2.e1.ucode,db3.e1.icode
quantity	db1.e1.qty,db2.e1.qty,db3.e1.qty
rest_site	db1.e1.site,db2.e1.site,db3.e1.rname
*dist_code	db2.e4.dcode,db3.e1.dcode
*order_level	db3.e1.olvl

Note: * indicates a new attribute.

ENTITY:DESC

Attribute	Maps To
item_code	db1.e2.icode,db2.e2.ucode,db3.e2.icode
description	db1.e2.desc,db2.e2.desc,db3.e2.desc

ENTITY:UNIT_PRICE

Attribute	Maps To
item_code	db1.e3.icode,db2.e3.ucode,db3.e3.icode
unit_price	db1.e3.price,db2.e3.price,db3.e3.price/10
dist_code	db2.e3.dcode,db3.e3.dcode

ENTITY:DIST_INFO

Attribute	Maps To
dist_code	db2.e4.dcode,db3.e4.dcode
dist_name	db1.e3.dname,db2.e4.dname,db3.e4.name
addr_code	db2.e4.address,db4.e5
telephone	db1.e3.tel,db2.e4.tel,db3.e4.tel

ENTITY:ADDR

Attribute	Maps To
addr_code	db3.e4.acode,db3.e5.acode
city	db3.e5.city
street	db3.e5.street

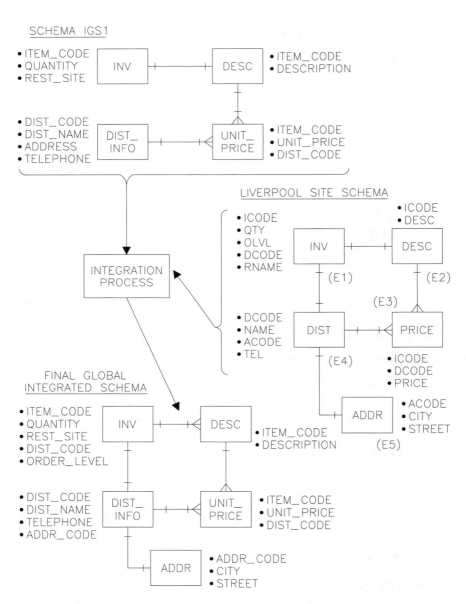

Figure 13.7 Integrating the intermediate schema with the Liverpool site schema

Semantic conflicts	The price attribute belonging to entity E3 in the Liverpool database refers to a 10-case shipment quantity. The price attributes in the other databases are based on a per-case shipment quantity. When referring to the attribute in this relation, we will have to specify a mapping algorithm.
Structure conflicts	The address attribute in the entity belonging to the Aberdeen site database is now an entire entity in the Liverpool database. The conflict was resolved by creating a new entity in the final intermediate schema and linking it to the other entities via the dist_code attribute.
Relationship conflicts	None.

The integration process not only generated the final intermediate schema but also enabled us to collect mapping and conflict information that can be stored in an auxiliary database.[6] We now proceed to design the final global schema by implementing it with the relational database model and the creation of the SQL DDL commands that will be used to create the definitions of each of the global tables. We will also create and examine a simple auxiliary database for this schema.

13.6 GLOBAL SCHEMA GENERATION

We are now at the last phase of our simplified design process. Two tasks must be accomplished in this last phase. First, the global schema must be generated. As we decided to implement the global schema with the relational model, we will generate the necessary SQL DDL command to create the relational tables for the global schemas. The definitions of each table are stored in a catalog at the global site so that the translator can use the definitions to localize each data object in a distributed query. Below are the five SQL DDL commands:

```
CREATE TABLE INVENTORY
     (
     ITEM_CODE       CHAR(10),
     QUANTITY        INT,
     REST_SITE       CHAR(80),
     DIST_CODE       CHAR(5),
     ORDER_LEVEL     INT,
     PRIMARY KEY(ITEM_CODE)
     );

CREATE TABLE DESCRIPTION
     (
     ITEM_CODE       CHAR(10),
     DESCRIPTION     CHAR(80),
     PRIMARY KEY(ITEM_CODE)
     );

CREATE TABLE UNIT_PRICE
     (
     ITEM_CODE       CHAR(10),
     UNIT_PRICE      DECIMAL,
     DIST_CODE       CHAR(5),
     PRIMARY KEY(ITEM_CODE)
     );

CREATE TABLE DIST_INFO
     (
     DIST_CODE       CHAR (5),
     DIST_NAME       CHAR(80),
     TELEPHONE       CHAR(8),
     PRIMARY KEY(DIST_CODE)
     );

CREATE TABLE ADDRESS
     (
     ADDR_CODE       CHAR(5),
     CITY            CHAR(40),
     STREET          CHAR(80),
     PRIMARY KEY(DIST_CODE)
     );
```

No rows are actually stored in the tables—their definitions are stored in the global site catalogs so that the global MDBMS layer can map the global tables and columns to their local schema name equivalents.

The mapping information is stored in a database that the literature calls an auxiliary database.[6] Locality information is also stored in this database, which is used to identify the components of a distributed query so that the subquery fragments can be generated and routed to each of the local sites. Based on the information collected during the design process, we now proceed to implement a simple auxiliary database for our system.

Auxiliary Database Implementation

Our simple auxiliary database will be made up of three tables. The first, GLOBAL_TABLE, contains the names of each of the tables that constitute the global database schema. This table contains the following columns:

GTBL_NAME	Name of the global table
SITE	Name of the local site(s) that contain rows referring to the table
MAPPING	Mapping method from global schema to local schema
LOCAL_NAME	Name of the table at each of the global sites
ALIAS	Alias for the local table name

Below is this table initialized with the values collected during the design process:

```
TABLE: GLOBAL_TABLES
GTBL_NAME       SITE      MAPPING       LOCAL_NAME      ALIAS
INVENTORY       S1        REL->REL      INV_TBL         E1
INVENTORY       S2        REL->HIER     INV_FILE        E1
INVENTORY       S3        REL->NET      INV_FILE        E1

DESCRIPTION     S1        REL->REL      INV_DESC        E2
DESCRIPTION     S2        REL->HIER     DESC_FILE       E2
DESCRIPTION     S3        REL->NET      DESC_FILE       E2

DIST_INFO       S1        REL->REL      INV_DIST        E3
DIST_INFO       S2        REL->HIER     DIST_FILE       E4
DIST_INFO       S3        REL->NET      DIST_FILE       E4

UNIT_PRICE      S2        REL->HIER     PRICE_FILE      E3
UNIT_PRICE      S3        REL->NET      PRICE_FILE      E3

ADDRESS         S3        REL->NET      ADDR_FILE       E5
```

The next table in our simple auxiliary database is called GLOBAL columns. It identifies each of the attributes for each of the relations in the global database. This table contains the following three columns:

GLOBAL_TBL   Name of the global database table
COLUMNS   Name of each column in the table
SEMANTICS   Description of the columns' domains

Below is this table initialized with the values collected during the design phase:

```
GLOBAL_COLUMNS
GLOBAL_TBL        COLUMNS          SEMANTICS
INVENTORY         ITEM_CODE        ITEM ORDER CODE
INVENTORY         QUANTITY         QUANTITY ON HAND AT A SITE
INVENTORY         REST_SITE        NAME OF THE RESTAURANT
INVENTORY         DIST_CODE        ITEM DISTRIBUTOR CODE
INVENTORY         ORDER_LEVEL      INVENTORY REORDER LEVEL

DESCRIPTION       ITEM_CODE        ITEM ORDER CODE
DESCRIPTION       DESCRIPTION      ITEM DESCRIPTION

UNIT_PRICE        ITEM_CODE        ITEM ORDER CODE
UNIT_PRICE        UNIT_PRICE       ITEM UNIT PRICE PER CASE
UNIT_PRICE        DIST_CODE        ITEM DISTRIBUTOR CODE

DIST_INFO         DIST_CODE        DISTRIBUTOR'S CODE
DIST_INFO         DIST_NAME        DISTRIBUTOR'S NAME
DIST_INFO         TELEPHONE        DISTRIBUTOR'S TELEPHONE NUMBER
DIST_INFO         ADDR_CODE        DISTRIBUTOR'S ADDRESS CODE

ADDRESS           ADDR_CODE        DISTRIBUTOR'S ADDRESS CODE
ADDRESS           CITY             DISTRIBUTOR'S CITY
ADDRESS           STREET           DISTRIBUTOR'S STREET ADDRESS
```

The final table in our auxiliary database contains detailed description and mapping information for all the columns in each table of the global database. Below are the columns for this table:

GLOBAL_TBL   Name of the global database table
COLUMN   Name of each column belonging to the global table
DB   Name of the local database that contains the column

ALIAS Alias of the local relation that contains the column

ATTRIB Name of the local attribute that maps to the global column

LEN Length of the column at the local site

TYPE Data type of the column at the local site

Below is a partial list of the entries in this table for the global relation UNIT_PRICE.

```
GLOBAL_MAPPING
GLOBAL_TBL    COLUMN       DB    ENTITY    ATTRIB    LEN     TYPE
UNIT_PRICE    ITEM_CODE    DB1   E1        ICODE     10      CHAR
UNIT_PRICE    ITEM_CODE    DB1   E2        ICODE     10      CHAR
UNIT_PRICE    ITEM_CODE    DB1   E3        ICODE     10      CHAR
UNIT_PRICE    ITEM_CODE    DB2   E1        UCODE     15      CHAR
UNIT_PRICE    ITEM_CODE    DB2   E2        UCODE     15      CHAR
UNIT_PRICE    ITEM_CODE    DB2   E3        UCODE     15      CHAR
UNIT_PRICE    ITEM_CODE    DB3   E1        ICODE     15      CHAR
UNIT_PRICE    ITEM_CODE    DB3   E2        ICODE     15      CHAR
UNIT_PRICE    ITEM_CODE    DB3   E3        ICODE     15      CHAR
UNIT_PRICE    UNIT_PRICE   DB1   E3        PRICE     8.2     DEC
UNIT_PRICE    UNIT_PRICE   DB2   E3        PRICE     8.2     DEC
UNIT_PRICE    UNIT_PRICE   DB3   E3        PRICE     10.2    DEC
UNIT_PRICE    DIST_CODE    DB2   E3        DCODE     5       CHAR
UNIT_PRICE    DIST_CODE    DB2   E4        DCODE     5       CHAR
UNIT_PRICE    DIST_CODE    DB3   E1        DCODE     10      CHAR
UNIT_PRICE    DIST_CODE    DB3   E3        DCODE     10      CHAR
UNIT_PRICE    DIST_CODE    DB3   E4        DCODE     10      CHAR
```

The data in the auxiliary database facilitate the translation and localization of global queries to query fragments for each site participating in the distributed query. Let's now examine the more formal design steps discussed by Özsu and Valduriez.[1]

13.7 FORMAL DESIGN STEPS

In this section I review the formal design steps discussed in Özsu and Valduriez. Figure 13.8 is a road map of the steps as they are grouped in Özsu and Valduriez.

Two main steps make up the design process. These are the first two steps in our simplified methodology. Let's look at the translation

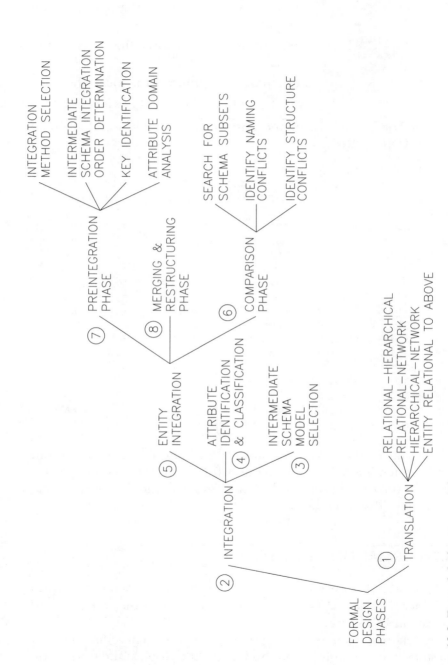

Figure 13.8 Formal design step road map

phase first, as it contains only one subtree. At this step, the designer selects the representation method to which each of the local schemas in the multi-database must translate. In Özsu and Valduriez,[1] the target model that was used was the entity-relationship model. In our example, we selected the relational model.

In this methodology, the integration phase is further subdivided into three steps:

1. Entity integration
2. Attribute identification and classification
3. Intermediate schema model selection

The entity integration phase is further subdivided into another three steps:

1. Preintegration
2. Merging and restructuring
3. Comparison

The preintegration phase is where the integration method is selected. (Recall that this can be the binary, ladder, or Nary strategy.) Additionally, at this phase the designer selects the schema integration order, identifies all the key attributes for each relation, and analyzes the attribute domains so as to search for semantic and naming conflicts.

The last two phases of the entity integration steps are the merging and restructuring phase and the comparison phase. The former implements the integration technique that was just selected. The latter examines each schema to search for conditions that can aid the integration process—for instance, the designer would like to identify schemas that are equivalent or subsets of each other. Structural conflicts are also identified during this phase. I've circled the steps in the diagram in the order of execution that a designer should follow to successfully design a global schema using this more formal method.

13.8 SUMMARY

This concludes our discussions on multi-database design methodology. I encourage the reader to examine the end notes for the finer points in the design process of multi-database systems. Özsu and

Valduriez contain discussions of the formal design steps that I used to derive the simple steps discussed in the beginning of the chapter.

In the next two chapters of the book, I show the reader how to implement algorithms for the major components of first an MDBMS and finally a federated database.

13.9 END NOTES

1. Özsu, M. Tamer, and P. Valduriez. *Principles of Distributed Database Systems*, Englewood Cliffs, NJ: Prentice Hall, 1991.

2. Batini, C., and M. Lenzirini. "A Methodology for Data Schema Integration in Entity-Relationship Model," *IEEE Transactions on Software Engineering* (November 1984): pp. 650–654.

3. Dayal, U., and H. Hwang. "View Definition and Generation for Databases Integration in Multibase: A System for Heterogeneous Distributed Database," *IEEE Transactions on Software Engineering* (November 1984): pp. 628–644.

4. Pu, C. "Superdatabases for Composition of Heterogeneous DB," *Procedings of the 4th International Conference on Data Engineering*, Los Angeles, CA (February 1988): pp. 548–555.

5. Batini, C., M. Lenzirini, and S. B. Navathe. "A Comparative Analysis of Methodologies for Database Schema Integration," *ACM Computing Survey*, vol. 18, no. 4 (December 1986): pp. 323–364.

6. Landers, T., and R. L. Rosenburg. *An Overview of Multibase in Distributed Databases*, Amsterdam: North-Holland, 1982, pp. 153–184.

14

Case Study 1: MDBMS Using OS/2 and OS/2 Database Manager

14.1 INTRODUCTION

In this chapter we examine a simple multi-database management system implemented in an IBM OS/2 local area network (LAN). The system has limited capabilities but illustrates some of the principal logic involved in generating instructions for local processing of subqueries and the subsequent routing of intermediate result sets.

The chapter begins by identifying basic assumptions and limitations of the system. Since we will be using the facilities and tools available in IBM's OS/2 environment, a section is included describing some of the features and components of this operating system (see Sections 14.2 and 14.3).

Section 14.4 describes the topology and architecture of the test environment and Sections 14.5 and 14.6, respectively, discuss the global and local system components. After all the basics and fundamental concepts have been discussed, Section 14.7 introduces the sequence of steps that is followed to process a distributed read-only query within this architecture.

Sections 14.8 and 14.9 include all of the algorithms for each major component together with the descriptions of the logic flow.

Section 14.10 discusses possible strategies and techniques for routing the final query results to the client.

I leave it to the reader to enhance the system by implementing the algorithms for global logging, recovery, and deadlock detection. Let's take a look at the system's basic functions and limitations.

14.2 BASIC ASSUMPTIONS AND LIMITATIONS

The system that we will design is based on a three-server LAN network. Each server utilizes IBM's OS/2 2.0 Operating System and OS/2's relational database engine, "Database Manager," as the database server. One of the servers is dedicated as a central control site where all global queries are accepted and parsed. The subfragments are then sent to the local sites involved in the query. It is the central site's responsibility to generate the execution strategy required to process the query.

The remaining two sites in the system serve as the "local sites" of the architecture. Their responsibilities are to execute the query fragments and generate the interim result sets that are shipped from site to site to perform distributed joins.

The limitations that I place on the system are that the queries can join only two remote tables at a time, the queries are read only, and that the facilities available with OS/2 interprocess communication tools be used. Additionally, the IMPORT/EXPORT facilities of OS/2 Database Manager are used to generate and transfer the interim result sets required to process joins.

The next section describes some of the basic concepts and features of OS/2 that we will use.

14.3 OS/2 AND DATABASE MANAGER BACKGROUND INFORMATION

In this section I will briefly introduce some concepts that a reader must be familiar with in order to follow the design steps. These concepts are:

1. Threads and processes
2. Dynamic link libraries
3. Queues
4. Named pipes

5.   EXPORT/IMPORT utilities

6.   Basic features of OS/2 Database Manager

Let us begin with processes and threads. Everyone should be familiar with the concept of a process. It is simply a program that is loaded into system memory and executed. A process is composed of one or more functions that are called in a specified order to accomplish a specific task. These functions are executed sequentially; that is, they are executed one at a time until the entire sequence is finished. It is possible to branch from one function to another. When this happens, the function that executes the branch operation is suspended until the function that was branched to finishes its task and terminates.

Threads are like functions except that they execute concurrently in an OS/2 process; that is, one can consider them processes within processes.

This concurrent execution of threads allows many sophisticated algorithms to be implemented. We will see their effectiveness when we use threads to monitor special communications channels called "named pipes." We will also put threads to work executing SQL functions against a local OS/2 database.

Dynamic link libraries are another feature available with OS/2. Unlike conventional libraries that are linked during the compilation of a program, they are linked at run time and can be shared by more than one process at the same time. Figure 14.1 shows two processes sharing a common dynamic link library (DLL for short) in order to submit queries against a database.

Queues are a familiar structure used to submit requests or information to a process by more than one process. Processes place items in a queue while another process reads the item from the queue. Figure 14.2 shows two threads manipulating queues.

Thread 1 reads information from queue 1 that was placed in the queue by some external agent. Thread 1 processes and perhaps modifies the information before placing it into queue 2 so that thread 2 can read it and further process it. We will be using this strategy throughout the component design of our multi-database management system.

A named pipe is simply a communications channel established between two cooperating processes at different sites. One process creates and monitors the pipe while the other process writes information to the pipe so that the first site can read it.

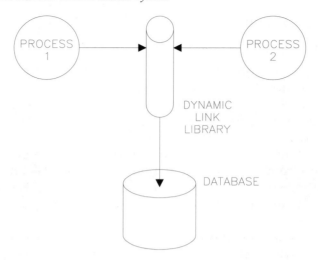

Figure 14.1 Dynamic linking

Figure 14.3 shows two processes transferring a file via a communications channel called a named pipe. At site 1, process 1 reads a file and writes it to the named pipe so that process 2 at site 2 can retrieve it and store it on its local disk.

Figure 14.4 shows an example of a process reading these export/import files to transfer them between sites. Process 1 exports rows from the database table and generates an export file that is read by thread 1. Thread 1 now sends the export file to site 2 via a named

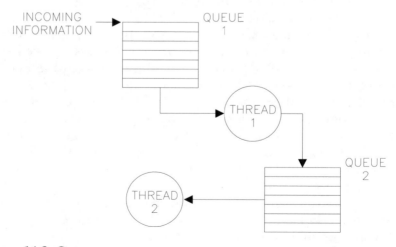

Figure 14.2 Queues

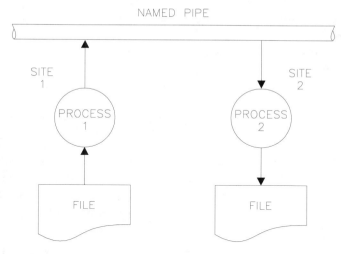

Figure 14.3 Named pipes

pipe. At site 2, thread 2 reads the file and stores it on disk. Once the file transfer is finished, thread 2 notifies process 2 that the new import file is available. Process 2 can now import it into a new database table. Once the new table is created, process 2 could use it to execute queries that involve joins with this new table. The scenario

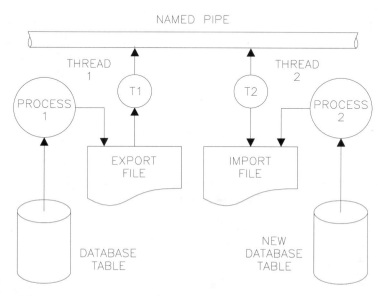

Figure 14.4 Import/export strategy

just described illustrates the steps that will be used to process distributed joins.

These features just discussed are all available with the OS/2 operating system.

14.4 EXAMPLE SEQUENCE OF OPERATION

Let's look at a simple distributed query and the steps that our system takes to process the requests. Assume that the query involves a join between two tables. Each table is situated in a database residing in a physically remote site. The following query is submitted to the system:

```
SELECT T1.C1,T2.C2,T2.C3
FROM T1,C2
WHERE T1.C1 = T2.C1
AND T2.C3 > 1000
```

Assume table T1 is situated at site 1. Its table cardinality is 10,000 rows, that is, CARD(T1) = 10,000.

Assume table T2 is situated at site 2. Its cardinality is 2,000 rows, that is, CARD(T2) = 2,000.

To process this query we must decompose it into two subqueries. Each subquery will have components local to one site. The interim results of these subqueries will have to be transferred to the other site in order to perform the distributed join. For our purposes, we will use the following simple rule to determine which site transfers its result set to the other:

"The site that produces the smallest result must transfer the result to its partner site."

Before we apply this rule, let's generate the subqueries required by each site. The query to be processed at site 1 reads as follows:

```
SELECT T1.C1,TSITE2.C2,TSITE2.C3
FROM T1,TSITE2
WHERE T1.C1 = TSITE2.C1
```

References to table TSITE2 and its columns refer to the table that will be created at SITE 1 to satisfy the distributed join. The table will be created with rows from an import file obtained from site 2.

The subquery to be processed at site 2 reads as follows:

```
SELECT T2.C1,T2.C2,T2.C3
FROM T2
WHERE T2.C3 > 1000
```

Notice the qualifying selectivity predicate "T2.C3 > 1000." (Notice also the inclusion of the key column T2.C1.) With our knowledge of the cardinality values of table T2 (T2 has 2,000 rows), we know that at most 1,000 rows will be generated when this predicate is used. (We are assuming that the values for column C3 are unique and evenly distributed between the values 1 and 2,000.) The query at site 1 will produce 10,000 rows. Logically, we wish to transfer the least amount of information, to keep communications cost to a minimum. The strategy that is adopted is to transfer the results of the subquery at site 2 to site 1. The join will be performed at site 1 and the results sent to the global site for final processing. The steps that must be followed at each site are summarized below.

Site 2 performs the following steps:

1. Let the subquery at site 2 be "SELECT T2.C1,T2.C2,T2.C3 FROM T2 WHERE T2.C3 > 1000."

2. Generate an export file with OS/2's export tool. The export tool uses the subquery defined above to generate the export file.

3. Transfer the newly exported file to site 1.

4. Erase the export file at site 2; it is no longer needed.

Site 1 performs the following steps:

1. Generate a query to retrieve final rows once the table from site 2 is retrieved and created at site 1. The following query is used: "SELECT C1,C2,C3 FROM FTABLE," where FTABLE is a table created during the processing to receive the final result set.

2. Create the new table called FTABLE with the following DDL SQL command:

```
CREATE TABLE FTABLE
       (C1, CHAR(10) NOT  NULL,
        C2, CHAR(5) NOT NULL,
        C3 INT NOT NULL);
```

3. Wait for the import file to arrive from site 2.

4.   Once the import file arrives, import it into a new table called TSITE2. Use OS/2's IMPORT facility and specify that the new table is to be created from the new import file.

5.   Execute the following SQL command to populate the final table with the desired results of the original query:

```
INSERT INTO FTABLE (C1,C2,C3)
SELECT T1.C1,TSITE2.C2,TSITE3.C3
FROM T1, TSITE2
WHERE T1.C1 = TSITE2.C1
```

(Step 5 resolves the distributed join.)

6.   Export the contents of FTABLE to an export file called FTABLE.IXF. Use the query generated in step 1.

7.   Transfer the new export table to the global site for final processing.

8.   Drop all temporary tables created to process this query.

9.   Drop all import/export files used to process this query.

The steps that were just discussed will be used to derive the algorithms executed at each site. These algorithms are introduced in Sections 14.7 and 14.9.

Let's next examine the communications topology that is used in our test case.

14.5 TEST TOPOLOGY AND ARCHITECTURE

The network topology that supports our simple multi-database system is depicted in Figure 14.5. As stated earlier, the architecture consists of three servers. The first server acts as the global control site, and the other two servers represent each of the "local sites" in the system.

As can be seen in the figure, each server uses IBM's OS/2 as its operating system. IBM's database product Database Manager serves as the relational database engine on each server. The global site contains a component called a GDBMS layer (global multi-database management system layer). This layer contains all of the components necessary to decompose a distributed query and generate an execution strategy. The local layers each contain a layer labeled

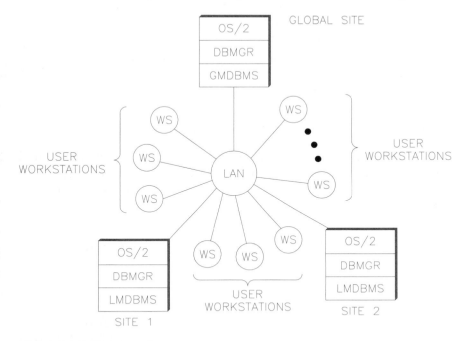

Figure 14.5 Test topology

"LMDBMS." This is the local multi-database management system layer. This layer contains all the components and data structures required to generate and route the intermediate result sets required to process the distributed joins.

The three servers are attached to an IBM token ring Local Area Network. Recall from Chapter 11 that this LAN can be part of a larger IBM SNA network. Attached to the LAN are multiple workstations where users can submit queries to the MDBMS via applications residing on their systems.

As we are working in an IBM architecture, the workstation can run either OS/2 or IBM's DOS. At each workstation is an application that has the capability of submitting distributed queries to the global control site. Each workstation has access to the global database schemas to be able to construct global queries on the global database. Let us investigate the components of the global schema.

Figure 14.6 contains a layout of the global schema situated at the server that acts as the global control site. As can be seen, it is made up of the two tables. The first table, GTBLCAT, contains global information as to the tables that make up our multi-database. This table contains the following columns:

site   Name of site where the table is located
tname   Name of the database table
dbname   Name of the database
card   Number of rows in the table
pkey   Name of the table's primary key

The second table that makes up our global schema is called GCOLCAT and contains global column information required to generate an execution strategy. The following columns make up this table:

cname   Name of the column in the table
tname   Name of the table that owns the column
ctype   Data type of the column
len   Length of the column in bytes

Before we continue, here's a word about the hardware required by each of the servers. Each server runs on an IBM PS-M90 or better with 16 megabytes of internal system memory and 300 megabytes of hard disk storage. Each of the workstations runs an IBM PS-M80 that

TABLE CATALOG: GTBLCAT

SITE	TNAME	DBNAME	CARD	PKEY
S1	T1	DB1	10,000	C1
S2	T2	DB2	2000	C1

COLUMN CATALOG: GCOLCAT

CNAME	TNAME	CTYPE	LEN
C1	T1	CHAR	10
C2	T1	CHAR	10
C3	T1	INT	—
C1	T2	CHAR	10
C2	T2	CHAR	5
C3	T2	INT	—
C4	T2	INT	—

Figure 14.6 The global schema

supports IBM DOS, OS/2, or Microsoft's Windows environment. We now proceed to the global components that make up the GMDBMS layer.

14.6 GLOBAL SYSTEM COMPONENTS

The global layer of our simple MDBMS performs the following basic functions:

1. Retrieve distributed queries from client workstations.
2. Decompose the global queries to multiple local subqueries to be executed at each of the two participating sites.
3. Generate and distribute the execution strategies for each site. (This includes the global site that has to process and route the final result rows to the requesting client.)
4. Process the final result table that is generated once the subqueries are run and the join table processed to produce the final results.

Figure 14.7 is a block diagram of the major components and communications channels of the global layer of our MDBMS. Let's examine the functionality of each component as a query is written to the request named pipe.

A thread labeled DQPT (distributed query processor thread) reads each of the distributed query requests and places them in a queue labeled the query request queue (QRQ). The monitor component continually reads this pipe and processes each request in two major steps.

The first step is to generate a query tree that contains all the objects referred to by the distributed query. This query tree is then passed to a function that generates a list of instruction packets for each of the steps involved in the execution of the local subquery at each site. Let's examine the query tree.

Figure 14.8 is a block diagram of the distributed query tree. The main component, labeled the query header, contains the following four members:

TID	Transaction ID
source	Name of the workstation that submitted the query. This name is used to route the final query results back to the requesting client.

final_ixf	Buffer that contains the name of the import/export files that will contain the query results. This file will be sent to the global site by one of the local sites after the distributed join is processed.
site_list	Pointer to a linked list of nodes that represents the sites involved in the processing of the distributed query.

The following C language structure can be used to implement this header:

```
struct QUERY_HEADER
    {
    int tid; // transaction id
    char source[80]; // name of client site
    char final_ixf[80]; // name of final export file
    struct SITE_LIST *pSiteList; // reference to list
                                 // containing subquery
                                 // site information

    };
```

Let's take a look at the elements that make up the site nodes of the site list. A typical node of the site contains the following members:

import_flag	Flag indicating that the site is involved in an import strategy; that is, it will import any temporary results that it requires to perform a distributed join.
export_flag	Flag indicating that the site must generate and transmit a temporary result table to another site that requires it to perform a distributed join.
cardinality	Variable containing the number of rows in the table at this site.
table_name	This member contains the name of the table situated at the site. This member also contains a list of column nodes that will make up the SQL SELECT command clause of the subquery that will be generated for the site.
predicates	This member contains a list of qualifying predicates that will be used in the WHERE clause belonging to the subquery for the site.

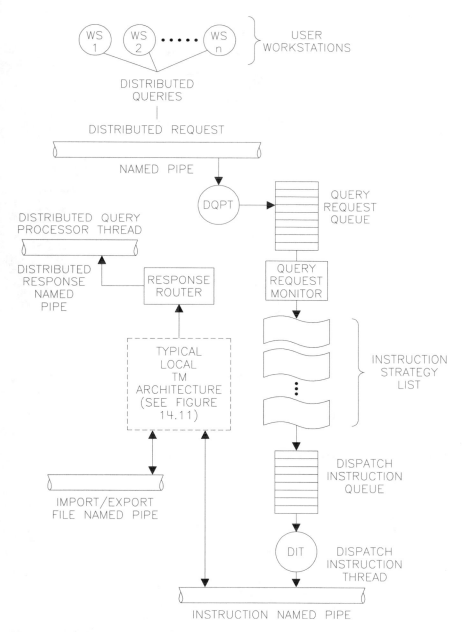

Figure 14.7 Global MDBMS components

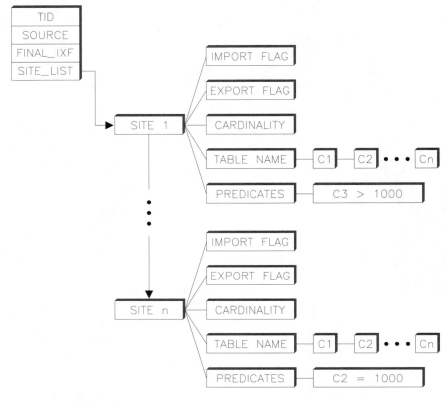

Figure 14.8 Distributed query tree

A C language structure that can be used to implement this structure is shown below:

```
struct SITE_LIST
     {
     BOOL input_flag;
     BOOL export_flag;
     LONG cardinality;
     struct TABLE_NAME *pTblList;
     struct PREDICATE *pPredList;
     struct SITE_LIST *NextNode;
     };
```

The C language structure for the TABLE_NAME member is

```
struct TABLE_NAME
     {
     char tbl_name[80];
```

```
struct COL_LIST *ColList;
struct TABLE_NAME *pNextNode;
};
```

Finally, the structures for the COLUMN_LIST and PREDI-CATE_LIST are shown below:

```
struct COL_LIST
    {
    char col_name[80];
    struct COL_LIST *NextNode;
    };

struct PRED_LIST
    {
    char pred_name[80];
    struct PRED_LIST *NextNode;
    };
```

From this list of information, the monitor can generate an execution strategy. The strategy is implemented as another linked list whose nodes contain identifying tokens, site information, and data (such as query formulas), which are routed to each site involved in the processing of the query. The following C language structure is used to build this list:

```
struct INST_PACKET
    {
    int trans_id;  // transaction id
    int inst_code; // instruction code
    char data[1024]; // information or instruction
    struct inst_packet *NextNode;
    };
```

The members of this structure are self-explanatory. The possible values for the inst_code member are

IXF_TABLE	Instruction code to generate an import/export table.
RESULT_TBL	Instruction code to create a table that will hold the final result rows once the distributed query is processed.
INSERT_QUERY	Instruction to generate a SQL INSERT command from the components of the distributed query and import table names.

EXP_TABLE	Instruction to generate an export table for transfer to a remote site involved in the processing of a distributed query.
TRANSFER_IXF	Instruction to transfer a generated import/export file to a remote site via an OS/2 named pipe.
DROP_TABLE	Instruction to drop a temporary table that was used in the processing of a distributed query.
ERASE_IXF	Instruction to erase an import/export file that was used in the processing of a distributed query.

Figure 14.9 is a block diagram of the import strategy instruction list sent to site 1. This follows the sequence depicted in our example in Section 14.4.

As can be seen, to process this subquery at site 1, the local MDBMS components must wait for an import file from site 2. Once the import file is received at site 1, it is imported into a new temporary table that is referenced by the SQL INSERT command that was generated in step 3. The temporary table that stores the final results is created by following the instructions in step 2. Step 3 executes the SQL INSERT command to populate the new table with the desired rows. Step 4 exports the final information into an export file. Step 5 transfers the file back to the global site. Steps 6 through 8 perform clean-up activities by deleting the old tables and temporary import/export files.

Figure 14.10 shows the three instructions that are sent to site 2 to generate the export file that will be imported into a new temporary table at site 1.

As can be seen, there are only three instructions to follow. Upon receiving this instruction list, site 2 first exports the required information via the OS/2 export utility. The utility is passed the supplied subquery as a parameter. Once the export file is created it is sent to site 1 (step 2) and finally the export file is erased in step 3 as it is no longer needed.

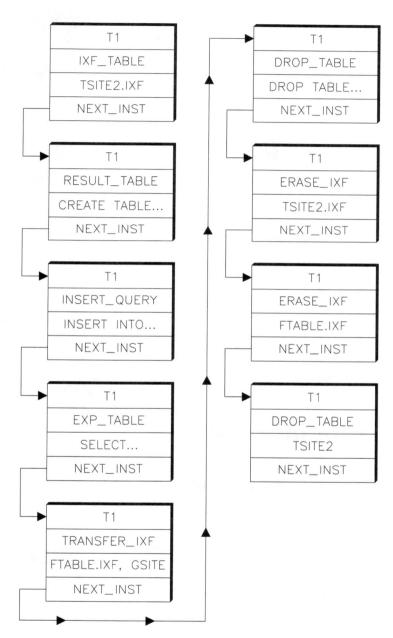

Figure 14.9 Import strategy list

377

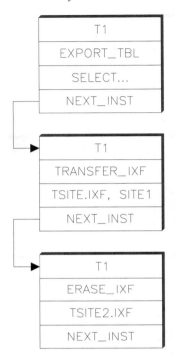

Figure 14.10   Export strategy list

14.7 GLOBAL ALGORITHMS

In this section we will discuss each of the following seven algorithms that make up the global multi-database system layer:

1. The GetDistQuery algorithm
2. The Monitor algorithm
3. The QHeaderGen algorithm
4. The ApplyStrategyRule algorithm
5. The GenImportStrategy algorithm
6. The GenExportStrategy algorithm
7. The InstDispThread algorithm

Each algorithm is used to implement either a function or an OS/2 thread. The algorithms are presented first and then a short description of the logic follows.

Algorithm: GetDistQuery

Implementation: THREAD

Purpose: Monitor a named pipe for incoming distributed queries from remote client workstations.

```
THREAD GetDistQuery()
    {
    while(FOREVER)
        {
        WaitForNamedPipe();
        item = ReadNamedPipe();
        copy(SQL_BUFFER,item);
        WriteItemToReqQueue(SQL_BUFFER);
        }
    }
```

Analysis: This thread implements a while() loop construct that forever iterates in order to monitor a named pipe for distributed requests submitted by client workstations at remote sites. As each query comes in, it is retrieved and placed in a holding queue until it is fetched by the monitor process.

Algorithm: Monitor

Implementation: THREAD

Purpose: Retrieve distributed queries from a queue and generate an import or export strategy depending on supplied strategy code.

```
THREAD Monitor()
    {
    StartThread(GetDistQuery());
    StartThread(InstDispThread());

    CreateQueue(ReqQueue);

    while(FOREVER)
        {
        query = ReadQueue(ReqQueue);
        QHeaderGen(query);

        if(site1.strategy_flag = IMP_STRATEGY)
            {
```

```
                    GenImportStrategy(site1,site2);
                    GenExportStrategy(site2);
                    }
            else
                    {
                    GenExportStrategy(site1);
                    GenImportStrategy(site2,site1);
                    }
            }
       }
```

Analysis: This process is the control point of the global MDBMS. As part of its initialization process, it starts all system threads and creates a queue that is used to store the incoming distributed queries as they are read from the named pipe. It then enters a continuous loop where it retrieves and processes user global queries. As each query is retrieved, it is passed to the QHeaderGen() function so that a query tree can be generated. Once the tree is generated, the monitor checks the strategy flags for each site involved in the query. Depending on the flag strategy, an import or export strategy is generated for each site.

Algorithm: QHeaderGen

Implementation: FUNCTION

Purpose: Generate an import or export strategy from the information supplied in the distributed query.

```
FUNCTION QHeaderGen(query)
    {
    // Variable list
    token;   // store individual tokens of the query
    tbl_list; // list of tables;
    cond_list; // list of qualifying query predicates
    site_list; // list of sites involved in the query
    sql_buf;   // scratch buffer for tokenizing query

    copy(SQL_BUF,query);

    // obtain first token
    token = GetToken(SQL_BUF,DelimiterList);

    while(token) // loop until no more tokens are found
        {
        if(compare(token,"SELECT") == TRUE)
```

```
                {
                // extract all columns in SQL SELECT clause
                while(compare(token,"FROM") == FALSE)
                    {
                    AddTokenToColList(token);
                    token = GetToken(SQL_BUF,DelimiterList);
                    }
                }
        else if(compare(token,"FROM") == TRUE)
            {
            // extract all tables in the FROM clause
            while(compare(token,"WHERE") == FALSE)
                {
                AddTokenToTblList(token);
                token = GetToken(SQL_BUF,DelimiterList);
                }
            }
        else if(compare(token,"WHERE") == TRUE)
            {
            // extract all WHERE clause predicates
            while(token)
                {
                BuildPredicateList(token);
                token = GetToken(SQL_BUF,DelimiterList);
                }
            }
        else
                ReportSyntaxError(query);
                // consult global catalogs so as to
                // identify sites that contain query
                // objects
                FindOutTableSites(tbl_list);
                AssignCollistToSites(col_list);
                AssignPredToSites(cond_list);
                GetTblCardinality(tbl_list);

                GenerateQryHeader();
                AssignTIDToQuery();
                ConectAllListsToQHeader();
    }
```

Analysis: This rather lengthy algorithm tokenizes the distributed query. As it retrieves each token, a check is made to see whether the token is part of the SELECT, FROM, or WHERE clause. During processing, lists are built to reflect the tables, columns, conditions, and sites that participate in the query. These lists are then used to generate the query header by attaching the various lists to the new empty query header. The query header is assigned a transaction ID and the strategy for each header is determined by applying the "STRATEGY RULE" discussed earlier.

The ApplyStrategyRuleFunction is passed the site list as its parameter. A check of the cardinalities of the tables involved in the sites is performed next. The site that contains the smallest table cardinality in its temporary result table (once any qualifying predicates are applied) is flagged as requiring an export strategy. The site with the largest table cardinality is flagged as requiring an import strategy. Upon returning from this function the monitor generates the appropriate strategy for each site.

Algorithm: ApplyStrategyRule

Implementation: FUNCTION

Purpose: Compare table cardinalities and set strategy flag to reflect application of the strategy rule.

```
FUNCTION ApplyStrategyRule(site_list)
     {
     site1 = site_list;
     site2 = site_list.NextNode;

     if(site1.card == site2.card)
         {
         site1.strategy_flag = EXP_STRATEGY;
         site2.strategy_flag = IMP_STRATEGY;
         }
     else
         {
         site1.strategy_flag = IMP_STRATEGY;
         site2.strategy_flag = EXP_STRATEGY;
         }
     }
```

Analysis: The cardinality of the tables at both sites is compared. If site 1 cardinality is smaller than site 2's cardinality, site 1 is elected to execute the export strategy by setting its strategy flag to the value "EXP_STRATEGY." The strategy flag for site 2 is set to the value "IMP_STRATEGY."

If the converse is true, site 1 is elected to execute the import strategy and site 2 is elected to execute the export strategy by setting the flags to the appropriate values.

Algorithm: GenImportStrategy

Implementation: FUNCTION

Purpose: Generate a set of import strategy instructions to be processed by a site involved in the processing of a portion of the distributed query. Store the instructions in a linked list.

```
FUNCTION GenImportStrategy(site1,site2)
    {
    // PHASE 1
    // Generate list of tables to import
    // for tables in site 2, add export table instruction
    inst_node = GetMemory();
    inst_node.TID = site1.TID;
    inst_node.inst_code = IXF_TABLE;
    copy(inst_node.data_buffer,site2.table_node);
    LinkNodeToList(inst_node);

    // PHASE 2
    // add an instruction node containing SQL DDL to
    // create the final result table
    inst_node.TID = site.TID;
    inst_node.inst_code = RESULT_TABLE;
    tbl_query = BuildFinalResultTable(site1.TID);
    copy(inst_node.data_buffer,tbl_query);
    LinkNodeToList(inst_node);

    // PHASE 3
    // create INSERT SQL command to populate the final
    // result table
    inst_node = GetMemory();
    inst_node.TID = site.TID;
    inst_node.inst_code = RESULT_TABLE;
    insert_sql = BuildInsertSqlCommand(site1.TID);
    copy(inst_node.data_buffer,insert_sql);
    LinkNodeToList(inst_node);

    // PHASE 4
    // generate export command to build the final
    // result export file
    inst_node = GetMemory();
    inst_node.TID = site.TID;
```

```
        inst_node.inst_code = EXPORT_IXF;
        export_sql = BuildExportFile(site1.TID);
        copy(inst_node.data_buffer,export_sql);
        LinkNodeToList(inst_node);

        // PHASE 5
        // generate the file transfer strategy
        inst_node = GetMemory();
        inst_node.TID = site.TID;
        inst_node.inst_code = TRANSFER_IXF;
        dest_site = GLOBAL_SITE;
        transfer_cmd = BuildTransferCmd(RESULT_IFX_NAME,
                                        dest_site);
        copy(inst_node.data_buffer,transfer _cmd);
        LinkNodeToList(inst_node);

        // PHASE 6
        // generate site clean-up instructions to remove table
        inst_node = GetMemory();
        inst_node.TID = site.TID;
        inst_node.inst_code = DROP_TABLE;
        copy(inst_node.data_buffer,FINAL_TBL_NAME;
        LinkNodeToList(inst_node);

        // PHASE 7
        // generate site clean-up instructions to remove
        // import/export files
        inst_node = GetMemory();
        inst_node.TID = site.TID;
        inst_node.inst_code = ERASE_IXF;
        copy(inst_node.data_buffer,FINAL_TBL_IXF;
        LinkNodeToList(inst_node);

        // PHASE 8
        // generate site clean-up instructions to remove
        // import/export files
        inst_node = GetMemory();
        inst_node.TID = site.TID;
        inst_node.inst_code = ERASE_IXF;
        copy(inst_node.data_buffer,TSITE2.IXF);
        LinkNodeToList(inst_node);
        }
```

Analysis: This algorithm generates a linked list that represents the import strategy scenario that a site must follow to process distributed joins. This strategy is assigned to sites whose table cardinality is greater than that of its partner site involved in the query. The algorithm follows the basic steps outlined in Section 14.4.

PHASE 1: Generate a list of tables to import.

PHASE 2: Generate an instruction to create the final result table.

PHASE 3: Generate an "INSERT" SQL command to populate the final result table.

PHASE 4: Generate an export command to create the export table with the final results.

PHASE 5: Generate the export file transfer strategy that uses named pipes.

PHASE 6: Generate site clean-up instructions to remove the temporary file.

PHASE 7: Generate site clean-up instructions to remove all import/export files.

Algorithm: GenerateExportStrategy(site)

Implementation: FUNCTION

Purpose: Create the linked list whose nodes contain the instruction codes and required data that constitute an export strategy.

```
FUNCTION GenerateExportStrategy(site_obj_list,site)
    {
    // PHASE 1
    // generate a list of tables to export
    inst_node = GetMemory();
    inst_node.TID = site.tid;
    inst_node.inst_code = EXP_TABLE;
    export_query = GenExportQuery();
    copy(inst_node.data_buffer,export_query);
    LinkNodeToList(inst_node);

    // PHASE 2
    // generate a file transfer strategy
    inst_node = GetMemory();
    inst_node.TID = site.tid;
    inst_node.inst_code = TRANSFER_IXF;
    transfer_cmd = BuildTransferCmd(RESULT_IXF_NAME,
                                    dest_site);
    copy(inst_node.data_buffer,transfer_cmd);
    LinkNodeToList(inst_node);

    // PHASE 3
    // generate site clean-up instruction
```

```
inst_node = GetMemory();
inst_node.TID = site.tid;
inst_node.inst_code = ERASE_IXF;
copy(inst_node.data_buffer,RESULT_IXF_NAME);
LinkNodeToList(inst_node);

AddInstListToDispositionQueue();
}
```

Analysis: This function generates the export strategy for the site whose table has the smallest cardinality. As we wish to minimize communication costs when transferring temporary result sets, we export tables from sites that can generate the smallest intermediate result tables after the qualifying predicates of the subquery are applied.

This algorithm performs the following three phases:

PHASE 1: Generate a list of tables to export.

PHASE 2: Transfer the exported files to the requesting site.

PHASE 3: Generate site clean-up instructions to remove export files after the file transfer is completed.

We will see in the next section how dedicated local threads perform these steps so as to generate the export files and then transfer them to their partner site over a named pipe.

Algorithm: InstDispatchThread()

Implementation: THREAD

Purpose: Monitor its queue for instructions to route to sites involved in the processing of a distributed query.

```
THREAD InstDispatchThread()
    {
    CreateInstructionQueue();

    while(FOREVER)
        {
        PeekInInstQueue();

        if(NUM_INST_PRESENT > 0)
            {
            inst_list = ReadInstQueue();
```

```
                    while(inst_list)
                        {
                        WriteItemToNamePipe();
                        inst_list = inst_list.NextNode;
                        }
                }
            }
        }
```

Analysis: This algorithm is rather simple. It is implemented as a thread and its function is to route instructions to the appropriate site. As part of its initialization process, it creates the instruction list request queue and begins to monitor it for instructions placed there by the monitor process. As instructions come in, the list is processed by sending each node to the specified site destination.

Now that we have examined all the global components of the global MDBMS layer, let's discuss the components and algorithms that make up the local layer of the MDBMS.

14.8 LOCAL SYSTEM COMPONENTS

We now turn our attention to the local architecture components of our simple MDBMS. Figure 14.11 is a block diagram depicting the various data structures and software modules used to process subqueries.

The reader should recall from the prior section that distributed queries are parsed and analyzed so that a linked list of instruction packets can be generated. These instructions are submitted to a named pipe for distribution to the two sites involved in the processing of the distributed query.

These packets are retrieved locally by the module called the Transaction Monitor (TM). It is the responsibility of this thread to examine each packet, set some flags, and deposit it into the queue belonging to one of the three local threads whose role is to execute subqueries against the local database, generate export files, or transfer import files to the other site.

Each of these threads owns one of the queues previously mentioned plus a linked list of pending instructions. These linked lists are accessed via semaphores, as more than one thread can alter the contents of these lists.

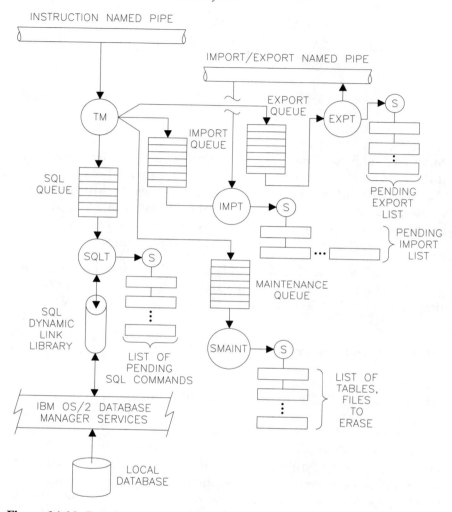

Figure 14.11 Local architecture components

Let's examine the sequence of events that occurs at a typical local site as it receives first an export strategy sequence of instructions, then an import strategy sequence. The reader should refer to Figure 14.11 as this discussion progresses.

Site 2 receives the export sequence of instructions described in the previous section and depicted in Figure 14.10. The following sequence of instructions is to be processed: EXPORT_TBL, TRANSFER_IXF, and ERASE.IXF.

The transaction monitor realizes that the first instruction must be processed by the SQL execution thread. (This thread is labeled SQLT in Figure 14.11.) The contents of the instruction packet are

1. Transaction TID
2. Instruction code (in this case it is EXPORT_TBL)
3. Query to be used in the generation of the export file

The transaction monitor places this instruction inside a queue belonging to the SQL thread. The second instruction is placed in the queue belonging to the export thread (labeled EXPT in Figure 14.11). The third instruction is placed in the queue belonging to the system maintenance thread (labeled SMAINT in Figure 14.11). It will be the responsibility of the SQLT thread to generate the export file by executing OS/2's export utility supplied with the OS/2 Database Manager product.

The SQLT will use the supplied query for selecting the necessary columns and rows. Once it is finished with the task, it notifies the export thread by gaining access to its linked list of pending export files and setting a flag in the node reserved for this file, as it is now available. Let's examine how the node in the export file pending list was inserted.

Recall that the transaction monitor analyzed the TRANSFER_IXF instruction and realized that the task must be processed by the export thread (labeled EXPT in Figure 14.11). The instruction is placed in the thread's queue.

The EXPT thread retrieves this instruction from its queue and generates a node for its export pending list by using the following C language structure to create a node for this list:

```
struct EXPORT_LIST
    {
    int tid;
    char expfname[20];
    char exfiledest[20];
    BOOL expfile_pres;
    struct EXPORT_LIST *NextNode;
    };
```

The name of the file is extracted from the data section of the instruction packet and copied to the expname structure member of the new node.

The destination site name is also retrieved from the data section of the instruction packet and copied to the expfiledest structure member. The flag expfilepres is set to FALSE indicating that the file has not yet been generated. It will be the responsibility of the SQL execution thread (labeled SQLT in Figure 14.11) to notify the export thread that the file has been generated and is now ready to be exported to the other site involved in the query. The SQLT thread accomplishes this notification by setting the expfilepres flag to TRUE.

Once this flag is set to TRUE, the EXPT thread sends the export file to its partner site and removes the node from the list. The EXPT thread notifies the SMAINT thread that the file can be deleted, as it is no longer required. This is accomplished in a similar manner by setting an equivalent flag in the SMAINT file list.

The last instruction in the sequence is the ERASE_IXF instruction. The transaction monitor places this instruction in the queue belonging to the system maintenance thread (labeled SMAINT in Figure 14.11). As was the case with the other three threads, it also has its own queue and pending file list. The name of the file to be deleted is placed in the list by allocating memory for and initializing the members of the following C language structure:

```
struct MAINT_LIST
    {
    BOOL obj_is_avail;
    BOOL obj_is_table;
    BOOL obj_is_file;
    char obj_name[20];
    struct MAINT_LIST *NextNode;
    };
```

The first structure member, obj_is_avail, is set to FALSE, as the export file has not yet been generated. If the object to be deleted is an export or import file, the obj_is_file member is set to TRUE and the obj_is_table structure member is set to FALSE. If the opposite condition holds TRUE, that is, the object is a temporary table that is no longer required, the obj_is_table structure member is set to TRUE and the obj_is_file structure member is set to FALSE. (This action is used as an indicator that the object must be deleted with a SQL DROP command.) The name of the object is copied to the obj_name structure member and the node is inserted into the maintenance list.

Let's review the sequence of events that was just described. Each instruction was placed in the queue belonging to its respective thread that is responsible for a specific task. In turn, each thread retrieves the instruction from its queue, creates a node for its instruction pending list, and waits for one of the other threads to notify it that the object is available for processing.

The first event that occurs in this sequence is that the SQLT thread generates the export file by using the supplied query. Once it generates the export file it notifies the EXPT thread that the file is available for export. Once the export thread EXPT receives this notification it exports the file and notifies the system maintenance thread SMAINT to go ahead and erase the file by setting the appropriate flags to TRUE.

The algorithms that perform these functions will be examined in Section 14.9. Let us now examine how the import strategy sequence is processed by these threads.

The sequence of instructions for the import strategy to be processed by site 1 was shown in Figure 14.9. The following instructions must be processed by the transaction monitor:

```
IXF_TABLE, RESULT_TABLE, INSERT_QUERY, EXP_TBL, TRANSFER_IXF,
DROP_TABLE, ERASE_IXF, ERASE_IXF, and DROP_TABLE
```

Loosely interpreted, these instructions state:

1. Wait for an import file called TSITE2.IXF from site 2.
2. Create a temporary table called TFINAL to hold the final results once the modified distributed query is executed.
3. Once the import file has been received and inserted into a new temporary table, execute the supplied SQL INSERT statement so that the table created in step 2 is populated with the rows generated by the join of the local table together with the table created from the import file received from site 2.
4. Create an export file from the new result table.
5. Transfer the export file to the global site.
6. Drop the imported ixf file.
7. Erase the imported ixf file.
8. Erase the exported ixf file.
9. Erase the table generated from the import file.

Each of the instructions is processed in basically the same manner as the instruction in the export sequence; that is, it is placed in the appropriate queue belonging to the threads responsible for processing each instruction. Each thread retrieves the instruction, generates a node for its pending list, and sets the appropriate flags indicating what the objects to be processed are and their availability status. As objects become available, the appropriate entries in the pending lists are modified to indicate that the objects can be processed.

Instruction 1 is processed by the import thread (IMPT). When the import file is received over the named pipe, the file is copied to disk and a new table is created that now contains the rows and columns stored in the import file. The import thread sets the appropriate flags in the SQL thread's pending list, indicating the table is available for performing the join.

Instructions 2 and 3 are processed by the SQL thread. This thread can immediately create the table that will hold the final results of the query. It must wait to execute the insert statement until the import file has been received from site 1 and transferred to a temporary table.

Once the table is available, the SQL INSERT command is executed, an export file is created by the SQL thread, and a notification is sent to the export thread to export the file to the global site via a named pipe. The sequence is implemented as a three-step export sequence that was previously described for site 2. Finally, steps 6, 7, 8, and 9 are processed by the system maintenance thread once all the import/export files and temporary tables have been processed. Let's take a look at the algorithms that perform the functions just described.

14.9 LOCAL ALGORITHMS

In this section, we examine the algorithms that are used to process the import and export instruction strategies. The reader will recall that the main components of the local multi-database system are implemented as threads. Figure 14.12 shows the first thread, the transaction monitor thread, whose responsibility is to retrieve instructions from the instruction named pipe and insert them in the queues of the threads that will perform the tasks specified by the instructions.

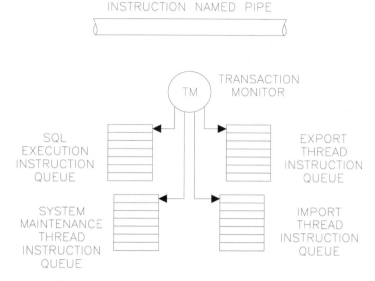

Figure 14.12 Local transaction monitor detail

Below is the algorithm used to implement this thread.

Algorithm: LocalTm()

Implementation: THREAD

Purpose: Monitor incoming named pipe for local subquery strategy instructions.

```
THREAD LocalTm()
    {
    while(FOREVER)
        {
        // read instruction named pipe
        PeekInInstNamedPipe();
        if(INSTRUCTION_IS_AVAILABLE)
            {
            ReadInstNamedPipe(instruction);
            ProcessInstruction(instruction);
            }
        }
    }
```

Analysis: Processing occurs in a continuous while(FOREVER) loop. The thread peeks inside an OS/2 named pipe. If any instructions are in the named pipe, they are read and placed in a buffer. The buffer is used as a parameter to a function called ProcessInstruction(). This function ensures that the instruction is placed in the proper queue for further processing. This function is explained below.

Algorithm: ProcessInstruction

Implementation: FUNCTION

Purpose: Place instructions in appropriate queues belonging to the threads responsible for performing the specified task.

```
FUNCTION ProcessInstruction(instruction)
    {
    switch(instruction.inst_code);
        {
        case IXF_TABLE:
            PlaceInstInImpThreadQueue(instruction);
            break;

        case RESULT_TABLE:
        case INSERT_QUERY:
        case EXP_TABLE:
            PlaceInstInSQLExecThreadQueue(instruction);
            break;

        case DROP_TABLE:
        case ERASE_IXF:
            PlaceInstInSysMaintThreadQueue(instruction);
            break;

        case TRANSFER_IXF:
            PlaceInstInExpThreadQueue(instruction);
            break;

        }
    }
```

Analysis: This function utilizes a C language switch-case construct to make calls to functions that place the instruction in the queue of the thread that is designed to perform the specific task specified by the instruction code. For example, if a "Wait for import file" instruction is received, a call is made to the PlaceInstInImpThreadQueue() function.

If an instruction is received to either create a result table, execute a SQL INSERT command, or export a table to an export file, then the instruction is placed in the SQLT thread's queue via a call to the PlaceInSQLExecThreadQueue() function. Instructions to drop tables, erase import/export files are placed in the SMAINT thread via a call to the PlaceInSysMaintThreadQueue() function. Finally, any instructions requesting import/export files to be transmitted to another site via a named pipe are placed in the export thread's queue by calling the PlaceInExpThreadQueue() function.

The architecture and the algorithm for the SQLEXEC thread is examined next. The components for this thread can be seen in Figure 14.13. The thread has its own request queue (SRQ) and a linked list of pending instructions that is to be executed once all the data objects are either imported or created.

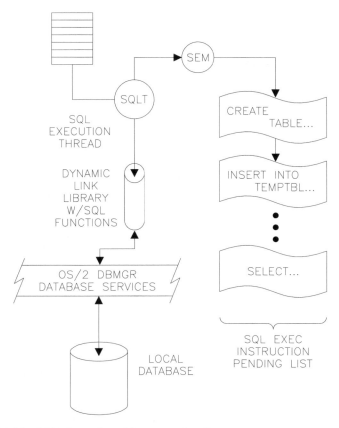

Figure 14.13 SQL thread architecture detail

The linked list is accessed by first requesting the semaphore used to coordinate access to the list between cooperating threads. Once a thread gains access to the semaphore, it can alter the linked list. It then releases the semaphore so other threads can modify the list.

The SQLT thread uses a dynamic link library (SQLDLL) that contains functions that execute SQL DML and DDL commands. These functions interface with IBM's OS/2 Database Manager database services to gain access to the local database. Let us examine the algorithms for this thread next.

Algorithm: SQLT

Implementation: THREAD

Purpose: Execute SQL DDL, DML commands and generate export/import files.

```
THREAD SQLT()
     {
    while(FOREVER)
         {
         RequestSem(SQLSEM);

         currnode = headnode;

         while(currnode)
              {
              switch(currnode.inst_code)
                   case RESULT_TABLE:
                        sql_execute(currnode.query);
                         break;

                   case EXP_TABLE:
                        sql_exec_exp(currnode,query,
                                     currnode.dest);
                        NotifyExpThread(currnode,dest,
                                        tid,exp_name);
                        currnode.inst_code =
                             PROCESS_COMPLETE;
                        break;

                   case INSERT_QUERY:
                        CheckIXFFiles(currnode);
                        break;

                   case PROCESS_COMPLETE:
                        DeleteNode(currnode);
                        break;
```

```
                }
           currnode = currnode.NextNode;
        }
        ReleaseSem(SQLSEM);
    }
```

Analysis: This thread is also implemented as a continuous while(FOREVER) loop. At each iteration, a request is made to obtain the semaphore that allows access to the SQL task list. Upon gaining access to the list, the thread starts at the head of the list and examines each node to see if any further processing can be performed.

A switch-case C language construct is entered and each of the following cases is examined and processed:

1. If the inst_code member of the current node is set to "RE-SULT_TABLE," a call is made to the sql_execute function passing the DDL SQL command that will be used to create the final result tables.

2. If the inst_code member is set to EXP_TABLE, a call is first made to the sql_exec_exp function to create the export file that will be sent back to the global site for final processing. Next, a call is made to the NotifyExpThread function, which updates the pending export list indicating that the file is now available for export. The inst_code member is now set to PROCESSING_COMPLETE.

3. If the inst_code member equals "INSERT_QUERY," a call is made to the CheckForIXFFiles() command. (This function is discussed next.)

4. If the inst_code member equals "PROCESS_COMPLETE," a call is made to the DeleteNode function to remove the current node from the list.

The CheckForIXFFile function is shown below.

Algorithm: CheckForImportFile

Implementation: FUNCTION

Purpose: Check that all import files are present so the the SQL INSERT command can be executed to populate the final result table with the desired data.

```
FUNCTION CheckForImportFiles(currnode)
    {
    if(currnode.all_ixf_avail == TRUE)
        {
        execute_sql(currnode.query);
        currnode.inst_code = EXP_TABLE;
        }
    else
        {
        // assume that once we examine this list all
        // import files are found to be present
        currnode.all_ixf_avail = TRUE;
        nodeimpflist = currnode.pIfxList;

        while(nodeimpflist)
            {
            if(nodeimpflist.ixf_pres == FALSE)
                {
                currnode.all_ixf_avail = FALSE;
                break;
                }
            }
        }
    }
```

Analysis: The function first checks to see if all the import files are present. If they are, the function executes the SQL INSERT query and sets the current node's inst_code member to EXP_TABLE so that during the next iteration of the loop the export file is created.

If the currnode.all_ixf_avail flag is set to FALSE, the function examines the list that shows all the pending import files required by the SQL insert command.

The currnode.all_ixf_avail flag is set to TRUE on the assumption that all the files will be present once the check sequence is complete. If even one file is found outstanding, the currnode.all_ixf_avail flag is set back to the FALSE indicator and the function breaks out of its loop and terminates.

Below are the C language functions used to implement the components of the SQL pending instruction list:

```
struct SQL_PENDING
    {
    int tid; // transaction code
    int inst_code; // instruction code
    char ftable_name[20]; // name of the final table
```

```
char *query; // memory address pointer to the query
BOOL all_ixf_avail; // import file availability flag
struct IXF_LIST *pIXFList; // pointer to import list
struct SQL_PENDING *NextNode; // next node in this list
};

struct IXF_LIST
    {
    char ixfname[20]; // name of import file
    BOOL ixf_pres;  // flag indicating import file
                    // availability status
    struct IXF_LIST *NextNode;  // pointer to next node
    };
```

Figure 14.14 is a block diagram for the export thread architecture. As was the case with the other threads, this thread owns a queue that contains any outstanding instructions submitted by the local transaction monitor. Each instruction is retrieved by the thread and in-

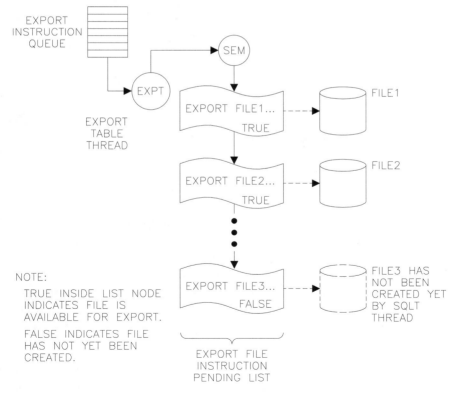

Figure 14.14 Export thread architecture

serted into the export file pending list. Access to this list is via the
EXPSEM semaphore. Below is the algorithm used to implement this
thread.

Algorithm: ExportThread()

Implementation: THREAD

Purpose: Check pending export file list. If any export files are
available for transfer, send them to the specified site and notify the
system maintenance thread so that they can be deleted.

```
THREAD ExportThread()
    {
    while(FOREVER)
        {
        RequestSem(EXPLISTSEM);
        node = head_pending_exp_list;

        while(node)
            {
            if(node.expfilepres == TRUE)
                {
                WriteNamedPipe(node.expfname,
                               node.expfiledest);
                NotifySysMainThread(DELETE_IXF,
                                    node.expname);
                }
            node = node.NextNode;
            }
        SemRelease(EXPLISTSEM);
        }
    }
```

Analysis: The thread enters the by now familiar while(FOREVER)
loop construct. Access to the export file pending list is requested by
attempting to access the EXPSEM semaphore. Once the semaphore
is obtained, the algorithm traverses the list checking the expfilepres
flag for each node. If this flag is set to TRUE, the export file is sent to
its destination via a named pipe and the system maintenance
thread's pending maintenance list is updated to reflect that the
export file can be deleted.

The algorithm and architecture for the import thread are examined next. Figure 14.15 is a block diagram of the major components
of the thread. The components are the same as in the other threads,

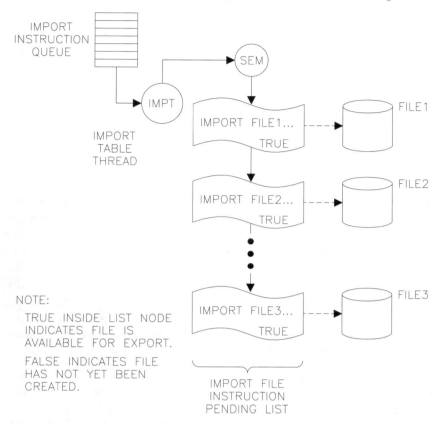

Figure 14.15 Import thread architecture

so I will not elaborate on them any further. Below is the algorithm used to implement this thread.

Algorithm: ImportThread

Implementation: THREAD

Purpose: Retrieve any incoming import files and convert them to relational tables.

```
THREAD ImportThread()
     {
     while(FOREVER)
          {
          PeekInNamedPipe();
          if(IMPORT_FILE_IS_AVAILABLE)
```

```
                              {
                              ReadInputFile();
                              StoreToDisk();
                              sql_exec_imp(import_name);
                              RequestSem(SQLSEM);
                              FindImpNameinSQLList(import_name);
                              impixfavail = TRUE;
                              ReleaseSem(SQLSEM);
                              }
                  }
      }
```

Analysis: This thread also uses the while(FOREVER) loop construct to monitor a named pipe for incoming import files. As files are found, they are read from the pipe, stored to disk, and imported to the temporary tables. The SQL thread's pending list is updated to reflect the presence of the newly imported table. This is accomplished by requesting access to the SQL thread's pending list via the SQLSEM semaphore. Once access is gained, a search through the list is made by searching for the filename in each node. Once the target node is found, the flag is set to TRUE and the semaphore is released so that the SQL thread can execute the SQL INSERT command.

The final algorithm that we examine is used to implement the SMAINT thread (the system maintenance thread). Recall that this thread's function is to drop old results and intermediate tables and to erase processed import/export files. The architecture for this thread is shown in Figure 14.16.

This thread's architecture is similar to that of the other threads. It accesses the SQL dynamic link library to execute the SQL DDL commands to drop relational database tables. The general utility library accessed by this thread contains functions to erase old import/export files once they are processed by the other threads.

Below is the C language structure used to implement the pending instruction list:

```
struct OBJ_MAINT
    {
    BOOL ObjFile; // flag indicating object is a file
    BOOL ObjTable; // flag indicating table object
    char objname[20]; // name of the object
    struct OBJ_MAINT *NextNode;
    };
```

The algorithm that can be used to implement this thread follows.

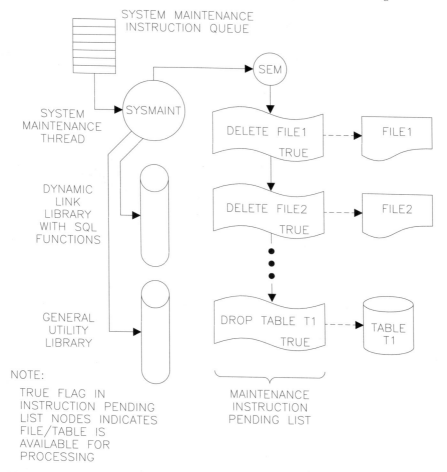

Figure 14.16 The system maintenance thread

Algorithm: SMAINT

Implementation: THREAD

Purpose: Drop old processed relational tables and import/export files used in the processing of query strategies.

```
THREAD SMAINT()
    {
    while(FOREVER)
        {
        RequestSem(SYSMSEM);
        currnode = head_maint_list;
```

```
while(currnode)
    {
    if(currnode.obj_processed == TRUE)
        {
        if(currnode.objfile == TRUE)
            {
            erase(currnode.objname);
            }
        else if(currnode.objtable == TRUE)
            {
            sql_exec_drop(currnode.objname);
            }
        DeleteNode(currnode);
        }
    currnode = currnode.NextNode;
    }
ReleaseSem(SYSMSEM);
}
```

Analysis: Within the familiar while(FOREVER) loop, the list containing objects to be erased or deleted is checked. Each node in the linked list is checked by examining the objprocessed flag. If the flag is set to TRUE, the object is either erased from disk (if it is an import/export file) or dropped from the database (if it is a relational table). This determination is made by checking the objfile and objtable flags in the current node being examined.

We have now completed examining the algorithms and data structures used to implement the local layer of our multi-database management system. Let us return to the global layer and examine how the final results are routed to the user who originally submitted the distributed query.

14.10 RESULT ROUTING STRATEGY

Up until now I have not mentioned how the final results get routed to the original requesting client. In this section we will introduce the architecture for the response router thread and the algorithms required to implement it.

Recall from Figure 14.7 that the global multi-database system layer also has a complete local MDBMS running at the global site. It behaves in the same manner as the components described in Section

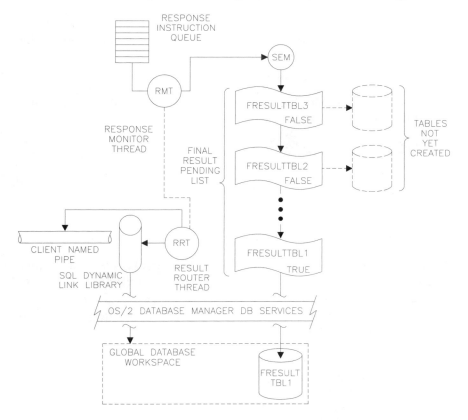

Figure 14.17 Response router architecture detail

14.10. Its role is to accept final result export files from the local site and convert them into tables. Each table is stored in a database called "The Global Database Workspace." This table, together with the components that make up the response router, can be seen in Figure 14.17.

Recall how the global layer generated a list of instructions that specified either an export strategy or an import strategy. These instructions were then routed to the appropriate sites for processing. For each transaction a special instruction packet containing the following information was generated:

TID	Transaction ID
client_site	Name of the client workstation that originated the request

final_result_tbl   Name of the final result table that will be stored in the global workspace once the transaction is completed

fquery   Query used to extract final results

The following C language structure is used to implement the instruction packet:

```
struct FINAL_PROCESSING
    {
    int tid;
    char client_site[20];
    char ftbl_name[20];
    char fquery[512];
    };
```

The strategy generator builds one of these packets for each transaction it processes and places the packet in the response instruction queue shown in Figure 14.17. The Response Router Thread (RRT) fetches the instructions from the queue and places the instructions into the pending list packet:

```
struct FRESULT_PENDING
    {
    int tid;
    char clientsite[20];
    char ftblname[20];
    char fquery[512];
    BOOL tableavail;
    struct FRESULT_PENDING *NextNode;
    }
```

This structure is identical to the first one except for the addition of a new member: tableavail. This flag is set to TRUE by the components of the local MDBMS that resides at the global site. In other words, when one of the local sites sends the import file containing rows for the final table, the local MDBMS will import the rows into the final result table and then set the tableavail flag to TRUE for the node that identifies the table.

Let's go back and see what the result router's next steps are once it has placed the final result packet in its pending linked list. Associated with the response monitor thread is a result router thread. It also has access to the pending list by periodically requesting the semaphore that protects the list. Each time it gains access, it checks each node in the list to see if the BOOL tableavail flag is set to TRUE. If it is, it proceeds to execute the query stored in the fquery member to extract the rows and columns from the new table that now exists in the global database workspace.

As each row is retrieved, the result router thread sends the information over a named pipe that the clients are monitoring. The client that submitted the request now retrieves the information and displays it to the user. Once all the rows have been sent to the client, the result router thread drops the table from the workspace and proceeds to search for other final result tables to process. Let's take a look at the algorithms for the result monitor thread and the result router thread.

Algorithm: RMT()

Implementation: THREAD

Purpose: Monitor the response instruction queue and place new instructions in the final result pending list.

```
THREAD RMT()
    {
    while(FOREVER)
        {
        PeekInRespQueue();
        if(RESPONSE_INST_AVAILABLE)
            {
            ReadInstruction();
            BuildPendingPacketNode();
            RequestSem(FINSTSEM);
            InsertNewPacket();
            ReleaseSem(FINSTSEM);
            }
        }
    }
```

Analysis: This thread also uses the familiar while(FOREVER) loop construct to monitor for the presence of new instructions in its queue. As instructions become available, they are read from the queue. A new pending instruction node is built, and its members are initialized with the information required to properly route the results to the client. The flag indicating the presence of the final result table is set to FALSE. The thread inserts the new packet at the tail of the pending list and proceeds to look for new instructions.

Algorithm: RRT()

Implementation: THREAD

Purpose: Monitor the Result Pending List for new nodes whose "Table Available" flag is set to TRUE. If the table is present, its contents are read and routed to the original requesting client.

```
THREAD RRT()
    {
    while(FOREVER)
        {
        RequestSem(FINSTSEM);
        currnode = head_query_list;
        while(currnode)
            {
            if(currnode.tableavail == TRUE)
                {
                execute_sql(currnode.fquery);
                while(ROWS_TO_PROCESS)
                    {
                    BuildRow();
                    SendRowToClient(clientsite);
                    }
                DropTable(FTBL_NAME);
                oldnode = currnode;
                currnode = currnode.NextNode;
                DeleteNode(oldnode);
                }
            else
                currnode = currnode.NextNode;
            }
        ReleaseSem(FINSTSEM);
        }
    }
```

Analysis: Within the while(FOREVER) loop, the thread requests access to the pending list by first obtaining the semaphore that protects the linked list. Having obtained access to the list, it checks each node in the list, looking for nodes whose tableavail flag is set to TRUE. If a node is found satisfying this condition, the query supplied in the node is executed. A while() loop is entered to retrieve a row at a time and send it to the client site that originally requested the query. Once all the rows are transmitted, the table is dropped from the workspace database. Reference to the current node is saved to a variable called "oldnode." The next node pointer to the list is retrieved and the node referred to by the oldnode variable is deleted from the list. The final result table for this distributed query is dropped from the workspace database.

The thread now continues checking all the nodes in the list until the tail of the list is reached. At this time the semaphore is released so that other threads waiting to update the list get a chance to access it. This concludes our discussion of the result routing mechanism for the global MDBMS layer.

One final note to the reader. You may have noticed that I refer to import/export files as "IXF" files. OS/2 Database Manager appends an "IXF" to the names of the files generated for import/export so as to identify the format of the file.

14.11 SUMMARY

This concludes our design of a simple MDBMS that processes distributed SQL queries. IBM's OS/2 environment was selected because of the many facilities provided for distributed processing architectures. Although this system processes queries that refer to only two distributed tables at a time, it is possible to extend the system by modifying the logic and components so that multiple tables at multiple sites are processed.

The algorithms introduced in this chapter were written in a pseudo C language style that the reader can easily translate to pure C. Additionally, the reader might wish to design dynamic link libraries that support other relational products for IBM's OS/2 environment such as Gupta's SQLBase product or Microsoft/Sybase's SQLServer product.

In Chapter 15 I will eliminate the global layer and introduce a local component that converts the system to a federated database.

15

Case Study 2: A Federated Architecture Using IBM's OS/2

15.1 INTRODUCTION

In this chapter the multi-database system introduced in Chapter 14 is modified to become a federated database. The chapter begins by describing the new overall modifications that have to be made at a high level. The three layers that constitute the federated architecture are introduced together with the limitations that are placed on the system.

In Section 15.3, I introduce some simple import and export schemas needed by the sites to process distributed queries submitted by client sites.

Section 15.4 introduces the concept of negotiating contracts between sites to obtain import tables necessary to process distributed joins. This concept is discussed in Deen.[1]

In our simple architecture, distributed query processing occurs in three scenarios: Section 15.5 discusses the first scenario, where all data objects referenced by the query are located at one site. Section 15.6 discusses the second scenario, where a contract must be negotiated with the remote site that participates in the federation in order to access distributed tables. Scenario 3 explains how a remote site fulfills a contract by supplying data it has agreed to export. This final scenario is discussed in Section 15.7.

This chapter concludes with an overall detailed view of the architecture, integrating all of the components.

15.2 GENERAL ARCHITECTURE MODIFICATIONS

Figure 15.1 shows the architecture of the federated database. The local multi-database components from the MDBMS discussed in Chapter 14 are retained, albeit with some minor modifications. The local operating system is still IBM's OS/2 and the local database manager is OS/2 Database Manager components.

Additions to the architecture include an import/export schema. The import schema defines the tables that are available at the remote site. The remote site has agreed to allow site 1 access to the local database. The tables that can be viewed are defined in site 1's import schema. The export schema, in turn, contains definitions for all the tables that site 1 has allowed site 2 to view. The import/export schemas will be discussed in more detail in the next section.

The global MDBMS from Chapter 14 has been eliminated and replaced with a layer labeled "Federated MGMT SYS" in Figure 15.1. The layers reside at each local site and communicate with each other

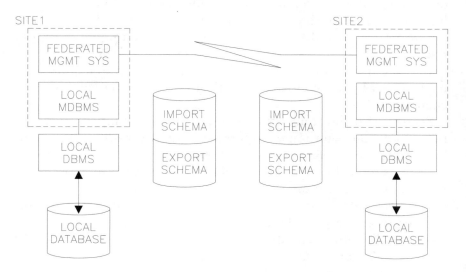

Figure 15.1 Replacing the global layer with local federated layers

IMPORT SCHEMA

IMP_TBL

SITE	TBLNAME	AVAIL

SITE2	T2	YES

IMP_COL

TBLNAME	COLNAME	TYPE	LEN
T2	C1	CHAR	20
T2	C2	CHAR	10
T2	C3	INT	2
T2	C4	CHAR	10

EXPORT SCHEMA

EXP_TBL

TBLNAME	AVAIL
T1	YES
T2	NO

EXP_COL

TBLNAME	COLNAME	TYPE	LEN
T1	C1	CHAR	20
T1	C2	CHAR	10
T1	C3	CHAR	20
T2	C1	CHAR	20
T2	C2	INT	2

Figure 15.2 The import/export schemas for site 1

over dedicated named pipes to negotiate contracts and transfer export files between sites.

The same basic methods of generating import and export strategies will be used. Some minor modifications to the local MDBMS have been made and are explained as each scenario is discussed. The rest of this chapter is dedicated to the components and algorithms that make up the federated management system layer at each site.

15.3 THE IMPORT/EXPORT SCHEMAS

The import/export schema for site 1 is implemented as four relational tables and is shown in Figure 15.2. Import information is contained in two tables. The first table, imp_tbl, defines the site name and table name that can be accessed at remote sites. This table contains the following columns:

site   Remote site name.

tblname   Name of the remote table.

avail   Availability status of the table. A table that is marked for export might be temporarily unavailable if the local site is updating, inserting, or deleting rows. Also, if the table is currently being reorganized or backed up, the administrator sets the avail flag to NO so that access is temporarily denied.

Table imp_col contains detailed information of the columns that are available in each of the imported tables. Columns in the imported table can be excluded by simply not mentioning them in the corresponding site's export schema. The columns that make up this table are

tblname   Table that owns the column.

colname   Name of the column.

type   Data type of the column.

len   Length of the column.

The table exp_tbl defines table information that is available for access by the other site. It contains the following columns:

tblname   Name of the table to be exported.

avail   Flag indicating whether or not the table is currently available for export.

The table that defines the columns for the tables that are to be exported is named exp_col. It contains the following columns:

tblname   Table that owns the column.

colname   Name of the column.

type   Data type of the column.

len   Length of the column.

Figure 15.3 shows the corresponding import/export schemas for site 2.

Notice that table T2, defined as an import table, is currently unavailable. This information was made known to site 2 when it attempted to negotiate a contract with site 1 to process a query. Contract negotiations are discussed in the next section.

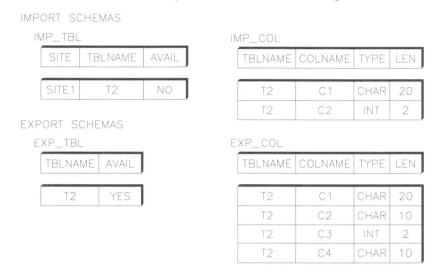

Figure 15.3 The import/export schemas for site 2

15.4 NEGOTIATING CONTRACTS

The concept of negotiating contracts between sites in a federated database is discussed in Deen.[1] For our purposes, the negotiation simply involves finding out if a table is available at a remote site. If the table is available, the supplier informs the requester of its availability and supplies a verification code to the requesting site. If the table is not available, the supplier can instruct the requester to wait and resubmit the request at a later time.

If the table is available, the requesting site sends the supplying site an SQL query that contains all the qualifying predicates. The supplier accepts the query and informs the requester of the name of the export file that will be transmitted over a dedicated named pipe once the query is executed. This export file will be built and delivered using the same export strategy that was used in the local MDBMS of Chapter 14. The requesting site uses the same import strategy of Chapter 14 to import the file into a new temporary table to be used in the distributed join.

At this point, the original query has been modified to include references to the newly imported table. At this stage, the contract is satisfied and terminated.

Let us now examine the three possible scenarios that our federated database management system must cope with.

15.5 SCENARIO 1: ALL DATABASE OBJECTS ARE LOCAL

In this section we examine the components and sequence of events that are used when a query references database objects that are all local to the site where the query is submitted. We will begin by inspecting the subsystems in the architecture responsible for the processing. Next, we define the sequence of events and conclude with the main algorithms that are required to implement the principal threads and functions. As in the previous chapter, the algorithms will be written in a pseudo C language style, which the reader can translate to pure C or C++.

Figure 15.4 shows the principal components and data structures for this scenario. A remote client workstation submits a query by writing it to the "Distributed Query Incoming Named Pipe." Inside the federated management system layer a thread called the query processor thread (QPT) retrieves the query and proceeds to create a query header as described in Chapter 14. The table list component of the query header is submitted to a thread named the Object Verifier Thread (OVT).

This thread examines the tables referenced in the query and compares them to the tables in its local database catalog. Since in this scenario all the objects referenced by the query are local to this site, no further processing or checking is required by this thread.

The thread requests access to the pending query list by requesting the semaphore that protects the list. Upon obtaining access, the QPT places a query execution packet in the list so that the result router thread (RRT) can process it.

The semaphore is released and the QPT returns to process the next incoming query.

The response router thread periodically checks its list to see if any queries are ready for execution. It requests access to the pending query list via the semaphore. Once it obtains access to the list it examines each node. Following is a C structure used to implement a typical node in the list:

```
struct PENDING_QUERY
    {
    int TID; // transaction id
```

```
BOOL delete_obj;   // flag indicating table can be deleted
BOOL table_avail;  // flag indicating that the table is
                   // available for processing
char query[512];   // query that when executed generates the
                   // final result set
char dest[20];     // name of requesting client workstation
struct PENDING_LIST *NextNode; // reference to the next
                               // node in the list
};
```

The QPT has set the table_avail flag to TRUE and copied the original query and destination site name to the query member and test member of this structure.

Upon examining this node, the RRT sees that the table_avail flag is set to TRUE. It proceeds to execute the query stored in the query structure member of the node and sends the resulting rows to the client site specified in the test structure member. The delete_object

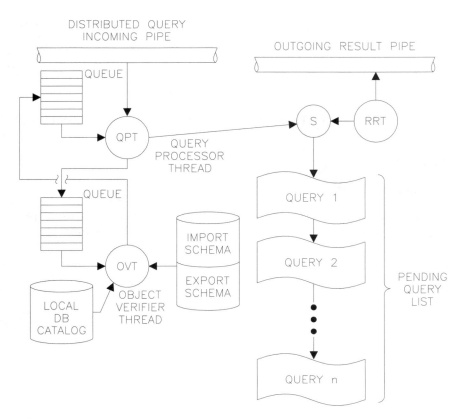

Figure 15.4 All database objects available locally (scenario 1)

flag is not set to TRUE, as the data come from a local table. Only temporary tables are deleted once they are processed.

Below is a summary of the sequence of events that was just discussed:

1. Workstation submits a distributed query on the named pipe.

2. The query processor thread parses the query and submits each query object (i.e., tables and columns) to the object verifier thread by placing them in its queue. (A packet called an OBJECT_VERIFICATION packet is generated for each object.)

3. The Object Verifier Thread (OVT) consults the local catalogs and import and export schemas for each object submitted in its request verification queue. If an object is available, the table_avail flag is set to TRUE in the object verification packet and the packet is returned to the query processor thread by placing it in the queue belonging to the QPT.

4. Once all the objects are examined, a check is made to see if all objects are available. In this scenario, they are all local so a result router packet is built.

5. The result router packet is placed in the Result Router Thread (RRT) for immediate execution and routing.

Below are the two principal algorithms used to implement the QPT and RRT.

Algorithm: QPT

Implementation: THREAD

Purpose: Accept incoming queries and determine whether they can be processed locally or if a contract has to be negotiated.

```
THREAD QPT()
    {
    while(FOREVER)
        {
        ReadClientNp(QUERY); // read named pipe for query
        QHeader_Gen(QUERY);  // generate a query header
        TABLE_NODE = HEAD_TBLLIST;
        while(TABLE_NODE)
            {
            VerifyTableNodeAvailability(TABLE_NODE);
            TABLE_NODE = TABLE_NODE.NextNode;
            }
```

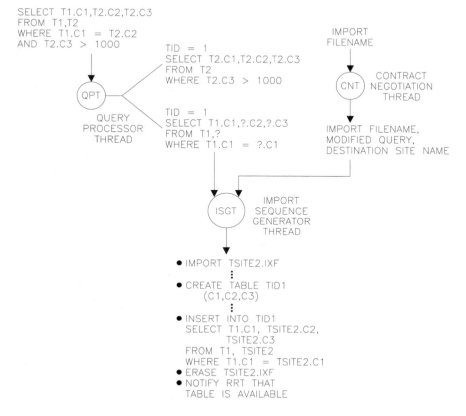

```
SELECT T1.C1,T2.C2,T2.C3
FROM T1,T2
WHERE T1.C1 = T2.C2                              IMPORT
AND T2.C3 > 1000                                 FILENAME
                     TID = 1
                     SELECT T2.C1,T2.C2,T2.C3
                     FROM T2                                 CONTRACT
                     WHERE T2.C3 > 1000          CNT    NEGOTIATION
       QPT                                               THREAD

       QUERY          TID = 1
     PROCESSOR        SELECT T1.C1,?.C2,?.C3     IMPORT FILENAME,
       THREAD         FROM T1,?                  MODIFIED QUERY,
                      WHERE T1.C1 = ?.C1         DESTINATION SITE NAME


                                    IMPORT
                            ISGT    SEQUENCE
                                    GENERATOR
                                    THREAD


                      ● IMPORT TSITE2.IXF
                        ⋮
                      ● CREATE TABLE TID1
                          (C1,C2,C3)
                        ⋮
                      ● INSERT INTO TID1
                         SELECT T1.C1, TSITE2.C2,
                                TSITE2.C3
                         FROM T1, TSITE2
                         WHERE T1.C1 = TSITE2.C1
                      ● ERASE TSITE2.IXF
                      ● NOTIFY RRT THAT
                         TABLE IS AVAILABLE
```

Figure 15.6 Scenario 2 sequence

file from site 2 is received and processed. (This query is then used in
the SQL INSERT command discussed in Chapter 14.) The CNT
begins the following dialog to negotiate the requisition of the desired import file:

```
Requesting Site (site1)        Supplying Site (site2)
PHASE 1            — is table T2 available? —>
                <— yes, here is your —–    PHASE 2
                   verification code
PHASE 3            — please execute this  —–>
                   query: SELECT ...
                <— OK, the import file —– PHASE 4
                   will be named ...
```

Once the name of the import file is known, it can be used to create
a temporary table and populated with the following SQL statements:

```
CREATE TABLE TID1
    (C1 CHAR(10), C2 CHAR(5), C3 INT);

INSERT INTO TID1 (C1,C2,C3)
    SELECT T1.C1,TSITE2.C2, TSITE2.C3
    FROM T1,TSITE2
    WHERE T1.C1 = TSITE2.C1;
```

The import filename, modified query, and destination site name are passed to the Import Sequence Generation Thread (ISGT) so that the import sequence shown in Figure 15.7 can be generated.

Once the import strategy is generated, it is passed to the Transaction Monitor Thread (TMT) of the local MDBMS so that each instruction in the import strategy can be executed. These remaining steps are the same as those described in Chapter 14. Let's examine the algorithm used by the Contract Negotiator Thread (CNT) next.

Algorithm: CNT()

Implementation: THREAD

Purpose: Open negotiations with the partner site in the federation to obtain the name of the import file that will be used to generate the temporary table. Once the name is obtained, supply the import strategy generator thread with the name of the file, a modified query to use in the "INSERT" SQL command, and the name of the destination client site that is to receive the results when the query is processed.

```
THREAD CNT()
    {
    while(FOREVER)
        {
        ReadQueryPacket();
        OBJ_AVAIL=ReqObjVerRemoteSite(tablename,vercode);
        if(OBJ_AVAIL == TRUE)
            {
            GenerateQueryForSite2(QPACKET.site2);
            Submit(query,vercode);
            WaitForImportName(imp_file_name);
            GenModeSql(qpacket,imp_file_name);
            SubmitModifiedSQLInsert(modsql,
                            imp_file_name,
                            destination);
            }
        else
            Reschedule(QPACKET);
        }
    }
```

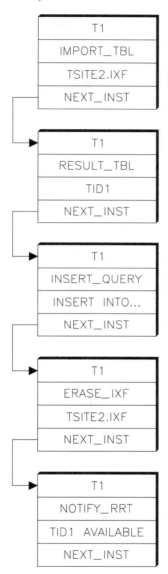

Figure 15.7   Import strategy list

Analysis: As was the case with the other threads we discussed, a while(FOREVER) loop is entered to process all query trees placed in the thread's instruction queue. As each tree is retrieved, the name of the required table is passed to a function that initializes contract negotiations with site 2. Upon return from the function, a verification code is returned in a variable called vercode. If the object is available, the algorithm performs the following steps:

1. Generates a query for site 2 to execute. This query will generate the export file at site 2 that will be sent to site 1. Site 1 will consider this file the import file.

2. Submit the query to site 2.

3. Wait for the name of the import file from site 2.

4. Once the import filename is available, it generates a modified query that references the name of the new table.

5. The new query, import file, and destination site name are passed to the import strategy thread.

If the table is not currently available, the contract negotiations are rescheduled for future processing. Let's now take a look at scenario 3, which discusses the architecture and algorithms required to implement the supplying end of the contract negotiations.

15.7 SCENARIO 3: EXPORT REQUESTED INFORMATION

In this section we examine the last scenario in the contract negotiation sequence between two sites participating in a federated database. Figure 15.8 shows the principal data structures and threads that

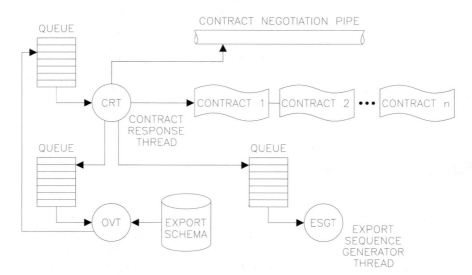

Figure 15.8 Supplying import file for negotiated contract (scenario 3)

participate in the preparation of export files that are to be shipped to
a requesting site.

The sequence begins by the Contract Response Thread (CRT)
retrieving a contract packet from the contract negotiation named
pipe. The following C language structure is used to create the packet
at the requesting site; it is retrieved at the supplying site using the
same format:

```
struct CONTRACT_TERM
    {
    int TID; // transaction ID
    int request_code; //type of request code
    char req_buffer[20]; // data pertinent to request
    char req_query[512]; // query for export file
    BOOL obj_avail; // flag indicating tables avail
    int vercode; // verification code
    };
```

The request code member identifies which phase of the contract
negotiations the packet represents. It can be one of the following
values:

QUERY_TBL_AVAILABLE (sent by requester)
QUERY_VER_CODE   (sent by supplier)
EXPORT_QUERY   (sent by requester)
IMPORT_NAME   (sent by supplier)

Figure 15.9 illustrates the simple dialog that occurs between two
sites negotiating for the required data. Basically, the requesting site
sends the participating site a packet containing the name of the table
that is required. The supplier checks if the table is available and
sends a verification code to the requester indicating that it has accepted the request. If the verification code is 0, it means that the

Figure 15.9 Contract negotiation dialog

table is currently not available and the requester should reschedule the request.

If the table is available, the requester sends the supplier a query that should be used for the construction of the export file. Upon receiving the query, the supplier of the table responds with the name of the import file that it will send to the requesting site.

A word of clarification is necessary before we continue. The supplier produces an export file using the export strategy sequence described in Chapter 14. Once this file is routed to the requesting site, it is considered an import file as the requesting site uses the import strategy to process the query.

Below is a summary of the events that occur in this scenario:

1. Remote federated site requiring data to perform a distributed join inquires if the table is available.

2. Thread CRESPT reads the pipe, submits the query object name to the Object Verifier Thread by placing it in its queue, and adds a node to the pending contracts list.

3. The OVT reads its queue. It sees it has a packet requesting export availability of a table.

4. The OVT looks at the export schema and sees that the table exists and is available. It sets a flag to TRUE in the CONTRACT_TERMS node, initializes the other members to the information in the original packet, and places the packet back inside the queue belonging to the CRESPT for inspection.

5. The CRESPT reads its queue, sees that the table object is available, and assigns a verification code to the contract. It now writes the response back to the remote site in the federation that originated the request.

6. The CRESPT updates the node in its pending contract list to reflect the newly assigned verification code that indicates the contract is approved and processing of the request should continue.

7. The site that sent the request sees the verification code and promptly submits the query that the supplier is to use to generate the export file.

8. The CRESPT now reads the query and checks the verification code of the query against the verification in its pending contracts list (just to make sure that the contract was approved).

The verification code for the request is found and the thread places the query in the Export Sequences Generator Thread's queue for further processing. An export filename is also generated.

9. The supplier now sends the Transaction ID, the verification code, and the name of the import file that is to be generated to the requesting site.

Let us now look at the principal algorithms used in this scenario, beginning with the OVT algorithm.

Algorithm: OVT

Implementation: THREAD

Purpose: Identify whether required objects are available for export or if they exist. The submitted requests come from the CRESPT and Query Processor Thread (QPT).

```
THREAD OVT()
    {
    while(FOREVER)
        {
        CheckObjVerQueue();
        switch(queryobj.requestcode)
            {
            CASE IS_COL_AVAIL:
                if(IsObjInColExpSchema() == TRUE)
                    QUERY_OBJ_AVAIL = TRUE;
                else
                    QUERY_OBJ_AVAIL = FALSE;
                PlaceObjInRequestorsQueue(queryobj,
                        requestor_id);
                break;

            CASE IS_TBL_AVAIL:
                if(IsObjInTblExpSchema() == TRUE)
                    QUERY_OBJ_AVAIL = TRUE;
                else
                    QUERY_OBJ_AVAIL = FALSE;
                PlaceObjInRequestorsQueue(queryobj,
                        requestor_id);
                break;
            }
        }
    }
```

Analysis: Like the other threads, the while(FOREVER) loop construct is implemented to perform the tasks specific to this thread. The OVT checks for objects in its queue. If any objects are found, they are looked up in the appropriate schema table. If the object is a column, the export column schema table is checked. If the object is a table, the export table schema table is checked. In either case, if the object is found, the obj_avail flag is set to TRUE, otherwise the flag is set to FALSE. The results are then written back to the queue belonging to the thread that made the request. This can be either the query processor's thread (QPT) or the contract response thread (CRT). This thread checks an indicator identifying the originator of the request. The C language structure used to place the requests in its queue is defined below:

```
struct IDENTIFY_OBJ
    {
    int TID;
    int Request_ID;
    int obj_type;
    char obj_name[20];
    BOOL obj_avail;
    };
```

Algorithm: CRESPT()

Implementation: THREAD, three auxiliary functions, one linked list protected by a semaphore, and one queue for requests submitted by the OVT.

Purpose: Negotiate contracts with remote sites participating in the federated database that require access to local information.

```
THREAD CRESPT()
    {
    while(FOREVER)
        {
        MonitorNamePipe();
        MonitorOBjRespQueue();
        ExecutePendingContracts();
        }
    }
```

Analysis: The thread implements a while(FOREVER) loop that makes calls to the following three functions:

1. MonitorNamePipe() This function checks to see if any new contracts are available in the named pipe. If any are present, they are retrieved for processing.

2. MonitorObjRespQueue() This function checks the queue for any objects that have been identified by the OVT.

3. ExecutePendingContract() Once all the objects requested by the partner site have been verified, this function processes the contract to produce the desired export files.

Algorithm: MonitorNamePipe()

Implementation: FUNCTION

Purpose: Check the contracts named pipe for any contract requests from the remote site that is participating in the federation.

```
FUNCTION MonitorNamedPipe()
    {
    ReadContractPacketFromNPipe();

    switch(cpacket.request_code)
        {
        CASE IS_COLUMN_AVAIL:
        CASE IS_TABLE_AVAIL:
            PlacePacketInOVTQueue(cpacket.req_buffer,
                                  cpacket.request_code);
            break;

        case EXEC_QUERY_REQUEST:
            if(VerifyVerCode(cpacket.vercode) == TRUE)
                {
                GenerateImpName();
                NotifyRequestor(imp_name,vercode);
                }
            else
                NotifyRequestor("ACCESS DENIED",
                                cpacket.tid);
            break;
        }
    }
```

Analysis: This function checks the contract named pipe for any new contract packets. If any are found, they are read from the pipe and the packet is identified as to whether it is asking for a table's export availability or a single column's availability. Single columns can be requested if only index information is required at a remote site to perform a join. If the request in the packet is an "execute query" request, the verification code is checked.

Algorithm: MonitorObjRespQueue()

Implementation: FUNCTION

Purpose: Check object response queue for availability of an object. If the object is available, assign a verification code and notify the requester that the contract was accepted.

```
FUNCTION: MonitorObjRespQueue()
    {
    ReadObjRespQueue(ExportObj)
    if(ExportObjInQueue == TRUE)
        {
        if(ExportObjAvail == TRUE)
            {
            AssignVerCode(exportobj.vercode);
            NotifyRequestor(exportobj);
            UpdateContractPendingList(ExportObj);
            }
        }
    }
```

Analysis: This function simply checks the thread's queue for any objects that have been verified as to their existence and their availability status for export. If the object is available, a check is made to see if all the objects referenced in the contract are available. If all are available, a verification code is assigned to the contract and the requester is notified as to the name of the import file it should begin to monitor for. The function updates the pending contract list to indicate the updated status of the contract.

Algorithm: ExecutePendingContracts

Implementation: FUNCTION

Purpose: Check pending contract list for entries whose request code is set to EXECUTE_NOW. If the verification code is set to this value, send the packet to the Export Sequence Generator Thread (ESGT) for processing.

```
FUNCTION: ExecutePendingContracts()
     {
     currnode = HeadPendingContractList;

     while(currnode)
          {
          if(currnode.request_code = EXECUTE_NOW)
               {
               PlaceInExpSeqQueue(currnode);
               oldnode = currnode;
               currnode = currnode.NextNode;
               DeleteNode(oldnode);
               }
          else
               currnode = currnode.NextNode;
          }
     }
```

Analysis: The function begins by initializing a variable to the head of the pending contracts list. It then examines each node in the list for any nodes whose request_code indicator is set to EXE-CUTE_NOW. If this condition is found, the entire node is placed in the queue belonging to the export sequence generator thread so that a list of export instructions can be generated. This logic follows the logic for the same algorithm explained in Chapter 14. A pointer to the current node is saved so that it can be used to delete the node. The address of the next node is obtained so that the rest of the list can be examined.

15.8 OVERVIEW OF THE ARCHITECTURE

Now that we have covered the three principal scenarios that are processed in our simple federated database architecture, let's wrap things up by taking an overall view of the components.

Figure 15.10 is a block diagram of a typical participating site in our two-site federation. The principal interfaces between each thread are the queues and linked lists used to either exchange processing instructions or update information packets.

Incoming queries are received by the Query Processor Thread (QPT) and submitted either directly to the RRT (if all the database objects are local) or to the Contract Negotiation Thread (CNT) (if some of the data objects are available at the remote site).

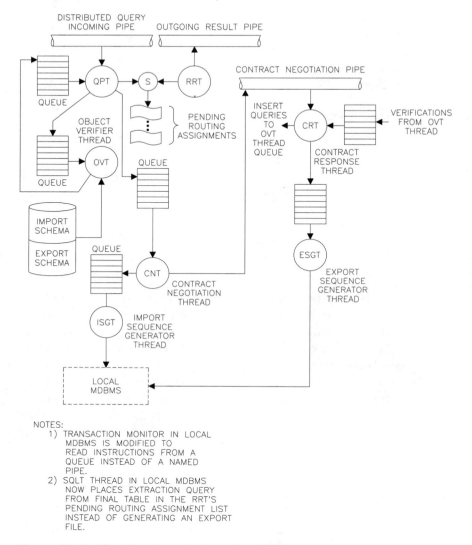

Figure 15.10 The complete federated architecture

Should the latter condition be the case, the CNT at the remote site negotiates with the CNT at the requesting site for access to all the required tables.

In our case, the negotiations are trivial. The remote site can access table information if the table is exportable and if it is currently available. A table might be rendered temporarily unavailable if the system has to perform maintenance or backup procedures on the table.

Should this be the case, the requesting site will be informed to resubmit the query later.

In a real federated system, the requester would poll other participating sites to see if they had the required information. Contract negotiations could also involve dialogs requesting bids from sites that could deliver the requested information at the lowest communications cost to the requester. The bidding site with the lowest cost would be awarded the contract. Data compression algorithms could be used to further reduce network traffic when export tables were being exchanged. Some sites might have more sophisticated compression facilities than other sites. This factor could be included as part of the bidding requirements.

The system just discussed was very simple, and severe limitations were imposed on the capabilities and functions to concentrate on the basic principles behind federated database implementation. (Besides, there's just so much one can squeeze inside a chapter!)

Although both sites used identical relational database engines (IBM's OS/2 Database Manager), it is possible to modify this design by including other vendors such as Informix, Gupta, or Microsoft/Sybase, who offer database engines for the OS/2 platform. Additionally, by including host-to-PC communications facilities, it would be possible to link our small database federation to host systems running nonrelational products.

Readers familiar with spreadsheet products such as Microsoft's Excel could think of ways of modifying the algorithms of this chapter so that workstations running Excel (or similar spreadsheets) could join the federation.

One last note: I chose IBM's OS/2 as the operating system for our small test system because of the rich supply of interprocess communications tools available with this platform. Other platforms that support concurrent or multi-processing (such as various implementations of the UNIX OS) can be used to implement this small database federation. IBM's OS/2 environment also offers a rich set of tools that can be used by developers to create dynamic link libraries. These DLLs contain communications functions for environments that support APPC, TCP/IP, and NetBIOS. This would enable our simple system to communicate with host systems or UNIX platforms.

15.9 SUMMARY

This concludes our exploration of distributed and multi-database architectures (with a small excursion into the realm of federated databases). (See Chapter 16 for information about object-oriented databases.) My original goal was to write a simple introduction and guide to a set of very complex disciplines. Hopefully, I've demystified some of the more theoretical and arcane aspects (such as relational algebra, horizontal and vertical table fragmentation, transaction serialization, and so on . . .). Many excellent references are included in the book so that the reader can explore the more formal discussions of the topics I've touched upon.

15.10 END NOTES

1. Deen, S. M., ed. *Cooperating Knowledge Based Systems*, New York: Springer-Verlag, 1991.

16

Object-Oriented Databases

16.1 INTRODUCTION

This is the last chapter of the book. We wrap things up by discussing object-oriented databases and how they relate to traditional relational databases, client/server environments, and distributed and federated architectures. We lay the groundwork by introducing key object-oriented concepts, such as classes, encapsulation, polymorphism, inheritance, and persistence. This discussion is followed by a review of the traditional data models discussed in the first part of the book so that we can tie them into the object model discussed in Section 16.4. The chapter concludes with hybrid database management systems, distributed objects (in particular, objects that are compliant with the Common Object Request Broker Architecture), and objects living in a federated architecture. Recall that federated architectures were covered in Chapter 15, so if you need a quick review, now's the time!

Let's begin our discussion by defining object-oriented technology. We will be using the C++ language as a point of reference and then relate it to traditional relational technology in order to bridge the gap between the two methodologies. Additionally, we wish to identify the features of object-oriented languages, since they are required in hybrid relational object database management systems.

As we proceed, we will see that an Object-Oriented Database Management System (OODBMS) contains an extended version of SQL, which can query not only traditional data types, such as numeric values and strings, but also complex data types, such as arrays, matrices, bit maps, and so forth. Additionally, this extended query language can access not only tables but classes as well. This means that OODBMS must also contain a class data dictionary in addition to the traditional system catalog tables found in RDBMS.

16.2 OBJECT-ORIENTED CHARACTERISTICS

Exactly what is object-oriented technology? What does it mean? Yes, it's just another way of modeling systems and data, but it is also a lot more. Objects allow you to design systems that are easier to implement and are also economical, since they allow you to reuse the objects in different designs, once the objects are tested, debugged, and operational. The best way to clear up the mystery is by identifying and explaining this methodology's key features:

1. Classes
2. Encapsulation
3. Polymorphism
4. Inheritance
5. Persistent Objects
6. Virtual Methods
7. Operator Overloading

Classes

The simplest way to describe a class is to say that it resembles a classic record (as in COBOL) or a structure (as in C++) that is enhanced with functions that act on the data. This is the simple description. A class is much more than this. Through various mechanisms, such as polymorphism, virtual methods, and encapsulation, it allows designers and programmers to create and use objects that hide information—the user is not aware of low-level details that support the class. This information hiding allows users of the class to concentrate on the components that they are interested in. Changes made to the "hidden" data are invisible and do not affect the users. Once the class is tested and debugged, it can be used over and over again. We will see what a class looks like later on in this section.

Encapsulation

This object-oriented feature allows data members and functions that act on the data to be combined or "encapsulated" into a single package called a class. This feature, particularly as implemented in C++, allows designers a high level of control as to how data are seen and manipulated. In C++, sections of the class can be specified as public, protected, and private. Public sections contain data and functions that all users of the class can access. The protected section contains data and functions that can only be accessed by classes that inherit features from a parent class. The private class is invisible to the user and can only be accessed by member functions of the class itself or by public functions that have been supplied by the designers of the class, with special logic that allows access to private data and/or functions in a controlled manner. We will see an example of a typical class in the next section of the chapter.

Polymorphism

Another important feature is polymorphism. This feature allows functions to take on different behavior, depending on their use, while maintaining the same name. The classic example is a function in a class that supports printers. By having a function called "print()," it is possible to create multiple functions, called print(), and to change the parameter list in order to support multiple printers. The environment that the function runs in can differentiate the multiple "print()" functions by their parameter signature, for example:

```
print(char *string);
print(char *string, float);
```

Although both functions have the same name, they have different parameter lists. The first function has only one parameter: a string. The second function has two parameters: a string and a floating-point value.

Inheritance

Another very important feature of object-oriented languages is the capability to derive classes from a base or "parent" class. This feature is basically the implementation of the generalization/specialization concept inherent in most data modeling methodologies. In the C++ programming language, a base class is created in order to provide generic data attributes and methods common to a set of entities. Child classes are then created and declared with a special syntax; these classes have the capability of inheriting (including) the features of the base class. The classic example of this feature uses the automotive motif: A "Car" class is created as the base class. This class contains the basic features of a car: an engine, number of doors, fuel system, four wheels, and so forth. A "Ferrari" class is a specialization of the base class. In this class you inherit the general features provided by the base class but also include features that distinguish a Ferrari from, let's say, a Mercedes.

Persistent Objects

This feature is just a fancy way of saying that an object will exist after the process that created it terminates. The object can be accessed and reused once the process that requires to access it is restarted on the system. Persistent objects are just files or, in the case of object-oriented systems, class objects that can be saved and restored between program executions. Accompanying these persistent objects is a class directory, which identifies them for easy retrieval. An index scheme is also available to improve the retrieval performance.

Virtual Methods

Virtual methods are used in the inheritance scheme supported by object-oriented languages. This mechanism allows a designer to implement methods within the classes participating in the inheritance tree that use the same name and parameter signature. Each class that implements the method is free to change the internal programming logic. Unlike polymorphic functions, virtual functions must have the same parameter scheme. (We will see examples of this later on in the chapter.)

Operator Overloading

This object-oriented programming feature gives programmers the capability to change or "overload" the functionality of common operators (such as "−, +, *, /, etc.) supported by the language. For instance, programmers can alter the meaning of "+" when they wish to concatenate two character strings. Normally, the addition symbol is used to add two new numerical values. With operator overloading it is possible to use the addition symbol to perform the string concatenation function described above, for example:

```
fullName = lastName + FirstName;
```

Let's continue by studying examples of the key object-oriented language features just described. We will be using some simple C++ language code fragments to illustrate the points just covered.

Examples of Classes

Below is an example of a class implemented with the C++ programming language:

```
class Employee{
   private:
       char lastName[20 + 1];         // employee last name
       char firstName[20 + 1];        // employee first name
       char employeeID[5 + 1];        // employee Identifier
       float salary;                  // employee salary
       char socialSecurity[11 + 1];   // social security number
       char deptID[5 +1];             // department ID

       void set_employeeID(char *empID){strcpy(employeeID,empID);}
       void set_deptID(char *dept_id){strcpy(deptID, dept_id);}


   public:
       Employee(char *dept_id, char *empID)
          {
          set_employeeID(empID);
          set_deptID(dept_id);
          }    // in-line function
       Employee(char *dept_id,float empSalary, char *empID);
          {
          set_employeeID(empID);
          set_deptID(dept_id);
          set_salary(sal);
          }    // in-line function

       ~Employee();

       void set_lastName(char *lName){strcpy(lastName,lName);}
```

```
void set_firstName(char *fName){strcpy(firstName,fName);}
void set_employeeID(char *empID){strcpy(employeeID,empID);}
void set_salary(float sal){salary = sal;}
void set_socialSecurity(char *soc_sec)
                          {strcpy(socialSecurity,soc_sec);}

char *get_lastName(void) return &lastName[0];}
char *get_firstName(void){ return &firstName[0];}
char *get_employeeID(void){ return &employeeID[0];}
float get_salary(void){return salary;}
char *get_socialSecurity(void){return &socialSecurity[0];}
char *get_deptID(void){return &deptID[0];}
};
```

Notice that the private section of the class contains all of the private data members plus two in-line functions, which are used to initialize the employee's department and identification number. The only way a programmer can access the data members is by the public in-line member functions. The only time that the employee's ID and assigned department are set is when the class object is created (instantiated). A special function called a constructor is automatically called each time an object is created. The constructor safely stores the department and employee ID. The only way to change these is to drop the object and recreate it with a new department and employee ID. In this particular implementation, we do not wish to allow any users of the class the capability to change either of these two fields. This is an example of encapsulation and information hiding!

Constructors can be identified as functions having the same name as the class they are contained in. A destructor is a class method that also has the same name as the class it can be found in except that it is preceded by a tilde ("~") character symbol. The purpose of the destructor is to perform any clean-up code, such as freeing memory or logging off of a database.

Examples of Polymorphism

The two constructors in our simple class are an example of polymorphism. Notice how the only way to differentiate between the functions is by their parameter signature:

```
Employee(char *dept_id, char *empID)
  {
  set_employeeID(empID);
```

```
        set_deptID(dept_id);
        }   // in-line function

    Employee(char *dept_id,float empSalary,
            char *empID);
        {
        set_employeeID(empID);
        set_deptID(dept_id);
        set_salary(sal);
        }   // in-line function
```

The first constructor requires a pointer to the dept_id and emp_id as its parameters. The second constructor also requires the dept_id and emp_id parameters, but it also requires the employee's salary as a passed parameter. Users of the class can create the object in one of two ways:

```
Employee empRecord("D0001","E000001");
```

or

```
Employee empRecord("D0001","E000001", 50000.00);
```

Notice how the constructors use the private and public in-line methods to initialize the private data members of the class. The set_salary() in-line method is public, since we wish to allow the employee to get a raise now and then. This would be accomplished with the following call:

```
empRecord->set_salary(55000.00);
```

Examples of Inheritance

The following class is used to enable a company to use not only employees but also contractors. Here we see an example of a specialization of an employee. The contractor has all the attributes of an employee with the additional attributes that apply to a contractor (such as vendor name):

```
class Contractor : public Employee
    {
    private:
        char vendorName[20 + 1]; // vendor name (i.e., consulting
                                 // firm name)
        char startDate[8 + 1];   // start date of contract
        char endDate[8 + 1];     // end date of contract
        float hourlyRate;        // hourly rate contractor
                                 // will charge
```

```
public:
    Contractor(char *vendor, char *sDate, char *eDate,
               float rate);
    ~Contractor();

    void set_vendorName(char *vendor)
                                    {strcpy(vendorName,vendor);}
    void set_startDate(char *sDate){strcpy(startDate,sDate);}
    void set_endDate(char *eDate){strcpy(endDate,eDate);}
    void set_hourlyRate(float rate){hourlyRate = rate;}

    char *get_vendorName(void){return vendorName;}
    char *get_startDate(void){return startDate;}
    char *get_endDate(void) {return endDate;}
    float get_hourlyRate(void) {return hourlyRate;}

};
```

What makes this a base class is the following syntax:

```
class Contractor : public Employee
```

It declares the Contractor class to be the child of the more general class: Employee. All public methods and data members declared in the public section of the base class can be accessed from the derived class. We can derive classes to as many levels as we wish in a parent-child hierarchy. Some systems allow multiple inheritance, which means that a derived class can have multiple parents. This capability is reminiscent of the old CODASYL Network data models!

Below is the code for the constructor for this class, showing how to pass parameters to the base class's constructor:

```
Contractor:: Contractor(char *vendor, char *sDate,
                        char *eDate, float rate,
                        char *dept_id, char *empID)
                  : (dept_id,empID)
  {
   set_vendorName(vendor);
   set_startDate(sDate);
   set_endDate(eDate);
   set_hourlyRate(rate);
  }
```

Although the Contractor's private data members are initialized in the usual fashion, with the public in-line member methods, we must also initialize some of the private data members of the base class. This is accomplished with the code appearing in bold text:

```
: (dept_id,empID)
```

Users would create a Contractor Object with the following code:

```
Contractor contractorRecord("ABC Consulting",
                            "8/28/95",
                            "12/20/95",
                            125.00,
                            "D0001",
                            "C0001");
```

The last two parameters, "D0001"—the department ID, and "C0001"—the contractor ID, automatically get passed to the base class constructor. Notice how the fact that the base class supplies overloaded constructors comes in handy. As contractors work on an hourly rate basis, we do not need to use the constructor that assigns a yearly salary rate!

Examples of Virtual Methods

Next, we take a look at an example of virtual methods. As stated earlier, we use virtual methods in an inheritance class hierarchy when we wish to execute the same function but at different levels of specialization. In this case, we add a virtual method called print-Record(). In the case of the employee class, we print out the employee's last name, ID, and department:

```
class Employee{
    private:
        char lastName[20 + 1];          // employee last name
        char firstName[20 + 1];         // employee first name
        char employeeID[5 + 1];         // employee Identifier
        float salary;                   // employee salary
        char socialSecurity[11 + 1];    // social security number
        char deptID[5 +1];              // department ID

        void set_employeeID(char *empID){strcpy(employeeID,empID);}
        void set_deptID(char *dept_id){strcpy(deptID, dept_id);}

    public:
        Employee(char *dept_id, char *empID)
```

```
        {
        set_employeeID(empID);
        set_deptID(dept_id);
        }    // in-line function
    Employee(char *dept_id,float empSalary, char *empID);
        {
        set_employeeID(empID);
        set_deptID(dept_id);
        set_salary(sal);
        }    // in-line function

    ~Employee();

    void set_lastName(char *lName){strcpy(lastName,lName);}
    void set_firstName(char *fName){strcpy(firstName,fName);}
    void set_employeeID(char *empID){strcpy(employeeID,empID);}
    void set_salary(float sal){salary = sal;}
    void set_socialSecurity(char *soc_sec)
                            {strcpy(socialSecurity,soc_sec);}

    char *get_lastName(void) return &lastName[0];}
    char *get_firstName(void){ return &firstName[0];}
    char *get_employeeID(void){ return &employeeID[0];}
    float get_salary(void){return salary;}
    char *get_socialSecurity(void){return &socialSecurity[0];}
    char *get_deptID(void){return &deptID[0];}

    virtual void printRecord(void);
  };

virtual void Employee::printRecord(void)
  {
  printf("Employee Id: %s\n"Employee Last Name:
            %s\nDepartment ID\n",
        get_lastName(),
        get_employeeID(),
        get_deptID());
  }
```

In the case of the contractor, we still wish to print out his/her last name, ID, and department. Additionally, we wish to print out the name of the vendor company supplying the contractor:

```
class Contractor : public Employee
  {
  private:
    char vendorName[20 + 1]; // vendor name (i.e., consulting
                             // firm name)
    char startDate[8 + 1];   // start date of contract
```

```
    char endDate[8 + 1];   // end date of contract
    float hourlyRate;      // hourly rate contractor will charge

public:
    Contractor(char *vendor, char *sDate, char *eDate,
               float rate);
    ~Contractor();

    void set_vendorName(char *vendor)
                                    {strcpy(vendorName,vendor);}
    void set_startDate(char *sDate){strcpy(startDate,sDate);}
    void set_endDate(char *eDate){strcpy(endDate,eDate);}
    void set_hourlyRate(float rate){hourlyRate = rate;}

    char *get_vendorName(void){return vendorName;}
    char *get_startDate(void){return startDate;}
    char *get_endDate(void) {return endDate;}
    float get_hourlyRate(void) {return hourlyRate;}
    virtual void printRecord(void);

};
```

Below is the code for the contractor class virtual function:

```
virtual void Contractor::printRecord(void)
    {
    printf("Contractor Id: %s\n"Contractor Last Name:
              %s\nDepartment ID\n",
        get_lastName(),
        get_employeeID(),
        get_deptID());
    printf("Vendor: %s\n", get_vendorName());
    }
```

Notice how we use in-line method functions from the base class in order to print out the contractor's last name, employee ID, and department. These methods do not appear anywhere in the Contractor class! We have access to them because the inheritance mechanism makes them available to us. In the example above, in order to print out the name of the contractor's vendor, we simply use the get_vendorName() in-line function to do the job.

Examples of Operator Overloading

The class example used when explaining operator overloading is the ability to concatentate two text strings by using the "+" addition operator as follows:

```
String fName("Angelo");
String lName("Bobak");
String fullName();

fullName = fName + lName;
```

Assume that the class String is defined as follows:

```
class String {
   private:
   char *buffer;

   public:
      String();
      String(char *string)
         {
         buffer = malloc(strlen(string) + 1);
         strcpy(buffer,string);
         }
      ~String(){delete buffer);}

    String& operator +(String &buf);
   };
```

For those of you not familiar with C = C++, malloc() is a function used to allocate memory and strcpy() is a function used to copy a character string into a memory buffer.

The overloaded operator "+" function would be implemented as follows:

```
String& String::operator +(String &buf)
   {
   // CODE to implement overloaded operator
   }
```

Overloaded operators are handy and typically are used with other traditional operator symbols to perform functions on user-defined classes.

16.3 METHODOLOGIES

As with any technology, there is an accompanying design methodology. Pioneers in object-oriented design methodologies are Grady Booch, James Rumbaugh, Yourdan/Coadd, and Shlear/Mellor, to name just a few. Generally, object-oriented analysis and design is an extension of traditional structured methodologies, such as entity-relationship diagramming and data-process flows. We will briefly discuss and examine examples of Grady Booch's design methodology, since it seems to be one of the currently more popular ones and is available on fairly inexpensive systems such as Microsoft Windows running on Intel 486 workstations.

Grady Booch Methodology

Although many design techniques exist, the prevalent methodology being used is that of Grady Booch. He represents classes and objects as "clouds" connected by lines with "adornments," which describe the relationship between the clouds. Figure 16.1 is an example of a class diagram, implemented with the Grady Booch methodology, that describes a small model of an enterprise.

The diagram can be read as follows: A group entity contains multiple departments. Each department is made up of employees and

Figure 16.1 Sample employee database

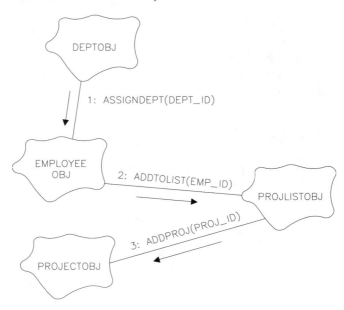

Figure 16.2 Assigning employees

each employee is assigned to a project by appearing on a project list. The project list is used to link (assign) an employee ID to a project ID. Additionally, a department is responsible for one or more projects.

Notice that each line has added symbols to further define the relationships between clouds. The dot and the box at the end of the group/department relationship mean that a group "has" or "owns" one or more department entities. Notice that the cardinality of this relationship is one to many. Does this look familiar? Of course it does—recall the traditional entity-relationship methodologies. Booch extends this methodology by allowing us to define the methods that act on each data attribute belonging to the entity—in our case, the object and its members. The filled-in dot at the originating end of the relationship means "has"; the box at the receiving end of the relationship means that the Department class is owned by reference. In programming languages, this implies a memory reference of some sort. A straight line is the simplest relationship. It implies that the classes are simply coupled. An empty dot at one end of a relationship means that the object uses the other object. In our diagram, a project list uses a project in order to link it to a customer.

Some of the clouds contain the attributes that can be found in the class. In the case of the project list class, I decided to display the employee ID and project ID attributes in the diagram. This is a feature of the CASE tool I used. Just by coincidence, I am using a tool called Rational Rose, which supports the Booch methodology. (As we all know, Grady Booch happens to be the resident scientist at that company!)

This methodology also supports another category of diagram called an object diagram. Object diagrams are used to show the messages that are passed between objects. Let's take a look at Figure 16.2, which illustrates the messages used to assign an employee to a department and then a project.

As can be seen, the objects pass messages to each other in order to accomplish the task. The department object passes a message called assignDept() to the employee object in order to assign the employee to a department. Notice that the department ID is passed as a parameter that is accepted and used by the employee object. The messages equate to methods that are part of the class receiving the message. Next, the employee object wishes to assign itself to a project. This is accomplished with the following three messages. First, the employee object passes the addToList() message to the project list object in order to include itself in the list. The message requires that the employee ID and project ID be included as a parameter. Upon receiving this message, the project list object must verify the project ID that is assigned to the employee. This is accomplished by a third message. The project list object asks the project object to verify that the project ID exists. Finally, the project object sends a message to the project list in order to acknowledge that the project ID linking the employee ID to the project exists. This is a typical sequence that is common in object-oriented applications.

Next, we examine a third diagram category called an interaction diagram. It is used to show the sequence of messages over time. This diagram can be seen in Figure 16.3.

Notice the sequence numbers on the messages. These were assigned when the object diagram just discussed was created. The labels of the columns identify the objects the messages are sent to, and the sequence of messages on the vertical axis represents the traffic over time. Readers will agree as to how much more powerful this methodology is compared to traditional entity-relationship techniques and structured data-process flow diagrams. Let's examine our

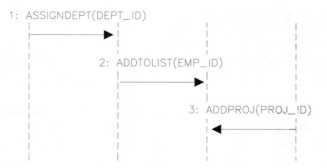

DEPTOBJ   EMPLOYEEOBJ   PROJLISTOBJ   PROJECTOBJ

1: ASSIGNDEPT(DEPT_ID)

2: ADDTOLIST(EMP_ID)

3: ADDPROJ(PROJ_ID)

Figure 16.3 Message traffic when assigning an employee

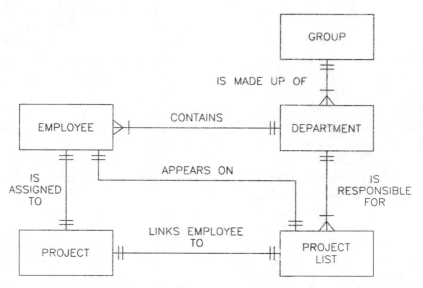

```
PROJECT NAME:     NEW PROJECT NAME
PROJECT PATH:     C:\ECWIN\DBBOOK\
CHART FILE:       ERD00001.ERD
CHART NAME:       SAMPLE EMPLOYEE DATABASE
CREATED ON:       JUL-13-1995
CREATED BY:       ANGELO R BOBAK
MODIFIED ON:
MODIFIED BY:
```

Figure 16.4 Model implemented with a traditional entity-relationship diagram

452

employee model as it would appear in a more traditional entity-relationship diagram.

Figure 16.4 shows our model implemented with a traditional entity-relationship diagram.

The reader will notice many similarities but also many differences. Entity-relationship diagrams show entities, relationships, and attributes together with data types and cardinalities. These diagrams do not contain methods that act on the data attributes and do not support any sort of message identification and sequencing. This is where object methodology enhances the modeling methodology.

At this stage, the reader may be asking, Why all this C++ code and discussions on object-oriented language features? I wanted to learn about object-oriented databases, not C++! Not only that, but I thought I would read about how they fit into distributed database architectures. Well, we will be discussing Hybrid Database Management Systems (HDBMS) and Object Database Management Systems (ODBMS). A requirement for each is that it supports a layer based on an Object-Oriented Programming Languages (OOPL). That's why we covered the main features first!

16.4 RELATIONAL, HIERARCHICAL, AND NETWORK MODELS (REVIEW)

In order to see how object-oriented databases interact with or use the more traditional data models, this section presents a brief review of the models presented in Chapter 3. We will see that object-oriented databases utilize all three types of models in one form or another. Usually, an advanced relational layer sits at the bottom of the model stack. By advanced, I mean that not only can it support traditional data types, but advanced data types, such as documents, bit maps, BLOBs, and arrays, are supported as well.

As stated earlier, both an extended SQL language and an object-oriented language sit on top of the relational layer in order to retrieve information, connect it, and build hierarchical and network models that allow fast navigation via memory pointers.

Review of the Relational Model

Recall that the relational model is the most powerful model to date, since it allows us to model almost any real-life situation. It is based on

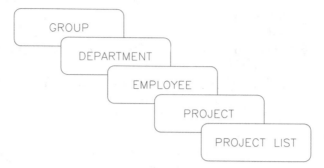

Figure 16.5 Example database (relational model)

the relational calculus, set theory, and the relational algebra. The basic components of a relational database are tables, attributes, and relationships. Relationships between tables are implemented via "joining" the participating tables. Joins are implemented via components of the Structured Query Language (SQL). Figure 16.5 shows the two-dimensional tables that constitute our example database.

Recall that by two-dimensional we mean rows and columns. We will see in later sections that hybrid relational database systems are based on several object layers that sit on top of the relational model.

Review of the Network Data Model

Next, we review the network model. Recall that the network model is the predecessor of the relational model and the successor of the

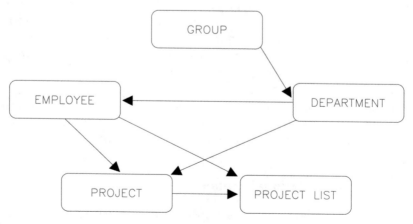

Figure 16.6 Example database (network model)

hierarchical model. Our old friends, the CODASYL committee, created the network model after a determination was made that the hierarchical model was not powerful enough to model real-world applications. Figure 16.6 depicts our sample database.

Notice that related files can have more than one parent. In our case, not only is a project sponsored by a department, but it is also assigned to one or more employees. Recall that navigation between records belonging to a related set of files is accomplished via pointers residing in special records called DBTG sets.

Review of the Hierarchical Model

Last, but not least, is our old friend, the hierarchical model. As the original database model, it was powerful for its time, but it only allowed relationships where parent entities could have multiple children, but children could have only one parent. Work-arounds to this problem involved splitting a database and connecting it via special records that allowed records residing in related files between the connected databases to be accessed. Figure 16.7 below shows our example database as a hierarchical model.

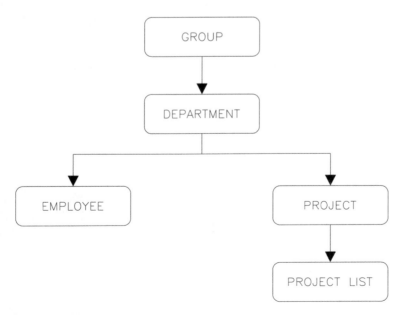

Figure 16.7 Example database (hierarchical model)

As in the network model, navigation between related entities is via pointers containing memory disk addresses that connect the related records. Notice the absence of some of the relationships that we were able to implement in the network model via DBTG sets. The relational model allowed us to implement relationships via mechanisms called joins. These SQL joins typically occurred between primary and foreign keys contained in the participating tables.

Hybrid Object/Relational Models as Stacks of Traditional Models

What do I mean by this subtitle? Simply that the underlying database is relational. The hybrid object/relational model will allow network or hierarchical or a combination of both data types to be created in the application space after having been loaded from a relational database that has been extended to support complex data types, such as bit maps, arrays, matrices, trees, and text documents. Figure 16.8 shows our example database as a network layer derived from an underlying relational layer.

The underlying data model is still relational, allowing us to perform SQL SELECTS, JOINS, and so forth. As objects are created, they are connected via pointers in order to present the user with a network model. This scheme can be stored in an extended data dictionary, which catalogs the classes and saves the hierarchical and network mappings.

Embedded in the objects could be structures implemented with the hierarchical model. For example, assume that a project involves

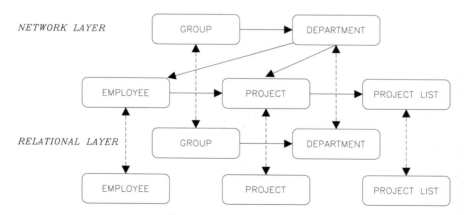

Figure 16.8 Network layer derived from an underlying relational layer

components and parts. Components can be composed of other components; components can also be composed of parts that are further composed of smaller parts. This type of model can best be represented as a hierarchy showing the decomposition of the components and parts used in a project. We now see how hybrid object/relational models are based on the three traditional models. Objects allow us to package the data plus the functions that act on the data in neat packages, which can then be assembled at whim into large complex systems. Objects can be used over and over again.

16.5 PURE OBJECT-ORIENTED DATABASE MANAGEMENT SYSTEMS

Pure Object-Oriented Database Management Systems (OODBMS) include many of the features just discussed. In particular, their most important features are the ability to store persistent objects, retrieve persistent objects, and provide a mechanism for manipulating objects via an object-oriented language. Figure 16.9 shows a high-level diagram of the major components of an object-oriented database management system.

Some systems provide an extended version of the Structured Query Language, which supports not only standard relational objects but also pure objects. The extended query is fed to a parser for syntax checking, parsing, and possibly scheduling. The class broker (a form of directory service) is consulted to find out where the

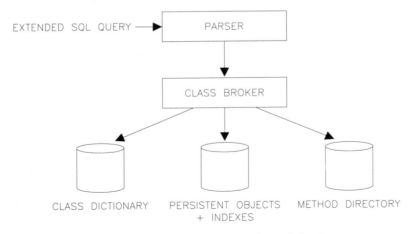

Figure 16.9 Major components of an object-oriented database management system

objects reside. The class broker provides the necessary links to the objects, indexes, and methods declared in the query. Recall that these objects may include attributes, complex data types such as matrices and arrays, bit maps, documents, and even multi-media objects. We will take a look at an example of an extended SQL query later on in this section, but first let's review the features that identify an object-oriented database management system from a plain relational database management system. We will see that an object-oriented language has an important role to play!

What Makes an OODBMS an OODBMS?

Basically there are two broad categories of requirements. First, it must add and support a level of object-oriented language that provides the features described in Section 16.2.

Second, it must support complex data types and allow retrieval and manipulation of the data types in a relational architecture. Traditional relational databases support data types such as character strings, variable character strings, and numeric data. Object-oriented databases must support more complex data types, such as bit maps for images and references to text files. Figure 16.10 depicts a typical layout for a row of a table that might be manipulated by an object-oriented database management system.

Notice how the record contains a mix of traditional and complex data types. This could be a record in an employee table. The first two fields show traditional data types, such as the employee ID and last name. Next comes a reference to a bit map. This could be a bit map containing an image of the employee that can be used for identification purposes. Next is the ID of the department where the employee

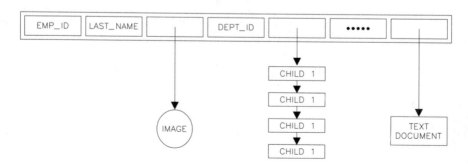

Figure 16.10 Records with complex data types

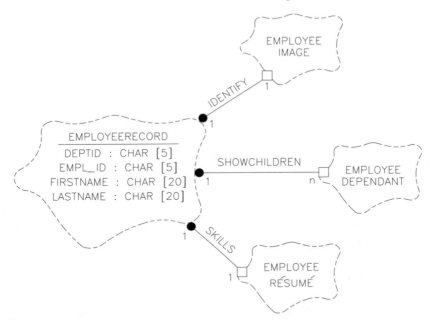

Figure 16.11 Complex employee record

works. Following this is a reference to an array containing the names of the employee's children (dependents). Other fields follow, leading finally to a field that refers to a document. This document could be a résumé or a document outlining the employee's skills. Figure 16.11 shows a class diagram depicting this record as an object model.

Compare this figure with Figure 16.10. The cloud diagram shows the main employee class, together with relationships to other classes containing the employee's image, dependent list, and résumé. Each class not only contains the data, but it also comes equipped with methods to access, load, and format the complex data types from the underlying database. For example, the employeeImage class will contain all methods to retrieve the image based on the employee ID and will then contain any methods that reference the APIs necessary to display the image on a terminal screen or print it out on a printer. Notice how navigation between these related objects is performed by pointers—hence, the network model. These classes could sit on top of a hybrid database that is both relational and object-oriented. It is considered relational because it contains traditional tables that store data in rows and columns. Additionally, it allows joins and other SQL commands in order to access the data stored in the RDBMS. The object-oriented flavor comes in when we add the layer that allows us to create classes and objects and manipulate them with an object-oriented language such as C++.

Do not forget that the object-oriented layer provides a mechanism for creating, saving, and loading persistent objects. Each persistent object is assigned a unique identity for easy retrieval.

16.6 HYBRID OBJECT/RELATIONAL DATABASE MANAGEMENT SYSTEMS

Hybrid Object/Relational Database Management Systems (HORDBMS) are a combination of pure object database management systems (described earlier) and traditional relational database management systems. Figure 16.12 shows the pure object DBMS that has been extended with links to a relational database management system.

The RDBMS itself has been extended to support advanced SQL queries that retrieve objects, bit maps, and complex data types, such as matrices and multimedia objects.

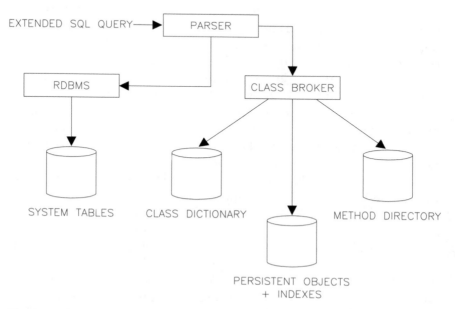

Figure 16.12 Hybrid object/relational DBMS

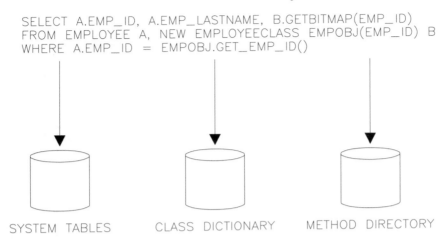

```
SELECT A.EMP_ID, A.EMP_LASTNAME, B.GETBITMAP(EMP_ID)
FROM EMPLOYEE A, NEW EMPLOYEECLASS EMPOBJ(EMP_ID) B
WHERE A.EMP_ID = EMPOBJ.GET_EMP_ID()
```

SYSTEM TABLES   CLASS DICTIONARY   METHOD DIRECTORY

Figure 16.13 Extended SQL select

Not only are the system tables (which describe relational tables, views, attributes, and indexes) a part of the data dictionary, but the class dictionary, object index, and method directory are also included.

Let's take a look at a possible syntax for a SQL query that has been extended in order to support objects. Figure 16.13 shows an example.

Notice that not only are we querying traditional columns, such as employee ID and employee last name, but also a bit map, which contains a picture of the employee for easy identification. The SQL SELECT clause has been extended so that class methods used to retrieve advanced data types are included in the selection list. The FROM clause has been extended in order to be able to reference objects and relational tables. In order to find the object, the parser and optimizer of the query engine must consult the class dictionary and method directory in order to retrieve the desired objects and functions that will load the objects from the persistent database. Notice the presence of the traditional system tables.

16.7 DISTRIBUTED OBJECTS AND CLIENT/SERVER

We've seen how object-oriented databases and hybrid object/relational databases handle objects. Our discussions were from the perspective of a single site or single hardware platform. How do we get

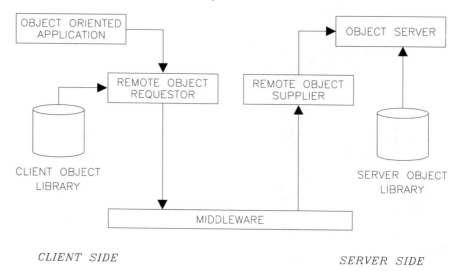

CLIENT SIDE   *SERVER SIDE*

Figure 16.14 Client/server objects (distributed objects)

objects to talk to each other across a LAN or WAN in order to complete a distributed transaction or other task? In this section, we take a high-level look at how objects can be distributed to perform services in a client/server architecture. In the next section, we see how an organization called the Object Management Group (OMG) derived an architecture called the Common Object Request Broker Architecture (CORBA) and how this architecture enables objects to hold dialogs over remote locations in order to complete tasks such as distributed transactions. We will see how CORBA is an excellent candidate for implementing federations of distributed cooperating databases, as discussed earlier in the book. Figure 16.14 shows a high-level diagram, which depicts the basic components required to implement distributed objects in a client/server environment.

As can be seen, an object-oriented application on a client workstation makes a request for a service provided by an object that resides on a remote server. The client and the server are connected by a LAN and some type of middleware, such as Open Client Database Connectivity (OCDBC). As far as the application is concerned, the object resides locally. All that the application has to do is find the object it needs in the local object library and it's on its way. Unknown to the application (and the user), what actually happens is that an intermediary process called a remote object requester receives the request, looks up the object's name in the local object library, and proceeds to link the local object with its counterpart on the server. The necessary preparation includes finding out the required parameters that must be sent to the server and the name of the object on the server that will provide the services. The request goes over the LAN via some preagreed protocol, is received by the server, and the necessary steps are then taken to link the two objects over the LAN so they can complete the requested task.

A process called the remote object supplier receives the request, looks up the object, makes sure that all parameters are supplied, and proceeds to inform the object server that a completed request came in. The object server links to a local object library and instantiates the desired object. This could be an object that completes a query against a local database or provides some information or access to a remote service, such as a stock ticker information provider. As stated earlier, OMG has provided an architecture called CORBA to enable the above scenario. Luckily for us, most of the major vendors are complying with components that support CORBA!

16.8 COMMON OBJECT REQUEST BROKER ARCHITECTURE

The key to the Common Object Request Broker Architecture (CORBA) is a component called an Object Request Broker (ORB). Basically, this component interacts with the client object-oriented application to process the request from the object. It begins by searching its object directory for available objects for the target object. Once the object is found, the ORB provides the necessary links to the middleware to initialize a dialog with its counterpart on the remote server that will provide the requested object and its services. Multiple remote object servers are also supported. Figure 16.15 shows a detailed diagram of the major components that make up the CORBA architecture.

The client application interfaces with the ORB via an interface mechanism. This interface is provided by an Interface Definition Language (IDL), which allows the client application access to the services provided by the ORB. The specification to the IDL is provided by CORBA. An example of an IDL is IBM's Distributed System Object Manager (DSOM), which provides an interface between OS/2 applications written in C to the object broker. The object broker can therefore accept requests, look up the desired object in a

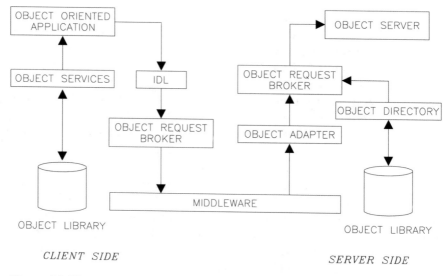

Figure 16.15 Common object request broker architecture (CORBA)

local directory, and pass the request to its counterpart ORB on the target server. At the target server, another CORBA-specified object called an Object Adapter (OA) receives the request and makes the necessary links to the local object request broker so that the selected object can be retrieved from a local object library and instantiated in order to provide the requested service. Easy, isn't it? Let's see how ORBs (and CORBA) can be used to implement a federated architecture, as described in Chapter 15.

16.9 DISTRIBUTED OBJECTS AND FEDERATIONS

Recall how federated architectures are composed of loosely connected, autonomous database platforms that have agreed to share some information via dictionary schemas called import/export schemas. Recall that the database sites making up the federation are heterogeneous; that is, they could very well use different data models and DBMS in order to carry out their activities. One site could be based on the relational model, such as a DB2 site. Another site could be IMS, based on the hierarchical model. To complicate matters even further, the third site could be based on IRMS, which supports a network model. As if this didn't complicate things enough, our

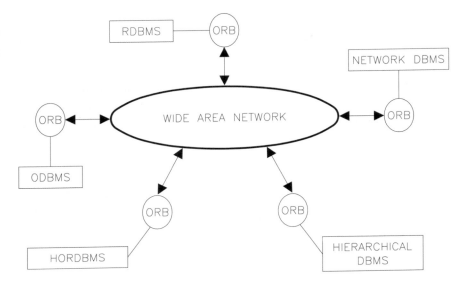

Figure 16.16 Distributed objects and federations

fourth participant in the federation is a new object-oriented database, which stores images, documents, and multi-media objects in a persistent database. Figure 16.16 shows a block diagram of such a federation.

As can be seen, the glue that ties everything together is CORBA's ORB. Each site has an ORB, which contains the proper services and objects that allow a cooperative dialog to occur whenever one or more sites in the federation want to share data or update each other's databases with new information. The ORBs have access to services that provide tools to enable communication over the middleware or middlewares that connect the various sites. One site might understand TCP/IP; another site might only understand an IBM or DEC protocol.

16.10 SUMMARY

Well, there you have it! We've discussed object-oriented languages by identifying their features. We've studied pure object-oriented databases and compared them to the traditional relational databases that are the foundation for today's information processing platforms.

We've seen how hybrid database management systems join both technologies by layering the features of object-oriented languages on top of relational architectures. We wrapped things up by applying objects to client/server and database federations.

I hope you enjoyed the book! It certainly was a lot of fun writing it. If anything, I learned some new tricks by studying the concepts of the pioneers in both the relational and object fields. Till the next time!

Index